THE OXFORD BOOK OF

EXILE

THE OXFORD BOOK OF

EXILE

Edited by

John Simpson

Oxford   New York

OXFORD UNIVERSITY PRESS

1995

Oxford University Press, Walton Street, Oxford OX2 6DP

Oxford New York
Athens Auckland Bangkok Bombay
Calcutta Cape Town Dar es Salaam Delhi
Florence Hong Kong Istanbul Karachi
Kuala Lumpur Madras Madrid Melbourne
Mexico City Nairobi Paris Singapore
Taipei Tokyo Toronto
and associated companies in
Berlin Ibadan

Oxford is a trade mark of Oxford University Press

Additional copyright information appears on pp. 345–51

First published 1995

British Library Cataloguing in Publication Data
Data available

Library of Congress Cataloging in Publication Data
The Oxford book of exile / edited by John Simpson.
p.   cm.
Includes bibliographical references (p.   ) and index.
1. Exiles—Literary collections.
2. Exile (Punishment)—Literary collections.
I. Simpson, John, 1944–
PN6071.E87094 1995   808.8'9920694—dc20   94–20999
ISBN 0–19–214221–6

10 9 8 7 6 5 4 3 2 1

Typeset by Graphicraft Typesetters Ltd., Hong Kong
Printed in Great Britain on acid-free paper by
Bookcraft (Bath) Ltd.
Midsomer Norton, Avon

CONTENTS

INTRODUCTION

Each of us is an exile: the thought is a hackneyed one, but it still retains a little force. We are exiles from our mother's womb, from our childhood, from private happiness, from peace, even if we are not exiles in the more conventional sense of the word. The feeling of looking back for the last time, of setting our face to a new and possibly hostile world is one we all know. It is the human condition; and the great upheavals of history have merely added physical expression to an inner fact. Thinking with longing of somewhere we can never return to becomes an obsession: no wonder that various of the people whose words and experiences appear on the pages that follow have tried to return, and have sometimes paid the penalty for doing so.

An anthology that was merely concerned with a standard definition of exile would, however, quickly become predictable; from Adam and Eve to Alexander Solzhenitsyn, there is a certain pattern. Accordingly, I have tried to stretch the definition of exile as far as possible without actually breaking it. I include not merely the more obvious political and religious exiles, but adventurers who threw everything up and headed out; misfits and ne'er-do-wells and those who were simply too intelligent or too restless or too awkward to stay at home like everyone else; debtors, pursued by the courts; writers who needed a quieter or a more stimulating atmosphere in which to work; refugees from bad weather, or bad cooking, or a bad past; people who merely turned in on themselves in order to block out the real world, or who created other and even more real worlds of their own; complainers and nuisances, maintainers of a stiff upper lip; men and women who returned home to their families and friends, or found things were worse at home than they had been in exile, or who never went home at all because they no longer felt the interest. There are small personal tragedies, and there are victims of the worst tragedies of modern times: the First World War, collectivization in Russia, the Holocaust, the Vietnam War, the clearances of indigenous peoples. But I have also added in a sprinkling of less serious figures: Casanova pestered by an innocent cleric as he escapes from prison, Bertie Wooster hunted down and exiled by his aunt. Exile can after all be a relief as well as a sadnesss.

It can also end in home-coming. Various figures reappear at times throughout this book, and most of them return from their exile in the end. The

Prodigal Son gets his fatted calf; Robinson Crusoe hangs up his goatskin hat and umbrella; Casanova has dinner with some of his former mistresses; Dreyfus leads a peaceful and forgotten existence; Nelson Mandela is released to become president. Yet I have tried to avoid too even and predictable a tone: we will also find two Jewish boys, survivors of the concentration camps, who are lucky to escape with their lives when they get back to their native Poland. Wherever possible I have used the words of the people involved, unless there was a better reason for quoting something about them. As a journalist I have a weakness for actuality, and a number of original documents have worked their way in, from the sentence on the Decembrists to the banning order on a South African dissident. A worse weakness has shown itself, however: in several cases I have included some passage from one of my own books. It was not, I hope, done out of vanity but because I could not find another way of illustrating a particular scene: the three future presidents of Argentina in an exiles' bar in Panama City, for instance, or the one-word answer from Ayatollah Khomeini when he was asked what it felt like to be returning to Iran.

Every now and then I would find myself edging away from the *Oxford Book of Exile* and veering too much towards the territory of a putative *Oxford Book of Alienation*; at that point I would delete the offending passages and head back to the central theme. Exile is a broader and more varied subject than alienation, and can take in the wit of Alexander Herzen, or the quiet despair of Oscar Wilde, sitting outside the Café de Flore in the Boulevard St Germain in the hope that someone will pay for his coffee, or the comfortable life of Sir Richard and Lady Burton in their *garçonnerie* in Trieste, as well as the angst of an Albert Camus and the wanderings of a Jack Kerouac. It can even include Edward Lear, who had a large circle of friends and was outwardly jolly and amusing, yet showed sudden glimpses in his nonsense verse of some inner flight from love and contentment. The intention behind the lateral thinking and the occasional leaps of logic was that ultimately this book might add up to a general, overall definition of the feeling and experience of exile, a pointillist impression of an experience each one of us has at least glimpsed.

All sorts of people have been kind enough to take an interest in this book, and it would be impossible to name them all, though all have my considerable gratitude. I should, however, mention Tim Gardam, who gave me at least a dozen ideas, Walter and Sylvia Lessing who gave me others, Clive Nettleton who lent me his banning order, Ruby Wax who talked to me about Evanston, Illinois, and Margaret Hardwidge who added a series of excellent suggestions, all of which I took. When I thought I would never be able to get the work done in time, Vivien Antwi and Gareth Nash stepped in and found the references I could only half-remember. They also suggested a sizeable number of ideas and passages, and without their help and enthusiasm the book would not have been completed. Sue Aldridge organized everything, from the ordering of books to the despatch of the manuscript, with her usual calm efficiency. Judith Luna was helpful, encouraging and persistent in just the right quantities, an excellent editor who kept her nerve even when I disappeared for long periods of time without breaking radio silence. Tira Shubart was, as always, an unflagging source of good ideas and practical assistance; without her this, like so many other things, would have been quite impossible and much less fun.

DRIVEN FORTH

To be wrenched from home, family, everything pleasant and familiar, and forced into a world that is cold and hostile, whether the expelling agent is the Angel of God or Stalin's NKVD: this is the defining experience of exile. The word itself carries powerful connotations of sorrow and alienation, of the surrender of the individual to overwhelming strength, of years of fruitless waiting. It was Victor Hugo who called exile 'a long dream of home'. There is also a lingering sense of defiance, a refusal to accept that what has happened can be permanent, an obsessive watch for any sign of weakness and decay in the enemy's camp which might permit an eventual return. But what lasts the longest is the shock of the original expulsion.

EXPELLED FROM PARADISE

And the LORD God called unto Adam, and said unto him, Where art thou?
And he said, I heard thy voice in the garden, and I was afraid, because I
was naked; and I hid myself.

And he said, Who told thee that thou wast naked? Hast thou eaten of the
tree, whereof I commanded thee that thou shouldest not eat?

And the man said, The woman whom thou gavest to be with me, she gave
me of the tree, and I did eat.

And the LORD God said unto the woman, What is this that thou hast done?
And the woman said, The serpent beguiled me, and I did eat.

And the LORD God said unto the serpent, Because thou hast done this,
thou art cursed above all cattle, and above every beast of the field; upon thy
belly shalt thou go, and dust shalt thou eat all the days of thy life:

And I will put enmity between thee and the woman, and between thy seed
and her seed; it shall bruise thy head, and thou shalt bruise his heel.

Unto the woman he said, I will greatly multiply thy sorrow and thy con-
ception; in sorrow thou shalt bring forth children; and thy desire shall be
to thy husband, and he shall rule over thee.

And unto Adam he said, Because thou hast hearkened unto the voice of thy
wife, and hast eaten of the tree, of which I commanded thee, saying, Thou
shalt not eat of it: cursed is the ground for thy sake; in sorrow shalt thou
eat of it all the days of thy life;

Thorns also and thistles shall it bring forth to thee; and thou shalt eat the
herb of the field;

In the sweat of thy face shalt thou eat bread, till thou return unto the
ground; for out of it wast thou taken: for dust thou art, and unto dust shalt
thou return.

And Adam called his wife's name Eve; because she was the mother of all
living.

Unto Adam also and to his wife did the LORD God make coats of skins,
and clothed them.

And the LORD God said, Behold, the man is become as one of us, to know good and evil: and now, lest he put forth his hand, and take also of the tree of life, and eat, and live for ever:

Therefore the LORD God sent him forth from the garden of Eden, to till the ground from whence he was taken.

So he drove out the man; and he placed at the east of the garden of Eden Cherubims, and a flaming sword which turned every way, to keep the way of the tree of life.

Genesis, 3

THEIR SOLITARY WAY

High in front advanced,
The brandished sword of God before them blazed
Fierce as a comet; which with torrid heat,
And vapour as the Lybian air adust,
Began to parch that temperate clime; whereat
In either hand the hastening angel caught
Our lingering parents, and to the eastern gate
Led them direct, and down the cliff as fast
To the subjected plain; then disappeared.
They looking back, all the eastern side beheld
Of Paradise, so late their happy seat,
Waved over by that flaming brand, the gate
With dreadful faces thronged and fiery arms:
Some natural tears they dropped, but wiped them soon;
The world was all before them, where to choose
Their place of rest, and providence their guide:
They hand in hand with wandering steps and slow,
Through Eden took their solitary way.

John Milton, *Paradise Lost*, Book XII, 1667

THE GHOST OF AENEAS'S WIFE URGES HIM TO LEAVE TROY

As I roamed on that endless, frenzied search through the city
    buildings,
There appeared before my eyes a piteous phantom, yes,
The very ghost of Creusa—a figure larger than life.

I was appalled: my hair stood on end, and my voice stuck
In my throat. It was she who spoke then, and thus relieved
    my pain:—
  Darling husband, it's madness for you to indulge your
    grief
Like this. These happenings are part of the divine
Purpose. It was not written that you should bring Creusa
Away with you; the great ruler of heaven does not allow it.
For you, long exile is destined, broad tracts of sea to be
    furrowed;
Then you will reach Hesperia, where Lydian Tiber flows
Gently through a land in good heart, and good men live.
There, your affairs will prosper; a kingdom, a royal bride
Await you. No more tears now for your heart's love, Creusa:
I shall not see the proud halls of the Myrmidons or Dolopes,
Nor work as a slave for Greek women—I, who am Dardan
And daughter-in-law to the goddess Venus.
No, the great Mother of the gods is going to keep me here.
Good-bye, Aeneas. Cherish our love in the son it gave us.
  With these words, though I wept and had so much to say
To her, she left me, fading out into thin air.
Three times I tried to put my arms round her neck, and three
    times
The phantom slipped my hands, my vain embrace: it was
    like
Grasping a wisp of wind or the wings of a fleeting dream.
So in the end I went back to my friends, the night being over.
I was astonished to find, when I got there, a great number
Of new arrivals come in, both women and men, a sorry
Concourse of refugees assembled for exile. From all sides
They'd come together, their minds made up, their belongings
    ready,
For me to lead them wherever I wished across the sea.
And now was the dawn star rising over the ridges of Ida,
Bringing another day. The Greeks were holding the gates of
The city in force. Troy was beyond all hope of aid.
I accepted defeat, picked up my father and made for the
    mountains.

                Virgil (70–19 BC), *Aeneid*, tr. C. Day-Lewis, 1967

ODYSSEUS REMEMBERS ITHACA

Odysseus talks to King Alcinous, who has given him shelter during his ten years' wandering after the siege of Troy

Many are the sorrows the gods of the sky have given me.
Now first I will tell you my name, so that all of you
may know me, and I hereafter, escaping the day without pity,
be your friend and guest, though the home where I live is far away
    from you.
I am Odysseus son of Laertes, known before all men
for the study of crafty designs, and my fame goes up to the heavens.
I am at home in sunny Ithaka. There is a mountain
there that stands tall, leaf-trembling Neritos, and there are islands
settled around it, lying one very close to another.

There is Doulichion and Same, wooded Zakynthos,
but my island lies low and away, last of all on the water
toward the dark, with the rest below facing east and sunshine,
a rugged place, but a good nurse of men; for my part
I cannot think of any place sweeter on earth to look at.
For in truth Kalypso, shining among divinities, kept me
with her in her hollow caverns, desiring me for her husband,
and so likewise Aiaian Circe the guileful detained me
beside her in her halls, desiring me for her husband,
but never could she persuade the heart within me. So it is
that nothing is more sweet in the end than country and parents
ever, even when far away one lives in a fertile
place, when it is in alien country, far from his parents.

       Homer (?8th century BC), *Odyssey*, Book IX, tr. Richmond Lattimore, 1991

A TROJAN SAILOR SINGS OF HOME

The sea shore, covered with Trojan tents. Trojan ships are visible in the harbour. It is night. A young Phrygian sailor sings as he rocks at the masthead of a ship. Two sentries are on guard at the back of the stage before the tents.

      HYLAS
      Oh echoing vale
      Where from first light
      I used to wander singing—alas!
      Will he sing again beneath your great trees,

Poor Hylas?
Rock gently on your mighty breast,
Eternal sea, the child of Dindyma.

Cool green branches,
Cherished retreat
From the day's heat—alas!
When will you restore your scented shade
To poor Hylas?
Rock gently on your mighty breast,
Eternal sea, the child of Dindyma.

Humble cottage
Where I received
My mother's last farewell—

1st SENTRY
He's dreaming of his homeland . . .

2nd SENTRY
Which he won't see again.

HYLAS
Alas!
Will he see your happy poverty again,
Poor Hylas? . . .
Rock gently on your mighty breast,
Eternal sea, the child . . .
He goes to sleep.

Hector Berlioz, *The Trojans*, Act V, 1858

OVID COMPLAINS TO THE EMPEROR AUGUSTUS

Banished from Rome in AD 8 for publishing a poem which was regarded as a scandalous incitement to adultery, Ovid was sent to live at Tomis, on the Black Sea. He exaggerates the unpleasantness of it shamelessly: Tomis is the modern Constanta, one of the most popular seaside resorts in eastern Europe.

This is the worst possible fate: not just to be forced out of Rome, but to have to live among barbarians. Not one else has been exiled so far from his native land, and no one else has been sent here, to the mouth of the Hister with its seven streams, crushed beneath the icy rod of the Parrhasian virgin. The waters of the Danube are scarcely enough to protect me from the tribes of the area: the Ciziges, the Colchi, the hordes of Teretei, the Getae. Other people have been exiled for offences that were far more serious, and none of them has been banished as far as I have. Nothing could be more alien to me than the cold of this place, or the hostile tribes, or the sea which freezes over. Here, on the ill-omened shore of the Euxene, the Roman Empire ends and the territory of the Basternae and the Sauromatae begins. This is the most distant region covered by the Ausonian law: it clings by its fingertips to the fringes of your empire.

And so, as a supplicant, I beg you to send me somewhere safer. Having already lost my homeland, I don't want to lose my peace of mind as well; and I am seriously afraid of all these tribes, which are only held back by the River Hister. Since I am your subject, it is not right that I should be in danger of capture by some enemy. While the Caesars rule Rome, a man of Latin blood must never be the prisoner of savages.

Ovid (43 BC–AD 18), *Tristia* I

THE TERRIBLE START TO THE JEWISH DIASPORA

In AD 70, after bitter fighting, the forces of the Roman general Titus, son of the Emperor Vespasian, captured Jerusalem. Those Jews who survived were forced into exile.

At dusk the slaughter ceased, but in the night the fire gained the mastery, and on the 8th of Gorpiaios the sun rose over Jerusalem in flames—a city that during the siege had suffered such disasters that if she had enjoyed as many blessings from her foundation, she would have been the envy of the world, and a city that deserved these terrible misfortunes on no other account than that she produced a generation such as brought about her ruin.

When Titus entered he was astounded by the strength of the city, and especially by the towers which the party chiefs in their mad folly had abandoned. Observing how solid they were all the way up, how huge each block of stone and how accurately fitted, how great their breadth and how immense their height, he exclaimed aloud: 'God has been on our side; it is God who brought the Jews down from these strongholds; for what could human hands or instruments do against such towers?' At that time he made many such remarks to his friends, and he set free all persons imprisoned by the party chiefs and found in the forts. Later, when he destroyed the rest of the City and pulled down the walls, he left the towers as a monument to his own luck, which had proved his ally and enabled him to overcome impregnable defences. . . .

All the prisoners taken from beginning to end of the war totalled 97,000; those who perished in the long siege 1,100,000. Of these the majority were Jews by race but not Jerusalem citizens: they had come together from the whole country for the Feast of Unleavened Bread and had suddenly been caught up in the war, so that first the overcrowding meant death by pestilence, and later hunger took a heavier toll. That so many could crowd into the City was shown by the census held in Cestius' time. Wishing to bring home the strength of the city to Nero, who despised the nation, Cestius instructed the chief priests to hold a census of the population, if it was possible to do so. They chose the time of the Passover Feast, at which sacrifice is offered from 3 to 5 p.m., and as it is not permissible to feast alone, a sort of fraternal group is formed round each victim, consisting of at least ten adult males, while many groups have twenty members. The count showed that there were 255,600 victims; the men, reckoning ten diners to each victim, totalled 2,700,000, all ceremonially clean; for persons suffering from leprosy, venereal disease, monthly periods, or any form of defilement were debarred from participation, as were the foreigners who came from abroad in large numbers to be present at the ceremonies.

But now fate had decreed that one prison should confine the whole nation and that a city solid with men should be held fast in war's embrace. No destruction ever wrought by God or man approached the wholesale carnage of this war. Every man who showed himself was either killed or captured by the Romans, and then those in the sewers were ferreted out, the ground was torn up, and all who were trapped were killed. There too were found the bodies of more than 2,000, some killed by their own hand, some by one another's, but most by starvation. So foul a stench of human flesh greeted those who charged in that many turned back at once. Others were so avaricious that they pushed on, climbing over the piles of corpses; for many valuables were found in the passages and all scruples were silenced by the prospect of gain. Many prisoners of the party chiefs were brought up; for not even at their last gasp had they abandoned their brutality. But God rewarded them both as they deserved: John, starving to death with his brothers in the sewers, after many scornful refusals at last appealed to the Romans for mercy, while Simon after battling long against the inevitable, gave himself up. John was sentenced to life-imprisonment, but Simon was kept for the triumphal procession and ultimate execution. The Romans now fired the outlying districts of the town and demolished the walls.

So fell Jerusalem in the second year of Vespasian's reign, on the 8th of Gorpiaios, captured five time before and now for the second time *utterly laid waste.*

Josephus (AD 37–? post 93), *The Jewish War*, tr. G. A. Williamson, 1981

LADY WEN-CHI IS KIDNAPPED BY BARBARIANS

Around AD *200, when the dynasty which ruled China was going through a period of weakness, a tribe of Mongolian nomads attacked the city of Ch'en-liu in modern Honan and captured Wen-Chi, the daughter of a leading statesman. She was carried off to Inner Mongolia and forced to marry one of the tribe's chiefs.*

Part I: The Abduction of Wen-Chi

The Han dynasty is in decline, the barbarians of the four quarters are
  hostile.
They have taken up arms, and there are constant wars.
My poor father and mother, who bore me and brought me up!
This is a time of partings and of turmoil.
All I knew of the world was what I had seen through gauze windows
  and mirrors;
I had thought the beaded curtains would protect me.
But then the barbarian horsemen rode into China.
Suddenly there were nomads everywhere.
Now my unhappy life is in danger from a sword-point,
And I have been carried off helplessly in the dust from the invaders'
  hooves.

Leaving China

They took me on horseback to the ends of the earth.
I prayed for death, but it did not come.
These barbarians stink; can they really be human?
When they enjoy themselves, or when they squabble, they are as
  terrible as jackals or wolves.
We head on to the farthest reaches of Tien-shan in the frost and sleet.
The people here are brutal and the land is desolate; we are
  approaching the territory of the barbarians.
The grey sky stretches for ten thousand miles, with not a bird to be
  seen.
The cold sands are unending, and you cannot tell one direction from
  another.

Camping in the Desert

I am like a prisoner in chains.
There is no one to confide my ten thousand fears to.

They can force me to work, they can cut my hair,
They can even eat my flesh and drink my blood:
Since all of this is death to me, I would not care.
But forcing me to marry is worse than killing me.
My beauty has been my undoing.
I hate being as weak and soft as water.

Longing for Home

The mountains and streams are so far behind us now, no one
    can remember them.
Where, on the far edge of the horizon, is my native land?
As a result of this terrible experience my spirits have left me,
And the wind and cold are slowly ruining my looks.
At night I dream of making the journey back.
In my half-conscious state maybe I can send my thoughts there?
No—there is no answer to my cries from the vast barbarian sky;
And yet the moon that shines there is our Chinese moon: it
    must surely recognize me?

> From 'Eighteen Songs of a Nomad Flute' by Liu Shang (*c.* AD 770), tr.
> John Simpson

THE PROPHET MAHOMET FLEES FROM MECCA TO MEDINA

The Hegira, or Flight, of the Prophet from the unbelievers of Mecca, accompanied by his faithful disciple Abu Beker, was the critical moment in the establishment of Islam. The year when it took place, AD 622, represents the start of the Muslim era.

He repaired immediately to the house of Abu Beker, and they arranged for instant flight. It was agreed that they should take refuge in a cave in Mount Thor, about an hour's distance from Mecca, and wait there until they could proceed safely to Medina: and in the meantime the children of Abu Beker should secretly bring them food. They left Mecca while it was yet dark, making their way on foot by the light of the stars, and the day dawned as they found themselves at the foot of Mount Thor. Scarce were they within the cave, when they heard the sound of pursuit. Abu Beker, though a brave man, quaked with fear. 'Our pursuers,' said he, 'are many, and we are but two.' 'Nay,' replied Mahomet, 'there is a third; God is with us!' And here the Moslem writers relate a miracle, dear to the minds of all true believers. By the time, say they, that the Koreishites reached the mouth of the cavern, an acacia tree had sprung up before it, in the spreading branches of which a pigeon had made its nest, and laid its eggs, and over the whole a spider had woven its web. When the Koreishites beheld these signs of undisturbed quiet, they concluded that no one could recently have entered the cavern; so they turned away, and pursued their search in another direction.

Whether protected by miracle or not, the fugitives remained for three days undiscovered in the cave, and Asama, the daughter of Abu Beker, brought them food in the dusk of the evenings.

On the fourth day, when they presumed the ardor of pursuit had abated, the fugitives ventured forth, and set out for Medina, on camels which a servant of Abu Beker had brought in the night for them. Avoiding the main road usually taken by the caravans, they bent their course nearer to the coast of the Red Sea. They had not proceeded far, however, before they were overtaken by a troop of horse, headed by Soraka Ibn Malec. Abu Beker was again dismayed by the number of their pursuers; but Mahomet repeated the assurance, 'Be not troubled; Allah is with us.' Soraka was a grim warrior, with shagged iron-gray locks, and naked sinewy arms rough with hair. As he overtook Mahomet, his horse reared and fell with him. His superstitious mind was struck with it as an evil sign. Mahomet perceived the state of his feelings, and by an eloquent appeal wrought upon him to such a degree, that Soraka, filled with awe, entreated his forgiveness; and turning back with his troop, suffered him to proceed on his way unmolested.

*

The Moslems of Mecca, who had taken refuge some time before in Medina, hearing that Mahomet was at hand, came forth to meet him at Koba; among these was the early convert Talha, and Zobeir, the nephew of Cadijah. These, seeing the travel-stained garments of Mahomet and Abu Beker, gave them white mantles, with which to make their entrance into Medina. Numbers of the Ansarians, or auxiliaries, of Medina, who had made their compact with Mahomet in the preceding year, now hastened to renew their vow of fidelity.

Learning from them that the number of proselytes in the city was rapidly augmenting, and that there was a general disposition to receive him favorably, he appointed Friday, the Moslem sabbath, the sixteenth day of the month Rabi, for his public entrance.

Accordingly, on the morning of that day he assembled all his followers to prayer; and after a sermon, in which he expounded the main principles of his faith, he mounted his camel Al Kaswa, and set forth for that city which was to become renowned in after ages as his city of refuge.

Boreida Ibn al Hoseib, with his seventy horsemen of the tribe of Saham, accompanied him as a guard. Some of the disciples took turns to hold a canopy of palm-leaves over his head, and by his side rode Abu Beker. 'Oh apostle of God!' cried Boreida, 'thou shalt not enter Medina without a standard;' so saying, he unfolded his turban, and tying one end of it to the point of his lance, bore it aloft before the prophet.

The city of Medina was fair to approach, being extolled for beauty of situation, salubrity of climate, and fertility of soil; for the luxuriance of its palm-trees, and the fragrance of its shrubs and flowers. At a short distance from the city a crowd of new proselytes to the faith, came forth in sun and dust to meet the cavalcade. Most of them had never seen Mahomet, and paid reverence to Abu Beker through mistake; but the latter put aside the screen of palm-leaves, and pointed out the real object of homage, who was greeted with loud acclamations.

In this way did Mahomet, so recently a fugitive from his native city, with a price upon his head, enter Medina, more as a conqueror in triumph than an exile seeking an asylum.

Washington Irving, 'The Life of the Prophet Mohammed', 1843

RELIGIOUS TERROR IN ENGLAND

The first part of Elizabeth I's reign had been marked by relative tolerance to Catholics. As the threat from Spain grew, however, and the Puritan influence on her government became stronger, new and more brutal laws were introduced. Well over a hundred Catholics were executed in England during her reign.

From 1559 to 1581, the charge upon which the martyrs were put to death was the second refusal to take the Oath of Supremacy. The other penalties were commonly confiscation of property, praemunire, imprisonment, and the payment of fines. Among those who were constituted within the Act of Supremacy were all who printed, imported, published, or disposed of, books maintaining papal authority. Gradually the apostolic zeal of the Seminary Priests and the enthusiasm created by the Jesuit Mission caused the Government to formulate laws which would affect those who were not bound to take the Oath of Supremacy; and the Act of 23 Eliz. c. i. (1581) made it high treason to absolve or to withdraw any one from the royal obedience or from the established religion. This Act caused many to leave the country, and though not affecting directly the Colleges at Rheims and Rome, made it impossible for the priests to stay more than three or four years in any given locality in England. The *Douay Diaries* mention constantly the coming of priests from the Missions, especially after the passing of the ferocious Act of 27 Eliz. c. i. (1585), which made the Priesthood itself sufficient cause for high treason and death. This Act was the parting of the ways. It marks the Government's firm determination to annihilate Catholicism in England.

Peter Guilday, *The English Catholic Refugees*, 1914

THE DETERMINATION OF THE PILGRIM FATHERS

From their temporary base at Leyden, Robinson and Brewster write to Sir Edwin Sandys, a member of the Council of the Virginia Company.

We are not like some, whom small things discourage, or small discontents cause to wish themselves at home again. We know what we can expect both in England and in Holland, and that we shall not improve our material well-being by our departure; whereas, should we be forced to return, we could not hope to regain our present position, either here or elsewhere during our lives, which are now drawing towards their periods.

These motives we have been bold to put to you, and, as you think well, to any other of our friends of the Council. We will not be further trouble-some, but with our humble duties to your Worship, and to any other of our well-willers of the Council, we take our leaves, committing you to the guidance of the Almighty.

Yours much bounden in all duty,

JOHN ROBINSON.

Leyden, Dec. 15th, 1617.   WILLIAM BREWSTER.

Bradfield's History of the Plymouth Settlement, 1608–1650, ed. Valerian Paget, 1909

THE TRIBULATIONS OF THE PILGRIMS

A large number of them had decided to take passage from Boston in Lincolnshire, and for that purpose had hired a ship wholly to themselves, and made agreement with the captain to be ready at a convenient place on a certain day to take them and their belongings. After long waiting and great expense—he had not kept day with them—he came at last and took them aboard at night. But when he had secured them and their goods he betrayed them, having arranged beforehand with the searchers and other officers to do so. They then put them in open boats, and there rifled and ransacked them, searching them to their shirts for money,—and even the women, further than became modesty,—and took them back to the town and made a spectacle of them to the multitude that came flocking on all sides to see them. Being thus rifled and stripped of their money, books, and other property, they were brought before the magistrates, and messengers were sent to inform the Lords of the Council about them. The magistrates treated them courteously, and showed them what favour they could; but dare not free them until order came from the council-table. The result was, however, that after a month's imprisonment, the majority were dismissed, and sent back to the places whence they came; but seven of the leaders were kept in prison, and bound over to the Assizes.

Next spring there was another attempt made by some of the same people, with others, to get over from a different place. They heard of a Dutchman at Hull who had a ship of his own belonging to Zealand, and they made an agreement with him, and acquainted him with their plight, hoping to find him more reliable than the English captain had been; and he bade them have no fear. He was to take them aboard between Grimsby and Hull, where there was a large common a good way from any town. The women and children, with all their effects, were sent to the place at the time arranged in a small bark which they had hired; and the men were to meet them by land. But it so happened that they all arrived a day before the ship came, and the sea being rough, and the women very sick, the sailors put into a creek hard by, where they grounded at low water. The next morning the ship came, but they were stuck fast and could not stir till about noon. In the meantime, the captain of the ship, seeing how things were, sent his boat to get the men aboard whom he saw were ready walking about the shore. But after the first boatful was got aboard and she was ready to go for more, the captain espied a large body of horse and foot, armed with bills and guns and other weapons,—for the country side had turned out to capture them. The Dutchman, seeing this, swore his country's oath, 'sacramente,' and having a fair wind, weighed anchor, hoist sail, and away! The poor men already aboard were in great distress for their wives and children, left thus to be captured, and destitute of help,—and for them-selves, too, without any clothes but what they had on their backs, and scarcely a penny about them, all their possessions being aboard the bark, now seized. It drew tears from their eyes, and they would have given anything to be ashore again. But all in vain, there was no remedy; they must thus sadly part. Afterwards they endured a fearful storm at sea, and it was fourteen days or more before they reached port, in seven of which they saw neither sun, moon, nor stars, being driven near the coast of Norway. The sailors themselves often despaired, and once with shrieks and cries gave over all, as if the ship had foundered and they were sinking without hope of recovery. But when man's hope and help wholly failed, there appeared the Lord's power and mercy to save them; for the ship rose again, and gave the crew courage to manage her . . .

The other men, who were in greatest danger, made shift to escape before the troops could surprise them, only sufficient staying to assist the women. But it was pitiful to see these poor women in their distress. What weeping and crying on every side: some for their husbands carried away in the ship; others not knowing what would become of them and their little ones; others again melted in tears, seeing their poor little ones hanging about them, crying for fear and quaking with cold! Being thus apprehended, they were hurried from one place to another, till in the end the officers knew not what to do with them; for to imprison so many innocent women and children only because they wished to go with their husbands, seemed unreasonable and would cause an outcry; and to send them home again was as difficult, for they alleged, as was the truth, that they had no homes to go to,—for they had sold or otherwise disposed of their houses and livings. To be short, after they had been thus turmoiled a good while, and conveyed from one constable to another, they were glad to be rid of them on any terms; for all were wearied and tired of them. Though in the meantime, they, poor souls, endured misery enough. So in the end, necessity forced a way for them . . .

> *Bradfield's History of the Plymouth Settlement, 1608–1650*, ed. Valerian Paget, 1909

SQUEEZED LIKE NETTLES

Sir Richard Cox, one of Cromwell's officials in County Cork, boasts of his services.

As to the enemy, I used them like nettles, and squeezed them (I mean their vagabond partyes) soe hard, that they could seldom sting; having, as I believe, killed and hanged no less than three thousand of them, whilst I stayed in the County of Cork; and taken from them in cattle and plunder, at least to the value of Twelve thousand pounds, which you will easily believe, when you know that I divided three hundred and eighty pounds between one troop (Colonel Townsend's) in the beginning of August. After which Colonel Beecher and the western gentlemen got a prey worth three thousand pounds, besides several other lesser preys, taken by small partyes, that are not taken notice of &c.

> Quoted in Thomas Addis Emmet, *Ireland under English Rule*, 1903

LIKE THE SLAVE HUNTS IN AFRICA

During Cromwell's wars in Ireland, and in particular after the sack of Drogheda and the murder of its inhabitants, slavery became a frequent punishment; and soon contractors were operating with official encouragement.

Ireland must have exhibited scenes in every part like the slave hunts in Africa. How many girls of gentle birth must have been caught and hurried to the private prisons of these men-catchers none can tell. We are told of one case. Daniel Connery, a gentleman of Clare, was sentenced . . . to banishment, in 1657, by Colonel Henry Ingoldsby, for harbouring a priest. 'This gentleman had a wife and twelve children. His wife fell sick and died in poverty. Three of his daughters, beautiful girls, were transferred to the West Indies, to an island called the Barbadoes; and there, if still alive (he says) they are miserable slaves.'

As one instance out of many:—Captain John Vernon was employed by the Commissioners for Ireland into England, and contracted in their behalf with Mr. David Sellick and Mr. Leader under his hand, bearing date the 14th September, 1653, to supply them with two hundred and fifty women of the Irish nation above twelve years, and under the age of forty-five, also three hundred men above twelve years of age and under fifty, to be found in the county within twenty miles of Cork &c. . . . To transplant them into New England . . . And (in 1655) to secure a thousand young girls ('Irish wenches' is Secretary Thurloe's term) to be sent there also. . . . Henry Cromwell answered that there would be no difficulty, only that force must be used in taking them; and he suggested the addition of from 1500 to 2000 boys of from twelve to fourteen years of age. . . . We could well spare them, he adds, and they might be of use to you; and who knows but it might be a means of making them Englishmen—I mean Christians? . . . The number finally fixed were 1000 boys, and 1000 girls, to sail from Galway October, 1655, the boys as bondsmen, probably, and the girls to be bound by other ties to these English soldiers in Jamaica. . . . In the course of four years they had seized and shipped about 6400 Irish men and women, boys and maidens, when on the 4th of March, 1656, all orders were revoked. . . . But at last the evil became too shocking and notorious, particularly when these dealers in Irish flesh began to seize the daughters and children of the English themselves, and to force them on board their slave ships; then, indeed, the orders, at the end of four years, were revoked.

John P. Prendergast, The Cromwellian Settlement in Ireland, 1875

THE TRIAL OF A HUGUENOT

Jean Mascarene, a wealthy Protestant from Paris, was charged with refusing to obey Louis XIV's new religious laws and found guilty. He was made a galley-slave, and later died as a result of the treatment he received.

May 7, 1687.

My dear wife, I have appeared before my judges when I least thought of doing so. Yesterday morning, while I was still in bed, the keeper came to apprise me that I must go to the Tournelle. So soon as I was dressed, and had made my prayer to God, imploring His grace to sustain me in this new trial, and asking the assistance of His Holy Spirit, that I might give a reason of my faith to those that might question me, my feet were put in fetters, and I was carried in a chair to the great door of the palace. From there I crossed the entire court on foot, and was led to the door of the bureau of the Tournelle, where I waited until M. Dupuy, who had been conducted thither before me, should be brought forth.

The inquiries concerning the proceedings soon came to an end. The president then asked me whether I purposed always to persist in my religion. I answered in the affirmative. Afterwards, another judge asked me what I had intended to do in the kingdom, seeing my religion was no longer tolerated within its bounds. To this I replied that my purpose was patiently to await whatever his majesty might ordain with reference to those who were not willing to abjure the [Reformed] religion. The president asked me if I did not know that it was forbidden by his majesty's last Edict to maintain any exercise of our religion, and if I did not perceive that therein I violated his majesty's orders. To this I answered that it was to the public exercise of our religion that the Edict referred, and that hence I was not in that case . . .

The president asked me for the second time whether I was wholly resolved to persist in my religion; to which I answered, Yes. After this another judge addressed me in the following terms: Enlightened as you are, you ought to profit by the light you possess, and acknowledge the truth of the Roman Catholic religion, and embrace it. We do not, said he, regard you as one of the criminals whom we are accustomed to see at our feet: yet we shall be constrained to judge you according to the king's declarations, and to condemn you to the penalties therein prescribed . . .

Finally, the president asked me for the third time if I were wholly resolved to persist in my religion? I replied that such was my resolution, and that I trusted that God would grant me grace to adhere to it. He inquired further if I knew to what I was condemned, and when I answered that I had been condemned by the first judge to the galleys, he asked me whether I were appellant? Upon my affirmative answer, he dismissed me, saying to me that the court would do me justice. I feel with joy that God strengthens me daily, and gives me grace to prepare for whatever issue with entire resignation to His will. You may imagine that I passionately desire to see you before my transportation. I do not think that I shall remain here long. I wish you every blessing.

> *The Torments of Protestant Slaves in the French King's Galleys, 1686–1707*, ed. Edward Arber, 1908

THE LOYALISTS ARE DRIVEN OUT OF AMERICA

The American War of Independence was a civil war as well as a struggle against the British. The Rebels or Whigs fought for political separation from Britain, the Tory Loyalists for a United Empire. The losers suffered heavily.

The treatment afforded the unfortunate Tories remains one of the most sordid chapters of American history. All sorts of malicious indignities were inflicted upon them in the name of patriotism. Tarring and feathering was a favourite sport of the mobs throughout the war. After the Declaration of Independence in 1776 each state enacted laws designating them as traitors. Thousands were deprived of their civil rights, debarred from earning a livelihood, robbed of their possessions, imprisoned, and finally banished from the land of their birth. Thousands of others left voluntarily to seek the protection of the British flag.

Because of proximity and climate, East Florida became the preferred asylum for southern Loyalists. This was an old Spanish colony which had been ceded to Britain after the Seven Years War. It was looked upon as a military outpost during Spanish rule and after two decades of British sovereignty the population was hardly more than that of the Bahamas. It had not joined the other colonies in revolt; in fact, throughout the war the inhabitants had shown no enthusiasm for the rebel cause. The harassed Tories of Georgia and the Carolinas saw that great empty space as a nearby, safe land of refuge. As their prospects deteriorated, they began to remove there by the hundreds. And when the British army abandoned their home states they poured into Florida in thousands.

Many of these Loyalists had owned sizeable estates, or were otherwise citizens of consequence in their communities. In Florida, and especially in St Augustine, they set about making new lives for themselves. They acquired land, built houses, developed plantations, and engaged in businesses and the professions.

The colony being British, they hoped to regain a sense of security and some semblance of their former fortunes. The Governor was informed that it was the King's wish that Florida should become a 'secure assylum for loyalists from the refractory colonists'. But fate had yet another blow in store for these wretched people. The Treaty of Versailles which restored the Bahamas to Britain also restored Florida to Spain. British residents were given eighteen months to settle their affairs and get out. . . .

In June 1783 the first batch of Loyalists arrived in Nassau from St Augustine. In charge of operations was Brigadier-General Archibald McArthur, and few men would have envied his job. It must be remembered that the great majority of these refugees were close to destitute. Many of them were to be recompensed for their losses by the British Government later, but for the moment only a few such as the Rolles and Kelsalls who went to Exuma could afford to charter vessels and provide for themselves on arrival.

McArthur had to supply transportation which was itself a formidable undertaking. But when the Loyalists and their slaves were put ashore in Nassau the real problems began. Shelter had to be provided where no shelter existed. Army tents and lean-tos of ships' sails, palmetto thatch, rough lumber or anything else that could be found, sprouted up all around the town. Almost every mouthful of food for this increasing mass of people had to be imported. Sometimes vessels bringing these precious cargoes were wrecked. When this happened, some of the refugees were reduced to near-starving conditions.

All through 1784 the exodus from Florida continued. But toward the end of that year the Governor gave notice that the last transport vessel would leave on 1 March 1785. Florida supplied by far the greatest number of immigrants, but some came from other places on the continent including a thousand or more from New York. The exact number of refugees who came to the Bahamas will never be known. Estimates range between 5000 and 7000 Loyalists and slaves.

Paul Albury, *The Story of the Bahamas*, 1975

THEY CALL THEM AMERICAN NEGROES

When the Europeans came,
when they brought their ships from Portugal,
the ship used to start its journey from Banjul,
then it went to Sanumunko Jammeh, and Mansa Demba Sanko,
and Samkala Marong, and Wali Mandeba, and Jata Sela.
Anyone who had slaves they collected them altogether
and took them to the places called Aladabara and Jufure

to sell them to the Portuguese.
Then the Portuguese put them in their ship
and left there and went to Jang Jang Bure.
When they arrived there they went
right to the slave house to collect slaves there
and take them to the Hollanders.
Then the Hollanders collected them and sent them to America.
It is because of this that slaves are plenty in America.

They call them American Negroes.

> Alhaji Fabala Kanuteh, from 'The Song of Alhaji Fabala Kanuteh', a Griot
> narrative from *The Griots*, Folkways Records, New York

THE HEAVY CHAINS OF SLAVERY

To his Excellency Thomas Gage Esq. Captain General and Governor in Chief
in and over this Province.
To the Honourable his Majestys Council and the Honourable House of Rep-
resentatives in General Court assembled May 25 1774

The Petition of a Grate Number of Blackes of this Province who by
divine permission are held in a state of Slavery within the bowels of a free
and christian Country
Humbly Shewing
That your Petitioners apprehind we have in common with all other men
a naturel right to our freedoms without Being depriv'd of them by our
fellow men as we are a freeborn Pepel and have never forfeited this Blessing
by aney compact or agreement whatever. But we were unjustly dragged by
the cruel hand of power from our dearest frinds and sum of us stolen from
the bosoms of our tender Parents and from a Populous Pleasant and plen-
tiful country and Brought hither to be made slaves for Life in a Christian
land. Thus we are deprived of every thing that hath a tendency to make life
even tolerable, the endearing ties of husband and wife we are strangers to
for we are no longer man and wife than our masters or mistresses thinkes
proper marred or onmarred. Our children are also taken from us by force
and sent maney miles from us wear we seldom or ever see them again there
to be made slaves of for Life which sumtimes is vere short by Reson of
Being dragged from their mothers Breest Thus our Lives are imbittered to
us on these accounts By our deplorable situation we are rendered incapable
of shewing our obedience to Almighty God how can a slave perform the
duties of a husband to a wife or parent to his child How can a husband

leave master to work and cleave to his wife How can the wife submit themselves to there husbands in all things How can the child obey thear parents in all things. There is a great number of us sencear . . . members of the Church of Christ how can the master and the slave be said to fulfil that command Live in love let Brotherly Love contuner and abound Beare yea onenothers Bordenes How can the master be said to Beare my Borden when he Beares me down whith the Have chanes of slavery and operson against my will and how can we fulfill our parte of duty to him whilst in this condition and as we cannot searve our God as we ought whilst in this situation. Nither can we reap an equal benefet from the laws of the Land which doth not justifi but condemns Slavery or if there had bin aney Law to hold us in Bondage we are Humbely of the Opinion ther never was aney to inslave our children for life when Born in a free Countrey. We therfor Bage your Excellency and Honours will give this its deer weight and consideration and that you will accordingly cause an act of the legislative to be pessed that we may obtain our Natural right our freedoms and our children be set at lebety at the yeare of twenty one for whoues sekes more petequeley your Petitioners is in Duty ever to pray.

> Herbert Aptheker, ed., *A Documentary History of the Negro People in the United States*, 1969

SENTENCED TO TRANSPORTATION IN AUSTRALIA

'It is therefore ordered and adjudged by this Court, that you be transported upon the seas, beyond the seas, to such place as His Majesty, by the advice of His Privy Council, shall think fit to direct and appoint, for the term of your natural life.' Or seven years, or fourteen—in any case, the shock of sentencing was dreadful. In law, seven years' banishment meant what it said; but what man could be certain of returning to England at the end of it? For many people, the sentence of transportation—whatever its announced length—must have seemed like a one-way trip over the edge of the world.

A man could bear it with dignity in the dock, but despair followed soon after. Anguish shows in the few surviving letters, like this one from a Lancashire weaver named Thomas Holden, who in the course of struggling for his rights as an early trade-unionist was convicted in 1812 of 'administering an illegal oath' to one Isaac Crompton in Bolton, Lancashire. It seems probable that Holden was a Luddite. He was also happily married. 'Dear Wife,' he wrote from a cell in Lancaster Castle,

Its with sorrow that I have to acquaint you that I this day receiv'd my Tryal and has receiv'd the hard sentance of Seven Years Transportation beyond the seas. . . . If

I was for any Time in prison I would try and content myself but to be sent from my Native Country perhaps never to see it again distresses me beyond comprehension and will Terminate with my life. . . . [T]o part with my dear Wife & Child, Parents and Friends, to be no more, cut off in the Bloom of my Youth without doing the least wrong to any person on earth—O my hard fate, may God have mercy on me. . . . Your affec. Husband until Death.

In April 1831 Peter Withers, the 'Swing' protestor from Wiltshire, wrote from the convict ship *Proteus* at Spithead to his wife Mary Ann:

My Dear Wife belive me my Hart is almost broken to think I must lave you behind. O my dear what shall I do i am all Most destracted at the thoughts of parting from you whom I do love so dear. Believe me My Dear it Cuts me even to the hart and my dear Wife there is a ship Come into Portsmouth harber to take us to New Southweals.

Inconceivable distances loom before Withers, who has never even been as far from home as London; and he tries to explain them, to normalize them by promising a fidelity that will annihilate separation:

it is about 4 months sail to that country But we shall stop at several cuntreys before we gets there for fresh water I expects you will eare from me in the course of 9 months. . . . you may depend upon My keeping Myself from all other Woman for i shall Never Let No other run into my mind for tis onely you My Dear that can Ease me of my Desire. It is not Laving Auld england that grives me it is laving my dear and loving Wife and Children, May God be Mersyful to me.

Many prisoners hoped their wives would go into Australian exile with them, although few actually did; it was hard to get passage out there, and tickets were far beyond the means of a worker's wife. 'I hope you will strain your utmost to keep my Company,' Thomas Holden wrote to his wife Molly as he was leaving for the hulks, 'and not let mee go without you for with your company I don't mind where I go nor what I suffer, if I have your Company to chear my allmost Broken Hart.' And later, from the hulk: 'My sorrow is greatly Encreased by parting with you, what Comfort can I enjoy when we are separate. . . . I could wish to know if you think you Could rise money to pay your passage & go with me.' She did not go. Neither did Mary Ann, Peter Withers's wife, despite his heart-wringing pleas:

We [h]ears we shall get our freedom in that Country, but if I gets my freedom evenso i am shure I shall Never be happy except I can have the Pleshur of ending my days with you and my dear Children, for I dont think a man ever loved a woman so well as I love you.
 My Dear I hope you will go to the gentlemen for they to pay your Passage over

to me when I send for you. How happy I shall be to eare that you are a-coming after me. . . . Do you think I shall sent for you except i can get a Cumfortable place for you, do you think that I wants to get you into Troble, do you think as I want to punish my dear Children? No my dear but if I can get a cumfortsable place should you not like to follow your dear Husband who Lovs you so dear?

There was no reply, and two years later Withers was writing to his brothers from Van Diemen's Land: 'I have sent 2 letters to My Wife an Cant get heny Answer from her Wich Causeth Me a great deal of unhapyness for i think she have quite forgotten me an I think she is got Marred to some other Man, if she is pray send me Word.' But there was still no word from her, and eleven years would pass before Mary Ann wrote in distress to her husband in Van Diemen's Land, asking to be reconciled.

> Robert Hughes, *The Fatal Shore: A History of the Transportation of Convicts to Australia, 1787–1868*, 1987

JIM JONES IS SENT TO BOTANY BAY

O listen for a moment, lads,
    And hear me tell my tale,
How o'er the sea from England's shore
    I was compelled to sail.

The jury says, He's guilty, sir,
    And says the judge, says he,
For life, Jim Jones, I'm sending you
    Across the stormy sea.

And take my tip before you ship
    To join the Iron Gang,
Don't be too gay at Botany Bay,
    Or else you'll surely hang.

Or else you'll hang, he says, says he,
    And after that, Jim Jones,
High up upon the gallows tree
    The crows will peck your bones.

You'll have no chance for mischief then,
    Remember what I say,
They'll flog the poaching out of you
    Out there at Botany Bay.

The winds blew high upon the sea,
　　And pirates came along,
But the soldiers on our convict ship
　　Were full five hundred strong.

They opened fire and somehow drove
　　That pirate ship away.
I'd rather have joined that pirate ship
　　Than come to Botany Bay.

For night and day the irons clang,
　　And like poor galley slaves
We toil and toil, and when we die
　　Must fill dishonoured graves.

But bye and bye I'll break my chains,
　　Into the bush I'll go
And join the brave bushrangers there—
　　Jack Donohoo and Co.

And some black night when everything
　　Is silent in the town
I'll kill the tyrants, one and all,
　　And shoot the floggers down.

I'll give the law a little shock,
　　Remember what I say,
They'll yet regret they sent Jim Jones
　　In chains to Botany Bay.

Anon.; from *How Strong the Roots: Poems of Exile*, ed. Howard Sergeant, 1981. Jack Donohoo was transported to Australia in 1825, but escaped. He was killed by the police five years later.

DOSTOEVSKY'S MOCK EXECUTION

Early in the morning of 22 December 1849 Fyodor Mikhailovich Dostoevsky, officially described as 'Lieutenant of Engineers, retired', was ordered out of his cell in the Petropavlovsky Fortress in the Imperial Russian capital, St Petersburg. He was then taken across the River Neva, by carriage in a convoy flanked by mounted Cossacks, to the Semyonovsky Square in the south of the city. Blinking in the wintry sunshine, the twenty-eight-year-old former army officer—and, it seemed, unsuccessful novelist—was paraded on the snow with twenty friends and former associates. They were surrounded on all four sides of the huge square by troops.

Dostoevsky and his friends had been arrested several months earlier for treason. Their conspiracy against the Russian state had consisted of little more than debating judicial reform, serf emancipation, socialism and revolution in informal discussion circles. But to discuss these subjects at all, however privately, in the Tsar-Emperor Nicholas I's later reign had been to take a grave risk. Perhaps the spice of danger had been the chief attraction to the young author, gambler and hypochondriac who now waited, shivering on the snow after embracing the other accused. Dostoevsky was fair-haired, freckled, with small, deep-sunk eyes under a high-domed forehead; shortish of stature, but broad-shouldered and of fairly strong build. He wore the rumpled civilian clothes in which the police had arrested him in the previous April. Paler even than usual after eight months in the dungeons, he formed with his friends a sharp contrast to the glittering battalions and squadrons massed on all sides. Orders cracked, drums rumbled ominously.

The presiding General stepped forward and began reading from a document. Only now did the twenty-one young men learn that they had been tried and condemned in their absence—to immediate death by firing squad! 'Criminal conversations . . . reading a felonious missive . . . full of impudent expressions directed against Supreme Authority and the Orthodox Church . . . plotting to write anti-government articles and to disseminate them by means of a home lithographic press': these were the main charges for which Dostoevsky personally had to pay the penalty!

That the young men were to be executed three at a time, with Dostoevsky himself in the second batch, soon became evident after they had been arrayed in the prescribed white 'shrouds' with long, trailing sleeves and hoods. The first victims were each secured to a post, their arms were bound behind their backs by the sleeves, and the hoods were pulled over their faces. At the word of command, three guards detachments took aim at almost point blank range and the order to fire was instantly expected. But then an aide-de-camp galloped across the square bearing a sealed packet. A drum roll halted the proceedings, and the condemned men heard the presiding General laboriously intone the last-minute commutation of their sentences: most to periods of *katorga* (Siberian hard labour and exile). Two days later the political criminal and future great novelist, his ankles secured by the customary fetters, had begun his two-thousand-mile journey to a new life as a convict at Omsk in Siberia.

The mock execution had been a cruel farce, deliberately staged to teach the culprits a lesson on the detailed instructions of the Emperor; he had, perhaps, even maliciously chosen the General, a notorious stutterer, who haltingly read out the sentence. Thus, at the whim of this crowned martinet, specialist in gallows humour and hounder of imaginative writers, did the young Dostoevsky spend several minutes in full expectation of imminent death. During that time, as he later indicated, all his previous life passed in review through his mind.

Ronald Hingley, *Dostoevsky: His Life and Work*, 1975

DEGRADING AN INNOCENT MAN

On Saturday 5 January 1895, at the Ecole Militaire in Paris, Alfred Dreyfus, having been found guilty of selling French military secrets to Germany, was publicly degraded before being sentenced to life imprisonment on Devil's Island. He was not a traitor; the secrets had been sold by another officer. But he was a Jew, and much of the case against him was rooted in anti-Semitism.

Bells sounded, military drums rolled, and four artillery soldiers, sabers in hand, led Dreyfus into the Cour Morland. Every regiment of the Paris garrison had been ordered to send two detachments to the ceremony—one of soldiers in arms, the other of young recruits. Like the ritualistic hazing process Dreyfus had known as a first-year cadet at the Ecole Polytechnique, the 'degradation' of an officer was a didactic ritual designed to instill the fear of humiliation. Moving diagonally across the courtyard's vast expanse and toward a general on horseback at its center, Dreyfus marched under the chiseled inscription 'Ecole Supérieure de Guerre.' It was the place where he had spent the most important part of his military career and where 'every wall, every stone, recalled images of his past.' Now, on a terrace 'which dominated the sad and imposing spectacle,' military students watched the traitor walk below. In lock-step with his guards, he stumbled briefly, then regained his balance. 'Look how he holds himself upright, the scum,' remarked someone in the distant crowd, but the nearly four thousand troops had been ordered to remain still and silent. The guards retreated, leaving their prisoner alone in front of General Darras and Vallecalle, the clerk of the Court-Martial. In a loud, clear voice Vallecalle read the act of judgment, saluted Darras, and stepped back. Dreyfus, heels together and at attention, remained silent. Standing in his stirrups, the general raised his sword, looked down at the prisoner, and announced, 'Alfred Dreyfus, you are not worthy of bearing arms. In the name of the French people, we degrade you!'

In fulfillment of the promise he had made to himself and his family, the prisoner broke his silence, raised both hands, forced his head even higher, and shouted: 'Soldiers, they are degrading an innocent man! Soldiers, they are dishonoring an innocent man! Long live France! Long live the Army!' Another silence followed, broken seconds later by the crowd beyond the courtyard gates chanting 'Death! Death!' Quickly a sergeant major approached Dreyfus and slashed the gold braids from his cap and uniform; he stripped the regiment numbers from his collar, ripped off his brass buttons and, kneeling down while the prisoner remained at strict attention, tore from Dreyfus's pants leg the red stripes he had worn since his entrance into the Ecole Polytechnique. Finally, he took the sword, broke it over his knee, pulled off the captain's scabbard and leather belt, and threw the pieces to the ground. With his kepi now misshapen and threads hanging from his uniform (his 'black rag'), Dreyfus repeated his protest: 'I am innocent!'

Stepping over the pile at his feet, he moved off the narrow cobblestone pathway that ran down the center of the Cour Morland and began the 'degradation parade' around the courtyard's muddy periphery. He knew the regulations and seemed to lead his guards 'like an officer commanding his squadron.' Soldiers gazed past him without a word, while dignitaries and journalists recorded their impressions. Maurice Paléologue, a diplomat from the Ministry of Foreign Affairs, had come to the degradation with Colonel Sandherr. Taken aback by Dreyfus's stiff, monotonous appeals, he told Sandherr: 'If I were innocent I would rebel, I would struggle.' 'It is clear that you do not know the Jews,' responded the officer. 'The race has neither patriotism, nor honor, nor pride. For centuries they have done nothing but betray.' A journalist covering the event for *La Croix* would call Dreyfus's shout of 'Long live France!' the 'last kiss of Judas,' and the reporter from *La Libre Parole* said that 'it was not a man being degraded for an individual error, but an entire race whose shame was laid bare.'. . .

When Dreyfus passed a special section reserved for officers' wives, the women began their own chants, and one, near the parade line, spat in the prisoner's face. Moving on, he called out, 'I swear on my wife and children that I am innocent! Long live France!' At the high gate facing the Place de Fontenoy, Dreyfus stopped and turned to the crowd. Police agents tried to push spectators back from the iron bars, but they surged forward and greeted the prisoner's protests with a torrent of hisses and shouts of 'Traitor! Traitor! Death to the Jew!' Nearing the end of his march, Dreyfus stopped again in front of the press: 'Tomorrow you will tell all of France that I am innocent,' he said. But the journalists, like the coterie of army wives, broke the silence that reigned within the courtyard and lashed back: 'Shut up, you wretch! Coward! Judas! Filthy Jew!' For the first time, Dreyfus interrupted his litany and cried out, 'You have no right to insult me!' But he was moved on by the Republican Guard, handcuffed, and pushed into the waiting prison wagon. The driver, who later called it 'the most beautiful day of my life,' whipped his horses into a gallop and headed north toward the Avenue Bosquet and the Pont de l'Alma. The entire spectacle had taken ten minutes.

Michael Burns, *Dreyfus: A Family Affair 1789–1945*, 1992

THE LIVING WILDE RISES FROM HIS TOMB

After being released from Reading Gaol in 1897, Oscar Wilde went to live for a time on the French coast. This merely left him open to the unkindness of former friends.

Dieppe, as he had feared, was not the best place for him. His friends might greet him effusively, other English tourists would not. He soon discovered that he could not rely upon the freemasonry of fellow artists, who could be as hypocritical as the inartistic in their gratuitous preference, as Wilde expressed it, for Messalina over Sporus, that is, for heterosexual debauchery over homosexual. As it happened, Dieppe was then full of artists, including three Englishmen and a Frenchman he had known well: Walter Sickert, Charles Conder, Beardsley, and Jacques-Emile Blanche. All were so eager to demonstrate that they were Bohemians that they became prigs. Sickert had reason to be grateful to Wilde for many acts of kindness to him and his family: now he shunned his old friend. Beardsley and Conder, walking with Blanche and aware that Blanche wished to show sympathy for Wilde, steered Blanche into a side street to prevent a meeting. Wilde may not have observed this cut, though one feels he observed every cut, but soon after, as he was sitting in front of the Café Suisse, he caught sight of Blanche, walking this time with Sickert, and beckoned to him. (Blanche had begun their friendship in 1883 by painting a picture of a young woman reading Wilde's *Poems*, and they had been on excellent terms for years.) But he ignored Wilde's signal and passed by as if he had not seen it. Wilde took great offense and made no further overtures.

As for Beardsley, he had profited from Wilde's kindness, which he returned by insisting that Wilde should not be published in the *Yellow Book* if he were to illustrate it. At this time, moreover, he was being supported financially by André Raffalovich (whom he called 'Mentor'), and that sworn enemy of Wilde would have resented any friendship between them. Yet circumstances threw the two men together, and Beardsley was unable to resist at least one cordial meeting at a dinner party on 19 July 1897. On 3

August Wilde persuaded Beardsley to 'buy a hat more silver than silver.' Then Wilde invited him to dinner at Berneval, and Beardsley snubbed him by not showing up and by leaving Dieppe for Boulogne soon after, complaining of some members of the society there. 'It was *lâche* of Aubrey,' Wilde commented, playing snob to Beardsley's snub: 'If it had been one of my own class I might perhaps have understood it. I don't know whether I respect most the people who see me or those who don't. But a boy like that, whom I made! No, it was too *lâche* of Aubrey.' 'To be spoken of, and not to be spoken to, is delightful,' he wrote ironically to Ada Leverson. But to the Ranee of Sarawak he sent a message, 'Tell her that horrible as are the dead when they rise from their tombs, the living when they come out from their tombs are more horrible still.'

Richard Ellmann, *Oscar Wilde*, 1987

COLLECTIVIZATION COMES TO THE TOWN OF ROSLAVL

Preparations for deportation began on February 15, 1931. Lists of all kulaks and well-to-do peasants were collected from the village soviets. But these lists, the OGPU emissary complained, 'failed to provide the information necessary to do the impending job.' Consequently, personal questionnaires were circulated to 215 potential victims under the guise of checking the correctness of their tax liabilities. On March 18, the raitroika reviewed the questionnaries and condemned seventy-four households to liquidation. On the evening of March 19, the raitroika assembled its emissaries at a central point, gave them instructions, and assigned two households to each emissary. The operation was to be completed that same night. But 'not all went smoothly.' In a number of cases the emissaries stalled, conducted drawn-out meetings with poor peasants, and in general 'failed to arrange the job in a tightly conspiratorial fashion.' As a result kulaks were forewarned, and the emissaries failed to find those marked for deportation. Some emissaries allowed 'tearful goodbyes to be drawn out' during which many able-bodied men slipped away. A number of kulaks succeeded in smuggling their property to poorer relatives. All in all, thirty-two families were deported from the raion; the rest fled, and the OGPU head stated that measures were being taken to find them. He complained that many emissaries had made 'grave mistakes'; the wife of one emissary, a Komsomol, publicly expressed grief and sympathy for the deported. 'We are no longer people,' she was quoted as having said; 'we are animals.' But most Komsomols were lauded for having done an outstanding job, 'better than that of responsible officials.' According to the report, poor peasants were 'generally pleased' with the progress of events. But middle peasants were 'confused and unnerved.' 'Our turn will come soon,' they kept repeating. . . .

According to this report, the deportations brought an atmosphere of panic to the towns as well as to the villages. Some workers 'do not sleep nights,' waiting to be taken away, or expecting some of their relatives to be taken. 'All my acquaintances have already been taken away,' one commented, '. . . the most terrible thing is that no one knows where he is taken to; people have been brought to the verge of complete passivity; no matter what one does to them, they don't care any more; earlier an arrested man was led by two militiamen; now one militiaman may lead groups of people, and the latter calmly walk and no one flees.' The report cited a 'characteristic' case where one citizen came to the raion procuracy and begged to be deported together with the kulaks, reasoning that he would at least have a chance to start a 'less hectic life.'

Manifestations of sympathy for the deported were widespread, even in the cities. Groups of women watching the departure of the deported commented: 'It is in vain that these poor families are so mistreated . . . they have been suffering for the last two years . . . everything was in any case taken away from them through taxes . . . this is horrifying . . . children are taken together with adults . . . with only what is on their backs . . . It is impossible to comprehend why all this is happening to the people . . .' 'Hearsay' is reproduced by the OGPU to the effect that 'deportee-families are separated . . . with mothers in one rail-car, husbands and children in other cars. Mothers are hysterical, tearing hair from their heads.'

Merle Fainsod, *Smolensk under Soviet Rule*, 1958

HOLOCAUST

Rivka Yosselevska was forced to kneel in an open grave with a large number of other Jews. They were then shot. Rivka was wounded in the head, but not seriously, and managed to crawl out of the grave.

I was searching among the dead for my little girl, and I cried for her—Merkele was her name—Merkele! There were children crying, 'Mother!' 'Father!'—but they were all smeared with blood and one could not recognise the children. I cried for my daughter. From afar I saw two women standing. I went up to them. They did not know me, I did not know them, and then I said who I was, and then they said, 'So you survived.' And there was another woman crying, 'Pull me out from amongst the corpses, I am alive, help!' We were thinking how could we escape from the place. The cries of the woman, 'Help, pull me out from the corpses!' We pulled her out. Her name was Mikla Rosenberg. We removed the corpses and the dying people who held on to her and continued to bite. She asked us to take her out, to free her, but we did not have the strength.

And thus we were there all night, fighting for our lives, listening to the cries and the screams and all of a sudden we saw Germans, mounted Germans. We did not notice them coming in because of the screamings and the shoutings from the bodies around us.

The Germans ordered that all the corpses be heaped together into one big heap and with shovels they were heaped together, all the corpses, amongst them many still alive, children running about the place. I saw them. I saw the children. They were running after me, hanging on to me. Then I sat down in the field and remained sitting with the children around me. The children who got up from the heap of corpses.

Then Germans came and were going around the place. We were ordered to collect all the children, but they did not approach me, and I sat there watching how they collected the children. They gave a few shots and the children were dead. They did not need many shots. The children were almost dead, and this Rosenberg woman pleaded with the Germans to be spared, but they shot her.

They all left—the Germans and the non-Jews from around the place. They removed the machine guns and they took the trucks. I saw that they all left, and the four of us, we went on to the grave, praying to fall into the grave, even alive, envying those who were dead already and thinking what to do now. I was praying for death to come. I was praying for the grave to be opened and to swallow me alive. Blood was spurting from the grave in many places, like a well of water, and whenever I pass a spring now, I remember the blood which spurted from the ground, from that grave.

I was digging with my fingernails, trying to join the dead in that grave. I dug with my fingernails, but the grave would not open. I did not have enough strength. I cried out to my mother, to my father, 'Why did they not kill me? What was my sin? I have no one to go to. I saw them all being killed. Why was I spared? Why was I not killed?'

Martin Gilbert, *The Holocaust*, 1987

BANISHED TO THE COUNTRYSIDE BY THE CULTURAL REVOLUTION

In 1969 my parents, my sister, my brother Jin-ming, and I were expelled from Chengdu one after another, and sent to distant parts of the Sichuan wilderness. We were among millions of urban dwellers to be exiled to the countryside. In this way, young people would not be roaming the cities with nothing to do, creating trouble out of sheer boredom, and adults like my parents would have a 'future.' They were part of the old administration which had been replaced by Mao's Revolutionary Committees, and packing them off to the sticks to do hard labor was a convenient solution.

According to Mao's rhetoric, we were sent to the countryside 'to be reformed.' Mao advocated 'thought reform through labor' for everyone, but never explained the relationship between the two. Of course, no one asked for clarification. Merely to contemplate such a question was tantamount to treason. In reality, everyone in China knew that hard labor, particularly in the countryside, was always punishment. It was noticeable that none of Mao's henchmen, the members of the newly established Revolutionary Committees, army officers—and very few of their children—had to do it.

The first of us to be expelled was my father. Just after New Year 1969 he was sent to Miyi County in the region of Xichang, on the eastern edge of the Himalayas, an area so remote that it is China's satellite launch base today. It lies about 300 miles from Chengdu, four days' journey by truck, as there was no railway. In ancient times, the area was used for dumping exiles, because its mountains and waters were said to be permeated with a mysterious 'evil air.' In today's terms, the 'evil air' was subtropical diseases.

A camp was set up there to accommodate the former staff of the provincial government. There were thousands of such camps throughout China. They were called 'cadres' schools,' but apart from the fact that they were not schools, they were not just for officials either. Writers, scholars, scientists, teachers, doctors, and actors who had become 'useless' in Mao's knownothing new order were also dispatched there.

Among officials, it was not only capitalist-roaders like my father and other class enemies who were packed off to the camps. Most of their Rebel colleagues were also expelled, as the new Sichuan Revolutionary Committee could not accommodate anything like all of them, having filled its posts with Rebels from other backgrounds like workers and students, and with army men. 'Thought reform through labor' became a handy way of dealing with the surplus Rebels. In my father's department only a few stayed in Chengdu. Mrs. Shau became deputy director of Public Affairs on the Sichuan Revolutionary Committee. All Rebel organizations were now disbanded.

The 'cadres' schools' were not concentration camps or gulags, but they were isolated places of detention where the inmates had restricted freedom and had to do hard labor under strict supervision. Because every cultivable area in China is densely populated, only in arid or mountainous areas was there space to contain the exiles from the cities. The inmates were supposed to produce food and be self-supporting. Although they were still paid salaries, there was little for them to buy. Life was very harsh.

In order to prepare for his trip, my father was released from his place of detention in Chengdu a few days before his departure. The only thing he wanted to do was to see my mother. She was still being detained, and he thought he might never see her again. He wrote to the Revolutionary Committee, as humbly as he could, begging to be allowed to see her. His request was turned down.

The cinema in which my mother was being kept was on what used to be the busiest shopping street in Chengdu. Now the shops were half empty, but the black market for semiconductor parts which my brother Jin-ming frequented was nearby, and he sometimes saw my mother walking along the street in a line of detainees, carrying a bowl and a pair of chopsticks. The canteen in the cinema did not operate every day, so the detainees had to go out for their meals from time to time. Jin-ming's discovery meant we could sometimes see our mother by waiting on the street. Occasionally she did not appear with the other detainees, and we would be consumed by anxiety. We did not know that those were the times when her psychopath guard was punishing her by denying her permission to go and eat. But perhaps the next day we would catch sight of her, one among a dozen or so silent and grim-looking men and women, their heads bowed, all wearing white armbands with four sinister black characters: 'ox devil, snake demon.'

I took my father to the street for several days running, and we waited there from dawn till lunchtime. But there was no sign of her. We would walk up and down, stamping our feet on the frost-covered pavement to keep warm. One morning, we were again watching the thick fog lift to reveal the lifeless cement buildings, when my mother appeared. Having seen her children many times on the street, she looked up quickly to see whether we were there this time. Her eyes met my father's. Their lips quivered, but no sounds came out. They just locked eyes until the guard shouted at my mother to lower her head. Long after she had turned the corner, my father stood gazing after her.

Jung Chang, *The Wild Swans: Three Daughters of China*, 1991

THE DALAI LAMA, NEWLY ESCAPED FROM THE CHINESE, SETTLES IN INDIA

There was no interference from Delhi over how I and the growing numbers of Tibetans conducted our lives. In accordance with popular requests, I had begun to give weekly audiences in the grounds of Birla House. This gave me the opportunity to meet a variety of people and tell them about the real situation in Tibet. It also helped me begin the process of removing the protocol which did so much to separate the Dalai Lama from his people. I had a strong feeling that we should not cling to old practices that were no longer appropriate. As I often reminded people, we were now refugees.

To this end, I insisted that all formality should be deliberately reduced and made clear that I no longer wanted people to perform the old courtesies. I felt this was especially important when dealing with foreigners. They would be much more likely to respond to genuine worth if they found it. It is very easy to put others off by remaining aloof. So I was determined to be entirely open, to show everything and not to hide behind etiquette. In this way I hoped that people would relate to me as one human being to another.

I also stipulated that whenever I received anybody, he or she should sit on a chair of equal height, rather than one lower than mine as was customary. At first, even I found this rather difficult as I did not have much self-confidence, but it grew from then on. And despite the misgivings of some of my older advisers, I think the only people who were discomfited by these principles were occasional new arrivals from Tibet who did not know that the Dalai Lama no longer lived the way they were used to.

Life at Birla House was hardly conducive to formality anyway. It was neither especially grand nor large and at times it became quite crowded. I shared it with my mother as well as my household, and the remainder of my officials lived very close by. This was the first time in my life that I had seen so much of my mother. I very much enjoyed her company.

In addition to reducing formality, our tragedy also gave me the opportunity greatly to simplify my own personal life. In Lhasa I had had many possessions which were of little use, but it was very difficult to give them away. Now, I possessed almost nothing and I found it much easier to pass on things that were given to me if they could be of use to my fellow refugees.

> The Dalai Lama, *Freedom in Exile: The Autobiography of His Holiness the Dalai Lama of Tibet*, 1990

NELSON MANDELA IS SENTENCED TO LIFE IMPRISONMENT

The trial of Mandela and his co-defendants for sabotage—the allegation was that they had plotted at the town of Rivonia, outside Johannesburg, to carry out a campaign of violence against the state—ended on 11 June 1964. One of his supporters, Aggery Klaaste, records the scene.

I'll never forget . . .

The voices of the crowd raised in song outside the Palace of Justice on Verdict Day . . . in the Rivonia Trial at Pretoria . . . the priest who led them in song as they waited for the judgement . . . and the way they burst into 'Nkosi Sikelele' as Winnie Mandela appeared on the steps.

The way Hilda Bernstein rushed up to her husband Rusty when he was found Not Guilty . . . and the expression on her face when, two minutes later, he was re-arrested and the police pulled her away.

The bewildered look on the face of old Mrs Mandela—Nelson Mandela's mother—who had come all the way from Umtata to hear her son found guilty of sabotage and sentenced to life imprisonment.

And the way her daughter-in-law, Winnie, looked after her inside and outside the court.

The expressions on the faces of the accused men when the verdict of Guilty was given—Nelson smiling to his wife; Walter Sisulu waving; Kathy Kathrada shrugging his shoulders. And the way they looked on sentence day—Nelson Mandela in new dark suit taking notes; Sisulu fined down to thinness; Dennis Goldberg, cheerful and almost chubby; Govan Mbeki listening, hand cupped to ear; Raymond Mhlaba staring at the proceedings.

The exchange between Dr Percy Yutar, the prosecutor, and Mr Alan Paton, who gave evidence in mitigation.

The biting sarcasm when Dr Yutar, questioning Mr Paton on his forecast of sabotage, asked: 'So you are a prophet?' And the quiet dignity with which Paton replied: 'Yes, a prophet.'

The quiet voice of Mr Justice de Wet saying: 'The sentence is life imprisonment on all counts for the accused.'

The hush in the court that followed—an almost deathlike, motionless silence. Then the eight men in the dock—who had stood erect showing no sign of emotion—turning to the packed courts and smiling.

The moment when their wives and relatives and friends caught their last glimpse of them as they descended from the court.

The car back-firing like a pistol shot. We all stepping briskly back. A police dog barking back. And somebody nervously whispering 'Sharpeville!' But a police captain near me, his row of buttons gleaming, standing impassive and aloof.

The women—in their black and green uniform—standing quietly, almost bored as the time crept to noon. Then 12.15 and the inevitable policeman and his dog walking up and down the pavement again.

The first spectator walking out of the Palace. We all looking anxiously at her, she saying, 'Amandla!' The crowd saying 'Amandla!' if doubtfully.

The ripple that went through the dense crowd as She walked out. Winnie Mandela. A whisper of 'life' passing from mouth to mouth as in a movie.

Those who stood next to Winnie say there were tears in her eyes. Yet there was no weeping.

Fatima Meer, *Higher Than Hope,* 1990

AS EASY AS PICKING CHERRIES

Pastora, a twelve-year-old refugee from the civil war of the 1980s in El Salvador, tells her story to the writer's daughter Patricia in the safety of a camp in Honduras.

The National Guard swept through one day, in a typical 'search and destroy' operation, and caught her entire family in their peasant hut. One of the soldiers knocked her mother unconscious with his rifle butt, another shot her father through the head and then killed her two small brothers, who were screaming, while Pastora, huddling in a corner under the bed, watched the carnage.

She and her mother managed to escape, hiding in a *tatus*, or manmade cave, until the last of the Guards had passed through. Little by little, other survivors of the massacre came out of their hiding places and, without burying their dead, commenced their exodus at nightfall. Their flight, in single file, toward the Lempa River which forms the border between Honduras and El Salvador in that region, was a nightmare that has been repeated thousands of times since then. It is known, with typical Salvadoran black humor, as *la guinda*, which means, 'as easy as picking cherries.'

When babies cried, their mothers would stop their mouths so the Guards wouldn't hear them, or offer them their dry breasts to stop their whimpering from hunger, thirst and fright. One small boy would not stop screaming until his father, in desperation, stuffed a handkerchief in his mouth, and he died of asphyxiation. During four terror-filled days and arduous nights of forced marching, they followed the banks of the Lempa, nourishing themselves on roots and leaves and an occasional wild berry. During the days of hiding, helicopter gunships patrolled overhead, firing rockets at anything that moved. At night, the adults took turns carrying the wounded in makeshift litters.

On the morning of the fifth day, a detachment of Guards appeared ahead of them, cutting off their retreat, and they were forced to cross the river into Honduras. Those who could, swam across. The others clung to rotting logs, and someone had brought an inner tube and a rope for such an eventuality. There were more deaths at the crossing: a number of small children, some of the wounded and one pregnant woman.

It has been five years now since Pastora arrived at Colomoncagua. A schoolteacher at the camp taught her and the other children to read, and she in turn taught her mother and is now teaching smaller children and adults the elements of literacy. As if that were not enough, Pastora developed the poetic itch. She writes poems about her dead father and brothers, about the importance of learning to read (the illiteracy rate in the encampment has dropped from eighty to less than thirty percent), about the threatened resettlement in El Salvador that the refugees dread. She began to write rhymed verse without anyone teaching her, and when she writes about the New Society, her words take on a prophetic ring.

She sent me half a dozen of her poems with Patricia—a fraternal gesture from one poet to another—and I had them published in a Managua literary supplement. Much, much later, Patricia wrote me that another human rights delegate had personally delivered the published poems to Pastora, who was delighted—as any poet would be—at her early recognition.

Claribel Alegria, in *You Can't Drown the Fire: Latin American Women Writing in Exile*, ed. Alicia Partnoy, 1989

SINGER OF WIND AND RAIN

Salem Jubran was born in 1941 in Upper Galilee. His home was incorporated into the new state of Israel seven years later.

> You can uproot the trees
>   from my village mountain
>   which embraces the moon
> You can plough my village houses under
>   leaving no trace of their walls
> You can confiscate my rebec,
>   rip away the chords and burn the wood
>
> but you cannot suffocate my tunes —
> for I am the lover of this land
> and the singer of wind and rain.

Salem Jubran, tr. Lena Jayyusi and Naomi Shihab Nye, in *An Anthology of Modern Palestinian Literature*, ed. Salma Khadra Jayyusi, 1992

FALLING FROM POWER

Long before the rise of Periclean Athens, exile was the price
exacted for political failure. Set against the other punishments
available, it was mild; where they can, governments prefer to
avoid the bad luck or the bad precedent which murder or
execution might create. The possibility of overthrow, whether as
a result of discontent at home or invasion from abroad, is a
constant accompaniment of political power, and kings,
presidents, dictators and their ministers, if they are wise, will
always prepare a foreign haven for themselves in case things
turn nasty. In the seventeenth and eighteenth centuries the
French court always had its quota of refugee monarchs,
pretenders and princes. In the Second World War there were
enough exiled monarchs in London, it was said, to form a
football team complete with reserves. In 1989 the appalling
Mengisthu Haile Miriam, President of Ethiopia, who had
murdered the Emperor Haile Selassie (another wartime exile)
and buried the dismembered corpse under his personal latrine,
escaped by driving the presidential Rolls Royce up the ramp into
a transport plane which then flew him to exile in Zimbabwe.
The difference between the royal exiles in Paris and London and
the bloodstained tyrant of Ethiopia is immense, but the penalty
they all endured was the same. And guilty exiles seemed to
survive just as long into calm old age as innocent ones.

CORIOLANUS IS BANISHED FROM ROME

SICINIUS   For that he has,
   As much as in him lies, from time to time
   Inveighed against the people, seeking means
   To pluck away their power, as now at last
   Given hostile strokes, and that not in the presence
   Of dreaded justice, but on the ministers
   That doth distribute it, in the name o'th' people,
   And in the power of us the tribunes, we
   E'en from this instant banish him our city
   In peril of precipitation
   From off the rock Tarpeian, never more
   To enter our Rome gates. I'th' people's name
   I say it shall be so.
ALL [THE CITIZENS] It shall be so,
   It shall be so. Let him away. He's banished,
   And it shall be so.
COMINIUS
   Hear me, my masters and my common friends.
SICINIUS
   He's sentenced. No more hearing.
COMINIUS   Let me speak.
   I have been consul, and can show for Rome
   Her enemies' marks upon me. I do love
   My country's good with a respect more tender,
   More holy and profound, than mine own life,
   My dear wife's estimate, her womb's increase,
   And treasure of my loins. Then if I would
   Speak that—
SICINIUS   We know your drift. Speak what?

BRUTUS

There's no more to be said, but he is banished,
As enemy to the people and his country.
It shall be so.

ALL [THE CITIZENS] It shall be so, it shall be so.

CORIOLANUS

You common cry of curs, whose breath I hate
As reek o'th' rotten fens, whose loves I prize
As the dead carcasses of unburied men
That do corrupt my air: I banish you.
And here remain with your uncertainty.
Let every feeble rumour shake your hearts;
Your enemies, with nodding of their plumes,
Fan you into despair! Have the power still
To banish your defenders, till at length
Your ignorance—which finds not till it feels—
Making but reservation of yourselves,
Still your own foes, deliver you
As most abated captives to some nation
That won you without blows! Despising
For you the city, thus I turn my back.
There is a world elsewhere.

>   *Exeunt Coriolanus, Cominius, and Menenius,*
>   *with the rest of the Patricians. The Citizens*
>   *all shout, and throw up their caps*

AEDILE

The people's enemy is gone, is gone.

ALL THE CITIZENS

Our enemy is banished, he is gone. Hoo-oo!

SICINIUS

Go see him out at gates, and follow him
As he hath followed you, with all despite.
Give him deserved vexation. Let a guard
Attend us through the city.

ALL THE CITIZENS

Come, come, let's see him out at gates. Come.
The gods preserve our noble tribunes! Come.   *Exeunt*

>   William Shakespeare, *Coriolanus*, Act III, 1607–9

THE MISFORTUNES OF THE EMPEROR VALERIAN

Valerian ruled Rome from AD 253 to 260. He unwisely led his army against the Persians and was defeated. It was the start of a long period of indignity, which did not end with his death.

The particulars of this great event are darkly and imperfectly represented; yet by the glimmering light which is afforded us, we may discover a long series of imprudence, of error, and of deserved misfortunes on the side of the Roman emperor. He reposed an implicit confidence in Macrinus, his Prætorian præfect. That worthless minister rendered his master formidable only to the oppressed subjects, and contemptible to the enemies of Rome. By his weak or wicked counsels the Imperial army was betrayed into a situation where valour and military skill were equally unavailing. The vigorous attempt of the Romans to cut their way through the Persian host was repulsed with great slaughter; and Sapor, who encompassed the camp with superior numbers, patiently waited till the increasing rage of famine and pestilence had ensured his victory. The licentious murmurs of the legions soon accused Valerian as the cause of their calamities; their seditious clamours demanded an instant capitulation. An immense sum of gold was offered to purchase the permission of a disgraceful retreat. But the Persian, conscious of his superiority, refused the money with disdain and, detaining the deputies, advanced in order of battle to the foot of the Roman rampart and insisted on a personal conference with the emperor. Valerian was reduced to the necessity of entrusting his life and dignity to the faith of an enemy. The interview ended as it was natural to expect. The emperor was made a prisoner, and his astonished troops laid down their arms. . . .

The voice of history, which is often little more than the organ of hatred or flattery, reproaches Sapor with a proud abuse of the rights of conquest. We are told that Valerian, in chains but invested with the Imperial purple, was exposed to the multitude, a constant spectacle of fallen greatness; and that whenever the Persian monarch mounted on horseback he placed his foot on the neck of a Roman emperor. Notwithstanding all the remonstrances of his allies, who repeatedly advised him to remember the vicissitude of fortune, to dread the returning power of Rome, and to make his illustrious captive the pledge of peace not the object of insult, Sapor still remained inflexible. When Valerian sank under the weight of shame and grief, his skin, stuffed with straw and formed into the likeness of a human figure, was preserved for ages in the most celebrated temple of Persia, a more real monument of triumph than the fancied trophies of brass and marble so often erected by Roman vanity. . . .

The emperor Gallienus, who had long supported with impatience the censorial severity of his father and colleague, received the intelligence of his misfortunes with secret pleasure and avowed indifference. 'I knew that my father was a mortal,' said he, 'and since he has acted as becomes a brave man, I am satisfied.' Whilst Rome lamented the fate of her sovereign, the savage coldness of his son was extolled by the servile courtiers as the perfect firmness of a hero and a Stoic.

Edward Gibbon, *The Decline and Fall of the Roman Empire*, 1788

LI PO, BANISHED FROM THE CAPITAL, LOOKS BACK

Homeless, exiled, I climb Sin-Ping tower.
It is late on in the dying year,
The sun is declining in the sky
And the dark river runs gloomy and slow.

A cloud moves across the forests on the mountain;
Wild geese fly off down the river.
Up here I can see for ten thousand miles,
But I do not see the end of my sorrows.

Li Po (701–62), *Collected Poems*, 1986, tr. John Simpson

RICHARD II ABASES HIMSELF

KING RICHARD
What must the King do now? Must he submit?
The King shall do it. Must he be deposed?
The King shall be contented. Must he lose
The name of King? A God's name, let it go.
I'll give my jewels for a set of beads,
My gorgeous palace for a hermitage,
My gay apparel for an almsman's gown,
My figured goblets for a dish of wood,
My sceptre for a palmer's walking staff,
My subjects for a pair of carvèd saints,
And my large kingdom for a little grave,
A little, little grave, an obscure grave;
Or I'll be buried in the King's highway,
Some way of common trade where subjects' feet
May hourly trample on their sovereign's head,

For on my heart they tread now, whilst I live,
And buried once, why not upon my head?
Aumerle, thou weep'st, my tender-hearted cousin.
We'll make foul weather with despisèd tears.
Our sighs and they shall lodge the summer corn,
And make a dearth in this revolting land.
Or shall we play the wantons with our woes,
And make some pretty match with shedding tears;
As thus to drop them still upon one place
Till they have fretted us a pair of graves
Within the earth, and therein laid? 'There lies
Two kinsmen digged their graves with weeping eyes.'
Would not this ill do well? Well, well, I see
I talk but idly and you mock at me.
Most mighty prince, my lord Northumberland,
What says King Bolingbroke? Will his majesty
Give Richard leave to live till Richard die?
You make a leg, and Bolingbroke says 'Ay'.

NORTHUMBERLAND
My lord, in the base court he doth attend
To speak with you. May it please you to come down?

KING RICHARD
Down, down I come like glist'ring Phaethon,
Wanting the manage of unruly jades.
In the base court: base court where kings grow base
To come at traitors' calls, and do them grace.
In the base court, come down: down court, down
    King,
For night-owls shriek where mounting larks should
    sing.   *Exeunt King Richard and his party*

William Shakespeare, *Richard II*, Act III, 1595

THE FATE OF THE BYZANTINE ROYAL FAMILY

When Constantinople fell to the Turks in 1453, the Emperor Constantine XI Palaiologos was killed as he fought to defend the city walls. His relatives and servants faced a difficult time.

There were not very many of them. The poorer folk had to remain in the East and suffer whatever might befall. Of the greater figures that had played a part in the drama a few accepted voluntarily life under the Sultan. Many more were detained by imprisonment or were put to death. The rest sought refuge in Italy.

The two old Imperial dynasties were soon reduced to virtual extinction. Of the Emperor Constantine's surviving brothers the Despot Demetrius was at first treated kindly by the Sultan. He was given an appanage out of the lands that had belonged to the Gattilusi, the town of Enos and the islands of Lemnos and Imbros and parts of Thasos and Samothrace. They brought him an annual income of six hundred thousand pieces of silver, half from the islands and half from Imbros. In addition, a hundred thousand pieces were sent him annually from the Sultan's mint. For seven years he lived quietly at Enos with his wife Zoe and her brother, Matthew Asen, who in the old days had been his governor at Corinth and now was in charge of the local salt monopoly. He spent his days in enjoying the pleasures of the hunt and of the table and in giving much of his wealth to the Church. In 1467 his appanage was suddenly taken from him. According to the story which Phrantzes believed, Matthew's underlings had tampered with the revenue due to the Sultan from the salt-pans, and Matthew and Demetrius held responsible. Matthew's fate is unrecorded. Demetrius was deprived of his revenues and sent to live in poverty at Didymoticum. There one day the Sultan who was passing by noticed him and felt pity for him. He was made an annual allowance of fifty thousand silver pieces, to be paid out of the Imperial corn monopoly. It was not for long. He and his wife both soon took monastic vows. He died in a monastery in Adrianople in 1470 and she survived him only for a few months. Their one child, Helena, had been officially taken into the Sultan's harem; but it seems that she preserved her virginity and lived in her own residence at Adrianople. She died a few years before her parents, leaving her jewels and her robes to the Patriarchate.

Steven Runciman, *The Fall of Constantinople*, 1975

MARY QUEEN OF SCOTS DECIDES TO SEEK REFUGE IN ENGLAND

Mary preferred to throw a veil in her own mind over these last Scottish sufferings, which had been a prelude to the long years of English imprisonment. Immediately after the flight, in June 1568, she gave a description of it to her uncle in France: 'I have endured injuries, calumnies, imprisonment,' she wrote, 'famine, cold, heat, flight not knowing whither, 92 miles across the country without stopping or alighting, and then I have had to sleep upon the ground and drink sour milk, and eat oatmeal without bread, and have been three nights like the owls. . . .' Queen Mary fled first to

Dumfries, a journey of about sixty miles; by tradition Lord Herries led her down through the unfrequented passes of the Glenkens and along the west bank of the River Ken. They paused to rest at the head of the valley of the Tarff, at a point now named Queen's hill. The Dee was crossed just beyond the village of Tongland, where her escort destroyed the ancient wooden bridge to avoid pursuit; close by, at Culdoach, Mary received the reviving bowl of sour milk which she mentioned to her uncle. Having rested at Herries's own castle of Corrah on the way, the queen finally reached the Maxwell castle of Terregles.

It was here at Terregles that the critical decision was taken to flee further on into England. The decision was made by the queen alone. She herself described dolefully to Archbishop Beaton in Paris how her supporters had cautioned her piteously not to trust Queen Elizabeth, since the English in the past had savagely imprisoned a Scottish sovereign, in the shape of James I, and even her own father had not trusted himself to meet Henry VIII at York. The general view was that she should either stay in Scotland—where Herries guaranteed that she could hold out for at least another forty days— or go to France and hope to rally some support there. In retrospect, either course would seem to have been more sensible than seeking an English refuge. We cannot tell what considerations weighed with Mary Stuart to choose it nevertheless, what dreams of friendship and alliance with Elizabeth still possessed her; yet the siren song of Elizabeth's friendship, the mirage of the English succession, were still strong enough in this moment of decision to blot out the stable image of the proven friendship of France, where Mary had actually lived for thirteen years, and which could still be so easily sought from a western port of Scotland, the sea-route past Wales and Cornwall which Mary had taken years before as a child. In France Mary had the inalienable estates and incomes of a queen dowager of the country; as a Catholic queen fleeing from a Protestant country, she had every reason to expect the support of her brother-in-law, Charles IX, and Queen Catherine, to say nothing of her Guise relations, of whom the latest scion Henry, duke of Guise, was just rising into a manhood which promised to be as glorious as that of his father Duke Francis. Even if Elizabeth had shown stronger support for Mary against her rebels in the short interval since Carberry Hill than the French king, the patent fact that Mary was a Catholic whereas her insurgents were Protestants meant that the French would in the long run always have a vested interest to help the Scottish queen as their co-religionist.

In place of friendly France, Mary Stuart chose to fling herself upon the mercy of unknown England, a land where she had no party, no money, no estates, no relatives except her former mother-in-law, Lady Lennox, who hated her and Queen Elizabeth herself, whom she had never met personally, and whose permission she had not even obtained to enter the country. As decisions go, it was a brave one, a romantic one even, but under the circumstances it was certainly not a wise one. No human character is static. Different circumstances develop different aspects of the same personality. Perhaps ten months in prison had served to bring out in Mary's nature that streak either of the romantic or of the gambler, which leads the subject fatally on ever to prefer hope and high adventure to the known quantity, and which Mary Stuart passed on so dramatically to many of her later Stuart descendants. From now on, like all captives, Mary Stuart was to live of necessity far more in the world of dreams, than in that of reality. Her confinement in Lochleven seemed to have already begun the process of attrition in her powers of judgement. The queen herself summed up the subject of her fatal decision in a sentence at the end of a letter to Beaton towards the end of her life as sad as any she ever wrote: 'But I commanded my best friends to permit me to have my own way. . . .'

Antonia Fraser, *Mary Queen of Scots*, 1969

OUR SEA-SORROW

PROSPERO   I pray thee mark me.
I, thus neglecting worldly ends, all dedicated
To closeness and the bettering of my mind
With that which but by being so retired
O'er-priced all popular rate, in my false brother
Awaked an evil nature; and my trust,
Like a good parent, did beget of him
A falsehood, in its contrary as great
As my trust was, which had indeed no limit,
A confidence sans bound. He being thus lorded
Not only with what my revenue yielded
But what my power might else exact, like one
Who having into truth, by telling oft,
Made such a sinner of his memory
To credit his own lie, he did believe
He was indeed the Duke. Out o'th' substitution,
And executing th'outward face of royalty
With all prerogative, hence his ambition growing—
Dost thou hear?

MIRANDA   Your tale, sir, would cure deafness.

PROSPERO

To have no screen between this part he played
And him be played it for, he needs will be
Absolute Milan. Me, poor man—my library
Was dukedom large enough—of temporal royalties
He thinks me now incapable; confederates,
So dry he was for sway, wi'th' King of Naples
To give him annual tribute, do him homage,
Subject his coronet to his crown, and bend
The dukedom, yet unbowed—alas, poor Milan—
To most ignoble stooping.

MIRANDA   O the heavens!

PROSPERO

Mark his condition and th'event, then tell me
If this might be a brother.

MIRANDA   I should sin
To think but nobly of my grandmother.
Good wombs have borne bad sons.

PROSPERO   Now the condition.

This King of Naples, being an enemy
To me inveterate, hearkens my brother's suit;
Which was that he, in lieu o'th' premises
Of homage and I know not how much tribute,
Should presently extirpate me and mine
Out of the dukedom, and confer fair Milan,
With all the honours, on my brother. Whereon,
A treacherous army levied, one midnight
Fated to th' purpose did Antonio open
The gates of Milan; and, i'th' dead of darkness,
The ministers for th' purpose hurried thence
Me and thy crying self.

MIRANDA   Alack, for pity!
I, not rememb'ring how I cried out then,
Will cry it o'er again; it is a hint
That wrings mine eyes to't.

PROSPERO [*sitting*]   Hear a little further,
And then I'll bring thee to the present business
Which now's upon's, without the which this story
Were most impertinent.

MIRANDA   Wherefore did they not
That hour destroy us?
PROSPERO   Well demanded, wench;
My tale provokes that question. Dear, they durst not,
So dear the love my people bore me; nor set
A mark so bloody on the business, but
With colours fairer painted their foul ends.
In few, they hurried us aboard a barque,
Bore us some leagues to sea, where they prepared
A rotten carcass of a butt, not rigged,
Nor tackle, sail, nor mast—the very rats
Instinctively have quit it. There they hoist us,
To cry to th' sea that roared to us, to sigh
To th'winds, whose pity, sighing back again,
Did us but loving wrong.
MIRANDA   Alack, what trouble
Was I then to you?
PROSPERO   O, a cherubin
Thou wast that did preserve me. Thou didst smile,
Infusèd with a fortitude from heaven,
When I have decked the sea with drops full salt,
Under my burden groaned; which raised in me
An undergoing stomach, to bear up
Against what should ensue.

William Shakespeare, *The Tempest*, Act I, 1611

OVER THE SEA TO SKYE

After his defeat at Culloden and the collapse of the 1745 Rebellion, Bonnie Prince Charlie made his escape to the Hebrides. On South Uist his guide was Neil MacEachain, who took him to seek help from his cousin, the 24-year-old Flora MacDonald.

As Flora tells the story in her journal, written some years afterward, she had taken the sheep to graze on Sheaval and was asleep. Shortly before midnight on June 20, her cousin MacEachain came to the shieling door and woke her up to tell her that the Prince and O'Neill were outside and wanted to speak with her. Writing in the third person, Flora continues: 'She was surprised and wanted to know what they had to say to her but went out fast as she could throw on some of her cloaths and met the collonel at the door, leaving the prince behind the hutt.' (What Flora meant to say was that O'Neill had stationed Charles behind the shieling out of sight.) O'Neill asked when troops were due to pass by that way, and Flora told him it would be on Sunday—in less than forty-eight hours. O'Neill then launched into a description of Hugh MacDonald's plan for the Prince's escape to Skye. Since Flora wished to return to that island, Hugh would issue a pass for his stepdaughter to show to any guards she encountered on the way. Naturally, he would not want her to travel alone, so the pass would make provision for an accompanying maid and manservant. MacEachain would fill the latter requirement. The maid was to be Charles dressed in women's clothing.

Flora was stunned. This was the first she had heard of any such plan, and she refused outright to be party to such a dangerous plot. When O'Neill, a blustering, badgering man, persisted, Flora protested that if such a dangerous cargo were conveyed to Skye, she would bring ruination to her chieftain, Sir Alexander MacDonald (who was then at Fort Augustus). O'Neill then told her that MacDonald's wife, Lady Margaret, had been sending brandy, shirts, and money from Skye for the past two weeks and had promised to give them protection. But still, as Flora wrote, she had 'many qualms and objections.' One concern was for her reputation, since she would be the only woman involved in the escapade. But O'Neill had an answer for that: He said he would marry Flora himself if she felt her honor and good name were at stake.

Flora . . . stood her ground. At this point O'Neill gave a low whistle, signaling the hidden Charles to show himself. He told Flora that even if she would not help on his account, she could hardly refuse the Prince himself. 'Don't think, sir,' she retorted, 'that I am quite so fainthearted as that comes to.'

The sight of the royal personage was hardly awe-inspiring. Charles was ragged, dirty, sunburned, and dissipated from bouts with diarrhoea (and doubtless too much drinking), and his feet and legs were contused and bleeding. Ridiculously, he still clutched the periwig he had brought from France, which now housed a colony of lice. Speaking in Italian (he had seen service in Italy for the King of Spain), Colonel O'Neill related what had transpired between him and Flora. Charles turned to Flora and said he had met her stepfather when he first arrived in Scotland and thought very highly of him. He was sure that Hugh wished him well since he had promised passes for his escape, and he impressed upon the girl, who was only two years younger than himself, 'the sense he would always retain of so conspicuous a service.' O'Neill also assured Flora of 'the honour and immortality that would redound to her by such a glorious action.' Perhaps the Prince's physical distress touched Flora MacDonald, for by the time the men left her that night, she had agreed at least to speak to her stepfather on the matter. . . .

Flora hastily put together the clothes Charles was to wear and packed a dinner of roasted bullock, heart, and liver with a few bottles of wine and set off on Saturday evening for Rossinish. . . . Flora also carried a letter for her mother, Marion. This was subsequently destroyed, but later Flora approved this version of what its contents had been:

My dear Marion:
I have sent your daughter from this country lest she should be in any way frightened with the troops lying here. She has got one, Betty Burke, an Irish girl, who, she tells me, is a good spinster. If her spinning please you, you can keep her till she spin all your lint, or if you have any wool to spin, you may employ her. I have sent Neil MacEachain along with your daughter and Betty Burke to take care of them.
I am, Your dutiful husband,
Hugh MacDonald.

'Betty Burke' put on a long white linen dress sprigged with lilac, a cap and apron, a quilted petticoat, and a hooded cape. A bonnet was also made for the Prince, 'but he could not keep his hands from adjusting his headdress,' said MacEachain, 'which he cursed a thousand times.' Charles tried to hide a brace of pistols under his petticoat, but Flora insisted he give them to Angus and Penelope, saying they would give him away if he were searched. The Prince retorted that if he were to be examined that closely he would be discovered anyway, but he armed himself instead with a short stout cudgel concealed under his cloak. MacLeod of Gualtergill and his boatmen had already been detained for questioning and were aboard the prison ship *Furnace*, but Flora had been able to obtain another boat, described as 'a shallop of nine cubits,' and four MacDonald boatmen for the crossing to Skye . . .

It was actually the Prince who kept watch by Flora's weary head during their storm-tossed crossing of the Sea of the Hebrides. Having been up the last two nights sewing, she fell asleep while Charles sang Jacobite songs, such as 'The Twenty-ninth of May' from the rising of 1715 and 'The King Shall Enjoy His Own Again':

> For who better may our high sceptre sway
> Than he whose right it is to reign
> Then look for no peace for the wars will never cease
> Till the King shall enjoy his own again.

Susan Maclean Kybett, *Bonnie Prince Charlie*, 1988

THE DEFEATED NAPOLEON COMPLAINS OF HIS TREATMENT BY THE BRITISH

I here protest solemnly, in the face of Heaven and of mankind, against the violence done me, against the violation of my most sacred rights, in disposing by force of my person and my liberty.

I came voluntarily on board the *Bellerophon*; I am not a prisoner; I am the guest of England. I came on board even at the instigation of the Captain who said he had the orders of his Government to receive me, and to conduct me to England with my suite if that was agreeable to me. I presented myself in good faith to place myself under the protection of the laws of England. Once on board the *Bellerophon* I was on the hearth of the British people. If the Government when giving orders to the Captain of the *Bellerophon* to receive me and my suite intended merely to lay a snare for me, it has forfeited its honour and disgraced its flag. If this act should be consummated it will be in vain for the English to boast to Europe of their loyalty, their laws, their liberty. British good faith will be gone in the hospitality of the *Bellerophon*. I appeal to history; it will say that an enemy who for twenty years made war against the British nation, came freely, in his misfortune, to seek an asylum under her laws. What more brilliant proof could he give of his esteem and his confidence? But what return did England make to such magnanimity? They feigned to proffer a hospitable hand to that enemy, and when he had delivered himself up in good faith, they sacrificed him.

NAPOLEON.

Correspondance de Napoleon Ier, 1870

A DICTATOR LIVES OUT HIS DAYS BY THE SEA

Juan Manuel de Rosas ruled the Republic of Buenos Aires—later Argentina—with efficient ferocity from 1835 to 1852. After humiliating the Catholic Church and defeating Britain and France in the first Battle of the River Plate, he lost power and settled near Southampton on the south coast of England.

> In the drawing room's quiet
> whose rigorous clock scatters
> its unclouded and ordinary time
> on the desolate white
> that swathes the mahogany's red heat,
> a voice, reproachful and tender,
> pronounced that familiarly sinister name.
> Straightway his tyrannical image
> loomed huge on the moment,

not like marble profiled by a forest,
but shadowy, vast, and remote
like a darkening mountain.
Conjecture and memory
flowed in on that casual utterance
like a bottomless echo.
Famous in infamy,
his name once could ravage a city,
rally the gaucho's idolatry,
and stab horror in history.
We lose count of those corpses today,
crime is more piecemeal
if we weigh Time's ferocity into the balance—
the unwearied immortality
that decimates men without ever declaring its guilt,
the festering wound
where all a world's bloodshed awaits the last of the gods
to seal the world's sores on the last of all days.
Perhaps Rosas
was only the implacable butcher our grandfathers thought him;
I think of him now, like ourselves, as
a creature of chance enclosed in an action's parentheses:
he lived out the everyday anguish of things
and for better or worse troubled
the age's uncertainty.

Today an ocean's span divides
what is left of his bones from his country;
today, grief-stricken or dry-eyed, the living
may grind both his night and his nullity under their heels.
Even God has forgotten him,
and to delay his eternal extinction
for a pittance of hatred
is to turn our contempt into charity now.

Jorge Luis Borges, *Poems*, tr. Ben Belitt, 1972

NAPOLEON III, DEFEATED AND ILL, FINDS POPULARITY IN ENGLAND

The Emperor, a prisoner of the Prussians after the disastrous Battle of Sedan in 1870, was deposed by the French National Assembly the following year and

*driven out, together with the Empress Eugénie. He came to England, as he had
during his two previous periods of exile from France.*

Chislehurst, fifteen miles form central London, was still right out in the
Kent countryside in 1871. Camden Place was on the edge of the common.
It was said to have been the house of the antiquary William Camden in the
sixteenth century, and was certainly the home in the middle of the eighteenth century of Lord Camden, the Lord Chancellor, who took his title
from the name of the house; but it was completely rebuilt during the
nineteenth century. In 1813 a notorious murder was committed in the house,
the master and mistress being battered to death by a manservant whom they
had caught trying to rob them. Queen Victoria, who visited Eugénie at
Camden Place soon after she arrived there, described it as 'that small house',
and referred to 'the poor Emperor's humble little rooms'; but the house
had twenty rooms, apart from the kitchens, and stood in pleasant grounds
with lawns hidden by trees from the public view. Louis Napoleon lived
there with Eugénie and the Prince Imperial, Prince Joachim Murat, Conneau,
Corvisart, his secretaries Filon and Franceschini Piétri, and a household of
thirty-two other ladies and gentlemen and twenty-three servants. The total
inmates of the house, including Louis Napoleon and his family, were entered as sixty-two in the census return of 1871.

Most of the servants at Camden Place were French, but seven of them
were British. One of these was a girl of twenty named Hannah Wilton, who
in the summer of 1872 stole seven £20 notes from Louis Napoleon's cash
box and gave them to her boy friend. Hannah and her friend were arrested
when they bought a coat priced at twenty-four shillings from a tailor in
Cheapside and offered one of the stolen £20 notes in payment. Louis
Napoleon wrote to the magistrate at Sidcup who tried the case and asked
him to deal leniently with the girl. Her friend was acquitted, but Hannah
was found guilty of larceny. The magistrate said that in view of the Emperor's plea on her behalf he would deal with her as leniently as possible,
and sentenced her to three months' imprisonment instead of the six months
which he would otherwise have given her.

For the third time Louis Napoleon was an exile in England, but his life
was very different now from what it had been in 1839 and 1846, when he
had gone to the opera and the theatres and the town and country houses
of the aristocracy, and had lived a gay social life. Now he was in poor health
and saddened in spirit; but he was still reasonably active during his first year
in England. In April 1871, Eugénie wrote to Queen Victoria that 'the Emperor
still suffers, but his condition is not alarming'.

Five days after he arrived at Camden Place, the Prince of Wales called on him, and on 27 March he was taken by special train to Windsor to meet Queen Victoria. He met her again in July in the house of Prince and Princess Christian of Schleswig-Holstein, her son-in-law and daughter, at Frogmore near Windsor, and she visited him at Camden Place on 20 April 1872, which was his sixty-fourth birthday. She would have come more often had it not been for one great difficulty: the Emperor liked very hot rooms, and the Queen liked very cold rooms. Their mutual friend, Lady Sydney, mentioned the matter to the Duc de Bassano, who assured her that the Empress disliked the Emperor's overheated rooms as much as the Queen did. . . .

He was . . . popular with the ordinary non-political British working man. In June 1871 the workmen employed by the contractor of the sewage works for the Greenwich District Board stopped outside the gates of Camden Place on their annual excursion to Sidcup and serenaded the Emperor with 'God Save the Queen' and 'Auld Lang Syne'. Louis Napoleon walked down to the gate with Eugénie and the Prince Imperial and was welcomed by the firm's solicitor, who stated in a prepared little speech that they knew that the Emperor was a friend of England and that they hoped that he would soon be restored to the throne of France. . . .

Apart from his visits to Windsor and Frogmore, Louis Napoleon took the Prince Imperial to visit his old acquaintance Angela Burdett-Coutts at Holly Lodge, her house in Highgate, and occasionally visited high-ranking officers at Woolwich. He was once taken by the Prince of Wales to the Marlborough Club, and in August 1871 went with Eugénie and the Prince Imperial to visit the famous steamship the *Great Eastern*, at Sheerness. He and Eugénie spent a few days that month at Cowes with Eugénie's Spanish nieces. They went yachting with an American girl, Jennie Jerome, who was soon to become Lady Randolph Churchill and the mother of Sir Winston Churchill. She had been presented to Louis Napoleon at the Tuileries, and was shocked to see how 'old, ill and sad' he looked as he leaned against the mast on the yacht. 'Even in my young eyes', she wrote in later years, 'he seemed to have nothing to live for.'

Jasper Ridley, *Napoleon III and Eugénie*, 1979

WINSTON CHURCHILL LEAVES THE GOVERNMENT AND GOES TO THE TRENCHES

Having become the scapegoat for the British failure in the Dardanelles and resigning as First Lord of the Admiralty, Churchill found he had been left out

of Asquith's inner cabinet. He decided to make a break with politics; he did not, he said, want to remain in well-paid inactivity.

Churchill had decided to join his Regiment in France. Before going he gave a small farewell luncheon party at 41 Cromwell Road. Asquith's daughter Violet, who was among those present, later recalled, 'Clemmie was admirably calm and brave, poor Eddie blinking back his tears, the rest of us trying to "play up" and hide our leaden hearts. Winston alone was at his gayest and his best.'

On the morning of November 18, in the uniform of a Major in the Queen's Own Oxfordshire Hussars, Churchill left London for the Western Front. Clementine had given him a little pillow to make his nights more comfortable. That evening Masterton-Smith wrote to her from the Admiralty, 'With those of us who shared his life here he has left an inspiring memory of high courage and tireless industry, and he carries with him to Flanders all that we have to give him—our good wishes.'. . . .

To his mother, Churchill wrote on November 24, while in reserve billets for forty-eight hours, 'Do you know I am quite young again.' Two days later, back in his dugout in the front line, he was annoyed to receive an order to go to a point some way behind the line, where he would be collected by a car and driven to a meeting with the Corps Commander. Churchill was now a serving officer and must obey. As he set off, the Germans began shelling the front-line trenches. 'I just missed a whole bunch of shells which fell on the track a hundred yards behind me,' he told Clementine. Then, after an hour walking away from the front 'across sopping fields on which stray bullets are always falling, along tracks periodically shelled', he reached the crossroads at which the Corps Commander's car was to collect him. But it had been 'driven off' by shells, and a Staff Officer who arrived to tell Churchill this informed him that the General had only wanted a chat 'and that another day would do equally well'.

Angry at a wasted journey, Churchill made his way back to his dugout, a further hour walking 'across the sopping fields now plunged in darkness'. 'You may imagine,' he told Clementine, 'how I abused to myself the complacency of this General—though no doubt kindly meant—dragging me about in wind & rain for nothing.' Then, reaching the front-line trenches, he learned that a quarter of an hour after he had left them 'the dugout in which I was living had been struck by a shell which burst a few feet from where I would have been sitting', smashing the structure and killing one of the three men who were inside. 'When I saw the ruin I was not so angry with the General after all.'. . .

After a week of marches, drills and inspections, trench discipline, gas-helmet training, and rifle and grenade practice at Moolenacker Farm, Churchill learned that there was to be an extra week in reserve. 'I am sorry there is this further delay,' he wrote to his wife, 'for a war without action is really a dreary affair. But these boys were evidently delighted.' The men were also delighted at Churchill's attitude to discipline. Ascertaining by his first question that one troublemaker up before him had fought at Loos, Churchill dismissed the charge against him. The officers were uneasy at this leniency, but Robert Fox, a twenty-year-old machine-gunner who had likewise fought at Loos, later recalled that 'Churchill was scrupulously fair to any man before him on a charge.' He had heard Churchill cross-examine a sergeant who had brought a man up before him 'with all the skill of a counsel at the Bar. The evidence did not satisfy him, so he dismissed the charge.'

'I have reduced punishment both in quantity & method,' Churchill told Clementine on January 16. He was also concerned, as he had been when Home Secretary, with the entertainment of those whose lives were restricted or confined. That evening he organised a combined sports day and concert for his men. 'I think they want nursing & encouraging more than drill-sergeanting.' Mule-races, pillow-fights, obstacle-races, all were provided, followed by a concert. 'Such singing you never heard. People sang with the greatest courage who had no idea either of words or tune.' The concert was followed by a banquet, during which the men gave a special cheer for Clementine. 'Poor fellows,' he told her, 'nothing like this had ever been done for them before. They do not get much to brighten their lives—short though they may be.'

Martin Gilbert, *Churchill: A Life*, 1991

KERENSKY LEAVES RUSSIA FOREVER

Alexander Kerensky, a Petrograd lawyer, became the head of the Provisional Government which took over power from Tsar Nicholas II in February 1917. Faced with continued military defeat and economic chaos, it became weaker and weaker. After nine months the Bolsheviks, led by Lenin and Trotsky, over-threw it almost without a struggle in the October Revolution. Kerensky, accompanied by his friend and adviser, made his escape from Petrograd.

On the day of departure, Fabrikant and I arrived at the Arkhangelsk Station while it was still daylight. We had no difficulty in identifying two uniformed Serbian officers, and these led us unobtrusively to the right platform, where we mingled with a crowd of passengers. The train was filled to capacity, but we were assigned seats in a second-class compartment that was evidently reserved for officers. It was quite obvious that several of them became aware of my identity. The voyage seemed endless. The one-track Murmansk line had innumerable sidings. For no apparent reason we spent hours waiting at junctions. I seemed to us that the train hardly ever moved. But we did not complain. After all, there was no hurry, and outside was an intoxicating northern spring. We enjoyed the long stops at night, when the train came to a standstill in some clearing in the midst of a dense forest. It reminded me of the white nights in Petrograd. But here nature was more mysterious, the northern stillness and the pale light of the nights held a very special charm. Yesterday did not seem to exist, and we did not feel like speaking or thinking of the future. We were in complete harmony with the natural beauties around us, and we felt at one with the mysterious forest.

I have no exact recollection of how long it took, but the journey must have lasted about ten days. Finally we reached Murmansk, then a drab, deserted town. All the passengers went straight to the port, which was occupied by the Allies, although the town itself was under Soviet administration and we had to pass a Soviet checkpoint. The Soviet soldiers barely glanced at our documents. Then we filed past an Allied officer who checked our names against a list. My companion and I were met by two French naval officers who took us to their cruiser, *General Hobe*. On board, a Serbian officer handed our real documents and visas to the commander. Throughout our journey these papers had been kept by the head of the 'extraterritorial' train. As I left my native land it did not even occur to me that I might never set foot on it again, and all my thoughts were for the future.

The French naval command welcomed us very warmly. It was a new experience to be completely relaxed. There was no longer any need to be constantly on the alert.

'You'd probably like to rest, wouldn't you?' asked one of the officers.

'No, thanks. I'd like to go to the barber.'

'What for?'

'I am sick and tired of my disguise. I want to be my own self again.'

There was an outburst of laughter. A few minutes later I found myself in the skilled hands of a barber and my locks and beard were scattered all over the floor.

> Alexander Kerensky, *The Kerensky Memoirs: Russia and History's Turning-Point*, 1966

TROTSKY, OUSTED BY STALIN IN 1929, IS NOT A WELCOME GUEST

Even before his deportation from Odessa he had asked the Politbureau to obtain for him a German entry permit. He was told that the German

Government—a Social Democratic Government headed by Hermann Mueller—had refused. He was half convinced that Stalin cheated him; and so when soon afterwards Paul Loebe, the Socialist Speaker of the Reichstag, declared that Germany would grant Trotsky asylum, he at once applied for a visa. He was not deterred by the 'malicious satisfaction with which . . . newspapers dwelt on the fact that an advocate of revolutionary dictatorship was obliged to seek asylum in a democratic country'. This lesson, they said, should teach him 'to appreciate the worth of democratic institutions'. The lesson was hardly edifying, however. The German Government first asked him whether he would submit to restrictions on his freedom of movement. He answered that he was prepared to refrain from any public activity, to live in 'complete seclusion', preferably somewhere near Berlin, and devote himself to literary work. Then he was asked whether it would not be enough for him to come for a short visit, just to undergo medical treatment. When he replied that having no choice he would content himself even with this, he was told that in the government's view he was not so ill as to require any special treatment. 'I asked whether Loebe had offered me the right of asylum or the right of burial in Germany. . . . In the course of a few weeks the democratic right of asylum was thrice curtailed. At first it was reduced to the right of residence under special restrictions, then to the right of medical treatment, and finally to the right of burial. I could thus appreciate the full advantages of democracy only as a corpse.'

The British House of Commons discussed Trotsky's admission as early as February 1929. The Government made it clear that it would not allow him to enter. The country was just about to have an election and the Labour Party was expected to return to office. Before the end of April two leading lights of Fabianism, Sidney and Beatrice Webb, arrived in Constantinople and respectfully asked Trotsky to receive them. Despite old political animosities he entertained them courteously, eagerly enlightening himself on the economic and political facts of British life. The Webbs expressed their confidence that the Labour Party would win the election, whereupon he remarked that he would then apply for a British visa. Sidney Webb regretted that the Labour Government would depend on Liberal support in the Commons, and the Liberals would object to Trotsky's admission. After a few weeks Ramsay MacDonald did indeed form his second government with Sidney Webb, now Lord Passfield, as one of his Ministers.

Early in June, Trotsky applied to the British Consulate in Constantinople and cabled a formal request for a visa to MacDonald. He also wrote to Beatrice Webb, in terms as elegant as witty, about their talks at Prinkipo and the attraction that Britain, especially the British Museum, exercised on him. He appealed to Philip Snowden, the Chancellor of the Exchequer, saying that political differences should not prevent him from visiting England just as they had not prevented Snowden from going to Russia when Trotsky was in office; 'I hope to be able soon to return you the kind visit you paid me in Kislovodsk', he telegraphed George Lansbury. It was all in vain. However, it was not the Liberals who objected to his admission. On the contrary, they protested against the attitude of the Labour Ministers; and Lloyd George and Herbert Samuel repeatedly intervened, in private, in Trotsky's favour. 'This was a variant', he commented, 'which Mr. Webb did not foresee.' On and off, for nearly two years, the question was raised in Parliament and in the Press. H. G. Wells and Bernard Shaw wrote two statements of protest against the barring of Trotsky; and J. M. Keynes, C. P. Scott, Arnold Bennett, Harold Laski, Ellen Wilkinson, J. L. Garvin, the Bishop of Birmingham, and many others appealed to the Government to reconsider their decision. The protests and appeals fell on deaf ears. 'This "one act" comedy on the theme of democracy and its principles . . .', Trotsky observed, 'might have been written by Bernard Shaw, if the Fabian fluid which runs in his veins had been strengthened by as much as five per cent of Jonathan Swift's blood.'

Isaac Deutscher, *The Prophet Outcast: Trotsky 1927–1940*, 1963

EDWARD VIII EXPLAINS HIS ABDICATION

Ten o'clock arrived. Sir John Reith, Director-General of the BBC, announced:
'This is Windsor Castle. His Royal Highness Prince Edward.'

Tense listeners heard a door close. Then in the well-known voice he began his last message to the peoples he had served:

'At long last I am able to say a few words of my own.

'I have never wanted to withhold anything, but until now it has not been constitutionally possible for me to speak.

'A few hours ago I discharged my last duty as King and Emperor, and now that I have been succeeded by my brother, the Duke of York, my first words must be to declare my allegiance to him.

'This I do with all my heart.

'You all know the reasons which have impelled me to renounce the Throne, but I want you to understand that in making up my mind I did not forget the country or the Empire, which as Prince of Wales and lately as King I have for 25 years tried to serve.

'But you must believe me when I tell you that I have found it impossible to carry the heavy burden of responsibility and discharge my duties as King as I would wish to do without the help and support of the woman I love.

'And I want you to know that the decision I have made has been mine and mine alone. This was a thing I had to judge entirely for myself. The other person most nearly concerned has tried up to the last to persuade me to take a different course.

'I have made this, the most serious decision of my life, only upon a single thought—of what would in the end be best for all.

'This decision has been made less difficult to me by the sheer knowledge that my brother, with his long training in the public affairs of this country and with his fine qualities, will be able to take my place forthwith without interruption or injury to the life and progress of the Empire.

'And he has one matchless blessing, enjoyed by so many of you, and not bestowed on me, a happy home with his wife and children.

'During these hard days I have been comforted by Her Majesty, my mother, and by my family. The Ministers of the Crown, and in particular Mr. Baldwin, the Prime Minister, have always treated me with full consideration. There has never been any constitutional difference between me and them, and between me and Parliament.

'Bred in the constitutional traditions by my father, I should never have allowed any such issue to arise. Ever since I was Prince of Wales, and later on when I occupied the Throne, I have been treated with the greatest kindness by all classes of people, wherever I have lived or journeyed throughout the Empire. For that I am very grateful.

'I now quit altogether public affairs, and I lay down my burden. It may be some time before I return to my native land, but I shall always follow the fortunes of the British race and Empire with profound interest, and if at any time in the future I can be found of service to His Majesty in a private station I shall not fail.

'And now we all have a new King. I wish him and you, his people, happiness and prosperity with all my heart. God bless you all. GOD SAVE THE KING!'

A moment later all the BBC transmitters closed down.

> J. Lincoln White, *The Abdication of Edward VIII: A Record*, 1937

THE ARCHBISHOP OF CANTERBURY, COSMO LANG, DISAPPROVES

Strange and sad it is that [the King] should have sought his happiness in a manner inconsistent with the Christian principles of marriage, and within a social circle whose standard and way of life are alien to all the best instincts and traditions of his people.

Statement, December 1936

THE WIT AND RACONTEUR, GERALD BULLET, RESPONDS

My Lord Archbishop, what a scold you are!
And when your man is down how bold you are!
Of charity how oddly scant you are!
How Lang, O Lord, how full of cantuar!

Private conversation, December 1936

SIR JOHN REITH IS EDGED OUT OF THE BBC

On 3 June [1939], Gerald Beadle, then Controller, West Region, was up from Bristol for the day. He put his head round the Director-General's door and proposed lunch at his club. Reith said that would suit him very well as he had an early-afternoon appointment. In the taxi he told Beadle that he was going to see the Prime Minister. 'It looks like the sack,' he said.

Reith's appointment was in fact with Sir Horace Wilson: 'It was as feared. The Prime Minister and the Secretary of State for Air had authorised him to "instruct me to go to Imperial Airways—tomorrow if possible".' It would be a full-time job, and there would therefore be no question of outside interests. Reith wriggled, but was uncomfortably aware that he was not wriggling very effectively. After fifty minutes he played a last despairing card:

I managed to collect myself to the extent of telling Wilson that if the Prime Minister wished me to do this or that I would presumably, in such days as these, do it; but I must have it direct from him, especially as I was so utterly reluctant. There was the clue to the monstrous pusillanimity. If the Prime Minister wished me to do something I must do it. Atrophy of self-interest and intelligence.

The conversation with Chamberlain was rather absurd: 'I asked if he was instructing me to go. He said he wasn't using that word. So I asked if he wanted me to go. He said again that was maybe too strong but that if I went he would be very glad.' This exercise in logic-chopping lasted no more than four minutes. Reith then went off to the Athenaeum to discuss details with Sir George Beharrell, the Imperial Airways acting chairman. . . .

The following week he had a telephone call from [Ronald] Norman [BBC Chairman]. A Governor had pointed out that his resignation had not been put in writing at any time—would he mind tidying up that small detail

for them? This request roused Reith to a new pitch of rage and bitterness
and the reply he dashed off was full of savage mockery:

'Just for tidyness' sake,' you said—well, my desire for tidyness is often thought to be
exaggerated, but no tidyness issue seems to warrant any risk of an extension of the
misunderstanding and unpleasantness which have gathered round my departure . . .

Having tonight announced your betrothal to the attractive young suitor of your
choice, were you fearful that the morning would find a dissolute old wretch on the
doorstep claiming restitution of his rights?

Now then—

I resign
I shall resign
I have resigned.

There it is—in all three tenses . . .

Is that sufficient? Or should there be another sentence renouncing all and every
claim on the body and absolving it from liability of every sort? . . .

The following day he entered his fiftieth year. He lived until he was eighty-
one, but there would be nights even in extreme old age when he dreamt
that he was back in Broadcasting House.

Ian McIntyre, *The Expense of Glory: A Life of John Reith*, 1993

A PROPITIOUS BAR

The pattern of modern Argentine politics was established in the unlikely
surroundings of a Panama City nightclub in 1956. Perón, gloomy, exiled,
and a widower, would make his way into the Happy Land Bar each evening,
and would sit down to watch the floorshow. The star, in what was not a
particularly elevated form of show business, was a 25-year-old dancer, María
Estela Martínez. She was handsome in something of the way Evita had been
handsome, and the ex-President, at sixty, found her sharp-witted and amusing. Her friends called her Isabelita, and she was later to marry him and one
day to succeed him as President of Argentina. But as Perón sat at his
accustomed table and watched her go through her routines, the Happy
Land Bar contained, not two future Presidents of Argentina, but three—the
third being the bar's manager, Raúl Lastiri. He allied himself with Isabelita,
and shared in the rise of her fortunes and those of Perón; and eventually,
before *El Líder* returned, he became head of the Chamber of Deputies. In
1973, when Héctor Cámpora had been elected President and stood down in
Perón's favour, Lastiri served as a stand-in for the four months from July

to October. The former manager of the Happy Land Bar was indirectly to have a baleful influence on his country's future.

Lastiri's father-in-law, José López Rega, was an obscure ex-corporal in the Argentine police who left the force in 1960 and started writing books about the occult, one of which he declared had been co-authored by the Archangel Gabriel. He went bankrupt, and escaped to Brazil, where a business partner of his introduced him to Brazilian-African magic: a variety of voo-doo. By 1966 he was ready for higher things, and, banking on the link between his son-in-law Raúl Lastiri and Perón, he travelled to the Iron Gate in Madrid and was taken on as a kind of servant. Soon he was carrying out more delicate tasks: once, for instance, he persuaded Isabelita to return to Perón after their marriage had broken down. Later, when a scandal erupted in an Argentine bank run by the Peronist unions, he turned up with a suitcase full of money and smoothed out the problem. After the trium-phant return from exile, López Rega's influence grew even more. Now he was in charge of Perón's medical treatment, and there were stories that he and Isabelita, his close ally, would force Perón to sign documents, refusing to give him the rich caramel delicacy, *dulce de leche*, unless he agreed. From the beginning of 1974 to Perón's death the following July, only the two of them had access to him.

John Simpson and Jana Bennett, The Disappeared, 1985

THE AYATOLLAH GOES TO FRANCE

In the autumn of 1978, when the turmoil in Iran was growing worse, the Shah put great pressure on the government of Iraq, dominated by Vice-President Saddam Hussein, to get rid of Ayatollah Khomeini, the leading Iranian dissident cleric who had taken refuge in the holy city of Najaf. It proved a costly mistake. In Najaf, Khomeini had been largely hidden from the world. Now he went to Paris, and everything would change.

On 6 October 1978, Khomeini arrived at Paris-Orly. His flowing robes and black turban drew a good deal of attention in the airport terminal, but he kept his eyes on the ground the entire time, determined not to allow anything that was evil to impinge on his consciousness. And as Bani-Sadr drove him to his own flat in the featureless suburb of Cachan he resolutely refused to look out of the window. Their route did not take them to the centre of Paris, and Khomeini never visited, let alone saw, the city whose environs provided the springboard for his return.

They waited at Cachan for several days, while the local building firm in

Neauphle belatedly finished the conversion work on the house where the exile was to live. Even nowadays there is a mild sense of scandal in the village about the work that was required. The workmen had, for instance, to dismantle the modern lavatory and replace it with the type that has no seat, just two porcelain steps on either side of a hole in the ground; the same firm had removed precisely that kind of lavatory from a dozen houses in the area over the previous decade. Planning permission for these and other changes, which would normally have taken weeks, was arranged in a day; and four new telephones and two telex lines were installed with extraordinary speed. The hand of the Quai d'Orsay was detected in all of this. Khomeini had always refused to use a telephone, but at the age of 78 he learned the advantages of instant communication. From then on he was in regular, though never daily, contact through his lieutenants with those who were preparing for the Revolution in Iran itself.

But if Neauphle made it easier for him to communicate with his followers in Iran, it also brought him to the attention of the world at large. During the summer a French television team had penetrated to Najaf to try to interview him, only to find that forty Iraqi soldiers were deployed around his house to stop them. In Neauphle there were no barriers of any kind. In the first ten days he was there, he complied with his undertaking to the French government not to make political statements in public. But the French press, radio and television did not give up their efforts to persuade him to speak to them; and on 17 October he talked for the first time directly to a Western audience.

The second French television channel, *Antenne-2*, filmed a rather stilted interview with him that day, in which he said he was prepared to urge his followers towards armed insurrection against the Shah, who was, he said, kept in power by the United States; the central themes of the next few months were present from the beginning of his time in the West. During the 105 days from this *début* to the time of his return, he gave 132 interviews: a remarkable rate of activity for a man in his eighth decade.

John Simpson, *Behind Iranian Lines*, 1988

THE SHAH LEAVES IRAN FOR THE LAST TIME

On January 16 the Shah and the Empress, Farah Diba, left the Niavaran Palace for the last time. Instead of flying straight to the United States, the Shah had decided at the last minute to accept an invitation from Anwar Sadat of Egypt to pause briefly in Aswan.

For the Queen the last few months had been perhaps harder than for the

Shah himself. 'There wasn't really five minutes of breathing calmly,' she said later. 'If we had ten to twenty minutes, we were happy.' While the court crumbled around them and advisers fled, she had become more and more vital to the Shah, lending him continual strength. In 1978 he came to depend on her almost completely.

Like him, she had been against destroying the revolution with massive bloodshed. And like him, she was uncertain whether they should leave. At one stage she says she suggested that he go and she stay, for the sake of those who believed in them. He refused and said they must leave together.

Officers of the Imperial Guard and the servants lined up on the palace steps, weeping, to say good-bye. Some of them held the Koran over the Shah's head, to give him its customary protection on his journey, and wailed as the royal party left by helicopter for the airport. It had been literally years since the Shah had driven in the streets of Teheran. Occasionally he went by car to the nearby homes of members of his family. Otherwise it was everywhere by air. His view of Iran had almost always been from the sky.

They landed close to the Imperial Pavilion. The Shah said later that he noticed the terrible wind and the gloomy sight of the planes grounded by strikes.

In the pavilion he made a little speech to a few reporters. 'As I said when this [new] government was formed, I am feeling tired and need a rest. I also stated that when I felt that things were going well and the government was settled I would take a trip and that trip starts now. . . .'

Asked how long he would be away he said softly, 'I don't know.'

He then waited for his new prime minister, Shapour Bakhtiar, who had been imprisoned several times during his reign, and in whose hands he was now leaving the country.

The Shah did not like Bakhtiar—'I had always considered him an Anglophile and an agent of British Petroleum.' (Perhaps therefore he thought his appointment would please the British.) But he still would not leave until Bakhtiar had been confirmed by the Majles. He asked his staff to telephone back to the city, but all the lines from his pavilion at the airport were cut. They had to use the guards' radio, which was patched through to army headquarters and thence to the Majles.

Finally the news crackled through that Bakhtiar had indeed been confirmed. A helicopter was sent for him and shortly afterwards it clattered down on the tarmac. Bakhtiar, a thin, nervous but very elegant man who looked like a French aristocrat, with a trim mustache and superbly cut clothes, entered the pavilion and bowed before his King.

'Now you have everything in your hands,' said the Shah. 'I hope you will succeed. I entrust Iran to you and to God.' Within days Bakhtiar would be swept away in the whirlwind of the ayatollah's return. He was the Kerensky of the Iranian revolution.

The Shah and his party, dressed against the wind, began to walk toward the plane. In front of the blue-and-white 707, he stopped for the final farewells. As neatly dressed as ever, his striped tie showing through the lapels of his overcoat, he stood stiffly, his left foot slightly forward, as if ready to walk quickly away. Several generals soon to lose their lives bent to kiss his right hand. One fell on the ground to kiss his feet and the Shah bent awkwardly to fetch him up. In his left hand, the Shah gripped his spectacles. He had barely slept for days and his white face was dominated by his broad, dark eyebrows, which were locked together in an expression suggesting both grief and incomprehension. Beside him the Empress's face was stretched taut with misery.

Almost everyone was weeping, even Bakhtiar, who, perhaps alone of those on the tarmac, had wanted the Shah to leave. Almost all the military men had begged him to stay. The Shah's own eyes were wet. This was not the first time that his officers had seen him show such emotion. He said to the commander of the Imperial Guard, 'Do whatever you consider necessary. I hope people are not killed.' Later he wrote, 'I was completely overwhelmed by the expressions of loyalty given to me when I left. There was a poignant silence broken by sobs.'

It was just two in the afternoon when the Shah and the Empress and their small entourage finally took off. When the news was broadcast on Teheran radio a few moments later, the city erupted in joy. Car horns were blared for minutes on end, headlights were flashed, people danced and sang and shouted, 'The Shah is gone. He's not coming back.' Boys gave V signs; girls and young women in chadors laughed, danced, and shouted, 'Everyone is free now.' People waved gladiolus, carnations, portraits of Ayatollah Khomeini, crying, 'By the force of Khomeini, the Shah has fled.'

Statues of the Shah and his father were torn to the ground; newspapers with huge headlines 'THE SHAH HAS GONE' were at once printed and distributed by the armload, to be enthusiastically seized and read.

Meanwhile, the Shah's 707, with the Shah himself at the controls, climbed and turned away toward the West, the source of many of his dreams and illusions, and now the object of hatred of many of his people.

William Shawcross, *The Shah's Last Ride*, 1989

GETTING OUT

The Prodigal Son is a distinct sub-species of the exile: impelled to escape by a restless desire for excitement, and a belief that things must surely be better somewhere else. By no means all Prodigals are actually prodigal—most lack the money of the original—but there is always a touch of innate wildness about them. They are not leaving for a visit, they are making their escape, running from the ordinary tameness of everyday life, the constrictions of a boring marriage, a decent, uninspiring job or dull, worthy, religious parents. They are self-exiles, and society judges them harshly because they have judged society harshly.

And yet there is always a twinge of admiration in the way we regard the prodigals; like prisoners who lack the courage for the leap over the wire ourselves, we know that their act of escape makes it easier for us to endure our own chains. That is why Robinson Crusoe is a familiar character wherever books are read and why the parable of the Prodigal Son is one of the three most quoted passages in the Bible.

AND TOOK HIS JOURNEY

A certain man had two sons: And the younger of them said to his father, Father, give me the portion of goods that falleth to me. And he divided unto them his living.

And not many days after the younger son gathered all together, and took his journey into a far country, and there wasted his substance with riotous living.

Luke, 15

THE ADVENTURES OF A SEVENTH SON

On the last day of January 1709, Captain Woodes Rogers, then commander-in-chief of two privateers of Bristol, and himself in the *Duke* (a ship of 320 tons, 30 guns and 117 men), sighted Juan Fernandez. For master of the *Duke* he had Dampier himself, who meanwhile had been marooned on the island of Nicobar, whence he escaped in a cockleshell canoe whose gunwale was only three inches above the water-line, and had also been wrecked on Ascension. Rogers had come to Juan Fernandez to water. The next evening lights were seen on shore and surmised to be those of French ships lying at anchor.

As a matter of fact, they were the watch fires of a sailor named Alexander Selcraig, or Selkirk, who on the following morning was brought off in the ship's pinnace amid a cargo of shell-fish. He was clothed in goatskins, and 'looking wilder than the first owners of them'. It is our first glimpse of one who was destined to become the prince and prototype of all castaways.

Like Hans Andersen and so many folk-tale heroes, he was the son—and the seventh son—of a cobbler. He was born at Largo, a sea-village in Fife. There to-day stands his effigy in stone, gazing—like Martin Behaim's at Nuremberg and Drake's at Plymouth—(and a little ironically, one might suppose) on the haunts of his youth. When he was nineteen he was cited for misbehaviour in kirk and ran away to sea. Six years afterwards he came home again, but quarrelled with his brothers, once more decamped, and in the spring of 1703 shipped with Captain William Dampier as sailing master of the galley, the *Cinque Ports,* Dampier himself being in command of the *St. George.* Having arrived, in a leaky ship, at Juan Fernandez, after a bitter altercation with his commander, and at his own suggestion—of which he speedily repented—Selkirk was marooned on Más-á-tierra in September 1704.

He landed there a man much richer in this world's goods than the Mosquito Indian. He had a sea chest, clothes, bedding, a firelock, a pound of gunpowder, a bag of bullets, flint and steel, some tobacco, a hatchet, a knife, a kettle, a Bible, mathematical instruments and some books of devotion. Yet in spite of these luxuries, after four years and four months' solitude, Selkirk told Rogers his story in a Scots English so broken and rusty for want of use as to be hardly intelligible. 'We could scarce understand him . . . he seemed to speak his words by halves.'

Walter de la Mare, *Desert Islands,* 1930

A BAD OMEN FOR THE START OF ROBINSON CRUSOE'S CAREER

Without asking God's blessing, or my father's, without any consideration of circumstances or consequences, and in an ill hour, God knows, on the first of September, 1651, I went on board a ship bound for London. Never any young adventurer's misfortunes, I believe, began sooner, or continued longer than mine. The ship was no sooner gotten out of the Humber, but the wind began to blow, and the waves to rise in a most frightful manner; and as I had never been at sea before, I was most inexpressibly sick in body, and terrified in my mind. I began now seriously to reflect upon what I had done, and how justly I was overtaken by the judgment of heaven for my wicked leaving my father's house, and abandoning my duty; all the good counsel of my parents, my father's tears and my mother's entreaties, came now fresh into my mind, and my conscience, which was not yet come to the pitch of hardness which it has been since, reproached me with the contempt of advice, and the breach of my duty to God and my father.

All this while the storm increased, and the sea, which I had never been upon before, went very high, though nothing like what I have seen many times since; no, nor like what I saw a few days after. But it was enough to affect me then, who was but a young sailor, and had never known anything of the matter. I expected every wave would have swallowed us up, and that every time the ship fell down, as I thought, in the trough or hollow of the sea, we should never rise more; and in this agony of mind I made many vows and resolutions, that if it would please God here to spare my life this one voyage, if ever I got once my foot upon dry land again, I would go directly home to my father, and never set it into a ship again while I lived; that I would take his advice, and never run myself into such miseries as these any more. Now I saw plainly the goodness of his observations about the middle station of life, how easy, how comfortably he had lived all his days, and never had been exposed to tempests at sea, or troubles on shore; and I resolved that I would, like a true repenting prodigal, go home to my father.

These wise and sober thoughts continued all the while the storm continued, and indeed some time after; but the next day the wind was abated and the sea calmer, and I began to be a little inured to it. However, I was very grave for all that day, being also a little seasick still; but towards night the weather cleared up, the wind was quite over, and a charming fine evening followed; the sun went down perfectly clear, and rose so the next morning; and having little or no wind, and a smooth sea, the sun shining upon it, the sight was, as I thought, the most delightful that I ever saw. . . . In a word, as the sea was returned to its smoothness of surface and settled calmness by the abatement of that storm, so the hurry of my thoughts being over, my fears and apprehensions of being swallowed up by the sea being forgotten, and the current of my former desires returned, I entirely forgot the vows and promises that I made in my distress. I found indeed some intervals of reflection, and the serious thoughts did, as it were, endeavour to return again sometimes; but I shook them off, and roused myself from them as it were from a distemper, and applying myself to drink and company, soon mastered the return of those fits, for so I called them, and I had in five or six days got as complete a victory over conscience as any young fellow that resolved not to be troubled with it could desire.

Daniel Defoe, *Robinson Crusoe*, 1719

A LONGING TO GO TO SEA

In 1822 John Nicol wrote a remarkable account of his life at sea, a life which took him from whale-hunting off Greenland to trading voyages in the South Seas and service as a steward on a convict ship to Australia.

I was born in the small village of Currie, about six miles from Edinburgh, in the year 1755. The first wish I ever formed was to wander, and many a search I gave my parents in gratifying my youthful passion.

My mother died in child-bed, when I was very young, leaving my father in charge of five children; two died young, and three came to man's estate. My oldest brother died of his wounds in the West Indies, a Lieutenant in the Navy; my younger brother went to America, and I have never heard from him. Those trifling circumstances I would not mention, were I not conscious that the history of the dispersion of my father's family is the parallel of thousands of the families of my father's rank in Scotland.

My father, a cooper to trade, was a man of talent and information, and made it his study to give his children an education suited to their rank in life; but my unsteady propensities did not allow me to make the most of the schooling I got. I had read Robinson Crusoe many times over, and longed to be at sea. We had been living for some time in Borrowstownness. Every moment I could spare was spent in the boats or about the shore. . . . I chose the profession of a cooper, to please my father. I was for some time with a friend at the Queensferry, but not agreeing with him, I served out my tedious term of apprenticeship at Borrowstownness. My heart was never with the business; while my hands were hooping barrels my mind was at sea, and my imagination in foreign climes.

Soon as my period of bondage expired, I bade my friends farewell, and set out to Leith with a merry heart, and after working journeyman a few months, to enable me to be a proficient in my trade, I entered on board the Kent's Regard, commanded by Lieutenant Ralph Dundas; she was the tender at this time (1776) stationed in Leith Roads.

Now I was happy, for I was at sea. To me the order to weigh anchor and sail for the Nore was the sound of joy; my spirits were up at the near prospect of obtaining the pleasures I had sighed for since the first dawn of reason. To others it was the sound of woe, the order that cut off the last faint hope of escape from a fate they had been impressed into much against their inclination and interest. I was surprised to see so few, who, like myself, had chosen it for the love of that line of life. Some had been forced into it by their own irregular conduct, but the greater number were impressed men.

The Life and Adventures of John Nicol, Mariner, 1822

IN FAR EXILE AT SEA

What pen can well report the plight
Of those that travel on the seas?
To pass the weary winter's night,
With stormy clouds, wishing for day;

With waves that toss them to and fro,
Their poor estate is hard to show.

When boistering winds begin to blow
On cruel coasts, from haven we;
The foggy mist so dims the shore
That rocks and sands we may not see;
Nor have no room on seas to try,
But pray to God and yield to die.

When shoals and sandy banks appear
What pilot can direct his course?
When foaming tides draw us so near,
Alas! what fortune can be worse?
Then anchors hold must be our stay,
Or else we fall into decay.

We wander still from luff to lee,
And find no steadfast wind to blow;
We still remain in jeopardy,
Each perilous point is hard to show;
In time we hope to find redress,
That long have lived in heaviness.

O pinching, weary, loathsome life,
That travel still in far exile.
The dangers great on seas be rife,
Whose recompense doth yield but toil.
O Fortune, grant me my desire:
A happy end I do require.

When frets and spates have had their fill
And gentle calm the coast will clear,
Then haughty hearts shall have their will,
That long have wept with morning cheer;
And leave the seas with their annoy,
At home at ease to live in joy.

From J. O. Halliwell, *The Early Naval Ballads of England*, 1841

THE WILD GEESE

*For more than a century, the English wars in Ireland created enormous de-
population. From the Elizabethan invasion to the surrender of Limerick in*

1691, hundreds of thousands of men left Ireland, many of them to fight in the armies of France, Spain, and Austria.

For many of the poorer classes, military service in Flanders seemed to be an alternative to starvation or at least tremendous economic misery at home. The devastation of Munster after the Desmond rebellion has been well documented, and the subsequent 'unseasonable harvest' in 1586 left Munster, according to Lord Deputy Perrot, 'destitute both of corn, beef, and all other victual for men and horses'. It was therefore in this context that the vice-president of Munster, Thomas Norreys, wrote to the lord deputy in December 1585 that many of his company of soldiers 'hoping to better their estates are ronne frome me into Flanders or other places'.

Many, besides soldiers, also sought refuge abroad throughout the late 1580s and 1590s because of the prevailing social and economic conditions. The problem of Irish migrants was particularly acute in England after the Desmond rebellion. A private letter of one M. de Mauvissière to an Archibald Douglas in November 1585 remarked on the commonplace sight of 'exiled Irishmen, who solicit alms in England'. The problem had obviously reached crisis proportions in 1587, when the lords of the council in England demanded of the lord deputy, that order be given 'unto the Governors and Counsell in Munster and the principall officers of the corporate townes in those partes for the receyvinge and bestowing of the poore Irish people . . . to be transported backe into that Realme'. In future 'the officers of the portes' were to ensure that no more 'poore Irish' were transported from Ireland to England. The order however did not prove an effective deterrent, for in 1591 the lords of the council again complained of the

great nombers of vagrant and masterless persons of the Irish byrthe that a long tyme, contrarie to good orders and lawes in that behalf provided go begging in and about the cittie of London and the subburbes thereof.

Grainne Henry, *The Irish Military Community in Spanish Flanders*, 1992

IRISH VOLUNTEERS FOR THE FRENCH ARMY SAIL FROM CLARE

See, cold island, we stand
Here to-night on your shore,
To-night, but never again;
Lingering a moment more.
See, beneath us our boat
Tugs at its tightening chain,

Holds out its sail to the breeze,
Pants to be gone again.
Off then with shouts and mirth,
Off with laughter and jests,
Mirth and song on our lips,
Hearts like lead in our breasts.
Death and the grave behind,
Death and a traitor's bier;
Honour and fame before,
Why do we linger here?
Why do we stand and gaze,
Fools, whom fools despise,
Fools untaught by the years,
Fools renounced by the wise?
Heartsick, a moment more,
Heartsick, sorry, fierce,
Lingering, lingering on,
Dreaming the dreams of yore;
Dreaming the dreams of our youth,
Dreaming the days when we stood
Joyous, expectant, serene,
Glad, exultant of mood,
Singing with hearts afire,
Singing with joyous strain,
Singing aloud in our pride,
'We shall redeem her again!'
Ah, not to-night that strain,—
Silent to-night we stand,
A scanty, a toil-worn crew,
Strangers, foes in the land!
Gone the light of our youth,
Gone for ever, and gone
Hope with the beautiful eyes,
Who laughed as she lured us on;
Lured us to danger and death,
To honour, perchance to fame,—
Empty fame at the best,
Glory half dimmed with shame.
War-battered dogs are we,
Fighters in every clime,

> Fillers of trench and of grave,
> Mockers, bemocked by time.
> War-dogs, hungry and grey,
> Gnawing a naked bone,
> Fighters in every clime,
> Every cause but our own.

Lady Mary Carboy, 'Clare Coast', 1843

AN ENGLISH ACTRESS EXPLAINS WHY SHE PREFERS VENICE

The actress and opera singer Mrs Tofts, after being treated rather critically on the London stage, went to Italy where she claims they appreciate her much more.

Venice, July 10 N[ew] S[tyle]

Mr Spectator,

I take it extremely ill, that you do not reckon conspicuous persons of your nation are within your cognizance, though out of the dominions of Great Britain. I little thought, in the green years of my life, that I should ever call it an happiness to be out of dear England; but as I grew to woman, I found myself less acceptable in proportion to the increase of my merit. Their ears in Italy are so differently formed from the make of yours in England, that I never come upon the stage but a general satisfaction appears in the countenance of the whole people. When I dwell upon a note, I behold all the men accompanying me with heads inclining, and falling of their persons on the side, as dying away with me. The women too do justice to my merit, and no ill-natured worthless creature cries 'the vain thing' when I am rapt up in the performance of my part, and sensibly touched with the effect my voice has upon all who hear me. I live here distinguished as one whom nature has been liberal to in a graceful person, and exalted mien, and heavenly voice. These particularities in this strange country are arguments for respect and generosity to her who is possessed of them. The Italians see a thousand beauties I am sensible I have no pretence to, and abundantly make up to me the injustice I received in my own country, of disallowing me what I really had. The humour of hissing, which you have among you, I do not know any thing of; and their applauses are uttered in sighs, and bearing a part at the cadences of voice with the persons who are performing. . . .

The whole city of Venice is as still when I am singing as this polite hearer was to Mrs Hunt. But when they break that silence, did you know the pleasure I am in, when every man utters his applauses, by calling me aloud, 'The Dear Creature! The Angel! The Venus! What attitudes she moves with!—Hush, she sings again!' We have no boisterous wits who dare disturb an audience, and break the public peace merely to show they dare. Mr Spectator, I write this to you in haste, to tell you I am so very much at ease here, that I know nothing but joy; and I will not return, but leave you in England to hiss all merit of your own growth off the stage. I know, sir, you were always my admirer, and therefore I am yours,

CAMILLA

P.S. I am ten times better dressed than ever I was in England.

Letter to the *Spectator*, 29 July 1712

CASANOVA ESCAPES FROM PRISON IN VENICE

On the night of 31 October 1756 Casanova, after being denounced to the State Inquisitors for possessing illegal books and spending fifteen months in the terrible prison known as The Leads, finally manages to break out. He takes with him, almost it seems for comic relief, a monk called Father Balbi.

I got out the first, and Father Balbi followed me. Soradaci who had come as far as the opening, had orders to put the plate of lead back in its place, and then to go and pray to St Francis for us. Keeping on my hands and knees, and grasping my pike firmly I pushed it obliquely between the joining of the plates of lead, and then holding the side of the plate which I had lifted I succeeded in drawing myself up to the summit of the roof. The monk had taken hold of my waistband to follow me, and thus I was like a beast of burden who has to carry and draw along at the same time; and this on a steep and slippery roof.

When we were half-way up the monk asked me to stop, as one of his packets had slipped off, and he hoped it had not gone further than the gutter. My first thought was to give him a kick and to send him after his packet, but, praised be to God! I had sufficient self-control not to yield to it, and indeed the punishment would have been too heavy for both of us, as I should have had no chance of escaping by myself. I asked him if it were the bundle of rope, and on his replying that it was a small packet of his own containing a manuscript he had found in one of the garrets under the Leads, I told him he must bear it patiently, as a single step might be our destruction. The poor monk gave a sigh, and he still clinging to my waist we continued climbing.

After having surmounted with the greatest difficulty fifteen or sixteen plates we got to the top, on which I sat astride, Father Balbi imitating my example. Our backs were towards the little island of St George the Greater, and about two hundred paces in front of us were the numerous cupolas of St Mark's Church, which forms part of the ducal palace, for St Mark's is really the Doge's private chapel, and no monarch in the world can boast of having a finer. My first step was to take off my bundle, and I told my companion to do the same. He put the rope as best he could upon his thighs, but wishing to take off his hat, which was in his way, he took hold of it awkwardly, and it was soon dancing from plate to plate to join the packet of linen in the gutter. My poor companion was in despair.

'A bad omen,' he exclaimed; 'our task is but begun and here am I deprived of shirt, hat, and a precious manuscript, containing a curious account of the festivals of the palace.'. . .

Without an instant's delay and in dead silence, I made haste to descend the stairs, the monk following me. Avoiding the appearance of a fugitive, but walking fast, I went by the Giants' Stairs, taking no notice of Father Balbi, who kept calling out 'To the church! to the church!'

The church door was only about twenty paces from the stairs, but the churches were no longer sanctuaries in Venice, and no one ever took refuge in them. The monk knew this, but fright had deprived him of his faculties. He told me afterwards that the motive which impelled him to go to the church was the voice of religion bidding him seek the horns of the altar.

'Why didn't you go by yourself?' said I.

'I did not like to abandon you;' but he should rather have said, 'I did not like to lose the comfort of your company.'

The safety I sought was beyond the borders of the Republic, and thitherward I began to bend my steps. Already there in spirit, I must needs be there in body also. I went straight towards the chief door of the palace, and looking at no one that might be tempted to look at me I got to the canal and entered the first gondola that I came across, shouting to the boatman on the poop,—

'I want to go to Fusina; be quick and call another gondolier.'

This was soon done, and while the gondola was being got off I sat down on the seat in the middle, and Balbi at the side. The odd appearance of the monk, without a hat and with a fine cloak on his shoulders, with my unseasonable attire, was enough to make people take us for an astrologer and his man.

As soon as we had passed the custom-house, the gondoliers began to row with a will along the Giudecca Canal, by which we must pass to go to Fusina or to Mestre, which latter place was really our destination. When we

had traversed half the length of the canal I put my head out, and said to
the waterman on the poop,—

'When do you think we shall get to Mestre?'

'But you told me to go to Fusina.'

'You must be mad; I said Mestre.'

The other boatman said that I was mistaken, and the fool of a monk, in
his capacity of zealous Christian and friend of truth, took care to tell me
that I was wrong. I wanted to give him a hearty kick as a punishment for
his stupidity, but reflecting that common sense comes not by wishing for
it I burst into a peal of laughter, and agreed that I might have made a
mistake, but that my real intention was to go to Mestre. To that they
answered nothing, but a minute after the master boatman said he was ready
to take me to England if I liked.

'Bravely spoken,' said I, 'and now for Mestre, ho!'

> Jacques Casanova de Seingalt (1725–98), *Memoirs*, vol. ii, tr. Arthur Machen,
> 1894

TOM JONES GOES OUT INTO THE WORLD

Jones received his effects from Mr Allworthy's early in the morning, with
the following answer to his letter.

'SIR,

'I am commanded by my uncle to acquaint you, that as he did not proceed to
those measures he hath taken with you, without the greatest deliberation, and after
the fullest evidence of your unworthiness, so will it be always out of your power to
cause the least alteration in his resolution. He expresses great surprize at your
presumption in saying, you have resigned all pretensions to a young lady, to whom
it is impossible you should ever have had any, her birth and fortune having made
her so infinitely your superior. Lastly, I am commanded to tell you, that the only
instance of your compliance with my uncle's inclinations, which he requires, is, your
immediately quitting this country. I cannot conclude this without offering my advice,
as a Christian, that you would seriously think of amending your life: that you may
be assisted with grace so to do, will be always the prayer of

'Your humble servant,

'W. BLIFIL.'

Many contending passions were raised in our hero's mind by this letter;
but the tender prevailed at last over the indignant and irascible, and a flood
of tears came seasonably to his assistance, and possibly prevented his misfortunes from either turning his head, or bursting his heart.

He grew, however, soon ashamed of indulging this remedy; and starting up, he cried, 'Well then, I will give Mr Allworthy the only instance he requires of my obedience. I will go this moment—but whither?—why, let Fortune direct; since there is no other who thinks it of any consequence what becomes of this wretched person, it shall be a matter of equal indifference to myself. Shall I alone regard what no other?—Ha! have I not reason to think there is another?—One whose value is above that of the whole world!—I may, I must imagine my Sophia is not indifferent to what becomes of me. Shall I then leave this only friend—and such a friend? Shall I not stay with her?—Where? How can I stay with her? Have I any hopes of even seeing her, tho' she was as desirous as myself, without exposing her to the wrath of her father? And to what purpose? Can I think of soliciting such a creature to consent to her own ruin? Shall I indulge any passion of mine at such a price?—Shall I lurk about this country like a thief, with such intentions?—No, I disdain, I detest the thought. Farewell, Sophia; farewell most lovely, most beloved—' Here passion stopped his mouth, and found a vent in his eyes.

And now, having taken a resolution to leave the country, he began to debate with himself whither he should go. *The world*, as Milton phrases it, *lay all before him*; and Jones, no more than Adam, had any man to whom he might resort for comfort or assistance. All his acquaintance were the acquaintance of Mr Allworthy, and he had no reason to expect any countenance from them, as that gentleman had withdrawn his favour from him. Men of great and good characters should indeed be very cautious how they discard their dependents; for the consequence to the unhappy sufferer is being discarded by all others.

What course of life to pursue, or to what business to apply himself, was a second consideration; and here the prospect was all a melancholy void. Every profession, and every trade, required length of time, and what was worse, money; for matters are so constituted, that 'nothing out of nothing' is not a truer maxim in physics than in politics; and every man who is greatly destitute of money, is on that account entirely excluded from all means of acquiring it.

At last the ocean, that hospitable friend to the wretched, opened her capacious arms to receive him; and he instantly resolved to accept her kind invitation. To express myself less figuratively, he determined to go to sea.

This thought indeed no sooner suggested itself, than he eagerly embraced it; and having presently hired horses, he set out for Bristol to put it in execution.

Henry Fielding, The History of Tom Jones, a Foundling, 1749

THE YOUNG BOSWELL IS DELIGHTED TO BE IN LONDON

James Boswell writes to his friend John Johnston of Grange in Scotland.

London, 20 Novr. 1762

My Dear Friend: At last I am got to this great Metropolis the object of my wishes for so long; The Place where I consider felicity to dwell and age to be a stranger to. I am all in a flutter of joy. I am full of fine wild romantic feeling to find myself realy in LONDON. O Johnstone my worthy friend! I wish you was with me to partake of my happiness. I wrote a line to you from Durham reproving you for neglecting to come to town Indeed my friend it hurt me; that we did not meet and bid a cordial adieu. I am sure it would hurt you more when you came to Edinburgh and found that I was gone. However let this be forgot and let us consider how to be most happy in time to come. You must write to me a great deal write freely and easily and if you are old it will releive you to open your heart. I shall burn all your letters that have any thing of that kind in them. I shall keep a journal of every day; and send it to you weekly so as to come on Saturday night and comfort you on Sunday. I know every thing that I write must please you. I must first hear from you, and get your exact address that my packets may go safe. I shall send you franks. Address for me at Mr. Douglasse's Surgeon Pallmall London. This Gentleman has kindly insisted that I shall stay in his house till I get a lodging to my mind.

Expect a longer letter soon. I ever am your very affectionate friend

JAMES BOSWELL

James Boswell and John Johnston of Grange: Correspondence, ed. Ralph S. Walker, 1966

NOT TO RESIDE IN ENGLAND AGAIN

Lord Byron was separated from his wife in 1816 and decided to go and live in Venice. Once there, he wrote this letter to his friend Douglas Kinnaird on 27 November 1816.

I meant to have given up gallivanting altogether—on leaving your country—where I had been totally sickened of that & every thing else—but I know not how it is—my health growing better—& my spirits not worse—the 'besoin d'aimer' came back upon my heart again—after all there is nothing like it.——So much for that matter.——I hear you are in a room with Dibdin & Fanny Kelly—& the Devil knows whom—Humph!——I hear also that at the meeting or in the committee—you said that I was coming back in spring—it is probable—& if you have said so I *will* come—for sundry reasons—to see my daughter—my sister—and my friends—(and not least nor last—yourself) to renew my proxy (if Parliament be dissolved) for the Whigs—to see Mr. Waite & Mr. Blake—and the newest play—and the S[ub] committee—and to sell Newstead (if I can) but not to reside in England again—it neither suits me—nor I it—my greatest error was remaining there—that is to say—my greatest error but *one*—my ambition—if ever I had merits—is over—or at least limited—if I could but remain as I now am—I should not merely be happy—but *contented* which in my mind is the strongest & most difficult attainment of the two—for any one who will hazard enough may have moments of happiness.——I have books—a decent establishment—a fine country—a language which I prefer—most of the amusements & conveniences of life—as much of society as I choose to take—and a handsome woman—who is not a bore—and does not annoy me with looking like a fool & ⟨pretending⟩ setting up for a sage.—Life has little left for my curiosity—there are few things in it of which I have not had a sight and a share—it would be silly to quarrel with my luck because it did not last—& even that was partly my own fault.——If the present does—I should not fall out with the past:—and if I could but manage to arrange my pecuniary concerns in England—so as to pay my debts—& leave me what would be here a very fair income—(though nothing remarkable at home) you might consider me as posthumous—for I would never willingly dwell in the 'tight little Island'.—— Pray write to me a line or two addressed to Venice—*Poste Restante*—I hope to remain here the winter— remember me to Maria—and believe me yrs. ever & truly & affectly.

B

Lord Byron: Selected Letters and Journals, ed. Leslie A. Marchand, 1982

DON JUAN LEAVES HIS NATIVE COUNTRY

Juan embark'd—the ship got under weigh,
   The wind was fair, the water passing rough;
A devil of a sea rolls in that bay,
   As I, who've cross'd it oft, know well enough:
And, standing upon deck, the dashing spray
   Flies in one's face, and makes it weather-tough:
And there he stood to take, and take again,
His first—perhaps his last—farewell of Spain.

I can't say but it is an awkward sight
   To see one's native land receding through

The growing waters—it unmans one quite;
   Especially when life is rather new:
I recollect Great Britain's coast looks white,
   But almost every other country's blue,
When, gazing on them, mystified by distance,
We enter on our nautical existence.

Lord Byron, 'Don Juan', Canto II, 1819–24

BEAU BRUMMEL'S BROKEN FORTUNES

Calais, May 22, 1816.

Here I am restant for the present, and God knows solitary enough in my existence. Of that, however, I should not complain, for I can always employ resources within myself, was there not a worm that will not sleep, called conscience, which all my endeavours to distract, all the strength of coffee, with which I constantly fumigate my unhappy brains, and all the native gaiety of the fellow who brings it to me, cannot lull to indifference beyond the moment; but I will not trouble you upon that subject.

You would be surprised to find the sudden change and transfiguration which one week has accomplished in my life and *propria persona*. I am punctually off the pillow at half-past seven in the morning. My first object—melancholy, indeed, it may be in its nature—is to walk to the pier-head and take my distant look at England. This you may call weakness; but I am not yet sufficiently master of those feelings which may be called indigenous to resist the impulse.

The most of my day is filled with strolling an hour or two round the ramparts of this dismal town, in reading, and the study of that language which must hereafter be my own, for never more shall I set foot in my own country. I dine at five, and my evenings have as yet been occupied in writing letters.

The English I have seen here—and many of them known to me—I have cautiously avoided; and with the exception of Sir W. Bellingham and Lord Blessington, who have departed, I have not exchanged a word. Prince Esterhazy was here yesterday, and came into my room unexpectedly without my knowing he was here. He had the good nature to convey several letters for me upon his return to London. So much for my life hitherto on this side of the water.

As to the alteration in my looks, you will laugh when I tell you your own head of hair is but a scanty possession in comparison with that which now crowns my pristine baldness; a convenient, comely scalp, that has divested me of my former respectability of appearance (for what right have I now to such an outward sign?) and if the care and distress of mind which I have lately undergone had not impressed more ravages haggard and lean than my years might justify upon my unfortunate phiz, I should certainly pass at a little distance for *five-and-twenty.*

Carlo Maria Franzero, *The Life and Times of Beau Brummell,* 1958

THE BEAU'S EFFECTS

A Catalogue
of
A very choice and valuable assemblage
of
Specimens of the rare old Sèvres Porcelaine,
Articles of Buhl Manufacture,
Curiously Chased Plate,
Library of Books,
Chiefly of French, Italian and English Literature, the best
Editions, and in fine condition.
The admired Drawing of the Refractory School Boy, and
others, exquisitely finished by Holmes, Christall,
de Windt, and Stephanoff.
Three capital double-barrelled Fowling Pieces,
By Manton.
Ten dozen of capital Old Port, sixteen dozen of Claret
(Beauvais), Burgundy, Claret and Still Champagne,
The whole of which have been nine years in bottle in the
Cellar of the Proprietor;
Also, an
Assortment of Table and other Linen, and some
Articles of neat Furniture;
The genuine property of
A MAN OF FASHION,
Gone to the Continent;
Which,
By order of the Sheriff of Middlesex!
Will be sold by Auction
By Mr. Christie,
On the premises, No. 13 Chapel Street, Park Lane,
On Wednesday, May 22nd, and the following day.

Carlo Maria Franzero, *The Life and Times of Beau Brummell,* 1958

A PAIR OF LITTLE MONSTERS

Captain Sir Richard Burton, the explorer, was the son of a man who was chronically short of money and lived on the Continent as a result. Burton and his brother were brought up in France, 'like wild beasts', he said, and were brought back by their disapproving grandmother to school in England.

Landing in England was dolorous. Grandmamma Baker inflated her nostrils, and, delighted at escaping from those *crapauds* and their kickshaws, quoted with effusion her favourite Cowper, 'England, with all thy faults, I love thee still.' The children scoffed. The air of Brighton, full of smoke and blacks, appeared to them unfit for breathing. The cold grey seas made them shudder. In the town everything appeared so small, so prim, so mean, the little one-familied houses contrasting in such a melancholy way with the big buildings of Tours and Paris. We revolted against the coarse and half-cooked food, and, accustomed to the excellent Bordeaux of France, we found port, sherry, and beer like strong medicine; the bread, all crumb and no crust, appeared to be half baked, and milk meant chalk and water. The large joints of meat made us think of Robinson Crusoe, and the vegetables *cuite à l'eau*, especially the potatoes, which had never heard of '*Maître d'hôtel*,' suggested the roots of primitive man. Moreover, the national temper, fierce and surly, was a curious contrast to the light-hearted French of middle France. A continental lady of those days cautioned her son, who was about to travel, against ridicule in France and the *canaille* in England. The little children punched one another's heads on the sands, the boys punched one another's heads in the streets, and in those days a stand-up fight between men was not uncommon. Even the women punched their children, and the whole lower-class society seemed to be governed by the fist. . . .

Before the year concluded, an attack of measles broke out in the school, several of the boys died, and it was found necessary to disperse the survivors. We were not hard-hearted, but we were delighted to get home. We worked successfully on the fears of Aunt G., which was assisted by my cadaverous appearance, and it was resolved to move us from school, to our infinite joy. My father had also been thoroughly sick of 'Maids of Honour Row' and 'Richmond Green.' He was sighing for shooting and boar-hunting in the French forests, and he felt that he had done quite enough for the education of the boys, which was turning out so badly. He resolved to bring us up abroad, and picked up the necessary assistance for educating us by tutor and governess. . . .

As soon as I was well enough to travel, the family embarked at the Tower Wharf for Boulogne. We boys scandalized every one on board. We shrieked, we whooped, we danced for joy. We shook our fists at the white cliffs, and loudly hoped we should never see them again. We hurrah'd for France, and hooted for England, 'The Land on which the Sun ne'er sets—nor rises,' till the sailor who was hoisting the Jack, looked upon us as a pair of little monsters. In our delight at getting away from school and the stuffy little island, we had no idea of the disadvantages which the new kind of life would inflict on our future careers. We were too young to know. A man who brings up his family abroad, and who lives there for years, must expect to lose all the friends who could be useful to him when he wishes to start them in life. The conditions of society in England are so complicated, and so artificial, that those who would make their way in the world, especially in public careers, must be broken to it from their earliest day. The future soldiers and statesmen must be prepared by Eton and Cambridge. The more English they are, even to the cut of their hair, the better. In consequence of being brought up abroad, we never thoroughly understood English society, nor did society understand us. And, lastly, it is a *real* advantage to belong to some parish. It is a great thing, when you have won a battle, or explored Central Africa, to be welcomed home by some little corner of the Great World, which takes a pride in your exploits, because they reflect honour upon itself. In the contrary condition you are a waif, a stray; you are a blaze of light, without a focus. Nobody outside your own fireside cares.

Sir Richard Burton, *Life*, ed. Lady Isabel Burton, 1893

HECTOR BERLIOZ LEAVES HOME WITH HIS MOTHER'S CURSE

My mother was therefore convinced that in deciding to become a composer (which to the French means the theatre) I was setting my feet on the broad road that leads to disgrace in this world and damnation in the next. The moment she got wind of what was happening her whole soul rose in righteous indignation. I could tell from her wrathful expression that she knew, so I thought it politic to avoid her and lie low until the time came for me to leave. But within a few minutes she followed me to my retreat and confronted me, her eyes blazing, every gesture betraying the intensity of the emotion that gripped her. 'Your father,' she said, addressing me by the formal you, 'has been so weak as to consent to your returning to Paris. He encourages you in your wicked, foolish ideas. I shall not have this sin to lay to my charge. I absolutely forbid you to go.'

'Mother!'

'Yes, I forbid you and, Hector, I implore you not to persist in this madness. Look, I kneel—I, your mother, I clasp your knees and humbly beg you to renounce it.'

'For God's sake, Mother, let me raise you to your feet, I can't bear it.'

'No, I will kneel.' Then, after a moment's silence: 'Wretched boy, you refuse? You can stand there unmoved while your mother kneels before you? Very well, go! Drag yourself through the gutters of Paris, besmirch our name, kill your father and me with shame and sorrow. I shall not set foot in this house again until you have left it. You are my son no longer. I curse you!'

One would hardly believe it possible that even the combination of religious fanaticism with the very grossest contempt for the artistic profession that provincial narrowmindedness is capable of could lead to such a scene, between so affectionate a mother as mine and so devoted a son as I had always been. It was a moment of horror, a scene of grotesque and exaggerated violence that I shall never forget, and to it more than to anything I owe my deep hatred of those crass medieval prejudices which still survive in most of the provinces of modern France.

The ordeal did not end there. My mother had gone; she had taken refuge at Le Chuzeau, a country house of ours near La Côte. When the time came for me to leave, my father decided we should make a last effort to get her to bid me goodbye and retract the bitter things she had said. He and I and my two sisters went to Le Chuzeau. My mother was sitting in the orchard under a tree, reading. When she saw us she got up and ran off. We waited for some time; we went after her; my father called out; my sisters and I were in tears. It was hopeless. I had to go away without embracing my mother, without a word or a look from her, and with all the weight of her curse upon me.

Hector Berlioz (1803–69), *Memoirs*, tr. David Cairns, 1969

DOSTOEVSKY ESCAPES HIS DEBTS WITH A EUROPEAN TOUR

You know how I left and for what reasons. There were two main reasons: (1) to save not only my health, but my very life. My fits had already begun to recur every week, and to feel and to be so acutely *aware* of this nervous and *brain* disorder was unbearable. My mind was actually beginning to be affected—that is the truth. I was conscious of it, and my nervous disorder drove me sometimes to moments of madness. The 2nd reason was the circumstances in which I found myself: My creditors wouldn't wait any longer and, by the time I was leaving, Latkin and then Pechatkin had already started proceeding against me, and I just escaped arrest. I must say, though (and this is not just a pretty phrase or empty words), that to be in *debtors' prison* would have been very useful to me from one point of view: Reality, material, a second *House of the Dead*, in brief, there could have been at least 4 or 5 thousand rubles' worth of material there. Only I had just got married and, besides, would I have pulled through a stifling summer in the Tarasov establishment? This posed an insoluble problem. If I were unable to write at Tarasov's, as my fits grew worse and worse, how would I manage to pay off my debts? And the burden had grown to awful proportions. So I left, but I left with death in my heart. I did not believe in living abroad, i.e., I believed that the moral effect of living abroad would be very bad: alone, *away from my material,* with a young creature who with naive joy eagerly looked forward to sharing my nomadic life; but I could see that in this naive joy there was much inexperience and youthful impulsiveness, and that worried and tormented me a great deal. . . .

Finally, our loneliness in Dresden wore down both Anna Grigorevna and myself. Above all, there were the following facts: (1) From the letters forwarded to me by Pasha (he has only written to me once), it turns out that the creditors have started proceedings against me (therefore, *I cannot return to Russia before paying the debts* [)]. (2) My wife has realized she is pregnant. (*Please keep this* between us. It will be nine months in February, which is one more reason why we cannot go back.) (3) The question arises —what will happen to my Petersburg relatives, to Emiliya Fyodorovna, to Pasha, and to a few others? Money, money, but there is no money! (4) If we must hibernate, let it be in the south. Anyway, I want to show Anna Grigorevna some things, to distract her, to take her around a bit. So we have decided to spend the winter somewhere in Switzerland or Italy. But there is no money—whatever we have borrowed has already been spent. I wrote to Katkov, described the whole situation, and asked him for another 500-ruble *advance.* And what do you think—he sent it to me! What a wonderful man he is! There is a man with a heart for you!

> Fyodor Dostoevsky (1821–81), *Selected Letters,* ed. Joseph Frank and David
> I. Goldstein, tr. Andrew T. MacAndrew, 1987

1838: THE TREK SPIRIT

The Boers hated boundaries. They had grown up with a sense of spaciousness that was part of their concept of freedom, and they hated being enclosed and restricted in their ability to move on and appropriate a new farm for each newly grown man. Above all they hated being interfered with in the regulating of their own affairs on their own farms. That was a kind of sacrilege. The long years of neglect had left them with a sense of total autonomy on their own domains, to intrude on which was to violate a free man's fundamental rights.

When the Dutch government had tentatively tried to introduce some small degree of administrative control toward the end of the eighteenth century, the Trekboers had rebelled and declared two independent republics in the outlying districts of Swellendam and Graaff-Reinet. Now this rebelliousness surged up again as the British drew their boundaries and imposed their regulations. Like the children of Israel they murmured against the alien rulers who afflicted them with these burdens. And the *trekgees*— the trek spirit—was upon them: the old urge if one was dissatisfied with anything to take one's wagons and one's span of oxen and one's horses and servants and households goods and go; to trek on under the clear blue skies in this endless land to some new ground where one's authority and independence would once again be unchallenged.

There were some genuine grievances, particularly over the abolition of slavery, and much has been made of them. The British offered compensation, a pro rata share of £20 million that was being divided among nineteen slave colonies, but it had to be collected in London. London! How was a Boer to get to London? There were agents offering to do the collecting but they had to be paid a commission. In the end very little compensation was received. Some Boers were too incensed to accept anything at all.

But the worst bitterness was over the imperial government's piecemeal granting of rights to people of colour. There was the right of a Khoikhoi servant to lodge a complaint against his master and take him to court, which had so enraged Freek Bezuidenhout. In 1828 Ordinance 50 ended the pass system for Khoikhoi and manumitted slaves and gave them equal legal status with whites. Six years later slavery itself was abolished. The cumulative effect represented the threat of *gelykstelling*, or equalizing, which the Boers considered an affront to their inherited principles.

'The shameful and unjust proceedings with reference to the freedom of the slaves,' cited Anna Steenkamp, niece of Trek leader Piet Retief, in a famous exposition of the grievances that caused the Boers to leave their homes. 'And yet it is not so much their freedom which drove us to such lengths as their being placed on an equal footing with Christians, contrary to the laws of God and the natural distinction of race and religion, so that it was intolerable for any decent Christian to bow down beneath such a yoke; wherefore we rather withdrew in order thus to preserve our doctrines in purity.'. . .

History is in the eye of the beholder. To the blacks the Great Trek was a time of defeat and dispossession. 'The northward march of the Voortrekkers was a gigantic plundering raid,' declared Dr. Abdul Abdurahman, a black political figure of the early twentieth century. 'They swept like a desolating pestilence through the land, blasting everything in their path and pitilessly laughing at ravages from which the native races have not yet recovered.'

To Afrikaners it was a sacred saga, a thunderous reenactment of the story of Exodus during which God made known his will to his chosen people and brought them out from under the burdens of the British through trial and tribulation into their promised land. It was a 'pilgrimage of martyrdom' they had to undertake to escape persecution 'until every portion of that unhappy country had been painted red with blood, not so much of men capable of resistance as with that of our murdered and defenceless women and children.' And as they went they were followed by the British army, like that of Pharaoh, and were beset everywhere by the unbelieving black 'Canaanites.'

Thus the prisms of perspective on either side of the bitter-almond hedge.

There is little evidence that Piet Retief and the other Voortrekkers saw it in such apocalyptic terms as they went their way. They were simple folk, fed up with the interfering British and their *kaffirboetie* ('nigger-loving') ideas, and they were intent on moving on to where they could be on their own to deal with the blacks as they pleased.

Allister Sparks, *The Mind of South Africa*, 1990

THE PASSAGE OF TIME

He travelled.

He came to know the melancholy of the steamboat, the cold awakening in the tent, the tedium of landscapes and ruins, the bitterness of interrupted friendships.

He returned.

He went into society, and he had other loves. But the ever-present memory of the first made them insipid; and besides, the violence of desire, the very flower of feeling, had gone. His intellectual ambitions had also dwindled. Years went by; and he endured the idleness of his mind and the inertia of his heart.

Gustave Flaubert, *A Sentimental Education*, 1869

FLEEING FROM COMMITMENT

I

On the Coast of Coromandel
Where the early pumpkins blow,
In the middle of the woods
Lived the Yonghy-Bonghy-Bò.

Two old chairs, and half a candle,—
One old jug without a handle,—
    These were all his worldly goods:
    In the middle of the woods,
    These were all the worldly goods,
  Of the Yonghy-Bonghy-Bò,
  Of the Yonghy-Bonghy-Bò.

II

Once, among the Bong-trees walking
  Where the early pumpkins blow,
    To a little heap of stones
  Came the Yonghy-Bonghy-Bò.
There he heard a Lady talking,
To some milk-white Hens of Dorking,—
    ' 'Tis the Lady Jingly Jones!
    'On that little heap of stones
    'Sits the Lady Jingly Jones!'
  Said the Yonghy-Bonghy-Bò,
  Said the Yonghy-Bonghy-Bò.

III

'Lady Jingly! Lady Jingly!
  'Sitting where the pumpkins blow,
    'Will you come and be my wife?'
  Said the Yonghy-Bonghy-Bò.
'I am tired of living singly,—
'On this coast so wild and shingly,—
    'I'm a-weary of my life:
    'If you'll come and be my wife,
    'Quite serene would be my life!'—
  Said the Yonghy-Bonghy-Bò,
  Said the Yonghy-Bonghy-Bò.

IV

'On this Coast of Coromandel,
  'Shrimps and watercresses grow,
    'Prawns are plentiful and cheap,'
  Said the Yonghy-Bonghy-Bò.
'You shall have my Chairs and candle,

'And my jug without a handle!—
    'Gaze upon the rolling deep
    ('Fish is plentiful and cheap)
    'As the sea, my love is deep!'
Said the Yonghy-Bonghy-Bò,
Said the Yonghy-Bonghy-Bò.

V

Lady Jingly answered sadly,
    And her tears began to flow,—
        'Your proposal comes too late,
        'Mr. Yonghy-Bonghy-Bò!
'I would be your wife most gladly!'
(Here she twirled her fingers madly,)
        'But in England I've a mate!
        'Yes! you've asked me far too late,
        'For in England I've a mate,
        'Mr. Yonghy-Bonghy-Bò!
        'Mr. Yonghy-Bonghy-Bò!'

VI

'Mr. Jones—(his name is Handel,—
    'Handel Jones, Esquire, & Co.)
        'Dorking fowls delights to send,
        'Mr. Yonghy-Bonghy-Bò!
'Keep, oh! keep your chairs and candle,
And your jug without a handle,—
        'I can merely be your friend!
        '—Should my Jones more Dorkings send,
        'I will give you three, my friend!
        'Mr. Yonghy-Bonghy-Bò!
        'Mr. Yonghy-Bonghy-Bò!'

VII

'Though you've such a tiny body,
    'And your head so large doth grow,—
        'Though your hat may blow away,
        'Mr. Yonghy-Bonghy-Bò!
'Though you're such a Hoddy Doddy—

'Yet I wish that I could modi-
  'fy the words I needs must say!
  'Will you please to go away?
  'That is all I have to say—
 'Mr. Yonghy-Bonghy-Bò!
 'Mr. Yonghy-Bonghy-Bò!'

VIII

Down the slippery slopes of Myrtle,
  Where the early pumpkins blow,
    To the calm and silent sea
  Fled the Yonghy-Bonghy-Bò.
There, beyond the Bay of Gurtle,
Lay a large and lively Turtle;—
    'You're the Cove,' he said, 'for me
    'On your back beyond the sea,
    'Turtle, you shall carry me!'
  Said the Yonghy-Bonghy-Bò,
  Said the Yonghy-Bonghy-Bò.

IX

Through the silent-roaring ocean
  Did the Turtle swiftly go;
    Holding fast upon his shell
  Rode the Yonghy-Bonghy-Bò.
With a sad primæval motion
Towards the sunset isles of Boshen
    Still the Turtle bore him well.
    Holding fast upon his shell,
    'Lady Jingly Jones, farewell!'
  Sang the Yonghy-Bonghy-Bò,
  Sang the Yonghy-Bonghy-Bò.

X

From the Coast of Coromandel,
  Did that Lady never go;
    On that heap of stones she mourns
  For the Yonghy-Bonghy-Bò.
On that Coast of Coromandel,
In his jug without a handle

Still she weeps, and daily moans;
On that little heap of stones
To her Dorking Hens she moans,
For the Yonghy-Bonghy-Bò,
For the Yonghy-Bonghy-Bò.

Edward Lear (1812–88), 'The Courtship of the Yonghy-Bonghy-Bò'

EDWARD LEAR

Left by his friend to breakfast alone on the white
Italian shore, his Terrible Demon arose
Over his shoulder; he wept to himself in the night,
A dirty landscape-painter who hated his nose.

The legions of cruel inquisitive They
Were so many and big like dogs: he was upset
By Germans and boats; affection was miles away:
But guided by tears he successfully reached his Regret.

How prodigious the welcome was. Flowers took his hat
And bore him off to introduce him to the tongs;
The demon's false nose made the table laugh; a cat
Soon had him waltzing madly, let him squeeze her hand;
Words pushed him to the piano to sing comic songs;

And children swarmed to him like settlers. He became a land.

W. H. Auden, 'Edward Lear', from *Collected Poems*, 1986

THE DEPARTURE

I ordered my horse to be brought from the stables. The servant did not
understand my orders. So I went to the stables myself, saddled my horse,
and mounted. In the distance I heard the sound of a trumpet, and I asked
the servant what it meant. He knew nothing and had heard nothing. At the
gate he stopped me and asked: 'Where is the master going?' 'I don't know,'
I said, 'just out of here, just out of here. Out of here, nothing else, it's the
only way I can reach my goal.' 'So you know your goal?' he asked. 'Yes,'
I replied, 'I've just told you. Out of here—that's my goal.'

Franz Kafka (1883–1924), *The Complete Short Stories*, tr. Tania and James
Stern, 1991

THE YOUNG TROTSKY WAKES UP LENIN

I arrived in London from Zurich by way of Paris, in the autumn of 1902. I think it was in October, early in the morning, when a cab, engaged after I had resorted to all sorts of pantomime, drove me to the address written on a slip of paper. My destination was Lenin's house. I had been instructed before I left Zurich to knock on the door three times. The door was opened by Nadyezhda Konstantinovna, who had probably been wakened by my knocking. It was early, and any one used to civilized ways would have waited quietly at the station for an hour or two, instead of knocking at the door of a strange house at such an unearthly hour. But I was still impelled by the force that had set me off on my journey from Verkholensk. I had disturbed Axelrod in Zurich in the same barbarous way, although that was in the middle of the night, instead of at dawn. Lenin was still in bed, and the kindly expression of his face was tinged with a justifiable amazement. Such was the setting for our first meeting and conversation. Both Vladimir Ilyich [Lenin] and Nadyezhda Konstantinovna already knew of me from Kler's letter, and had been waiting for me.

I was greeted with: 'The Pero has arrived!' At once I unloaded my modest list of impressions of Russia: the connections in the South are bad, the secret *Iskra* address in Kharkov is wrong, the editors of the *Southern Worker* oppose amalgamation, the crossing at the Austrian frontier is in the hands of a student at the *gymnasium* who refuses help to followers of the *Iskra*. The facts in themselves were not of a sort to fill one with much hope, but there was faith enough to make up for it, and to spare.

Either the same or the next morning, Vladimir Ilyich and I went for a long walk around London. From a bridge, Lenin pointed out Westminster and some other famous buildings. I don't remember the exact words he used, but what he conveyed was: 'This is their famous Westminster,' and 'their' referred of course not to the English but to the ruling classes. This implication, which was not in the least emphasized, but coming as it did from the very innermost depths of the man, and expressed more by the tone of his voice than by anything else, was always present, whether Lenin was speaking of the treasures of culture, of new achievements, of the wealth of books in the British Museum, of the information of the larger European newspapers, or, years later, of German artillery or French aviation. They know this or they have that, they have made this or achieved that—but what enemies they are! To his eyes, the invisible shadow of the ruling classes always overlay the whole of human culture—a shadow that was as real to him as daylight.

The architecture of London scarcely attracted my attention at that time. Transferred bodily from Verkholensk to countries beyond the Russian border which I was seeing for the first time, I absorbed Vienna, Paris and London in a most summary fashion, and details like the Westminster Palace seemed quite superfluous. It wasn't for that, of course, that Lenin had taken me out for this long walk. His object was to become acquainted with me, and to question me. His examination, it must be admitted, was very thorough indeed.

Leon Trotsky, *My Life*, 1929

THE BROKEN MEN (1902)

For things we never mention,
  For Art misunderstood—
For excellent intention
  That did not turn to good:
From ancient tales' renewing
  From clouds we would not clear—
Beyond the Law's pursuing
  We fled, and settled here.

We took no tearful leaving.
  We bade no long good-byes.
Men talked of crime and thieving.
  Men wrote of fraud and lies.
To save our injured feelings
  'Twas time and time to go—
Behind was dock and Dartmoor,
  Ahead lay Callao!

The widow and the orphan
  That pray for ten per cent
They clapped their trailers on us
  To spy the road we went.
They watched the foreign sailings
  (They scan the shipping still),
And that's your Christian people
  Returning good for ill!

God bless the thoughtful islands
  Where never warrants come;

God bless the just Republics
 That give a man a home,
That ask no foolish questions,
 But set him on his feet;
And save his wife and daughters
 From the workhouse and the street.

On church and square and market
 The noonday silence falls;
You'll hear the drowsy mutter
 Of the fountain in our halls.
Asleep amid the yuccas
 The city takes her ease—
Till twilight brings the land-wind
 To the clicking jalousies.

Day long the diamond weather,
 The high, unaltered blue—
The smell of goats and incense
 And the mule-bells tinkling through.
Day long the warder ocean
 That keeps us from our kin,
And once a month our levée
 When the English mail comes in.

You'll find us up and waiting
 To treat you at the bar;
You'll find us less exclusive
 Than the average English are.
We'll meet you with a carriage,
 Too glad to show you round,
But—we do not lunch on steamers,
 For they are English ground.

We sail o' nights to England
 And join our smiling Boards—
Our wives go in with Viscounts
 And our daughters dance with Lords,
But behind our princely doings,
 And behind each coup we make,
We feel there's Something Waiting,
 And—we meet It when we wake.

Ah, God! One sniff of England—
 To greet our flesh and blood—
To hear the traffic slurring
 Once more through London mud!
Our towns of wasted honour—
 Our streets of lost delight!
How stands the old Lord Warden?
 Are Dover's cliffs still white?

Rudyard Kipling (1865–1936)

EDWARD VII ESCAPES FROM VICTORIAN VALUES

He was particularly fond of France. He paid regular visits to the Riviera where he engaged with relish in the annual battle of the flowers, once dressed as Satan complete with scarlet robes and horns, and where he played roulette '*comme d'habitude*'. He was even more frequently to be seen in Paris, where he sometimes stayed at the Ritz or the Hôtel de l'Ambassade, but usually at the Bristol, being known there as the Earl of Chester or the Duke of Lancaster, a title which Lord James of Hereford, for one, considered him unjustified in using as it properly belonged to the descendants of John of Gaunt and did not go with the Duchy.

As Prince of Wales he had loved to go for walks in the Bois de Boulogne and down the Champs Elysées, to sail up and down the Seine, to stroll along the boulevards, looking into the shop windows in the rue de la Paix, buying shirts at Charvet's, jewellery at Cartier's, handkerchiefs at Chaperon's and hats at Genot's. He had enjoyed meals at his favourite restaurants—Magny's, Léon's and Durand's, the Voisin, the Bignon, the Café Américain, the Café des Ambassadeurs and the Café de la Paix. He had wandered into one or other of the clubs of which he was a member—the Jockey Club, the Yacht Club de France, the Cercle des Champs Elysées, the Union Club, the Nouveau and the Rue Royale. Almost every evening he had been to the theatre—the Théâtre Français, the Théâtre des Variétés, the Gymnase, the Vaudeville, the Odéon, the Palais Royal, the Nouveautés, the Renaissance or the Porte St Martin. Afterwards he had paid calls backstage with friends from the Jockey Club, or he had gone to the Épatant for a game of baccarat, or to 16 rue de la Pépinière for '*une soirée intime*', or to the cabaret at the Lion d'Or, the Bouffes-Parisiens or the Moulin Rouge. Once he had played the part of the murdered prince in Sardou's *Fedora* while Sarah Bernhardt wept over him. And he had entertained Bernhardt and other actresses in the Café Anglais in the 'Grand Seize', an exotic private room hung with red wall paper and gold hieroglyphics, furnished with gilt chairs and a crimson sofa, and softly lit by gasoliers.

He had made elaborate efforts to give the slip to the indefatigable French detectives who, to his extreme annoyance, followed him everywhere, suitably disguised, even to the extent of wearing clothes appropriate to the different parts of the theatres to which they were assigned and taking their wives with them to restaurants. Occasionally the Prince's carriage had suddenly rattled off at such a pace from the Hôtel Bristol that the police had lost track of him. But generally they managed to keep up with him and were able to submit reports of meetings with celebrated beauties in the Jardin des Plantes, of long afternoons spent with his intimate friends, the Comtesse Edmond de Pourtalès in the rue Tronchet, the Baronne Alphonse de Rothschild in the Faubourg St Honoré, and the Princesse de Sagan on the corner of the Esplanade des Invalides.

The police had watched him on his visits to Mme Kauchine, a Russian beauty who rented a room in the Hôtel du Rhin; to 'the widow Signoret', mistress of the Duc de Rohan; to a certain 'Dame Verneuil' who had an apartment on the second floor at 39 rue Lafayette; to the Baronne de Pilar at the Hôtel Choiseul; to Miss Chamberlayne (described in 1884 as his '*maîtresse en titre*') at the Hôtel Balmoral; to unidentified ladies in the Hôtel Scribe and the Hôtel Liverpool in the rue de Castiglione. The police had been particularly concerned by his visits to the Hôtel de Calais, where he often spent most of the night with a mysterious woman known to the chambermaid as Mme Hudrie, 'a very beautiful woman, aged about thirty, tall, slim, blonde, remarkable for her magnificent colouring and her perfect elegance . . . usually dressed in white satin, but always in black when she meets the Prince'. This turned out to be the Comtesse de Boutourline, wife of the Prefect of Moscow, sister-in-law of General Boutourline, formerly military attaché at the Russian Embassy in London, and granddaughter of Princess Bobinska, with whom she claimed to be staying in the rue de Chateaubriand, though the police discovered that she was actually living in a house belonging to the Comte de Guinsonnas.

The Prince had spent other evenings with the delightful English courtesan, Catherine Walters; and had visited his favourite brothel, Le Chabanais, where the chair upon which he sat with his chosen young women was still displayed over a generation later to the brothel's customers. He had gone to the Maison Dorée with the Duc de Gramont to meet the generous, passionate and consumptive Giulia Beneni, known as La Barucci, who arrived very late and, on being reprimanded by the Duke, turned her back on the royal visitor, lifted her skirts to her waist and said, 'You told me to show him my best side.' He had asked also to meet La Barucci's rival, Cora Pearl, who had appeared before him naked except for a string of pearls and a sprig of parsley.

Christopher Hibbert, Edward VII: A Portrait, 1991

THE UNSPEAKABLE FR. ROLFE

Frederick William Rolfe (1860–1913) shortened his first name to give the impression that he was a Catholic priest, and at other times wrote under the name 'Baron Corvo'. He was a drifter, a pederast, a sufferer from persecution mania, and a leech who attached himself to people and invariably ended the relationship on poisonous terms. He also wrote one extraordinary work of literature, Hadrian VII. *In Venice he was given shelter by Dr and Mrs van Someren.*

Various watermen warned Mrs van Someren that her guest bore a bad character; and rumours from other quarters reached the Doctor's ears. But Rolfe behaved with such discretion and aloofness that his hosts, disbelieving the reports, regarded him as a maligned man; Dr van Someren even agreed to allow him a small sum weekly for stamps and tobacco. As the winter wore away Rolfe was still working indefatigably at his new book. He had taken up his residence at the Palazzo Mocenigo in the July of 1909; the spring of 1910 found him still there. And then, in an unlucky moment for himself, Rolfe was moved by natural author's vanity to satisfy Mrs van Someren's equally natural curiosity.

She had made numerous vain efforts to persuade him into allowing her to see the manuscript on which he was working, efforts which he had politely withstood. Unexpectedly, however, one afternoon he yielded, and placed in her hands a bulky bundle of closely written sheets, the first part of his book, exacting only the condition that she would say nothing of what it contained to her husband. The condition was granted; but as Mrs van Someren read she soon saw that it must be retracted: for, as she turned the manuscript pages written in vermilion ink, she recognized first one and then another and then another of her friends and acquaintances, pitilessly lampooned in this 'Romance of Modern Venice', *The Desire and Pursuit of the Whole*. With perverse and brilliant ingenuity, Rolfe had woven his life and letters into this story of himself (as Nicholas Crabbe, the hero) pursued and thwarted by the members of the English colony. The book was not completed; and, rancid with libel as it was, might never be published; but it was clearly impossible for the friend of Lady Layard, Canon Ragg, Horatio Brown and the rest of the English residents to share responsibility for it by sheltering the author while he finished it. So Mrs van Someren instantly told Rolfe, adding that she must let her husband decide what action should be taken. The Doctor, when he learned how his long hospitality had been requited, issued an ultimatum: the manuscript must be abandoned, or its author must leave the house. Rolfe was equally prompt in his decision: next morning he took his few belongings and his cherished romance to the Bucintoro Club; that night he walked the streets. It was early March and bitterly cold. A month later he collapsed, and was taken to that Hospital which, in his libellous book, he had so bitterly attacked. Exposure and insufficient food had induced pneumonia. He was given the Last Sacraments; but he did not die.

A. J. A. Symons, The Quest for Corvo, 1934

THE ELATION OF LEAVING HITLER'S BERLIN

Friends came to say goodbye to us, tears were shed. I laughed and was calm, I left alone with one small suitcase.

Downstairs I encountered a surprise. A Nazi wearing a civilian overcoat over his uniform was standing in front of the shingle for my practice. He fixed me with a stare—and followed me to the subway. He waited to see which train I would take and then entered the same compartment. I got out to change trains and he got out too. At least I immediately caught on to *this* situation. He followed me. We came to a crowd getting off an arriving train, I ran down the steps to another platform and traveled first in one, then in another direction to my destination, the Möcken Bridge at Potsdamer Platz. I wanted to reach the Anhalter station. A train was leaving from there for Stuttgart around ten o'clock. I booked a sleeping berth; I carried that ticket in my wallet for the entire twelve years of emigration; I have taken it out now, it's with my other papers. As the train departed, I stood at the window in the corridor. It was dark. I had traveled this stretch many times. I loved the lights of the city. It was always the same when I arrived back in Berlin and saw them: I would take a deep breath, I felt good, I was at home. So I set off, I lay down to sleep. A strange situation that had nothing to do with me, really.

A few hours in Stuttgart; it's peaceful, the Nazis are calling assembly meetings—a comedy, why am I leaving? Ridiculous; I'll be embarrassed by this later. We come to Überlingen, I spend the night there, then cross the lake to Kreuzlingen. I cross the border by car; everything goes smoothly.

In Kreuzlingen I visited a sanatorium physician whom my wife and I had visited the year before (what a happy time that had been). Now I show up as a refugee, a role that seems absurd, meaningless to me. But who was it who was fleeing? And from what? Everything looked so peaceful, so normal, totally normal. I saw myself as ridiculous. I was ashamed to tell him the story. But he thought foresight preferable to hindsight.

So there I was, as if on an unexpected vacation. I wrote letters home. Until one day I was summoned outside the sanatorium; someone was asking for me. It was (I am superstitious about numbers, but not overly so) the third day of the third month, March of 1933. I had noted the date that morning as I was reading the newspaper. What does it signify, what will it bring?

Outside stood my entire family, with the exception of one son. And then it became a different situation entirely. My wife was in tears; she described the awful things that were occurring in Berlin, the things she had heard in the train. The whole family was in danger, she said; they couldn't have remained there.

So here they were. It frightened me, this day of March 3, 1933. But I got over it; I had other worries: where we were to live, for instance, or going for walks, or conversations and plans. Had I left the country for good or was I merely waiting to return? I didn't know. And I wasn't much concerned.

My wife recognized the reality of the situation, she knew that she had left her home and that our children had been uprooted from everything they knew, she saw the mountain of worries, the clouds of uncertainty—she wept a great deal; I in comparison (being who I was) was elated. Yes, elated. . . .

During those months I kept remembering words from Schiller's *The Diver*: 'But all was for his best, he was carried on high!'

But what was 'best'? Everything in Germany had become unbearable, not only politically but spiritually. It was as though the political chaos and the stagnation had taken hold of spiritual life and paralyzed it. I fought it in my own way. Finally, at the end of 1932, a vision appeared to me that I could not rid myself of: an ancient and obsolete god approaching his own demise leaves his domicile in heaven and descends to the people of earth to rejuvenate himself and to do penance for his past sins. Once a god and ruler, he is now a human being like everyone else (*Babylonian Journey*). It was my foreboding and anticipation of exile.

Exile: the separation and isolation, the escape from the dead end—this descent appeared to be for my 'best.' Something in me sang, 'It carried me on high. . . .' I couldn't help it. I was in an exalted state (it also affected the book that I worked on for a year).

And so I went into exile. That's the way it was when I took my leave.

Alfred Doblin, *Destiny's Journey*, tr. Edna McCown, 1992

A MAGIC LAND

Late afternoon had come. The country had closed in around them. The train was winding through a pleasant, romantic landscape of hills and woods. In the slant of evening and the waning light there was a sense of deep, impenetrable forest and of cool, darkling waters.

They had long since passed the frontier, but the woman, who had been looking musingly and a little anxiously out of the window, hailed the conductor as he passed along the corridor and asked him if they were really in Belgium now. He assured her that they were . . .

The woman had her hand upon her breast, and now when the conductor had gone she sighed slowly with relief. Then, quietly and simply, she said:

'Do not misunderstand me. I am a German and I love my country. But— I feel as if a weight has lifted from me *here*.' She put her hand upon her breast again. 'You cannot understand, just how it feels to us, but—' and for a moment she was silent, as if painfully meditating what she wished to say. Then, quickly, quietly: 'We are so happy to be—*out*!'

Out? Yes, that was it. Suddenly George knew just how she felt. He, too, was 'out' who was a stranger to her land, and yet who never had been a stranger in it. He, too, was 'out' of that great country whose image had been engraved upon his spirit in childhood and youth, before he had ever seen it. He, too, was 'out' of that land which had been so much more to him than land, so much more than place. It had been a geography of heart's desire, an unfathomed domain of unknown inheritance. The haunting beauty of that magic land had been his soul's dark wonder. He had known the language of its spirit before he ever came to it, had understood the language of its tongue the moment he had heard it spoken. He had framed the accents of its speech most brokenly from that first hour, yet never with a moment's trouble, strangeness, or lack of comprehension. He had been at home in it, and it in him. It seemed that he had been born with this knowledge.

He had known wonder in this land, truth and magic in it, sorrow, loneliness, and pain in it. He had known love in it, and for the first time in his life he had tasted there the bright, delusive sacraments of fame. Therefore it was no foreign land to him. It was the other part of his heart's home, a haunted part of dark desire, a magic domain of fulfilment. It was the dark, lost Helen that had been forever burning in his blood—the dark, lost Helen he had found.

And now it was the dark, found Helen he had lost. And he knew now, as he had never known before, the priceless measure of his loss. He knew also the priceless measure of his gain. For this was the way that henceforth would be forever closed to him—the way of no return. He was 'out'. And, being 'out', he began to see another way, the way that lay before him. He saw now that you can't go home again—not ever. There was no road back. Ended now for him, with the sharp and clean finality of the closing of a door, was the time when his dark roots, like those of a pot-bound plant, could be left to feed upon their own substance and nourish their own little self-absorbed designs. Henceforth they must spread outward—away from the hidden, secret, and unfathomed past that holds man's spirit prisoner— outward, outward towards the rich and life-giving soil of a new freedom in the wide world of all humanity. And there came to him a vision of man's true home, beyond the ominous and cloud-engulfed horizon of the here and now, in the green and hopeful and still-virgin meadows of the future.

'Therefore,' he thought, 'old master, wizard Faust, old father of the ancient and swarm-haunted mind of man, old earth, old German land with all the measure of your truth, your glory, beauty, magic, and your ruin; and dark Helen burning in our blood, great queen and mistress, sorceress—dark land, dark land, old ancient earth I love—farewell!'

Thomas Wolfe, You Can't Go Home Again, 1940

THE PROBLEMS OF WRITING POETRY IN WARTIME

W. H. Auden and Christopher Isherwood had decided, not long before Evelyn Waugh began writing Put Out More Flags, *that they could not possibly stay in England once war had been declared. They left for America.*

'When we say that Parsnip can't write in war-time Europe, surely we mean that he can't write as he has written up till now? Mightn't it be better for him to stay here, even if it meant holding up production for a year or so, so that he can *develop?*'

'Oh, I don't think Parsnip and Pimpernell *can* develop. I mean an organ doesn't *develop*; it just goes on playing different pieces of music but remains the same. I feel Parsnip and Pimpernell have perfected themselves as an instrument.'

'Then suppose Parsnip were to develop and Pimpernell didn't. Or suppose they developed in different directions. What would happen then?'

'Yes, what would happen then?'

'Why does it take two to write a poem?' asked the red-headed girl.

'Now Julia, don't short circuit the argument.'

'I should have thought poetry was a one-man job. Part-time work at that.'

'But Julia, you'll admit you don't know very much about poetry, dear.'

'That's exactly why I'm asking.'

'Don't pay any attention, Tom. She doesn't really want to know. She's only being tiresome.'

Evelyn Waugh, Put Out More Flags, 1943

LORD MARCHMAIN AND HIS MISTRESS IN VENICE

I was full of curiosity to meet Lord Marchmain. When I did so I was first struck by his normality, which, as I saw more of him, I found to be studied. It was as though he were conscious of a Byronic aura, which he considered to be in bad taste and was at pains to suppress. He was standing on the balcony of the saloon and, as he turned to greet us, his face was in deep shadow. I was aware only of a tall and upright figure.

'Darling papa,' said Sebastian, 'how young you are looking!'

He kissed Lord Marchmain on the cheek and I, who had not kissed my father since I left the nursery, stood shyly behind him.

'This is Charles. Don't you think my father very handsome, Charles?'

Lord Marchmain shook my hand.

'Whoever looked up your train,' he said—and his voice also was Sebastian's—'made a *bétise*. There's no such one.'

'We came on it.'

'You can't have. There was only a slow train from Milan at that time. I was at the Lido. I have taken to playing tennis there with the professional in the early evening. It is the only time of day when it is not too hot. I hope you boys will be fairly comfortable upstairs. This house seems to have been designed for the comfort of only one person, and I am that one. I have a room the size of this and a very decent dressing-room. Cara has taken possession of the other sizeable room.'

I was fascinated to hear him speak of his mistress so simply and casually; later I suspected that it was done for effect, for me.

'How is she?'

'Cara? Well, I hope. She will be back with us tomorrow. She is visiting some American friends at a villa on the Brenta canal. Where shall we dine? We might go to the Luna, but it is filling up with English now. Would you be too dull at home? Cara is sure to want to go out tomorrow, and the cook here is really quite excellent.'

He had moved away from the window and now stood in the full evening sunlight, with the red damask of the walls behind him. It was a noble face, a controlled one, just, it seemed, as he planned it to be; slightly weary, slightly sardonic, slightly voluptuous. He seemed in the prime of life; it was odd to think that he was only a few years younger than my father.

Lord Marchmain's mistress arrived next day. I was nineteen years old and completely ignorant of women. I could not with any certainty recognize a prostitute in the streets. I was therefore not indifferent to the fact of living under the roof of an adulterous couple, but I was old enough to hide my interest. Lord Marchmain's mistress, therefore, found me with a multitude of conflicting expectations about her, all of which were, for the moment, disappointed by her appearance. She was not a voluptuous Toulouse-Lautrec odalisque; she was not a 'little bit of fluff'; she was a middle-aged, well-preserved, well-dressed, well-mannered woman such as I had seen in countless public places and occasionally met. Nor did she seem marked by any social stigma. On the day of her arrival we lunched at the Lido, where she was greeted at almost every table.

'Vittoria Corombona has asked us all to her ball on Saturday.'

'It is very kind of her. You know I do not dance,' said Lord Marchmain.

'But for the boys? It is a thing to be seen—the Corombona palace lit up for the ball. One does not know how many such balls there will be in the future.'

'The boys can do as they like. We must refuse.'

'And I have asked Mrs Hacking Brunner to luncheon. She has a charming daughter. Sebastian and his friend will like her.'

'Sebastian and his friend are more interested in Bellini than heiresses.'

'But that is what I have always wished,' said Cara, changing her point of attack adroitly. 'I have been here more times than I can count and Alex has not once let me inside San Marco even. We will become *tourists*, yes?'

We became tourists; Cara enlisted as guide a midget Venetian nobleman to whom all doors were open, and with him at her side and a guide book in her hand, she came with us, flagging sometimes but never giving up, a neat, prosaic figure amid the immense splendours of the place.

Evelyn Waugh, *Brideshead Revisited*, 1945

SOPHIA LOREN—ALLEGED CONCUBINE

Criminal law in Italy allows any citizen, even anonymously, to charge any other citizen with a crime. Thus, when the public prosecutor received a letter from a Milanese woman named Luisa Brambilla, whom I had never met nor heard of, charging Carlo with the crime of bigamy and me with being a *concubina*, the prosecutor was obliged to proceed against us. In her letter, Signora Brambilla stated that as a married woman and a mother she was demanding criminal prosecution of us in order to save the institution of matrimony in Italy. The condemnation of the Catholic Church had now escalated itself into a crime.

Once the newspapers got hold of the story, Carlo and I were assailed from all sides. The prosecutor received supportive letters of denunciation from women all over Italy; I was particularly upset by a letter, condemning me, sent by a group of Pozzuoli women. We were also attacked by lawyers, doctors, and government officials, and even the august Roman Catholic Morality League accused us of 'bigamy and public adultery.' I was not aware that a single letter was received by the prosecutor which defended us.

At a preliminary hearing before a magistrate, none of these accusers showed up in the courtroom to repeat their denunciations in person, but Italian law did not compel them to. The magistrate signed the prosecutor's warrants, which meant that if we set foot in Italy we were subject to arrest and jail. The basis for the bigamy charge was simple: the Church had declared the Mexican divorce illegal. Therefore, when Carlo and I were married in Mexico, he was still married to his first wife. Italy, our homeland, had now shut its doors to us. We were exiles.

But for me, no matter what they said about me, no matter how harshly they judged us, my reaction was a defiance of all of them. When I know deep down that I am doing something that is right (in judging my own conscience, I am the sole arbiter of what is right), then I do not brood about what is appearing in the papers or try to analyze why they are per-secuting us or even try to justify myself. I am right and that's all there is to it. The courage of my conviction is what sustains me. I feel no guilt regardless of how sanctimoniously I am attacked. I do not bleed. I have no capacity for self-doubt.

I was making *A Breath of Scandal* in Vienna, with John Gavin and Maurice Chevalier, when an official invitation arrived to attend the Venice Film Festival. *Black Orchid* was in competition and I was a candidate for best actress award. But Carlo and I were wary of the possible consequences of entering Italy while under indictment as criminals. The festival invitation could have been a lure to capture us, confiscate our passports, and throw us into jail. Italian law did not permit a writ of habeas corpus, which meant that a prisoner could be held indefinitely without hearing or trial.

Carlo got in touch with the festival people and made a bargain: as the alleged bigamist, Carlo was the major criminal, and I, the alleged concu-bine, was the minor criminal; therefore only I, the minor criminal, would attend but with the assurance that the police would grant me free passage into and out of Italy. The festival officials gave us that assurance, but I can tell you it was a very apprehensive Sophia Loren who stepped off the train in the Venice railroad station. I half expected *carabinieri* to seize me and whisk me away.

My fears were groundless. Instead of *carabinieri*, there was a festive crowd of shouting, laughing, waving Italians to greet me, and a welcoming fleet of gondolas and motorboats in the Grand Canal, tooting boat horns and calling my name. It was altogether a triumphal return to Italy after an absence of four years—and my indictment as a public sinner did not seem to have dampened the ardor of the Venetians.

A. E. Hotchner, *Sophia: Living and Loving—Her Own Story*, 1979

A SONNET FOR EXILES

I praise all exiles, the Crusoes, Whittingtons,
Flying Dutchmen and Prodigal Sons
whose accents, flat-feet, or bloody-mindedness
kept them out of the village band.

I praise all those who weren't even wanted
by the third eleven, who never got cheques
to stay away from the family boardroom,
who left without flags or fond farewells

to build small lives in distant places
with only a chip on their backs. I point
to what States do best—sending off
the unwanted flotsam of their wars and debts,

that orphaned race who sail away to discover
the depths of their neglected grace.

Peter Bland, from *How Strong the Roots: Poems of Exile*, ed. Howard Sergeant, 1981

A BUBBLE ON THE TIDE

I packed a bag and was headed out. I was headed out down a long bone-white road, straight as a string and smooth as glass and glittering and wavering in the heat and humming under the tires like a plucked nerve. I was doing seventy-five but I never seemed to catch up with the pool which seemed to be over the road just this side of the horizon. Then, after a while, the sun was in my eyes, for I was driving west. So I pulled the sun screen

down and squinted and put the throttle to the floor. And kept on moving
west. For West is where we all plan to go some day. It is where you go
when the land gives out and the old-field pines encroach. It is where you
go when you get the letter saying: *Flee, all is discovered.* It is where you go
when you look down at the blade in your hand and see the blood on it.
It is where you go when you are told that you are a bubble on the tide of
empire. It is where you go when you hear that thar's gold in them-thar
hills. It is where you go to grow up with the country. It is where you go
to spend your old age. Or it is just where you go.

It was just where I went.

The second day I was in Texas. I was traveling through the part where
the flat-footed, bilious, frog-sticker-toting Baptist biscuit-eaters live. Then
I was traveling through the part where the crook-legged, high-heeled, gun-
wearing, spick-killing, callous-rumped sons of the range live and crowd the
drugstore on Saturday night and then all go round the corner to see epi-
sode three of 'Vengeance on Vinegar Creek,' starring Gene Autry as Borax
Pete. But over both parts, the sky was tall hot brass by day and black velvet
by night, and Coca Cola is all a man needs to live on. Then I was traveling
through New Mexico, which is a land of total and magnificent emptiness
with a little white filling station flung down on the sand like a sun-bleached
cow skull by the trail, with far to the north a valiant remnant of the heroes
of the Battle of Montmartre in a last bivouac wearing huaraches and ham-
mered silver and trying to strike up conversations with Hopis on street
corners. Then Arizona, which is grandeur and the slow incredulous stare of
sheep, until you hit the Mojave. You cross the Mojave at night and even
at night your breath rasps your gullet as though you were a sword swallower
who had got hold of a hack-saw blade by mistake, and in the darkness the
hunched rock and towering cactus loom at you with the shapes of a visceral,
Freudian nightmare.

Then California.

Then Long Beach, which is the essence of California. I know because I
have never seen any of California except Long Beach and so am not distracted by competing claims. I was in Long Beach thirty-six hours, and
spent all of that time in a hotel room, except for forty minutes in a barber-
shop off the lobby of the hotel.

I had had a puncture in the morning and so didn't hit Long Beach till
about evening. I drank a milk shake, bought a bottle of bourbon, and went
up to my room. I hadn't had a drop the whole trip. I hadn't wanted a drop.
I hadn't wanted anything, except the hum of the motor and the lull of the
car and I had had that. But now I knew that if I didn't drink that bourbon,

as soon as I shut my eyes to go to sleep the whole hot and heaving continent would begin charging at me out of the dark. So I took some, took a bath, and then lay on the bed, with my light off, watching the neon sign across the street flare on and off to the time of my heartbeat, and drinking out of the bottle, which, between times, I set on the floor by the bed.

I got a good sleep out of it. I didn't wake up till noon the next day. Then I had breakfast sent up and a pile of newspapers, for it was Sunday. I read the papers, which proved that California was just like any place else, or wanted to think the same things about itself, and then I listened to the radio till the neon sign began to flare on and off again to the time of my heartbeat, and then I ordered up some food, ate it, and put myself to sleep again.

The next morning I headed back.

I was headed back and was no longer remembering the things which I had remembered coming out.

For example. But I cannot give you an example. It was not so much any one example, any one event, which I recollected which was important, but the flow, the texture of the events, for meaning is never in the event but in the motion through event. Otherwise we could isolate an instant in the event and say that this is the event itself. The meaning. But we cannot do that. For it is the motion which is important. And I was moving. I was moving West at seventy-five miles an hour, through a blur of million-dollar landscape and heroic history, and I was moving back through time into my memory. They say the drowning man relives his life as he drowns. Well, I was not drowning in water, but I was drowning in West. I drowned westward through the hot brass days and black velvet nights. It took me seventy-eight hours to drown. For my body to sink down to the very bottom of West and lie in the motionless ooze of History, naked on a hotel bed in Long Beach, California.

Robert Penn Warren, All the King's Men, 1946

ON THE ROAD

My first ride was a dynamite truck with a red flag, about thirty miles into great green Illinois, the truckdriver pointing out the place where Route 6, which we were on, intersects Route 66 before they both shoot west for incredible distances. Along about three in the afternoon, after an apple pie and ice cream in a roadside stand, a woman stopped for me in a little coupe. I had a twinge of hard joy as I ran after the car. But she was a middle-aged woman, actually the mother of sons my age, and wanted somebody to help her drive to Iowa. I was all for it. Iowa! Not so far from Denver, and once I got to Denver I could relax. She drove the first few hours, at one point insisted on visiting an old church somewhere, as if we were tourists, and then I took over the wheel and, though I'm not much of a driver, drove clear through the rest of Illinois to Davenport, Iowa, via Rock Island. And here for the first time in my life I saw my beloved Mississippi River, dry in the summer haze, low water, with its big rank smell that smells like the raw body of America itself because it washes it up. Rock Island—railroad tracks, shacks, small downtown section; and over the bridge to Davenport, same kind of town, all smelling of sawdust in the warm midwest sun. Here the lady had to go on to her Iowa hometown by another route, and I got out.

The sun was going down. I walked, after a few cold beers, to the edge of town, and it was a long walk. All the men were driving home from work, wearing railroad hats, baseball hats, all kinds of hats, just like after work in any town anywhere. One of them gave me a ride up the hill and left me at a lonely crossroads on the edge of the prairie. It was beautiful there. The only cars that came by were farmer-cars; they gave me suspicious looks, they clanked along, the cows were coming home. Not a truck. A few cars zipped by. A hotrod kid came by with his scarf flying. The sun went all the way down and I was standing in the purple darkness. Now I was scared. There weren't even any lights in the Iowa countryside; in a minute nobody would be able to see me. Luckily a man going back to Davenport gave me a lift downtown. But I was right where I started from.

I went to sit in the bus station and think this over. I ate another apple pie and ice cream; that's practically all I ate all the way across the country, I knew it was nutritious and it was delicious, of course. I decided to gamble. I took a bus in downtown Davenport, after spending a half-hour watching a waitress in the bus-station café, and rode to the city limits, but this time near the gas stations. Here the big trucks roared, wham, and inside two minutes one of them cranked to a stop for me. I ran for it with my soul whoopeeing. And what a driver—a great big tough truckdriver with popping eyes and a hoarse raspy voice who just slammed and kicked at everything and got his rig under way and paid hardly any attention to me. So I could rest my tired soul a little, for one of the biggest troubles hitchhiking is having to talk to innumerable people, make them feel that they didn't make a mistake picking you up, even entertain them almost, all of which is a great strain when you're going all the way and don't plan to sleep in hotels. The guy just yelled above the roar, and all I had to do was yell back, and we relaxed.

Jack Kerouac, *On the Road*, 1957

A RUSSIAN ASKS FOR POLITICAL ASYLUM

Leonid Vladimirovich Finkelstein, a Soviet journalist, was allowed to go on an official trip to Britain in 1966. He took the opportunity of defecting.

It was a delightful group: very nice people, a privileged party travelling around England and Scotland. I decided to bide my time and wait until the penultimate day. It turned out that this day was set aside for shopping on our own; we had each been given the princely sum of £6.11s to spend—that was a lot in those days.

That day (28 June 1966) I waited outside our hotel, the Embassy in Bayswater Road, and observed everyone from the group leaving. The last person to leave was our 'escort' from the KGB. They were all going off to Oxford Street. I realized that I was free. I went to Charing Cross Station and put my suitcase in the Left Luggage, and was suddenly filled with the strangest sensation: my boats were burned.

I took my time, slowly drinking a Coca-Cola in Lyons Corner House, and then walked to the Home Office opposite the Cenotaph and came out with my prepared speech: 'I am a Soviet journalist seeking political asylum in this country.' Nobody reacted. They looked puzzled, and then gave me a card showing me the 76 bus route to Princes House, Holborn. I went out again, got on the bus, found Princes House, tried out my phrase again, and this time it worked.

Then I set about trying to get them to release my wife. Kosygin was about to visit Britain, so I wrote a letter that was published in thirty-eight newspapers all over the world asking for them to let her out. And they did. But the KGB got their own back. In the two months it took to organize her departure, they worked her over to such an extent that she was not herself when she eventually did get to the West. She was unable to settle down, and took advantage of a three-day absence on my part to go with our son to the Soviet Embassy and to be repatriated. Back in Moscow, she published a small interview in which she said she was unable to live in the capitalist world. In 1975 she emigrated to Israel and I managed to remake contact with my son. Now he has graduated from Harvard Business School and works in California. . . .

Despite my broadcasting on political subjects, I had no great problems from the Soviets. As everyone does, I received a summons from the KGB, but it does not mean anything. I realized I was not the sort of person to be hunted by them; there are many more important people higher up on their list! In fact, speaking out strongly on political matters actually helped me; it is in their nature to respect only strength and plain speaking and to have contempt for the weak. If you speak out, they respect you for it; otherwise, they destroy you. I decided that I was not going to spend my life hiding. One day I was giving a lecture at an Institute of Higher Education; I was being heckled by some members of the Communist Party of Great Britain. Afterwards one of them came up and asked me why I was living so openly—didn't I know that people like me were often killed in the West by Communists? I told him, as I tell everyone, that I did not come here to hide away: that if they're going to kill me, let them. In the meantime, I'm going to speak out.

> Michael Glenny and Norman Stone, *The Other Russia*, 1990

THEY DON'T HAVE PROBLEMS IN EVANSTON

The American comedienne Ruby Wax fled to England to escape the middle-class paradise of Evanston, Illinois.

I can't think of a reason why I would want to *stay* in Evanston. England is the kind of place where if you're unusual they crown you. If you're unusual in Evanston they stone you to death. I wouldn't have flourished there, so I had to go. In America they think they like individuality, but they don't really. Outside New York there's nothing in the atmosphere, just deadness. The only way to survive is either you have to fit in, or you have to be a shit-kicker. If you don't fit in, it's like something went wrong in the birth-canal.

Evanston was just like living in those sit-coms—the *Dick Van Dyke Show*, or *Leave It To Beavor*. They don't have problems in Evanston. Everyone's at peace there, you can walk up and down and see even black people having barbecues. There's nothing to rebel against. The brain can't take a situation of no conflict. My friends either became crackheads or else they became like their parents, who were like *their* parents. It was all a little too blissful. My parents wanted me to stay there, be married, become brain-damaged.

We had a big picture-window in Evanston, overlooking the lake. My mother used to put my dog Lumpi and me in the window to look cute, so she'd shave both our heads in the same way. People would come and park by the lake and I'd watch them necking. Then I'd go and knock on the car window just before they had intercourse and sell them lemonade, and they'd push handfuls of money at me to make me go away. Lumpi had to have cortizone injections every hour to keep him alive, but he was clinically dead anyway. The only function he had left was to lift his leg automatically every time he saw a tree.

My grandmother, who was crazy, lived with us. When the front-door bell rang, she'd answer the refrigerator. If she liked you, she'd hand you her false teeth, which was fine because they were always smiling. I'd pay fifty cents to have boys come home with me, and then my father would drive up in his eighty-foot Wiener Wagon that was shaped like a hot dog. People would park in the street outside just to watch our family. Everything about us was different. And you're asking me why I wanted to leave Evanston?

In conversation

POETRY OF DEPARTURES

Sometimes you hear, fifth-hand,
As epitaph:
He chucked up everything
And just cleared off,
And always the voice will sound
Certain you approve
This audacious, purifying,
Elemental move.

And they are right, I think.
We all hate home
And having to be there:
I detest my room,
Its specially-chosen junk,
The good books, the good bed,
And my life, in perfect order:
So to hear it said

He walked out on the whole crowd
Leaves me flushed and stirred,
Like *Then she undid her dress*
Or *Take that you bastard;*
Surely I can, if he did?
And that helps me stay
Sober and industrious.
But I'd go today,

Yes, swagger the nut-strewn roads,
Crouch in the fo'c'sle
Stubbly with goodness, if
It weren't so artificial,
Such a deliberate step backwards

To create an object:
Books; china; a life
Reprehensibly perfect.

Philip Larkin, Collected Poems, 1988

THE EXILE COMMUNITY

Societies, even the small and fractured societies which exiles create around themselves, quickly develop their own structures and rules. Those who conform to them look down on those who do not; those who do not conform, have to create structures and rules of their own. In late Victorian England there were more than three dozen distinct groups of exiles from Tsarist Russia; nowadays Iranians, Iraqis, Kurds and all sorts of other nationalities gather together for a while before breaking up into new groupings and compete for adherents as each new wave of dissidents arrives. Sometimes communities divide on issues which have deep significance for the future: the Russian Social Democrats spent long hours debating the value of violence and the role of the state, for instance. At other times the division can be more genial: refugees from apartheid who came to Britain often found themselves split over whether to boycott South African wine as well as the country's other exports. Some were purist about it, and refused to drink the wine just as they refused to eat the oranges; others would gather in private and crack open the vintages they had grown to love in South Africa and which now consoled them abroad. They had made many sacrifices for the anti-apartheid cause, but they were not able to make this final one.

STIFF UPPER LIPS IN THE DESERT

I can understand the sort of amazement of the Orientals at the scantiness of the retinue with which an Englishman passes the Desert, for I was somewhat struck myself when I saw one of my countrymen making his way across the wilderness in this simple style. At first there was a mere moving speck in the horizon; my party, of course, became all alive with excitement, and there were many surmises; soon it appeared that three laden camels were approaching, and that two of them carried riders; in a little while we saw that one of the riders wore the European dress, and at last the travellers were pronounced to be an English gentleman, and his servant; by their side there were a couple, I think, of Arabs on foot, and this was the whole party.

This Englishman, as I afterwards found, was a military man returning to his country from India and crossing the Desert at this part in order to go through Palestine. As for me, I had come pretty straight from England, and so here we met in the wilderness at about half way from our respective starting points. As we approached each other, it became with me a question whether we should speak; I thought it likely that the stranger would accost me, and in the event of his doing so, I was quite ready to be as sociable, and chatty as I could be, according to my nature; but still I could not think of any thing particular that I had to say to him; of course among civilized people, the not having anything to say is no excuse at all for not speaking, but I was shy, and indolent, and I felt no great wish to stop, and talk like a morning visitor, in the midst of those broad solitudes. The traveller, perhaps, felt as I did, for except that we lifted our hands to our caps, and waved our arms in courtesy, we passed each other, as if we had passed in Bond Street. Our attendants, however, were not to be cheated of the delight that they felt in speaking to new listeners, and hearing fresh voices once more. The masters, therefore, had no sooner passed each other than their respective servants quietly stopped and entered into conversation. As soon as my camel found that her companions were not following her, she caught the social feeling and refused to go on. I felt the absurdity of the situation, and determined to accost the stranger, if only to avoid the awkwardness of remaining stuck fast in the Desert, whilst our servants were amusing themselves. When with this intent I turned round my camel, I found that the gallant officer, who had passed me by about thirty or forty yards, was exactly in the same predicament as myself. I put my now willing camel in motion, and rode up towards the stranger, who seeing this, followed my example, and came forward to meet me. He was the first to speak; he was much too courteous to address me as if he admitted the possibility of my wishing to accost him from any feeling of mere sociability, or civilian-like love of vain talk; on the contrary, he at once attributed my advances to a laudable wish of acquiring statistical information, and, accordingly, when we got within speaking distance, he said, 'I dare say, you wish to know how the Plague is going on at Cairo?' and then he went on to say, he regretted that his information did not enable him to give me in numbers a perfectly accurate statement of the daily deaths; he afterwards talked pleasantly enough upon other, and less ghastly subjects. I thought him manly, and intelligent—a worthy one of the few thousand strong Englishmen, to whom the Empire of India is committed.

A. W. Kinglake, *Eothen*, 1844

COLONIAL NOSTALGIA

HOME. In Anglo-Indian and colonial speech this means England.

1837.—'Home always means England; nobody calls India *home*—not even those who have been here thirty years or more, and are never likely to return to Europe.'— *Letters from Madras*, 92.

1865.—'You may perhaps remember how often in times past we debated, with a seriousness becoming the gravity of the subject, what article of food we should each of us respectively indulge in, on our first arrival at home.'—*Waring, Tropical Resident*, 154.

So also in the West Indies:

c. 1830.—'... "Oh, your cousin Mary, I forgot—fine girl, Tom—may do for you at home yonder" (all Creoles speak of England as home, although they may never have seen it).'—*Tom Cringle*, ed. 1863, 238.

> *Hobson-Jobson: A Glossary of Colloquial Anglo-Indian Words and Phrases*, 1886.

WHERE THE ANGLO-INDIAN LIVED

BUNGALOW, s. H. and Mahr. *banglā.* The most usual class of house occupied by Europeans in the interior of India; being on one story, and covered by a pyramidal roof, which in the normal bungalow is of thatch, but may be of tiles without impairing its title to be called a *bungalow.* Most of the houses of officers in Indian cantonments are of this character. In reference to the style of the house, *bungalow* is sometimes employed in contradistinction to the (usually more pretentious) *pucka house*; by which latter term is implied a masonry house with a terraced roof. A *bungalow* may also be a small building of the type which we have described, but of temporary material, in a garden, on a terraced roof for sleeping in, &c., &c. The word has also been adopted by the French in the East, and by Europeans generally in Ceylon, China, Japan, and the coast of Africa.

Wilson writes the word *bānglā,* giving it as a Bengālī word, and as probably derived from *Banga,* Bengal. This is fundamentally the etymology mentioned by Bp. Heber in his *Journal* (see below), and that etymology is corroborated by our first quotation, from a native historian, as well as by that from F. Buchanan. It is to be remembered that in Hindustan proper the adjective 'of or belonging to Bengal' is constantly pronounced as *bangǎlā* or *banglā.* Thus one of the eras used in E. India is distinguished as the *Banglā* era. The probability is that, when Europeans began to build houses of this character in Behar and Upper India, these were called *Banglā* or 'Bengal-fashion' houses; that the name was adopted by the Europeans themselves and their followers, and so was brought back to Bengal itself, as well as carried to other parts of India. ['In Bengal, and notably in the districts near Calcutta, native houses to this day are divided into *ath-chala, chau-chala,* and *Bangala,* or eight-roofed, four-roofed, and Bengali, or common huts. The first term does not imply that the house has eight coverings, but that the roof has four distinct sides with four more projections, so as to cover a verandah all round the house, which is square. The *Bangala,* or Bengali house, or *bungalow* has a sloping roof on two sides and two gable ends. Doubtless the term was taken up by the first settlers in Bengal from the native style of edifice, was materially improved, and was thence carried to other parts of India. It is not necessary to assume that the first bungalows were erected in Behar.' (*Saturday Rev.,* 17th April 1886, in a review of the first ed. of this book).]

A.H. 1041 = a.d. 1633.—'Under the rule of the Bengalis (*darahd-i-Bangālīyān*) a party of Frank merchants, who are inbabitants of Sundíp, came trading to Sátgánw. One kos above that place they occupied some ground on the banks of the estuary.

Under the pretence that a building was necessary for their transactions in buying and selling, they erected several houses in the **Bengálí** style.'—*Bādshāhnāma*, in *Elliot*, vii. 31.

c. 1680.—In the tracing of an old Dutch chart in the India Office, which may be assigned to about this date, as it has no indication of Calcutta, we find at Hoogly: '*Ougli . . . Hollandze Iogie* . . . **Bangelaer** *of Speelhuys*,' i.e. 'Hoogly . . . Dutch Factory . . . **Bungalow**, or Pleasure-house.'

1780.—'To be Sold or Let, A Commodious **Bungalo** and out Houses . . . situated on the Road leading from the Hospital to the Burying Ground, and directly opposite to the Avenue in front of Sir Elijah Impey's House. . . .'—*The India Gazette*, Dec. 23.

1781–83.—'**Bungelows** are buildings in India, generally raised on a base of brick, one, two, or three feet from the ground, and consist of only one story: the plan of them usually is a large room in the center for an eating and sitting room, and rooms at each corner for sleeping; the whole is covered with one general thatch, which comes low to each side; the spaces between the angle rooms are *viranders* or open porticoes . . . sometimes the center *viranders* at each end are converted into rooms.'— *Hodges, Travels*, 146.

1784.—'To be let at Chinsurah . . . That large and commodious House. . . . The out-buildings are—a warehouse and two large *bottle-connahs*, 6 store-rooms, a cook-room, and a garden, with a **bungalow** near the house.'—*Cal. Gazette*, in *Seton-Karr*, i. 40.

Hobson-Jobson

THE BRITISH IN INDIA

Rudyard Kipling wrote this article for his newspaper, The Civil and Military Gazette *of Lahore, in January 1887, in imitation of a letter which an English visitor to India might write home. It was, perhaps, a device to enable him to make the kind of criticisms of his fellow Anglo-Indians which would have been hard for him to set out more openly.*

Men age very rapidly in India, and I have seen young men of even five and six and twenty wrinkled, and grey on the temples. Looking down a dinner table, it is curious to notice the decisiveness and look of energy in the faces of the men—especially the younger ones. In England there is a certain flat uniformity of unformedness about our young men that covers them all. The older men *invariably* talk of their own work or pay or prospects when two or three gather together; and the young men, if in the army, talk of their horses. In a country where every Englishman owns at least one horse, this is natural but monotonous. No one talks lightly and amusingly as in England. Every one works and talks and thinks about his work. It must be a ghastly existence, when the brain and body both begin to tire with the approach of old age. Very few Englishmen in India seem at all contented, though they are enthusiastic enough about their work—always their work; though, to do them justice, they don't talk about it with a capital W. . . .

You want to know what Anglo-Indian women are like? Well, they are very much like English ladies all the world over; but they aren't pretty. The climate kills good looks, and, taking one thing with another, they are as plain as they can be. Where they aren't plain, they are sickly and sallow. A little beauty goes a very long way in India. Nevertheless, they are exceedingly nice, and have much more individuality than English women. They know more of life, death, sickness and trouble than English women, I think; and this makes them broader in their views—though they talk about their servants as much as women do at home.

All the stuff that one hears and reads in England about their being 'fast' is utter rubbish. Of course there are some exceptions, but the bulk of them are a good deal steadier than women at home. Their life is very quiet, and everybody, everywhere, knows everything they do. Besides this, married couples live year after year alone by themselves in forsaken places, scores of miles away from anything like civilization; and I fancy that woman who has helped her husband through an abomination of desolation like this 'out-station' life, as they call it, gets to be exceedingly fond of him. This is rather curious, but I believe it to be the fact. If they were prettier, the English-women in India would be delightful. I admit that their 'belles' startle one rather. They would be out of consideration in a small county town in England. As a general rule, only the older women try to be 'fast', and their fastness is very modified; but is lasts for many years. Women of from forty to fifty and upwards—I'm not exaggerating, I assure you—are the Lillie Langtrys of India, and the youngest men are their worshippers in a luke-warm sort of way.

Nothing seems to impress the Anglo-Indians except their work. They call the Himalaya mountains—'the hills'; when a man dies he 'pegs out'; when he is ill he is 'sick'. When a mother nearly breaks her heart over the loss of her first child, they say 'she frets about it a little'. They are more than American in their curious belittling of everything, and they take everything as a matter of course, and when a man does anything great or heroic—and I have heard of some wonderfully grand things being done by officers and civil servants—they say 'not half bad'. That is their highest praise. I don't think you could startle an Anglo-Indian under any circumstances.

He is a very queer person, and I don't see what there is in his life worth living for. His amusements are very forlorn affairs, and there never seems to be any 'go' about him; though I have been told that this is not the case. All his jokes are old ones from England, and the local jokes can't be understood, unless you have been years in that particular place. He hasn't even any vices worth speaking of, and he smokes tobacco strong enough to blow your head off. Nearly all Anglo-Indians smoke heavily, and they all ride—down to the children. They have no notion of walking; but as a class they ride beautifully. I never wish to be better or more kindly entertained than I have been; but somehow their life repels me—it's so dreary. You would understand it better if you were out here. They don't seem to be paid as well as I expected, and the prices of any English-made things in India are absurdly high. All their money seems to go in insurance and remittances for their children; and you have no idea what they lose by exchange.

Thomas Pinney, ed., *Kipling's India: Uncollected Sketches 1884–88*, 1986

HOW THE ANGLO-INDIAN LIVED AND DIED

From time to time clouds of tawny dust rose from the ground without wind or warning, flung themselves tablecloth-wise among the tops of the parched trees, and came down again. Then a whirling dust-devil would scutter across the plain for a couple of miles, break, and fall outward, though there was nothing to check its flight save a long low line of piled railway-sleepers white with the dust, a chuster of huts made of mud, condemned rails, and canvas, and the one squat four-roomed bungalow that belonged to the assistant engineer in charge of a section of the Gaudhari State line then under construction.

The four, stripped to the thinnest of sleeping-suits, played whist crossly, with wranglings as to leads and returns. It was not the best kind of whist, but they had taken some trouble to arrive at it. Mottram of the Indian Survey had ridden thirty and railed one hundred miles from his lonely post in the desert since the night before; Lowndes of the Civil Service, on special duty in the political department, had come as far to escape for an instant the miserable intrigues of an impoverished native State whose king alternately fawned and blustered for more money from the pitiful revenues contributed by hard-wrung peasants and despairing camel-breeders; Spurstow, the doctor of the line, had left a cholera-stricken camp of coolies to look after itself for forty-eight hours while he associated with white men once more. Hummil, the assistant engineer, was the host. He stood fast and received his friends thus every Sunday if they could come in. When one of them failed to appear, he would send a telegram to his last address, in order that he might know whether the defaulter were dead or alive. There are very many places in the East where it is not good or kind to let your acquaintances drop out of sight even for one short week. . . .

'Hummil's the lucky man,' said Lowndes, flinging himself into a long chair. 'He has an actual roof—torn as to the ceiling-cloth, but still a roof— over his head. He sees one train daily. He can get beer and soda-water and ice 'em when God is good. He has books, pictures,'—they were torn from the *Graphic*,—'and the society of the excellent sub-contractor Jevins besides the pleasure of receiving us weekly.'

Hummil smiled grimly. 'Yes, I'm the lucky man, I suppose. Jevins is luckier.'

'How? Not—'

'Yes. Went out. Last Monday.'

'By his own hand?' said Spurstow quickly, hinting the suspicion that was in everybody's mind. There was no cholera near Hummil's section. Even fever gives a man at least a week's grace, and sudden death generally implies self-slaughter.

'I judge no man this weather,' said Hummil. 'He had a touch of the sun, I fancy; for last week, after you fellows had left, he came into the verandah and told me he was going home to see his wife, in Market Street, Liverpool, that evening.

'I got the apothecary in to look at him, and we tried to make him lie down. After an hour or two he rubbed his eyes and said he believed he had had a fit,—hoped he hadn't said anything rude. Jevins had a great idea of bettering himself socially. He was very like Chucks in his language.'

'Well?'

'Then he went to his own bungalow and began cleaning a rifle. He told the servant that he was going to shoot buck in the morning. Naturally he fumbled with the trigger, and shot himself though the head—accidentally. The apothecary sent in a report to my chief, and Jevins is buried somewhere out there. I'd have wired to you, Spurstow, if you could have done anything.'

'You're a queer chap,' said Mottram. 'If you'd killed the man yourself you couldn't have been more quiet about the business.'

'Good Lord! what does it matter?' said Hummil calmly. 'I've got to do a lot of his overseeing work in addition to my own. I'm the only person that suffers. Jevins is out of it,—by pure accident, of course, but out of it. The apothecary was going to write a long screed on suicide. Trust a *babu* to drivel when he gets the chance.'

'Why didn't you let it go in as suicide?' said Lowndes.

'No direct proof. A man hasn't many privileges in this country, but he might at least be allowed to mishandle his own rifle. Besides, some day I may need a man to smother up an accident to myself. Live and let live. Die and let die.'

'You take a pill,' said Spurstow, who had been watching Hummil's white face narrowly. 'Take a pill, and don't be an ass. That sort of talk is skittles. Anyhow, suicide is shirking your work. If I were Job ten times over, I should be so interested in what was going to happen next that I'd stay on and watch.'

Rudyard Kipling (1865–1936), 'At the End of the Passage'

A DIFFERENT INDIA

'I'd learned the rules, Mr Turner. The rules of the club. I'd learned them for Tusker's sake and when they made him a Lieutenant-Colonel at the end of Nineteen forty-five I thought: Perhaps the sun will come out again. But it didn't. We didn't even move out of Smith's hotel. We'd been billeted there from the day we arrived early in the war, two rooms, en-suite, the same ones the Bhoolabhoys now occupy as bedrooms. We used one as a living-room and the smaller as a bedroom. We didn't move because Tusker wouldn't. We could have moved into a bungalow of our own several times, but Tusker wouldn't. He said it was cheaper living there than running your own establishment—in those days he was very tight-fisted. In a way I respected this. I'd been brought up to know the value of money, too. Now he's tight-fisted again but that's because there's no alternative. He spent money like water, lost money, gambled money, made a fool of himself directly he left the army for commerce and we lived in Bombay. But that's another story. I mustn't talk to you about it.

'We didn't leave Smith's until the whole British–India thing was coming to an end and Tusker had agreed to stay on for a year or two. Rose Cottage was becoming vacant because Mildred had gone home and Colonel Layton and Sarah and Susan were moving down to Commandant House. We were offered it. For once I insisted. If we were going to stay after practically every other British family had gone then I wanted for once in my life a proper setting, Mr Turner. And for once Tusker didn't resist. He only grumbled a bit. I thought that was a good sign. I thought perhaps after all the sun would come out again, between us. But it didn't. Not really. Except once— and that paradoxically was after sunset.

'I remember the ceremony we had here in Pankot on Independence eve very clearly still, the evening of August fourteen, Nineteen forty-seven, down there on the parade ground of the Pankot Rifles. At sundown, they beat the retreat. After that we dined at Flagstaff House. Then we went back to the parade ground. It was quite chilly. We sat on stands put up for the occasion. The whole place was floodlit. There was still one small British contingent on station, a mixed bunch. They marched on last after all the Indian troops had marched on. There was a band. That was a pretty scratch affair too, but they seemed inspired by the occasion. They played all the traditional martial British music. Then there were some Indian pipers, and a Scottish pipe-major. They played "The Flowers of the Forest". One by one all the floodlights were put out leaving just the flagpole lit with the Union Jack flying from it. Colonel Layton and the new Indian colonel stood at attention side by side. Then the band played "Abide With Me". They still play that, Mr Turner, when they beat the retreat in Delhi on the eve of Republic Day.

'It was so moving that I began to cry. And Tusker put his hand in mine and kept it there, all through the hymn and when we were standing all through God Save the King, and all through that terrible, lovely moment when the Jack was hauled down inch by inch in utter, utter silence. The only sounds you could hear were the jackals hunting in the hills and the strange little rustles when a gust of wind sent papers and programmes scattering. There was no sound otherwise until on the stroke of midnight the Indian flag began to go up, again very slowly, and then the band began to play the new Indian national anthem and all the crowds out there in the dark began to sing the words and when the flag was up there flying and the anthem was finished you never heard such cheering and clapping. I couldn't clap because Tusker still had hold of my hand and didn't let go until all the floodlights came on again and the troops marched off to the sound of the band.'

Paul Scott, *Staying On*, 1982

COLONIAL ATTITUDES DIE HARD

There was much talk when Jane and Mary Ann Jenkins came home to Mount Kilimanjaro. Mary Ann had been gone for only two years in an American city no one ever heard of, called Cleveland; but Jane was away for twelve long years, cutting a swath in Europe, so the locals understood. Gone into the wide world, far from this mountain, to make their fortunes, and returned to the ancestral hotel with no fortune and unmarried, both of them. . . .

Jane stamped into the office where Mary Ann was bowed over a ledger, saying, 'There's an African drinking at the bar.'

Mary Ann went on, moving her lips, adding the long line of figures.

'Since when,' Jane said furiously, 'do Africans drink at our bar?'

'Since Independence,' Mary Ann said, still adding.

'It's the limit. Why do we put up with it?'

Mary Ann laid a ruler to mark her place and made a note. Then she turned to Jane. 'He's the M.P. for this district. A very nice man and an honest one. He even insists on paying for his beer. We're lucky he likes to stop in here when he's visiting his people.'

'Lucky?' Jane said with scorn. 'We certainly don't want African good will and a ghastly lot of African guests.'

'You fool,' Mary Ann said. 'We want African good will like mad. Haven't you heard about Independence? What do you keep under your peroxided hair? We're visitors here. It's not our colony, it's their country. If we insult Africans, we're out. Deported. They can do it and they do.'

'I never heard such rot. I'd rather sell the hotel than crawl to Africans.'

'Would you? Have you got a buyer? My God, how stupid can you be?'

Jane was too stunned by this turning worm to answer properly. Instead she said, 'I'm sure Daddy's put money aside.'

'Think again. They've ploughed the profits back so they could make a big fancy hotel for us, to keep us in our old age. Were you rude to him?'

'He smiled at me,' Jane said, furious again. 'I didn't say anything but I imagine he got the message.'

'Oh for God's sake. Now I'll have to go and try to make up for you. You tiresome dangerous half-wit.'

Jane brooded and fumed and sulked and, for once, her parents backed Mary Ann.

'We've had very few African guests,' Bob said. 'Mostly Ministers. Decent well-behaved chaps. Africans don't really like it here and it's quite expensive for them. But of course we do our best to make them happy if they come; we must, Jane. It's different from when you were a child. They don't want the hotel and they know we're useful for the tourist trade. But believe me, if we offended them, they wouldn't worry about anything practical, they'd kick us out.'

From spite, to show up Mary Ann and her parents, Jane unleashed all her charms and wiles on the next African guest. He was the new African, a young bureaucrat in a grey flannel suit. He came from the coast; there were ancient mixtures of Arab in his blood; he had a sharp nose and carved lips and a beautifully muscled slender tall body. With white skin, he would have resembled a Greek god as portrayed in the statues in the Rome museums which Jane had never visited. His name was Paul Nbaigu, a Christian like the Jenkins. He had a bureaucrat's job in the Ministry of Co-operatives and a European's taste for bathrooms and respectfully served food. Instead of staying with the African manager of a Co-op, he chose to do his inspector's round from Travellers' Rest. At the bar, where he was quietly drinking whisky and soda, splurging his pay on European pleasures, Jane joined him, introduced herself and smiled her best, sad, alluring, professional singer's smile. She might have been moaning more of the ritual blues' words: why doan yah luv me like yah useta do.

Jane suggested sharing his table at dinner, more spiteful bravado: let her family see what crawling to Africans looked like. Paul Nbaigu could not refuse but failed to appear honoured. Jane began to notice him.

'Where did you learn English?' Jane asked. 'You speak it perfectly.'

'Here and there. And at Makerere University.'

She could hardly inquire where he'd learned his table manners which were faultless. He began to notice Jane too, in particular the way she treated the waiter, not seeing the man, giving orders contemptuously. A small flame started to burn in the mind of Mr Nbaigu, who did not love white people though he did not specially love black people either.

'Where did you learn Swahili?' he asked.

'I was born here.'

'Upcountry Swahili,' Mr Nbaigu said mildly. 'On the coast, we rather make fun of it.'

Martha Gellhorn, The Weather in Africa, 1978

AN ENGLISH TEACHER ON THE PAMPAS

In the second half of the nineteenth century the British emigrated to Argentina in considerable numbers. At their hacienda on the cattle-plains W. H. Hudson's parents hired an itinerant schoolmaster for their children.

The feared man arrived, Mr. Trigg by name, an Englishman, a short, stoutish, almost fat little man, with grey hair, clean-shaved sunburnt face, a crooked nose which had been broken or was born so, clever mobile mouth, and blue-grey eyes with a humorous twinkle in them and crow's-feet at the corners. Only to us youngsters, as we soon discovered, that humorous face and the twinkling eyes were capable of a terrible sternness. He was loved, I think, by adults generally, and regarded with feelings of an opposite nature by children. For he was a schoolmaster who hated and despised teaching as much as children in the wild hated to be taught. He followed teaching because all work was excessively irksome to him, yet he had to do something for a living, and this was the easiest thing he could find to do. How such a man ever came to be so far from home in a half-civilized country was a mystery, but there he was, a bachelor and homeless man after twenty or thirty years on the pampas, with little or no money in his pocket, and no belongings except his horse—he never owned more than one at a time—and its cumbrous native saddle, and the saddle-bags in which he kept his wardrobe and whatever he possessed besides. He didn't own a box. On his horse, with his saddle-bags behind him, he would journey about the land, visiting all the English, Scotch, and Irish settlers, who were mostly sheep-farmers, but religiously avoiding the houses of the natives. With the natives he could not affiliate, and not properly knowing and incapable of understanding them he regarded them with secret dislike and suspicion. And by and by he would find a house where there were children old enough to be taught their letters, and Mr. Trigg would be hired by the month, like a shepherd or cowherd, to teach them, living with the family. He would go on very well for a time, his failings being condoned for the sake of the little ones; but by and by there would be a falling-out, and Mr. Trigg would saddle his horse, buckle on the saddle-bags, and ride forth over the wide plain in quest of a new home. With us he made an unusually long stay; he liked good living and comforts generally, and at the same time he was interested in the things of the mind, which had no place in the lives of the British settlers of that period; and now he found himself in a very comfortable house, where there were books to read and people to converse with who were not quite like the rude sheep- and cattle-farmers he had been accustomed to live with . . .

One afternoon we had a call from a quaint old Scotch dame, in a queer dress, sunbonnet, and spectacles, who introduced herself as the wife of Sandy Maclachlan, a sheep-farmer who lived about twenty-five miles away. It wasn't right, she said, that such near neighbours should not know one another, so she had ridden those few leagues to find out what we were like. Established at the tea-table, she poured out a torrent of talk in broadest Scotch, in her high-pitched cracked old-woman's voice, and gave us an intimate domestic history of all the British residents of the district. It was all about what de-lightful people they were, and how even their little weaknesses—their love of the bottle, their meannesses, their greed and low cunning—only served to make them more charming. Never was there such a funny old dame or one more given to gossip and scandal-mongering! Then she took herself off, and presently we children, still under her spell, stole out to watch her departure from the gate. But she was not there—she had vanished unaccountably; and by and by what was our astonishment and disgust to hear that the old Scotch body was none other than our own Mr. Trigg! That our needle-sharp eyes, concentrated for an hour on her face, had failed to detect the master who was so painfully familiar to us seemed like a miracle.

W. H. Hudson, Far Away and Long Ago, 1918

AN ANGLO-ARGENTINE OPENS UP

'Where's the Consulate? Is it the next turning on the left?'

'Yes, but we could take the second or third just as well and make a little turn. I enjoy your company, doctor. What did you say your name was?'

'Plarr.'

'Do you know what my name is?'

'Yes.'

'Mason.'

'I thought . . .'

'That's what they called me at school. Mason. Fortnum and Mason, the inseparable twins. It was the best English school in B.A. My career though was less than distinguished. A good word to get out so distinct . . . so well. The right measure you see. Not too much and not too little. I was never a prefect, and the marbles team was the only one I made. Not recognized officially. We were a snobbish school. All the same the headmaster, not the one I knew, that was Arden—we called him Smells—well, this new man wrote me a letter of congratulation when I became Honorary Consul. I wrote to him first, of course, and told him the glad news, so I suppose he couldn't very well ignore me altogether.'

'Will you tell me when we get to the Consulate?'

'We've passed it, old man, but never you mind. I've got a clear head. You just take another turn. First to the right and then left again. I'm in the sort of mood when I could drive like this all night. In sympathetic company. No need to pay attention to the one-way signs. Diplomatic privilege. The CC on the car. I can talk to you, doctor, as I can talk to no other man in this city. Spaniards. A proud people but they have no sentiment. Not as we English know it. No sense of Home. Soft slippers, the feet on the table, the friendly glass, the ever-open door. Humphries is not a bad chap—he's as English as you or me, or is he Scotch?—but he has the soul of a—pedagogue. Another good word that. He always tries to correct my morals, and yet I don't do much that's wrong, not really wrong. Tonight, if I'm a little pissed, it was the fault of the glasses. What's your other name, doctor?'

'Eduardo.'

'But I thought you were English?'

'My mother's Paraguayan.'

'Call me Charley. Would you mind if I called you Ted?'

'Call me what you like, but for God's sake tell me where the Consulate is.'

'The next corner. But don't go expecting too much. No marble halls, no chandeliers and potted palms. It's only a bachelor's digs—a bureau, a bedroom—all the usual offices of course. The best the buggers at home are ready to provide. No sense of national pride. Penny wise, pound foolish. You must come out to my camp—that's where my real home is. Nearly a thousand acres. Eight hundred anyway. Some of the best maté in the country. We could drive there now—it's only three quarters of an hour from here. A good night's sleep afterwards—a hair of the dog. I can give you real Scotch.'

'Not tonight. I have patients to see in the morning.'

They stopped outside an old colonial house with Corinthian pillars; the white plaster gleamed in the moonlight. On the first floor a flagstaff projected and a shield bore the Royal arms. Charley Fortnum swayed a little on the pavement, gazing up. 'Is it true?' he asked.

'Is what true?'

'The flagstaff. Isn't it leaning over a bit too much?'

'It looks all right to me.'

'I wish we had a simpler flag than the Union Jack. I hung it upside down once on the Queen's birthday. I could see nothing wrong with the bloody thing, but Humphries was angry—he said he was going to write to the Ambassador. Come up and have a glass.'

Graham Greene, The Honorary Consul, 1973

WE ARE NOT EXILES

Andrew Graham-Yooll, finding the military repression in his native Argentina increasingly dangerous, comes to London.

Victoria Station, Saturday. Struggle to get the children, cases, boxes, bags, dolls, off the train. Ahead is cousin Liz, waving, looking so lovely, so human—Laforgue comes to mind: there are three sexes, 'men, women and English girls'; cannot remember if he was trying to flatter or deprecate. Behind lies an overnight journey from the Gare du Nord, and far further back is Buenos Aires, left behind in a discreet hurry. My sister went to the airport convinced that she would not see us in years. My mother-in-law had dragged about a huge bag filled with disposable nappies, convinced that there was no such useful commodity in Britain; equally sure that our departure was for good, that we were lying when we said we would be back in a year. We were escaping just as she, in 1934, had fled her German-Jewish home in Warburg and gone to Argentina.

Every inch of a small Japanese tourist in front of us is searched by an officer with the polite indelicacy of the civil servant. We are waved by, thanks to the precaution taken by my father, a Scots immigrant, of registering me at birth at the British Consulate in Buenos Aires, thereby giving me the privileges of dual nationality.

We are not exiles; take note. There is a British passport to prove it, even if birth and a lifetime far away may deny it. I am at Victoria Station to do Britain a favour, bringing my charm, my family, my experience, and no money. We have arrived with plenty of advice: speak English with a clear accent; don't go to the dentist; avoid the medical bureaucracy. Life is easier with a white skin.

We have arrived as the country is struggling out of the political mediocrity and diplomatic incompetence of the Harold Wilson government.

But that does not matter, we are in London, *City of any Dream* according to the title of a glossy book we have left behind. The hotel guide says 'Dogs allowed' and 'No children'. When the accommodation desk finds a vacancy for us at a hotel on Belgrave Road, my son is told to call his mother and father. The boy quietly asks us if we have brought any birds. There is puzzlement, impatience at the inopportune enquiry; finally, a closer questioning of my son elicits the statement: 'The woman at the desk said "Fetch your parrots."'

We went to live in Colindale, on a quiet tree-lined street that looked part of a set from a British film of the 1950s: empty streets, pretty with shrubs and garden borders. Nobody seemed to live in the houses.

As soon as we had an address, the literature of exiles arrived in the post— the exile magazines which asked for subscriptions and then faded after three issues.

We read them with the curiosity of the detached. We were visitors, not exiles, in London for only one year because we were sure it would then be safe to go back. It was interesting to be able to read the reports and reviews without the need to disguise them inside another publication. In Buenos Aires they would have been intercepted. In London we could enjoy the advantages of distance; the chance to read and sleep in peace.

Purging the mind of fear was a slow process. Fear had become a habit, a state each got accustomed to and reacted to by reflex. The car that coasted up to the pavement still aroused suspicion; a glance at the occupants, their faces, their number was part of an automatic evaluation of the danger, immediately dispelled by the recollection that the street was in London, not Buenos Aires, and nobody was after us. A car parked in an empty street was approached with care; one that was in darkness with two occupants inside caused alarm—but the occupants in outline turned out to be the front seat head rests. The sight of a policeman provoked a small, sudden intake of breath before the image was mentally processed and explained as a Bobby, the best in the world. Our son, on seeing a man standing at his front gate, asked if he was the guard, the bodyguard. It took time to overcome the patterns of fear that had become part of daily living, and dying. It was not easy to comprehend that we were in a country where the ordinary individual fears the tax inspector more than the police.

> Andrew Graham-Yooll, *A State of Fear: Memories of Argentina's Nightmare*, 1986

THE IDEALISTS, FANATICS, AND THUGS OF GENEVA

Alexander Herzen (1812–70), the witty and improvident radical who had been imprisoned in his native Russia for his subversive writings as early as 1834, was a clear-sighted observer of the assorted revolutionaries who had flocked to Switzerland after the failure of the uprisings of 1848.

All *émigrés*, cut off from the living environment to which they have belonged, shut their eyes to avoid seeing bitter truths, and grow more and more acclimatised to a closed, fantastic circle consisting of inert memories and hopes that can never be realised.

If we add to this an aloofness from all who are not exiles and an element of exasperation, suspicion, exclusiveness and jealousy, this new, stiff-necked Israel becomes perfectly comprehensible.

The exiles of 1849 did not yet believe in the permanence of their enemies' triumph; the intoxication of their recent successes had not yet passed off, the applause and songs of the exultant people were still ringing in their ears. They firmly believed that their defeat was a momentary reverse, and did not move their clothes from their trunks to a wardrobe. Meanwhile Paris was under police supervision, Rome had fallen under the onslaught of the French, the brother of the Prussian King was brutally triumphing in Baden, and Paskevich in the Russian style had outwitted Görgei in Hungary by bribes and promises. Geneva was full to overflowing with refugees; it became the

Coblenz of the revolution of 1848. There were Italians from all parts; Frenchmen escaping from the Bauchart inquiry and from the Versailles trial; Baden militiamen, who entered Geneva marching in regular formation with their officers and with Gustav Struve; men who had taken part in the rising of Vienna; Bohemians and Poles from Posen and Galicia. All these people were crowded together between the Hôtel des Bergues and the Café de la Poste. The more sensible of them began to guess that this exile would not be over soon, talked of America, and went away. With the majority it was just the opposite, especially with the French who, true to their temperament, were in daily expectation of the death of Napoleon and the birth of a republic—some looking for a republic both democratic and socialistic, others for one that should be democratic and not at all socialistic.

A few days after my arrival, as I was walking in Les Paquis, I met an elderly gentleman who looked like a Russian village priest, wearing a low, broad-brimmed hat and a *black* white overcoat, and walking along with a sort of priestly unction; beside him walked a man of terrific dimensions, who looked as though he had been casually put together of huge chunks of human flesh. F. Kapp, the young writer, was with me.

'Don't you know them?' he asked me.

'No; but, if I'm not mistaken, it must be Noah or Lot out for a walk with Adam, who has put on a badly cut overcoat instead of his fig-leaves.'

'They are Struve and Heinzen,' he answered, laughing: 'would you like to make their acquaintance?'

'Very much.'

He introduced me.

The conversation was trivial. Struve was on his way home, and invited us to come in; so we went with him. His small lodging was crowded with people from Baden. A tall woman, very good-looking from a distance, with a mass of luxuriant hair flowing loose in an original fashion, was sitting in the midst of them; this was his wife, the celebrated Amalie Struve.

Struve's face made a strange impression on me from the very first; it expressed that moral rigidity which fanaticism gives to bigots and schismatics. Looking at his strong, narrow forehead, at the untroubled expression of his eyes, at his uncombed beard, his slightly grizzled hair, and his whole figure, I could have fancied that this was either a fanatical pastor of the army of Gustavus Adolphus who had forgotten to die, or a Taborite preaching repentance and communion in both kinds. There was a surly coarseness about the appearance of Heinzen, that Sobakevich of the German revolution; full-blooded and clumsy, he looked out angrily from under his brows, and was sparing of words. He wrote later on that it would be sufficient to *massacre two millions* of the inhabitants of the globe and the cause of revolution would go swimmingly. Anybody who had once seen him would not be surprised at his writing this.

> Alexander Herzen (1812–70), *My Past and Thoughts*, tr. Constance Garnett, 1968

SUPERHUMAN, BUT HOMELESS

Mikhail Alexandrovich Bakunin (1814–76) went into exile after fighting on the barricades in Leipzig and Prague in 1848. Engaging and disorganized, he advocated the notion of spontaneous agricultural anarchism, and borrowed money from everyone he knew. He seldom repaid them.

Bakunin recovered in our midst from nine years of silence and solitude. He argued, preached, gave orders, shouted, decided, arranged, organized, exhorted, the whole day, the whole night, the whole twenty-four hours on end. In the brief moments which remained, he would throw himself down at his desk, sweep a small space clear of tobacco ash, and begin to write five, ten, fifteen letters to Semipalatinsk and Arad, to Belgrade and Constantinople, to Bessarabia, Moldavia and White Russia. In the middle of a letter he would throw down his pen in order to refute some reactionary Dalmatian; then, without finishing his speech, he would seize his pen and go on writing. This of course was all the easier as he was writing and talking on the same subject. His activity, his leisure, his appetite, like all his other characteristics— even his gigantic size and continual sweat—were of superhuman proportions; and he himself remained, as of old, a giant with leonine head and tousled mane.

At fifty he was still the same wandering student, the same homeless Bohemian of the Rue de Bourgogne, caring nothing for the morrow, despising money, scattering it on all sides when he had it, borrowing indiscriminately right and left when he had none, with the same simplicity with which children take from their parents and never think of repayment, with the same simplicity with which he himself was prepared to give to anyone his last penny, reserving for himself only what was necessary for cigarettes and tea. He was never embarrassed by this mode of life; he was born to be the great wanderer, the great outcast. If anyone had asked him what he thought about the rights of property, he might have replied as Lalande replied to Napoleon about God: 'Sire, in the course of my career I have never found the slightest need to believe in Him.'

> Alexander Herzen (1812–70), *My Past and Thoughts*, tr. Constance Garnett, 1968

ON THE MOVE

The following is the list of addresses of Herzen's residences in London between 1852 and 1865:

25 Aug. 1852–20 Sept. (?) 1852	Morley's Hotel, Trafalgar Square.
20 Sept. (?) 1852–31 Oct. 1853	4, Spring Gardens.
31 Oct. 1853–(?) June 1854	25, Euston Square.
(?) June 1854–26 Dec. 1854	St. Helena Terrace, Richmond.
26 Dec. 1854–5 April 1855	Richmond House, Twickenham.
5 April 1855–5 Dec. 1855	Cholmondeley Lodge, Richmond.
5 Dec. 1855–10 Sept. 1856	1, Peterborough Villas, Finchley Rd.
10 Sept. 1856–11 Nov. 1858	Laurel House (Mr Tinkler's), High Street, Putney.
24 Nov. 1858–25 May (?) 1860	Park House, Percy Cross, Fulham.
25 May (?) 1860–15 Nov. 1860	10, Alpha Road, Regent's Park.
15 Nov. 1860–28 June 1863	Orsett House, Westbourne Terrace.
28 June 1863–(?) June 1864	Elmsfield House, Teddington.
(?) Sept. 1864–10 Nov. 1864	Tunstall House, Warwick Road, Maida Hill.
10 Nov. 1864–21 Nov. 1864	11, Eastbourne Terrace, Paddington.
22 Feb. 1865–15 March 1865	6, Rothesay Villas, Richmond.

'Herzen always used to say,' remarks Natalie Ogarev in her *Memoirs*, 'that there was such uniformity about the arrangement of the rooms, and even the position of the furniture, in English houses that he could find any room or any object blindfold.'

E. H. Carr, *The Romantic Exiles*, 1968

THE SPELL OF KOSSUTH'S ORATORY

The newspapers were lamenting in October [1851] that with the closing of the Crystal Palace there was nothing left for people to get excited about. Relief for this vacuum came rapidly on October 25th, when the exiled Hungarian national hero, Louis Kossuth, landed at Southampton. The story of Kossuth's progress through England and his reception in the various towns show how strong British sympathy still was for the revolutionaries of central Europe—the sympathy, that is, of the middle and lower classes. The upper classes viewed with alarm such public demonstrations on behalf of radical foreigners. Thus the *Daily News* championed Kossuth; the *Times* was coolly satirical, sometimes acidulous.

There was much in the career and personality of Kossuth to explain the storm of popular demonstrations which greeted him in England. During the fierce days of 1848–49 he had been the energetic leader of the Hungarian revolt against Austria. The new emperor, Francis Joseph, had proclaimed him a traitor. When the Hungarian revolt was defeated by the Austrian forces in 1849, Kossuth fled to Turkey. There he was honourably interned and at last allowed to embark for England.

Kossuth cast England under the spell of his oratory. During an earlier political imprisonment he had learned English with the aid of a volume of Shakespeare, and so he brought to his audiences now the full, rich flavour of their own Elizabethan heritage. He was a man of medium height, slight, with oval face, high forehead, and bluish-grey eyes. He wore whiskers and a heavy moustache. He delivered his speeches clearly and distinctly in his beautiful, logical, if somewhat florid, English, and a three-hour talk was not unusual for him. The fact that emotion occasionally overcame him as he spoke of the disgrace of his country did not at all reduce his effectiveness. From the beginning his audiences were huge and their enthusiasm unbounded.

The dignitaries of the various towns he visited delighted to honour him, until his tour, to the consternation of those who disapproved of him, took on the aspect of a semi-official series of municipal receptions. At Southampton the route of his entry into towns was lined by delighted crowds. He addressed them briefly from a balcony. When the band somewhat inappropriately played 'Auld Lang Syne,' the people joined in the chorus and Kossuth asked the Mayor what the air was that so awakened popular sympathy. The Mayor extricated himself by explaining that it was a song 'customarily sung on occasions of cordial welcome.' In the afternoon Kossuth addressed the Corporation in the Town Hall, and was presented with a large flag of the Hungarian Republic.

The triumphal tour began. The Corporation of London held a meeting in his honour, and his progress through the streets to the Guildhall was lined with cheering thousands of people. His audience greeted him with excited shouts. He next returned to Southampton, there to deliver a more elaborate three-hour speech, with Mr. Cobden and Lord Dudley Stuart on the platform as 'assistant guests.' Then next to Winchester, for a great banquet and attendant speechmaking on the part of many local and invited notables. Then to Manchester and Liverpool, and to Birmingham, where even the less sympathizing accounts placed the numbers of those who watched his procession under the triumphal arches at 75,000. Back again in London he addressed the Trades Unions at Copenhagen Fields, Islington. There 'respectable artisans'—some 12,000 of them—formed a huge parade in Russell Square and marched through the streets out to the Fields. The *Times* conservatively described the crowd as one of 25,000; the *Morning Chronicle* estimated it at 50,000; the demonstrators themselves at 100,000.

John W. Dodds, *The Year of Paradox*, 1953

MARXIST LIVING CONDITIONS

In 1921 a report came to light in the archives of the Prussian government from a police spy who had visited Marx's flat at 28 Dean Street, in London's Soho, in the autumn of 1852. The German spy disapproved of the conditions in which Marx lived, but seems to have liked the man himself.

At the head of the party is Karl Marx; his lieutenants are Engels, who lives in Manchester where there are thousands of German workmen; Freiligrath and Wolff (known as Lupus) are in London; Heine in Paris; Weydemeyer and Cluss in America; Bürgers and Daniels were his lieutenants in Cologne, and Weerth in Hamburg. All the rest were merely party members. The shaping and moving spirit, the real soul of the party, is Marx; therefore I will describe his personality so that you will have a better idea of him.

Marx is of middle height, 34 years old. Although in the prime of life, he is already turning gray. He is powerfully built, and his features remind you of Szemere very distinctly, only his complexion is darker, and his hair and beard quite black. Lately he does not shave at all. His large piercing fiery eyes have something demonically sinister about them. The first impression one receives is of a man of genius and energy. His intellectual superiority exercises an irresistible power on his surroundings.

In private life he is an extremely disorderly, cynical human being, and a bad host. He leads a real gypsy existence (*il mène une vie à la bohémien de l'intelligence*). Washing, grooming and changing his linen are things he does rarely, and he is often drunk. Though he is often idle for days on end, he will work day and night with tireless endurance when he has a great deal of work to do. He has no fixed times for going to sleep and waking up. He often stays up all night, and then lies down fully clothed on the sofa at midday and sleeps till evening, untroubled by the whole world coming and going through the room.

His wife is the sister of the Prussian Minister von Westphalen, a cultured and charming woman, who out of love for her husband has accustomed herself to his bohemian existence, and now feels perfectly at home in her poverty. She has two daughters and one son, and all three children are truly handsome and have their father's intelligent eyes.

As father and husband, Marx, in spite of his wild and restless character, is the gentlest and mildest of men. Marx lives in one of the worst, therefore one of the cheapest quarters of London. He occupies two rooms. The one looking out on the street is the salon, and the bedroom is at the back. In the whole apartment there is not one clean and solid piece of furniture. Everything is broken, tattered and torn, with a half inch of dust over everything and the greatest disorder everywhere. In the middle of the salon there is a large old-fashioned table covered with an oilcloth, and on it there lie manuscripts, books and newspapers, as well as the children's toys, the rags and tatters of his wife's sewing basket, several cups with broken rims, knives, forks, lamps, an inkpot, tumblers, Dutch clay pipes, tobacco ash— in a word, everything topsy-turvy, and all on the same table. A seller of secondhand goods would be ashamed to give away such a remarkable collection of odds and ends.

When you enter Marx's room smoke and tobacco fumes make your eyes water so much that for a moment you seem to be groping about in a cavern, but gradually, as you grow accustomed to the fog, you can make out certain objects which distinguish themselves from the surrounding haze. Everything is dirty and covered with dust, so that to sit down becomes a thoroughly dangerous business. Here is a chair with only three legs, on another chair the children are playing at cooking—this chair happens to have four legs. This is the one which is offered to the visitor, but the children's cooking has not been wiped away; and if you sit down, you risk a pair of trousers. But none of these things embarrass Marx or his wife. You are received in the most friendly way and cordially offered pipes and tobacco and whatever else there may happen to be; and eventually a spirited and agreeable conversation arises to make amends for all the domestic deficiencies, and this makes the discomfort tolerable. Finally you grow accustomed to the company, and find it interesting and original. This is a true picture of the family life of the Communist chief Marx.

Robert Payne, *Marx*, 1968

A FEW HUNDRED YARDS FROM BUCKINGHAM PALACE

A Prussian secret policeman, infiltrating the secret underworld of the post-1848 revolutionaries in London, finds a seething mass of would-be republicans.

There exist here 4 Socialist Republican Societies—two German, one Polish and one French, besides a Blood Red English secret Chartist Society.

A. One of the German Societies under Marx, Wolff, Engels, Vidil, meets at No. 20 Great Windmill St. on the first storey. It is divided again into three Sections. The Society B. is the most violent. The murder of Princes is formally taught and discussed in it. At a meeting held the day before yesterday at which I assisted and over which Wolff and Marx presided, I heard one of the Orators call out 'The Moon Calf will likewise not escape its destiny. The English Steel Wares are the best, the axes cut particularly sharp here, and the guillotine awaits every Crowned Head.' Thus the murder of the Queen of England is proclaimed by Germans a few hundred yards only from Buckingham Palace. The secret committee is divided again into two Sections, the one composed of the Leaders and the other of the so-called 'Blindmen' who are from 18 to 20 in number and are men of great daring and courage. They are not to take part in disturbances, but are reserved for great occasions and principally for the murder of Princes. 4 of these men are at Berlin. The German society A is in communication with Paris and with the Secret Chartist Society in London, of which Wolff and Marx are members. Wolff declared in the meeting of the evening before last 'The English want what we do, an Orator (of the Chartist Society) has loudly proclaimed, we want not only the Social Democratick Republick, *but something more.* You therefore see (said Wolff) that the English Mooncalf with Her Princely Urchins must go the way we mean to send all crowned Monarchs.' Upon which one well-dressed man cried out 'You mean hanging, Citizen—another the guillotine.'

The month of May or June was spoken of for striking the chief blow at Paris. Before the close of the meeting Marx told his audience that they might be perfectly tranquil, their men were everywhere at their Posts. The eventful moment was approaching and infallible measures are taken so that not one of the European crowned Executioners can escape. . . .

Robert Payne, Marx, 1968

TEA AND REVOLUTION: AN INVITATION

Commemoration of The
GREAT REVOLUTIONARY MOVEMENT OF 1848
ALLIANCE OF ALL PEOPLES
An
international
soirée
followed by
A Public Meeting
will be held at

St. Martin's Hall,
Long Acre
on
Tuesday, February 27, 1855

The following distinguished representatives of European
Democracy have been invited:

FRENCH: Louis Blanc, Victor Hugo, Barbès, Felix Pyat, Ledru-
Rollin, Raspail, Eugène Sue, Pierre Leroux.
GERMAN: Kinkel, Marx, Ruge, Schapper.
ITALIAN: Bianciani, Saffi, Mazzini.
HUNGARIAN: Teleki, Kossuth.
POLISH: Worcell, Zeno-Swientoslawski.
RUSSIAN: Herzen.
ENGLISH: W. Coningham, J. Finlen, Cooper, Mayne-Reid, J. Beal,
Gerald Massey.

Ernest Jones, President.
Alfred Tallandier, French Sec.
Dombrovski, Polish Sec.
M. Bley, German Sec.
B. Chapman, English Sec.

Tea on Table at Five. Doors open for meeting at half-past
Seven, to commence at Eight.

Double Tickets, 2*s.* 6*d.*; Single ditto. 1*s.* 6*d.*; meeting ditto, 3*d.*
Tickets may be had at St. Martin's Hall.

Quoted in E. H. Carr, *The Romantic Exiles*, 1968

THE TWENTY-SECOND DETONATOR

*Comrade Alexander Ossipon, special delegate of the Red Committee, has come
to the Silenus Restaurant in London to meet the Professor—a revolutionary,
and an expert in explosives. The Professor has a foolproof method to ensure he
is never arrested by the police.*

'I don't think there's one of them anxious to make that arrest. I don't think
they could get one of them to apply for a warrant. I mean one of the best.
Not one.'

'Why?' Ossipon asked.

'Because they know very well I take care never to part with the last
handful of my wares. I've it always by me.' He touched the breast of his
coat lightly. 'In a thick glass flask,' he added.

'So I have been told,' said Ossipon, with a shade of wonder in his voice. 'But I didn't know if—'

'They know,' interrupted the little man crisply, leaning against the straight chair back, which rose higher than his fragile head. 'I shall never be arrested. The game isn't good enough for any policeman of them all. To deal with a man like me you require sheer, naked, inglorious heroism.'

Again his lips closed with a self-confident snap. Ossipon repressed a movement of impatience.

'Or recklessness—or simply ignorance,' he retorted. 'They've only to get somebody for the job who does not know you carry enough stuff in your pocket to blow yourself and everything within sixty yards of you to pieces.'

'I never affirmed I could not be eliminated,' rejoined the other. 'But that wouldn't be an arrest. Moreover, it's not so easy as it looks.'

'Bah!' Ossipon contradicted. 'Don't be too sure of that. What's to prevent half-a-dozen of them jumping upon you from behind in the street? With your arms pinned to your sides you could do nothing—could you?'

'Yes; I could I am seldom out in the streets after dark,' said the little man impassively, 'and never very late. I walk always with my right hand closed round the india-rubber ball which I have in my trouser pocket. The pressing of this ball actuates a detonator inside the flask I carry in my pocket. It's the principle of the pneumatic instantaneous shutter for a camera lens. The tube leads up—'

With a swift disclosing gesture he gave Ossipon a glimpse of an india-rubber tube, resembling a slender brown worm, issuing from the armhole of his waistcoat and plunging into the inner breast pocket of his jacket. His clothes, of a nondescript brown mixture, were threadbare and marked with stains, dusty in the folds, with ragged button-holes. 'The detonator is partly mechanical, partly chemical,' he explained, with casual condescension.

'It is instantaneous, of course?' murmured Ossipon, with a slight shudder.

'Far from it,' confessed the other, with a reluctance which seemed to twist his mouth dolorously. 'A full twenty seconds must elapse from the moment I press the ball till the explosion takes place.'

'Phew!' whistled Ossipon, completely appalled. 'Twenty seconds! Horrors! You mean to say that you could face that? I should go crazy—'

'Wouldn't matter if you did. Of course, it's the weak point of this special system, which is only for my own use. The worst is that the manner of exploding is always the weak point with us. I am trying to invent a detonator that would adjust itself to all conditions of action, and even to unexpected changes of conditions. A variable and yet perfectly precise mechanism. A really intelligent detonator.'

'Twenty seconds,' muttered Ossipon again, 'Ough! And then—'

With a slight turn of the head the glitter of the spectacles seemed to gauge the size of the beer saloon in the basement of the renowned Silenus Restaurant.

'Nobody in this room could hope to escape,' was the verdict of that survey. 'Nor yet this couple going up the stairs now.'

The piano at foot of the staircase clanged through a mazurka with brazen impetuosity, as though a vulgar and impudent ghost were showing off. The keys sank and rose mysteriously. Then all became still. For a moment Ossipon imagined the overlighted place changed into a dreadful black hole belching horrible fumes choked with ghastly rubbish of smashed brickwork and mutilated corpses. He had such a distinct perception of ruin and death that he shuddered again. The other observed, with an air of calm sufficiency:

'In the last instance it is character alone that makes for one's safety. There are very few people in the world whose character is as well established as mine.'

Joseph Conrad, *The Secret Agent*, 1907

THE ARISTOCRATIC DUSTMEN OF CANNES

After the Revolution of 1917 the majority of the upper class of Tsarist Russia left the country. Many ended up in Shanghai, where they taught music or danced in the bars. The majority took refuge in Western Europe, and especially in France.

The Russian dustmen of Cannes were famous: they were very elegant and glamorous in their military tunics! Everyone loved them. I knew an English woman who lived below a Russian colonel who was working as a dustman, and he used to give her copies of the *Tatler* every week. She asked him why on earth he got the *Tatler*—'Oh, to keep track of my friends.'

Some of the French whom Russians had known before the war were very kind. My husband went instinctively to the Hôtel Meurice when he arrived. After three days he realized they were charging him the same price they had in 1914, despite the fact that in the meantime inflation had made that sum almost ridiculous. He couldn't pay the real price, so he left. Another friend went to Dusé to get some new shirts and he told them he owed them money from before the war. They told him they'd torn up all those bills. Nor did they want him to pay for the new shirts—he'd been a good customer in the past.

Russians adapted very quickly, but very few made fortunes. They're very bad at money. But they soon found jobs: couture for the women; nursing;

embroidery. The men started driving taxis, acting as guides for American tourists—anything. In Constantinople, when we were there, there was already a Russian restaurant—the Doré—with *baryshni* [well-brought-up girls] acting as waitresses. So there was no sitting around. But the Russian restaurants I knew in France mostly went bankrupt. People would be eating in front, while at the back there would be a room where old Russian generals would sit drinking vodka and eating the restaurant's food, talking politics and fighting battles: 'Now if I'd put my cavalry *there* and my guns *there* . . .'— it was a stock joke.

The women mostly started work first: the men had been through the war, then the Civil War—they were still dazed. But there was no loss of self-respect in taking any job that was going: 'Man must have bread!'

Mother and Father bought a farm and Father teamed up with a childhood friend he met. It was an absolute disaster. They knew nothing about farming. He'd been a soldier all his life. He did know something about horses, but not about cows. Then he trained dogs for a while. After that he collected bills for the Gas and Electricity Company. His friend Baron Prittwitz read the meters. They'd meet on the street: 'How are you, my dear fellow?' 'I live like a moth, you know—first I eat my trousers, then the jacket!' There was no gloom and no suicides. Russians become gloomy only when they have nothing to be gloomy about and have time to sit around and think.

For two years my cousin and I had private lessons. Then, aged fifteen, we were put into school with the *Sœurs Laïques*. That was very difficult. In maths and so on I had of course to translate from the Russian terms, despite the fact that my French was good. They were very strict and hypercritical, didn't even want you to laugh. And then they taught such rubbish about Russia—that Russian women were veiled, that they had to go round in closed carriages. How could we believe them about anything else when they taught things like that? One trouble was that people in the West tended to say to the Russian émigrés, 'Well, you got your just deserts,' because we had supposedly oppressed the people so terribly.

After that I went to the École des Arts Décoratifs, and then became a mannequin. For a while I worked as an extra for Rex Ingram's films—the whole of Russian Nice was working as extras. When he was making a film of *The White Devil* my father had a glorious two weeks. They made a village in the mountains above Cannes into a complete *aul* [Caucasian village] for the time of the making of the film, and he had the illusion that he was home again.

Around Cannes there were many Cossacks who kept chicken farms. They never learnt French—there was one famous mistranslation from Russian in an advertisement: '*Cosaque d'Amour Divorce les Poules*'. My nanny never learnt either French or English, although she died only twelve years ago— yet she always understood what was going on and somehow people understood her; and she always knew all the gossip. There were many like that.

> Countess Natalya Sumarokov-Elston; in Michael Glenny and Norman Stone,
> *The Other Russia*, 1990

THE REVOLUTION'S QUARRELS LINGER ON

Vladimir Nabokov, whose family were prominent liberals in Tsarist Russia, remained on good terms in exile with Alexander Kerensky when they both lived in New York. Kerensky headed the short-lived government which took power in February 1917 when Tsar Nicholas II abdicated. Many other Russian exiles blamed him for the Bolshevik revolution and everything that followed.

One day before the war Nabokov invited me to his home, he was a lecturer in those days and not too well off—he had a room in his sister-in-law's apartment, a walk-up on 60th Street on the fourth floor, near Madison Avenue. We were sitting around—it was quite late; I arrived only after most of the other guests had already left—when suddenly the doorbell rang. Heavy footsteps on the stairs. Nabokov said, 'That must be Alexander Fyodorovich.' The door opened and Kerensky said, as he looked around the room, 'Ah, I see that whenever I arrive somewhere all "decent" people leave!' It was said in such an amusing, self-deprecating way that I decided to stay and see what Kerensky was like at close quarters. Nabokov wanted to draw me into the conversation, and mentioned to Kerensky that I had been at the Lycée. 'Ah,' said Kerensky, 'did you leave Russia right after the February Revolution?' (I suppose he thought I was a confirmed monarchist.) I replied, 'No, I stayed until 1920 and lived right through the mess you created!' I immediately felt very ashamed of myself for this remark; he was, after all, a man considerably older than me, and I was a guest in someone else's house. When we were leaving, Kerensky offered me a lift home—at that time he was living in the house of a very rich American woman [and he] very kindly took me home in the chauffeur-driven car that his hostess had put at his disposal.

I met him later, too, here in America. I remember an occasion in 1927, when a book that he had written was translated into English and published. It was in the Century Theater, where Kerensky was to make a speech to an audience of Russian émigrés. The theatre was full, and I could only get a seat at the very back, but I saw Kerensky come on stage, to be greeted by a mixture of applause and a sort of hostile buzz. Then some woman came up on stage with a huge bouquet of red flowers. Kerensky accepted the bouquet with great pleasure, at which moment the woman gave him the most resounding box on the ears. The place immediately broke into an uproar; the police had to take action and they arrested the woman. It later transpired that her brother had been killed at the very beginning of the Revolution; he was a naval officer, who was killed by revolutionary sailors in Kronstadt . . .

> Dmitry Vladimirovich Lekhovich; in Michael Glenny and Norman Stone, *The Other Russia*, 1990

BRITISH STINGINESS

The Russian colony in London faithfully mirrored Tsarist society, starting with the Court.

The sister of the late Tsar, Grand Duchess Xenia Alexandrovna lived in a small villa. Modest, with sad, pensive eyes, and surrounded by her sons and grandsons, she would sometimes appear at church services. If what had happened in our country had happened in England, England's representatives would have met with generous hospitality in our palaces. Young émigrés would have been accepted, at State expense, into privileged educational institutions and our most brilliant regiments. Undoubtedly, King George would have liked to help his cousin the Grand Duchess, but in this matter it was necessary to reckon with Parliament, the democratic parties, parliamentary questions . . . Thanks be to God, the Grand Duchess did not have to suffer: her children, such as Prince Nikita Alexandrovich, did not disdain to take jobs in British firms and thereby contributed to the household expenses.

Under English law the Grand Duchess was accorded no privileges that were not possessed by an ordinary Russian refugee. Yet, when we saw her, none of us, whoever he might be, dared to speak of her as the 'former' Grand Duchess. She remained for us—and also, to their honour be it said, to the English—a Grand Duchess. She did not go out much, but kept within a small circle of friends. To be invited to her house was considered a great honour. . . .

The material situation of the colony was, of course, considerably better than that of Russians in Paris or, say, the Belgrade Russian colony. On the one hand, the British Government did not grant 'extensions' to residence permits as easily as other governments did; but, on the other hand, nowhere else, apparently, were Russian émigrés so free to take up occupation and engage in businesses, or to reside wherever they liked, as was the case in Britain. Here there was nothing comparable to the tedious restrictions on employment that prevailed in France, and we ought, of course, to have valued that circumstance very highly. Nor was there any obligation to go to the police station or to pay dues. That also counted for something.

None of the Russians made a grand, successful career in Britain. Still, P. L. Bark had a well-paid appointment in a bank, and some of the Russian Jews who had moved to Britain before the Revolution became prosperous. Professor Korenchevsky, honoured in scientific circles, commanded a big salary. Braikevich ran a building firm. All the rest made their living through various small-scale crafts and trade—millinery, underclothes and toilet articles. No work was below the dignity of an émigré: Admiral Smirnov, who had been Kolchak's Chief of Staff, lived by making ladies' hats; the Volkovs kept a restaurant; and the Golitsyns went into the antiques business.

> Pyotr Petrovich Shilovsky; in Michael Glenny and Norman Stone, *The Other Russia*, 1990

REMEMBERING PETERSBURG SUNSETS

When I chance to meet someone who has lived in Petersburg in the old days we touch off like this:

'And do you remember the Summer Garden?'

'Yes, yes, of course I do, and the Islands in the early autumn. That scent . . .' (associated, you perhaps reflect, with your first, and, as you then thought, your only love).

'And the white nights of Petersburg?'

'And the Palace Quay', you interrupt, 'that long pink-granite walk beloved of Pushkin, and that quite incredibly broad Nevski Prospekt on a cold winter afternoon, and the ice in early spring moving on the river, and the quay-side private palaces jostling each other in the dusk. Blocks of ice piling on one another; above, a small fugitive red sun.'

'Oh yes, oh yes! What memories it all brings back!' . . .

But how can I speak of something, to me particular, that sounds like nothing in particular: a drive—one of many to the Islands, where private carriages congregated on a Sunday afternoon in the late spring or early autumn (whereas driving up and down the full length of the Palace Quay, roughly between the Winter Palace and the British Embassy, was more of a winter pleasure). I still retain the feeling, as I alighted from my parents' carriage and stood and looked out to the Finnish Bay glowing in the evening sunlight, the feeling of bulging into open space; and, coloured by the setting sun and by a tragic sense of being fifteen and hopelessly in love with a girl of seventeen, it brings back to me the living breath of Petersburg. But how impart its essence? . . .

'And do you remember our Petersburg sunsets?' asks a Russian refugee.

'Oh, don't I!' says the other.

'The sky ashen and pink; the water a rosy mirror; the trees' silhouettes as if each cut out separately. The dark etching of the Kazan Cathedral against a pearly background . . .'

'Oh, don't speak of it! Don't. But when they light the lamps on the Troitski Bridge, what . . .?'

'And that bit of canal there by the Spasskaya . . .'

'And the heavy arch with the clock at the end of the Morskaya . . .'

'Don't!' . . .

William Gerhardie, 'Memories of St Petersburg', a BBC talk, 1953

A PAST OF TSARIST ADVENTURERS

On his father's side the novelist and broadcaster Michael Ignatieff, Canadian-born, comes from a family which produced ministers and diplomats for the Tsars; his mother's family are Scottish Canadians.

I heard very little Russian as a child: my father did not speak it at home. I went with him to the Russian church in the cities where I grew up—New York, Toronto, Ottawa, Belgrade, Paris, Geneva and London—and I was moved by the service because I did not understand it. Standing beside him in the church, watching him light his candles, say his prayers and sing in his deep vibrating voice, I always felt that he had slipped away through some invisible door in the air. Yet he kept his distance from the Russian émigré community, from their factional intrigues and antediluvian politics. He presented himself to the world throughout my childhood as the model of an assimilated Canadian professional. And to this day he is a much more patriotic and sentimental Canadian than I am. For him Canada was the country that gave him a new start. For me, being a Canadian was just one of those privileges I took for granted.

Father often met Soviet diplomats in his work and they always spoke Russian together. Yet the meetings were edgy. I remember one Soviet diplomat, dressed like a Zürich banker with a large black onyx ring on his finger, being introduced to both of us in a lobby of the United Nations building in New York. He doffed his astrakhan and in a great sweeping gesture said in English, 'As the son of a peasant I salute you.' Other Soviets treated the family past with the same mixture of respect and irony. In 1955, my father returned to the Soviet Union as part of an official Canadian delegation led by the Foreign Minister, Mike Pearson. The Soviet officials, led by Nikita Khrushchev himself, called my father *Graf* (Count) and took him aside and asked in all sincerity why he didn't come 'home' again and continue the diplomatic work of his grandfather instead of serving the diplomacy of a small satellite state of the Americans. But my father didn't feel at home at all in the Soviet Union of the 1950s. Even the moments of memoried connection were brief, as when he was shown into his room at the Hotel Astoria in Leningrad, frozen in its pre-revolutionary decor, and saw on the writing desk two silver bears exactly like two little bears that had once stood on his father's desk in the same city forty years before. On that visit, he also realized how archaic his Russian sounded to Soviet citizens and how rusty it had become. He found himself stumbling in his native tongue.

In my inability to learn Russian, I can now see the extent of my resistance to a past I was at the same time choosing as my own. The myths were never forced upon me so my resistance was directed not at my father or my uncles but rather at my own inner craving for these stories, at what seemed a weak desire on my part to build my little life upon the authority of their own. I wasn't sure I had the right to the authority of the past and even if I did have the right, I didn't want to avail myself of the privilege. Yet as one of my friends wryly says when I talk like this, no one ever gives up his privileges. So I used the past whenever I needed to, but with a guilty conscience. My friends had suburban pasts or pasts they would rather not talk about. I had a past of Tsarist adventurers, survivors of revolutions, heroic exiles. Yet the stronger my need for them, the stronger too became my need to disavow them, to strike out on my own. To choose my past meant to define the limits of its impingement upon me.

My father always said that I was more Mestchersky than Ignatieff, more like his mother than his father. Since he was more Ignatieff than Mestchersky, the statement underlined how complicated the ties of filiation really were between us. Inheritance is always as much a matter of anxiety as pride. If I was a Mestchersky what could I possibly make of myself? How could I ever master my temperament, that tightly strung bundle of fears and anxieties that seemed to have me locked in its grasp? From the beginning, the project of finding out about my past was connected to a struggle to master the anxiety of its influence.

I also found myself face to face with what I liked least about myself. My grandfather's favourite phrase was, 'Life is not a game, life is not a joke. It is only by putting on the chains of service that man is able to accomplish his destiny on earth.' When Paul talked like this, my grandmother Natasha always used to mutter, 'The Ignatieffs would make hell out of Paradise.'

Michael Ignatieff, *The Russian Album*, 1987

BOSTON BECOMES AN IRISH CITY

Other immigrants were drawn by the magic promise of the New World; the Irish were escaping from the horrors of death by starvation. Not many were adventurous, but, as we have seen, starving, fever-ridden, and with a high proportion of old people, widows, young children and invalids.

When the Americans first heard of the famine they subscribed generously, and in all they sent over a million dollars in food and money; but when it came to letting thousands of refugees into their country it was a different story. They had tried to discourage undesirable immigrants, even in the years before the famine, but it was still just as easy to sail to Canada, and then slip over the border. This they did in large numbers.

An odd thing about the Irish in America was that they mostly settled in towns. Back at home they would have done anything to find and keep a miserable plot, and land was scarce and very expensive. In the USA there were thousands of kilometres of undeveloped prairie, and they could have as much as they wanted for almost nothing. Instead, they chose to crowd together in the towns on the eastern seaboard.

There were several reasons for this. The only farming the Irish peasant understood was how to cultivate a potato patch with a spade. He knew little about wheat growing and nothing about cattle ranching. The wide, empty prairies would have terrified him had he gone far enough to see them. But these Irish were not pioneers, they were people running away, and it was enough for them to reach the USA at all. Having arrived in the crowded north-east, they were content to remain there, even though it meant staying in town. Not being enterprising they also felt the need to live with their own kind. They were quite unprepared to live among American families, and felt they had to have the comfort of Irish neighbours like themselves. Again, this could only be in town. Accordingly in many cities, large Irish *ghettoes* appeared, and they made serious problems for the Americans. We can see what happened in one particular town, Boston.

Early in the nineteenth century Boston was a pleasant place to live, and its citizens were prosperous. It was a port, so there was a good deal of commerce, and this brought the development of banking. Thus, Boston's leading citizens were either merchants or bankers, and there were a great many in these well-paid jobs. On the other hand, there were few really poor people. The only heavy industry was ship-building, in which many of the employees were skilled, and for the rest, the workmen tended to be master-craftsmen, owning their own small businesses and producing for the upper classes such goods as glass ware, high quality clothing and furniture.

Then the Irish arrived. Just after the famine, in 1850, there were already 35,000, and by 1855 there were 50,000. How was this multitude to earn a living?

The better of the girls and women were welcome, since the wealthy residents wanted servants, and American girls were not at all keen on this work. But now a merchant's wife could find all the domestic help she wanted, and at low wages too. The men among the Irish had more difficulty. There were jobs in the service trades that Americans did not want, such as being a waiter or a stable boy; there were the unskilled jobs in the ship-yards; fortunately there was a good deal of building going on so that men were needed for the heavy labour of digging foundations and carrying materials. But all these together were not nearly enough, and large numbers remained unemployed. . . .

Not surprisingly, the Irish lived wretchedly. They collected together where housing was cheap and, of course, bad. They lived in crumbling tenements that had once been fine houses, they lived in converted warehouses, wooden shacks, cellars and attics. To save rent they crowded in as closely as they could. They were almost without furniture, had little or no heating, and, what was worse, had poor water supplies with no proper sanitation.

Boston, once a healthy city, was now full of disease: smallpox, typhoid and tuberculosis. In 1849 there was a cholera epidemic, and most of the victims were Irish. The death rate for the whole town rose from about 20 per thousand in 1820 to 30 per thousand in 1850, but in the Irish districts, it was over 56 per thousand. An Irishman who came to Boston could not expect to live more than another fourteen years.

There was also a vast difference in outlook between the old Bostonians and the new. The Americans who were already there were descended from people like the Pilgrim Fathers—stern Puritans who believed in the virtues of soberness, hard work, clean living, and who looked on progress and pro-sperity as the rewards that God gave to a virtuous people. The newcomers were Catholics, peasants who had had little or no chance of education and who had lived through two famines in Ireland. They did not understand the outlook of the old Bostonians. They had no faith in progress. Why should they have, since they had no share in its rewards? The old Bostonians pressed for Negro emancipation, sanitary reform, compulsory state education; the Irish opposed them. The American Negro, set free in the south, would come north and compete for the unskilled jobs; sanitary reform cost money; compulsory education would rob them of their children's earnings.

So the Irish potato famine transformed the city of Boston. A small but prosperous trading town changed into a large industrial city. This brought increased wealth for the few, but the majority had to toil in poverty and misery. Above all, a city that had once been united was now divided against itself.

James McCartney, *The Development of Boston*, 1949

AN AMERICAN JOURNALIST DISAPPROVES OF AMERICANS WHO GO NATIVE

She rustled, she shimmered, in fresh, dove-coloured draperies, and Ralph saw at a glance that she was as crisp and new and comprehensive as a first issue before the folding. From top to toe she had probably no misprint. She spoke in a clear, high voice—a voice not rich but loud; yet after she had taken her place with her companions in Mr. Touchett's carriage she struck him as not all in the large type, the type of horrid 'headings,' that he had expected. She answered the enquiries made of her by Isabel, however, and in which the young man ventured to join, with copious lucidity; and later, in the library at Gardencourt, when she had made the acquaintance of Mr. Touchett (his wife not having thought it necessary to appear) did more to give the measure of her confidence in her powers.

'Well, I should like to know whether you consider yourselves American or English,' she broke out. 'If once I knew I could talk to you accordingly.'

'Talk to us anyhow and we shall be thankful,' Ralph liberally answered.

She fixed her eyes on him, and there was something in their character that reminded him of large polished buttons—buttons that might have fixed the elastic loops of some tense receptacle: he seemed to see the reflection of surrounding objects on the pupil. The expression of a button is not usually deemed human, but there was something in Miss Stackpole's gaze that made him, as a very modest man, feel vaguely embarrassed—less inviolate, more dishonoured, than he liked. This sensation, it must be added, after he had spent a day or two in her company, sensibly diminished, though it never wholly lapsed. 'I don't suppose that you're going to undertake to persuade me that *you're* an American,' she said.

'To please you I'll be an Englishman, I'll be a Turk!'

'Well, if you can change about that way you're very welcome,' Miss Stackpole returned.

'I'm sure you understand everything and that differences of nationality are no barrier to you,' Ralph went on.

Miss Stackpole gazed at him still. 'Do you mean the foreign languages?'

'The languages are nothing. I mean the spirit—the genius.'

'I'm not sure that I understand you,' said the correspondent of the *Interviewer*; 'but I expect I shall before I leave.'

'He's what's called a cosmopolite,' Isabel suggested.

'That means he's a little of everything and not much of any. I must say I think patriotism is like charity—it begins at home.'

'Ah, but where does home begin, Miss Stackpole?' Ralph enquired.

'I don't know where it begins, but I know where it ends. It ended a long time before I got here.'

'Don't you like it over here?' asked Mr. Touchett with his aged, innocent voice.

'Well, sir, I haven't quite made up my mind what ground I shall take. I feel a good deal cramped. I felt it on the journey from Liverpool to London.'

'Perhaps you were in a crowded carriage,' Ralph suggested.

'Yes, but it was crowded with friends—a party of Americans whose acquaintance I had made upon the steamer; a lovely group from Little Rock, Arkansas. In spite of that I felt cramped—I felt something pressing upon me; I couldn't tell what it was. I felt at the very commencement as if I were not going to accord with the atmosphere. But I suppose I shall make my own atmosphere. That's the true way—then you can breathe. Your surroundings seem very attractive.'

'Ah, we too are a lovely group!' said Ralph. 'Wait a little and you'll see.'

Henry James, *The Portrait of a Lady*, 1881

GERTRUDE STEIN'S HOME TOWN

America is my country and Paris is my home town and it is as it has come to be.

After all anybody is as their land and air is. Anybody is as the sky is low or high, the air heavy or clear and anybody is as there is wind or no wind there. It is that which makes them and the arts they make and and the work they do and the way they eat and the way they drink and the way they learn and everything.

And so I am an American and I have lived half my life in Paris, not the half that made me but the half in which I made what I made.

And why is Paris my home town, because after all that is just what it is, it is my home town.

It is very natural that every one who makes anything inside themselves that is makes it entirely out of what is in them does naturally have to have two civilizations. They have to have the civilization that makes them and the civilization that has nothing to do with them.

What is adventure and what is romance. Adventure is making the distant approach nearer but romance is having what is where it is which is not where you are stay where it is. So those who create things do not need adventure but they do need romance they need that something that is not for them stays where it is and that they can know that it is there where it is.

It has always been true of all who make what they make come out of what is in them and have nothing to do with what is necessarily existing outside of them it is inevitable that they have always wanted two civilizations. The Renaissance needed the greeks, as the modern painter needed the negroes as the English writers have needed Italy and as many Americans have needed Spain or France. There is no possibility of mixing up the other civilization with yourself you are you and if you are you in your own civilization you are apt to mix yourself up too much with your civilization but when it is another civilization a complete other a romantic other another that stays there where it is you in it have freedom inside yourself which if you are to do what is inside yourself and nothing else is a very useful thing to have happen to you and so America is my country and Paris is my home town.

Gertrude Stein, What Are Masterpieces, 1933

ERNEST HEMINGWAY GETS THE BENEFIT OF GERTRUDE STEIN'S LITERARY JUDGEMENT

It was easy to get into the habit of stopping in at 27 rue de Fleurus late in the afternoon for the warmth and the great pictures and the conversation. Often Miss Stein would have no guests and she was always very friendly and for a long time she was affectionate. When I had come back from trips that I had made to the different political conferences or to the Near East or Germany for the Canadian paper and the news services that I worked for she wanted me to tell her about all the amusing details. There were funny parts always and she liked them and also what the Germans call gallows-humour stories. She wanted to know the gay part of how the world was going; never the real, never the bad.

I was young and not gloomy and there were always strange and comic things that happened in the worst time and Miss Stein liked to hear these. The other things I did not talk of and wrote by myself.

When I had not come back from any trips and would stop in at the rue de Fleurus after working I would try sometimes to get Miss Stein to talk about books. When I was writing, it was necessary for me to read after I had written. It was necessary to get exercise, to be tired in the body, and it was very good to make love with whom you loved. That was better than anything. But afterwards, when you were empty, it was necessary to read in order not to think or worry about your work until you could do it again. I had learned already never to empty the well of my writing, but always to stop when there was still something there in the deep part of the well, and let it refill at night from the springs that fed it.

To keep my mind off writing sometimes after I had worked I would read writers who were writing then, such as Aldous Huxley, D. H. Lawrence or any who had books published that I could get from Sylvia Beach's library or find along the quais.

'Huxley is a dead man,' Miss Stein said. 'Why do you want to read a dead man? Can't you see he is dead?'

I could not see, then, that he was a dead man and I said that his books amused me and kept me from thinking.

'You should only read what is truly good or what is frankly bad.'

'I've been reading truly good books all winter and all last winter and I'll read them next winter, and I don't like frankly bad books.'

'Why do you read this trash? It is inflated trash, Hemingway. By a dead man.'

'I like to see what they are writing,' I said. 'And it keeps my mind off me doing it.'

'Who else do you read now?'

'D. H. Lawrence,' I said. 'He wrote some very good short stories, one called *The Prussian Officer*.'

'I tried to read his novels. He's impossible. He's pathetic and preposterous. He writes like a sick man.'. . . .

She was angry at Ezra Pound because he had sat down too quickly on a small, fragile and, doubtless, uncomfortable chair, that it is quite possible he had been given on purpose, and had either cracked or broken it. That he was a great poet and a gentle and generous man and could have accommodated himself in a normal-size chair was not considered. The reasons for her dislike of Ezra, skilfully and maliciously put, were invented years later.

It was when we had come back from Canada and were living in the rue Notre-Dame-des-Champs and Miss Stein and I were still good friends that Miss Stein made the remark about the lost generation. She had some ignition trouble with the old Model T Ford she then drove and the young man who worked in the garage and had served in the last year of the war had not been adept, or perhaps had not broken the priority of other vehicles, in repairing Miss Stein's Ford. Anyway he had not been *sérieux* and had been corrected severely by the *patron* of the garage after Miss Stein's protest. The *patron* had said to him, 'You are all a *génération perdue.*'

'That's what you are. That's what you all are,' Miss Stein said. 'All of you young people who served in the war. You are a lost generation.'

'Really?' I said.

'You are,' she insisted. 'You have no respect for anything. You drink yourselves to death . . .'

Ernest Hemingway, *A Moveable Feast*, 1964

WE RUINED OURSELVES

F. Scott Fitzgerald, in lachrymose mood, drafted this letter to his wife Zelda in the summer of 1930, while she was being treated in a clinic. He seems not to have sent it.

I know this then—that those days when we came up from the south, from Capri, were among my happiest—but you were sick and the happiness was not in the home.

I had been unhappy for a long time then—When my play failed a year and a half before, when I worked so hard for a year, twelve stories and novel and four articles in that time with no one believing in me and no one to see except you + before the end your heart betraying me and then I was really alone with no one I liked   In Rome we were dismal and was still working proof and three more stories and in Capri you were sick and there seemed to be nothing left of happiness in the world anywhere I looked.

Then we came to Paris and suddenly I realized that it hadn't all been in vain. I was a success—the biggest man in my profession everybody admired me and I was proud I'd done such a good thing. I met Gerald and Sara who took us for friends now and Ernest who was an equeal and my kind of an idealist. I got drunk with him on the Left Bank in careless cafés and drank with Sara and Gerald in their garden is St Cloud but you were endlessly sick and at home everything was unhappy. We went to Antibes and I was happy but you were sick still and all that fall and that winter and spring at the cure and I was alone all the time and I had to get drunk before I could leave you so sick and not care and I was only happy a little while before I got too drunk. Afterwards there were all the usuall penalties for being drunk.

Finally you got well in Juan-les-Pins and a lot of money came in and I made of those mistakes literary men make—I thought I was 'a man of the world—that everybody liked me and admired me for myself but I only liked a few people like Ernest and Charlie McArthur and Gerald and Sara who were my peers. Time goes bye fast in those moods and nothing is ever done. I thought then that things came easily—I forgot how I'd dragged the great Gatsby out of the pit of my stomach in a time of misery . . . By the time we reached the beautiful Rivierra I had developed such an inferiority complex that I couldn't fase anyone unless I was tight. I worked there too, though, and the unusual combination exploded my lungs.

You were gone now—I scarcely remember you that summer. You were simply one of all the people who disliked me or were indifferent to me. I didn't like to think of you—You didn't need me and it was easier to talk to or rather at Madame Bellois and keep full of wine. I was grateful when you came with me to the Doctors one afternoon but after we'd been a week in Paris and I didn't try any more about living or dieing. Things were always the same. The appartments that were rotten, the maids that stank—the ballet before my eyes, spoiling a story to take the Troubetskoys to dinner, poisoning a trip to Africa. You were going crazy and calling it genius—I was going to ruin and calling it anything that came to hand. And I think every-one far enough away to see us outside of our glib presentation of ourselves guessed at your almost meglomaniacal selfishness and my insane indulgence in drink. Toward the end nothing much mattered. The nearest I ever came to leaving you was when you told me you thot I was a fairy in the Rue Palatine but now whatever you said aroused a sort of detached pity for you. For all your superior observation and your harder intelligence I have a faculty of guessing right, without evidence even with a certain wonder as to why and whence that mental short cut came. I wish the Beautiful and Damned had been a maturely written book because it was all true. We ruined ourselves—I have never honestly thought that we ruined each other.

> F. Scott Fitzgerald, *Correspondence*, ed. Matthew J. Bruccoli and Margaret M. Duggan, 1980

EZRA POUND THINKS EXTREMELY WELL OF MUSSOLINI

Rapallo, 30 November

Dear Harriet: I have not, at the moment, any strong objection to visiting America. I shall probably be HORRIFIED if or when I do get there. It is probably infinitely worse than anything I am prepared for, despite my being prepared for ANYTHING within the range of my imagination. . . . But still . . . the risk is not a particular deterrent.————

As to lecture tour: the question is simply: what wd. it pay? I can not afford to do it on the cheap. If I blow all that energy, I have got to have a few years free from worry AFTER it.

Poverty here is decent and honourable. In America it lays one open to continuous insult on all sides, from the putridity in the White House down to the expressman who handles one's trunk.

I don't care to place my head under the guillotine or my feet under the trolley wheels.—/—/ . . .

I personally think extremely well of Mussolini. If one compares him to American presidents (the last three) or British premiers, etc., in fact one can not without insulting him. If the intelligentsia don't think well of him, it is because they know nothing about 'the state,' and government, and have no particularly large sense of values. Anyhow, WHAT intelligentsia?

What do the intelligentsia think of Henry Ford? He has given people a five day week, without tying it up in a lot of theoretical bunk. I can't imagine ANY labour party consenting to the results; it puts such a lot of 'secretaries' out of a job.

Re your question is it any better abroad for authors: England gives small pensions; France provides jobs. A ninth rate slob like Claudel gets a job as ambassador. Giraudoux, Morand, Cros, etc., etc., get quite comfortable posts. Italy is full of ancient libraries; the jobs are quite comfortable, not very highly paid, but are respectable, and can't much interfere with the librarians' time.

As to 'betterness,' if I were a citizen of any of these countries I wd. have some sort of appui, which is unthinkable in America. As for professorships??? I have not been overwhelmed with offers . . . I reckon the danger is not imminent.

Ezra Pound, Letters 1907–41, ed. D. D. Paige, 1951

IN BED WITH MONA

She talks to me so feverishly—as if there will be no tomorrow. 'Be quiet, Mona! Just look at me . . . *don't talk!*' Finally she drops off and I pull my arm from under her. My eyes close. Her body is there beside me . . . it will be there till morning surely . . . It was in February I pulled out of the harbor in a blinding snowstorm. The last glimpse I had of her was in the window waving good-bye to me. A man standing on the other side of the street, at the corner, his hat pulled down over his eyes, his jowls resting on his lapels. A fetus watching me. A fetus with a cigar in its mouth. Mona at the window waving good-bye. White heavy face, hair streaming wild. And now it is a heavy bedroom, breathing regularly through the gills, sap still oozing from between her legs, a warm feline odor and her hair in my mouth. My eyes are closed. We breathe warmly into each other's mouth. Close together, America three thousand miles away. I never want to see it again. To have her here in bed with me, breathing on me, her hair in my mouth—I count that something of a miracle. Nothing can happen now till morning . . .

I wake from a deep slumber to look at her. A pale light is trickling in. I look at her beautiful wild hair. I feel something crawling down my neck. I look at her again, closely. Her hair is alive. I pull back the sheet—more of them. They are swarming over the pillow.

It is a little after daybreak. We pack hurriedly and sneak out of the hotel. The cafés are still closed. We walk, and as we walk we scratch ourselves. The day opens in milky whiteness, streaks of salmon-pink sky, snails leaving their shells. Paris. Paris. Everything happens here. Old, crumbling walls and the pleasant sound of water running in the urinals. Men licking their mustaches at the bar. Shutters going up with a bang and little streams purling in the gutters. *Amer Picon* in huge scarlet letters. *Zigzag*. Which way will we go and why or where or what?

Mona is hungry, her dress is thin. Nothing but evening wraps, bottles of perfume, barbaric earrings, bracelets, depilatories. We sit down in a billiard parlor on the Avenue du Maine and order hot coffee. The toilet is out of order. We shall have to sit some time before we can go to another hotel. Meanwhile we pick bedbugs out of each other's hair. Nervous. Mona is losing her temper. Must have a bath. Must have this. Must have that. Must, must, must . . .

'How much money have you left?'

Money! Forgot all about that.

Hôtel des Etats-Unis. An *ascenseur*. We go to bed in broad daylight. When we get up it is dark and the first thing to do is to raise enough dough to send a cable to America. A cable to the fetus with the long juicy cigar in his mouth. Meanwhile there is the Spanish woman on the Boulevard Raspail—she's always good for a warm meal. By morning something will happen. At least we're going to bed together. No more bedbugs now. The rainy season has commenced. The sheets are immaculate. . . .

Henry Miller, *Tropic of Cancer*, 1965

AFRO-AMERICANS IN PARIS

It is estimated that there are five hundred American Negroes living in this city, the vast majority of them veterans studying on the G.I. Bill. They are studying everything from the Sorbonne's standard *Cours de Civilisation*

Française to abnormal psychology, brain surgery, music, fine arts, and literature. Their isolation from each other is not difficult to understand if one bears in mind the axiom, unquestioned by American landlords, that Negroes are happy only when they are kept together. Those driven to break this pattern by leaving the U.S. ghettos not merely have effected a social and physical leave-taking but also have been precipitated into cruel psychological warfare. It is altogether inevitable that past humiliations should become associated not only with one's traditional oppressors but also with one's traditional kinsfolk.

Thus the sight of a face from home is not invariably a source of joy, but can also quite easily become a source of embarrassment or rage. The American Negro in Paris is forced at last to exercise an undemocratic discrimination rarely practised by Americans, that of judging his people, duck by duck, and distinguishing them one from another. Through this deliberate isolation, through lack of numbers, and above all through his own overwhelming need to be, as it were, forgotten, the American Negro in Paris is very nearly the invisible man.

The wariness with which he regards his coloured kin is a natural extension of the wariness with which he regards all of his countrymen. At the beginning, certainly he cherishes rather exaggerated hopes of the French. His white countrymen, by and large, fail to justify his fears, partly because the social climate does not encourage an outward display of racial bigotry, partly out of their awareness of being ambassadors, and finally, I should think, because they are themselves relieved at being no longer forced to think in terms of colour. There remains, nevertheless, in the encounter of white Americans and Negro Americans the high potential of an awkward or an ugly situation.

The white American regards his darker brother through the distorting screen created by a lifetime of conditioning. He is accustomed to regard him either as a needy and deserving martyr or as the soul of rhythm, but he is more than a little intimidated to find this stranger so many miles from home. At first he tends instinctively, whatever his intelligence may belatedly clamour, to take it as a reflection on his personal honour and good-will; and at the same time, with that winning generosity, at once good-natured and uneasy, which characterises Americans, he would like to establish communication, and sympathy, with his compatriot. 'And how do *you* feel about it?' he would like to ask, 'it' being anything—the Russians, Betty Grable, the Place de la Concorde. The trouble here is that any 'it', so tentatively offered, may suddenly become loaded and vibrant with tension, creating in the air between the two thus met an intolerable atmosphere of danger.

The Negro, on the other hand, via the same conditioning which con-stricts the outward gesture of the whites, has learned to anticipate: as the mouth opens he divines what the tongue will utter. He has had time, too, long before he came to Paris, to reflect on the absolute and personally expensive futility of taking any one of his countrymen to task for his status in America, or of hoping to convey to them any of his experience. The American Negro and white do not, therefore, discuss the past, except in considerately guarded snatches. Both are quite willing, and indeed quite wise, to remark instead the considerably overrated impressiveness of the Eiffel Tower.

James Baldwin, *Notes of a Native Son*, 1964

A MOLE IN THE ENGLISH GOVERNMENT

Sir Henry Wotton, English ambassador in Venice and originator of the quip about being sent abroad to lie for one's country, gets wind in 1606 that one of King James I's ministers is a Spanish agent. He informs Sir Robert Cecil, the chief minister, about it, unaware that Cecil himself is receiving a pension from Spain and sends secret information to the Spanish embassy in London.

(Postscript.) MY VERY GOOD LORD,

It seemeth fit for me, out of that dispatch which was sent by Rouland Woodward, in all event to repeat this peculiarity received from the party at Milan. That one of his Majesty's counsel doth hold continual intelligence with the ambassador of Spain in England, who advertiseth the things that he receiveth first to Milan and from thence to Rome. The particular name he promised to signify unto me which he hath not yet done. And therefore, though I was bound in my allegiance to relate unto your Lordship what I had received, yet I very humbly beseech you to represent it for mine own defence with this addition unto his Majesty, that I was and am far from thinking it sufficient (without more particularity) to stain the reputation of any ordinary person, and much less of the most honourable.

Sir Henry Wotton (1586–1639), *Life and Letters*, ed. Logan Pearsall Smith, 1908

TRAPPING A TRAITOR

Somerset Maugham's alter ego from the First World War, Ashenden, is ordered by his spymaster, 'R', to make contact with a British living in Switzerland, Grantley Caypor.

Ashenden's instructions were to get acquainted with Caypor and see whether there was any chance that he would work honestly for the British: if he thought there was, he was entitled to sound him and if his suggestions were met with favour to make certain propositions. It was a task that needed tact and a knowledge of men. If on the other hand Ashenden came to the conclusion that Caypor could not be bought, he was to watch and report his movements. The information he had obtained from Gustav was vague, but important; there was only one point in it that was interesting, and this was that the head of the German Intelligence Department in Berne was growing restive at Caypor's lack of activity. Caypor was asking for a higher salary and Major von P. had told him that he must earn it. It might be that he was urging him to go to England. If he could be induced to cross the frontier Ashenden's work was done.

'How the devil do you expect *me* to persuade him to put his head in a noose?' asked Ashenden.

'It won't be a noose, it'll be a firing squad,' said R.

'Caypor's clever.'

'Well, be cleverer, damn your eyes.'. . .

Ashenden did not have to wait long. Next day he was sitting in the doorway of the hotel, drinking a cup of coffee and already half asleep after a substantial *mittagessen*, when the Caypors came out of the dining-room. Mrs. Caypor went upstairs and Caypor released his dog. The dog bounded along and in a friendly fashion leaped up against Ashenden.

'Come here, Fritzi,' cried Caypor, and then to Ashenden: 'I'm so sorry. But he's quite gentle.'

'Oh, that's all right. He won't hurt me.'. . .

'Please sit down,' said Ashenden.

'It's very good of you, I've lived so long on the Continent that I'm always forgetting that my countrymen are apt to look upon it as confounded cheek if you talk to them. Are you English, by the way, or American?'

'English,' said Ashenden.

Ashenden was by nature a very shy person, and he had in vain tried to cure himself of a failing that at his age was unseemly, but on occasion he knew how to make effective use of it. He explained now in a hesitating and awkward manner the facts that he had the day before told the landlady and that he was convinced she had already passed on to Caypor.

'You couldn't have come to a better place than Lucerne. It's an oasis of peace in this war-weary world. When you're here you might almost forget that there is such a thing as a war going on. That is why I've come here. I'm a journalist by profession.'

'I couldn't help wondering if you wrote,' said Ashenden, with an eagerly timid smile.

It was clear that he had not learnt that 'oasis of peace in a war-weary world' at the shipping-office.

'You see, I married a German lady,' said Caypor gravely.

'Oh, really?'

'I don't think anyone could be more patriotic than I am. I'm English through and through and I don't mind telling you that in my opinion the British Empire is the greatest instrument for good that the world has ever seen, but having a German wife I naturally see a good deal of the reverse of the medal. You don't have to tell me that the Germans have faults, but frankly I'm not prepared to admit that they're devils incarnate. At the beginning of the war my poor wife had a very rough time in England and I for one couldn't have blamed her if she'd felt rather bitter about it. Everyone thought she was a spy. It'll make you laugh when you know her. She's the typical German *hausfrau* who cares for nothing but her house and her husband and our only child Fritzi.' Caypor fondled his dog and gave a little laugh. 'Yes, Fritzi, you are our child, aren't you? Naturally it made my position very awkward. I was connected with some very important papers, and my editors weren't quite comfortable about it. Well, to cut a long story short I thought the most dignified course was to resign and come to a neutral country till the storm blew over. My wife and I never discuss the war, though I'm bound to tell you that it's more on my account than hers, she's much more tolerant than I am and she's more willing to look upon this terrible business from my point of view than I am from hers.'

'That is strange,' said Ashenden. 'As a rule women are so much more rabid than men.'

'My wife is a very remarkable person. I should like to introduce you to her. By the way, I don't know if you know my name. Grantley Caypor.'

'My name is Somerville,' said Ashenden.

> W. Somerset Maugham, 'The Traitor', from *The Complete Short Stories*, vol. ii, 1951

THE SPIES' WATERING-HOLE

The bar at the St George Hotel in pre-civil war Beirut was a famous centre for spies and secret agents of all kinds. Kim Philby was one of the habitués, and the barman later wrote this account of him.

The bar was full of spies—resident spies, visiting spies, Lebanese, Egyptian, British, American, Yugoslav and, undoubtedly, Russian spies. I personally know every spy discussed in this chapter and so, among other things, my judgement is highly subjective. There are many reasons why Kim Philby should head the list of bar spies. Not only was he the most famous among them, but his was an amazing career which continues to baffle and intrigue us. Much about this man and his activities remains unknown and is likely to stay that way. . . .

Kim always looked slightly dishevelled, an attractive man of letters in a sports jacket and corduroy trousers that had seen better days. His stammer and his tendency to speak in a soft, gravelly voice gave an impression of shyness. Together with his longer-than-average hair, a middle-age slouch and a naughty twinkle, they all added to his physical attractiveness. Women liked Kim and he returned the compliment. One might have called him a natural flirt; his very being carried a sexual suggestiveness. . . .

The one aspect of Philby's spy life which I can report with authority is the amount of American, CIA, hounding to which he was subjected until his defection. When CIA agent James Russell Barracks tried to hire me to monitor Philby, he told me that the Americans were keen to determine whether 'a relationship' existed between Kim and one of the bar's waiters, an Armenian with known leftist tendencies named Haig. I rejected Barracks' generous offer because I liked Kim and Haig and found the whole thing distasteful.

American interest in Philby manifested itself in many ways: Barracks openly wanted him watched, Fistere extended the rules of the game to the point of hiring Philby's daughter and Miles Copeland, by his own admission a major CIA operative during the Philby years in Beirut, maintained a curious friendship. But it didn't stop there; Molly Izzard, wife of Ralph and an author in her own right, gives innumerable examples of late-night telephone calls to their place every time Kim stayed with them. The callers were always 'drunken American ladies' who were checking on Kim's whereabouts. This degree of American attention to Philby amounted to merciless hounding. Miles Copeland himself attests to this in his book, *The Game of Nations*, and suggests that a great many people, British as well as American, were involved.

The British Philby-monitoring operation was much more subtle; it certainly didn't show its colours around the bar. However one felt about Kim, there was something beyond the naive in the American moves against him. Most were downright stupid, winning him the sympathy of a number of bar regulars, including some British journalists. Eventually, the belief in Kim's guilt or innocence practically divided along national lines, with the Americans believing he was guilty and the British defending him.

Said K. Aburish, *The St George Hotel Bar*, 1989

HE REMAINS AN ENGLISHMAN

The actress Coral Browne, visiting Moscow, meets the defector Guy Burgess. He asks her to order some suits for him from his London tailor, plus an Old Etonian tie.

CORAL. What do you miss most?

BURGESS. Apart from the Reform Club, the streets of London and occasionally the English countryside, the only thing I really miss is gossip. The comrades, though splendid in every other respect, don't gossip in quite the way we do, or about quite the same subjects.

CORAL. Pardon me for saying so, dear, but the comrades seem to me a sad disappointment in every department. There's no gossip, their clothes are terrible, and they can't make false teeth. What else is there?

BURGESS. (*Gently.*) The system. . . . Only, being English, you wouldn't be interested in that. (*Pause.*) What do people say about me in England?

CORAL. They don't much, any more. (*She gets up suddenly and starts frantically tidying up the room. Folding clothes, washing dishes. Sweeping. Burgess watches languidly.*) I thought of you as a bit like Oscar Wilde.

Burgess laughs.

BURGESS. No, no. Though he was a performer. And I was a performer. (*He is looking at himself in the glass.*) Both vain. But I never pretended. If I wore a mask, it was to be exactly what I seemed. And I made no bones about the other. My analysis of situations, the précis I had to submit at the Foreign Office, were always Marxist. Openly so. Impeccably so. (*She should be wiping the floor round his feet at this point, something very menial indeed.*) Nobody minded. 'It's only Guy.' 'Dear old Guy.' Quite safe. If you don't wish to conform in one thing, you should conform in all the others. And in all the important things I did conform. 'How can he be a spy? He goes to my tailor.' The average Englishman, you see, is not interested in ideas. Say what you like about political theory, and no one will listen. You could shove a slice of the Communist Manifesto in the Queen's Speech, and no one would turn a hair. Least of all, I suspect, HMQ. Am I boring you?

CORAL. It doesn't matter.

Fade in to Burgess at the piano, playing Elgar. Coral, having finished tidying up, sits. Then investigates the bookshelves. Takes a book out. Puts it back.

BURGESS. (*Shouting above the music.*) I'll think of 101 things to ask you when you've gone. How is Cyril Connolly?

CORAL. You've asked me that. I don't know.

BURGESS. (*Stopping playing.*) So little, England. Little music. Little art. Timid, tasteful, nice. But one loves it. Loves it. You see I can say I love London. I can say I love England. I can't say I love my country. I don't know what that means. Do you watch cricket?

CORAL. No. Anyway, it's changed.

BURGESS. Cricket?

CORAL. London.

BURGESS. Why? I don't want it to change. Why does anybody want to change it? They've no business changing it. The fools. You should stop them changing it. Band together.

CORAL. (*Getting up.*) Listen, darling. I'm only an actress. Not a bright lady, by your standards. I've never taken much interest in politics. If this is communism, I don't like it because it's dull. And the poor dears look tired. But then, Leeds is dull and that's not communism. And look at Australia. Only it occurs to me we have sat here all afternoon pretending that spying, which was what you did, darling, was just a minor social misdemeanour, no worse. And I'm sure in some people's minds much better than being caught in a public lavatory the way gentlemen in my profession constantly are, and that it's just something one shouldn't mention. Out of politeness. So that we won't be embarrassed. That's very English. We will pretend it hasn't happened, because we are both civilised people. Well, I'm not English. And I'm not civilised. I'm Australian. I can't muster much morality and outside Shakespeare the word treason to me means nothing. Only, you pissed in our soup and we drank it. So. Very good. Doesn't affect me, darling. And I will order your suit and your hat. And keep it under mine. Mum. Not a word. But for one reason: because I'm sorry for you. Now in your book . . . in your *real* book . . . that probably adds my name to the list of all the other fools you've conned. But you're not conning me, darling. Pipe isn't fooling pussy. I know.

Burgess's Apartment, Moscow.
It is empty, but the floor is strewn with cardboard boxes, a chaos of torn tissue-paper and opened parcels.

Moscow Street.
Burgess is walking down it alone. He is in his new clothes and very elegant. In Voice Over, Burgess is singing at the piano, with piano accordion accompaniment, the song from HMS Pinafore *which, as the scene progresses, is taken up by full chorus and orchestra.*

BURGESS. For he himself has said it,
    And it's greatly to his credit,
    That he is an Englishman.

For he might have been a Roosian,
A French or Turk or Proosian,
Or perhaps I-tal-ian.
But in spite of all temptations.
To belong to other nations,
He remains an Englishman.
He remains an Englishman.

Alan Bennett, 'An Englishman Abroad', from *Objects of Affection and Other Plays for Television*, 1982

EXILED IN THEIR OWN COUNTRY

*M*ore *people have probably been driven from their homes in Russia than any other country; and it was Russia which first showed under Tsardom that it was not necessary to force political dissidents out of the country in order to silence them, it was enough to send them as punishment to the farthest reaches of Siberia or Central Asia in what became known as 'internal' exile. Soon, however, it became clear that autocracy had created a rather different form of internal exile as well: the retreat into a world of one's own, the erection of barriers between external political reality and the way one chose to live the private life of the mind. There is, however, another and worse form of internal exile, the transformation of people into aliens in their own countries. It happened to the Aztecs and Incas as a result of the Spanish conquest; it happened through the colonial expansion of Europe into Asia and Africa, it happened in South Africa more intensely after the introduction of apartheid in 1948. Exiles abroad are at least as free as their host countries permit to think and act as they want. Internal exiles have no such freedom.*

In Hsü-chou, in the District of Ku-fêng
There lies a village whose name is Chu-ch'ên—
A hundred miles away from the county town,
Amid fields of hemp and green of mulberry-trees.
Click, click, the sound of the spinning-wheel;
Donkeys and oxen pack the village streets.
The girls go drawing the water from the brook;
The men go gathering fire-wood on the hill.
So far from the town Government affairs are few;
So deep in the hills, men's way are simple.
Though they have wealth, they do not traffic with it;
Though they reach the age, they do not enter the Army.
Each family keeps to its village trade;
Grey-headed, they have never left the gates.
Alive, they are the people of Ch'ên Village;
Dead, they become the dust of Ch'ên Village.
Out in the fields old men and young
Gaze gladly, each in the other's face.
In the whole village there are only two clans;
Age after age Chus have married Ch'êns.
Near or distant, they live in one clan;
Young or old, they move as one flock.
On white wine and brown fowl they fare
At joyful meetings more than 'once a week.'
While they are alive, they have no distant partings;
For marriage takes them no further than the next village.
When they are dead—no distant burial;
Round the village graves lie thick.
They are not troubled either about life or death;
They have no anguish either of body or soul.

And so it happens that they live to a ripe age
And great-great-grandsons are often seen.

I was born in the Realms of Etiquette;
In early years, unprotected and poor.
In vain I learnt to distinguish between Evil and Good;
Bringing myself only labour and toil.
The age we live in honours the Doctrine of Names;
Scholars prize marriages and rank.
With these fetters I gyved my own hands;
Truly I became a much-deceived man.
At ten years old I learnt to read books;
At fifteen, I knew how to write prose.
At twenty I was made a Bachelor of Arts;
At thirty I became a Censor at the Court.
Above, the duty I owe to Prince and parents;
Below, the ties that bind me to wife and child.
The support of my family, the service of my country—
For these tasks my nature is not apt.
  I reckon the time that I first left my home:
From then till now—fifteen Springs!
My lonely boat has twice sailed to Ch'u:
Four times through Ch'in my lean horse has passed.
I have walked in the morning with hunger in my face;
I have lain at night with a soul that could not rest.
East and West I have wandered without pause,
Hither and thither like a cloud adrift in the sky.
In the civil-war my old home was destroyed;
Of my flesh and blood many are scattered and parted.
North of the River, yes, and South of the River—
In both lands are the friends of all my life;
Life-friends whom I never see at all—
Whose deaths I hear of only after the lapse of years.
Sad at morning, I lie on my bed till dusk;
Weeping at night, I sit and wait for dawn.
The fire of sorrow has burnt my heart's core;
The frost of trouble has seized my hair's roots.
In such anguish my whole life has passed;
Long I have envied the people of Ch'ên Village.

Chinese Poems, tr. Arthur Waley, 1953

MARKED FOR LIFE

One of the fiercest political battles of eighth- and ninth-century Constantinople was between the worshippers of icons ('iconodules') and those who wanted to destroy them ('iconoclasts'). The penalties for nonconformity could be elaborate and unpleasant.

Two brothers from Palestine, the writer Theodore and the hymnographer Theophanes, . . . had together assumed the mantle of Theodore of the Studium, after the latter's death in 826, as principal champions of the iconodules. According to their own account, they were summoned to Constantinople, kept for a week in prison and then brought before the Emperor. When he asked them why they had entered the Empire in the first place, they refused to answer, whereupon they were beaten severely about the head. On the next day they were flogged, but still refused to renounce their views. Four days later still, Theophilus offered them their last chance: if they would consent to take communion just once with the iconoclasts, they would hear no more of the matter. But they only shook their heads. And so, by the imperial command, they were laid across a bench while an abusive lampoon was tattooed across their faces. It was not, Theophilus admitted, a very good lampoon; but it was good enough for them. A free translation, thoughtfully provided by Professor Bury—complete with its majestic mixed metaphor in the second line—confirms the Emperor's opinion:

> In that fair town whose sacred streets were trod
> Once by the pure feet of the Word of God—
> The city all men's hearts desire to see—
> These evil vessels of perversity
> Where driven forth to this our City where,
> Persisting in their wicked, lawless ways,
> They are condemned and, branded in the face,
> As scoundrels, hunted to their native place.

The tenor of the Emperor's questions—as well as that of this deplorable doggerel—suggests that not the least of the two brothers' offences was the fact that they were foreign immigrants who had, in Theophilus's eyes, entered the Empire deliberately to stir up trouble. They were not, however, returned to Palestine as the last line claims, but were imprisoned in the small Bithynian town of Apamea. Here Theodore died; his brother survived to become, in happier times, Bishop of Nicaea.

John Julius Norwich, *Byzantium: The Apogee*, 1989

THE BARBAROUS BEHAVIOUR OF THE CRUSADERS

When I was visiting Jerusalem, I used to go to al-Aqṣā mosque, where my Templar friends were staying. Along one side of the building was a small oratory in which the Franj had set up a church. The Templars placed this spot at my disposal that I might say my prayers. One day I entered, said *Allāhu akbar*, and was about to begin my prayer, when a man, a Franj, threw himself upon me, grabbed me, and turned me toward the east, saying, 'Thus do we pray.' The Templars rushed forward and led him away. I then set myself to prayer once more, but this same man, seizing upon a moment of inattention, threw himself upon me yet again, turned my face to the east, and repeated once more, 'Thus do we pray.' Once again the Templars intervened, led him away, and apologized to me, saying, 'He is a foreigner. He has just arrived from the land of the Franj and he has never seen anyone pray without turning to face east.' I answered that I had prayed enough and left, stunned by the behaviour of this demon who had been so enraged at seeing me pray while facing the direction of Mecca. . . .

In Nablus I had the opportunity to witness a curious spectacle. Two men had to meet each other in individual combat. The cause of the fight was this: some brigands among the Muslims had invaded a neighbouring village, and a farmer was suspected of having acted as their guide. He ran away, but was soon forced to return, for King Fulk had imprisoned his children. 'Treat me fairly', the farmer had asked him, 'and allow me to compete against my accuser.' The king then told the lord who had been granted this village as a fiefdom, 'Bring the man's adversary here.' The lord had selected a smith who worked in the village, telling him, 'It is you who will fight this duel.' The possessor of the fiefdom wanted to make sure that none of his peasants would be killed, for fear that his crops would suffer. I looked at this smith. He was a strong young man, but was constantly asking for something to drink, whether he was walking or sitting. As for the accused, he was a courageous old man who stood snapping his fingers in a gesture of defiance. The viscount, governor of Nablus, approached, gave each man a lance and shield, and had the spectators form a circle around them.

The struggle was joined. The old man forced the smith back, pressed him towards the crowd, and then returned to the centre of the arena. There was an exchange of blows so violent that the rivals seemed to form a single column of blood. The fight dragged on, despite the exhortations of the viscount, who was anxious to hasten its conclusion. 'Faster', he shouted at them. The old man was finally exhausted, and the smith, taking advantage of his experience in handling the hammer, dealt him a blow that knocked the old man down and caused him to lose his lance. . . . The smith then finished off his opponent with a thrust of his lance. A rope was immediately wound around the neck of the corpse, with was dragged to a gallows and hanged. In this example you may see what justice is among the Franj!

Amin Maalouf, *The Crusades Through Arab Eyes*, tr. Jon Rothschild, 1984

HUMILIATING THE INCA

A few months after the execution of the Inca monarch Atahuallpa in 1533, his nephew Manco was crowned as his successor by the Spanish conquistadors who had captured the Inca Empire Manco. At first he co-operated with them, but their gross ill-treatment of him would later force him to escape to the rain forest, where he created a small Inca empire of his own.

The abuse of the Inca increased during his captivity. Manco was later reported to have said that 'he was urinated upon by Alonso de Toro, [Gregorio] Setiel, Alonso de Mesa, Pedro Pizarro and [Francisco de] Solares, all citizens of this city. He also said that they burned his eyelashes with a lighted candle.' Manco said on another occasion: 'I rebelled more on account of the abuses done to me than because of the gold they took from me, for they called me a dog and they struck me, and took my wives and the lands that I farmed. I gave Juan Pizarro 1,300 gold bricks and two thousand golden objects: bracelets, cups and other pieces. I also gave seven gold and silver pitchers. They said to me: "Dog, give us gold. If not, you will be burned."' Cristóbal de Molina reported that 'they stole everything he had, leaving him nothing. They kept him imprisoned for many days on this occasion, guarded day and night. They treated him very, very disgracefully, urinating on him and sleeping with his wives, and he was deeply distressed.' Almagro's son repeated these accusations and added that Manco's persecutors 'urinated and spat in his face, struck and beat him, called him a dog, kept him with a chain round his neck in a public place where people passed.' These squalid reports were all repeated by men who hated the Pizarros, but they had a basis of truth. A royal emissary, Bishop Berlanga, reported to the King: 'Any claim that the Inca should serve no one has been a fraud. For the Governor has exploited him, and so have any others who wished.'

John Hemming, *The Conquest of the Incas*, 1970

A PHILOSOPHICAL OUTSIDER

Benedict Spinoza was born in Amsterdam in 1632, the son of a prominent Jewish figure. Spinoza was a gentle yet determined man, and his philosophical opinions, which brought about his lapse from the orthodox faith, caused great scandal. He became a lens-maker and died in The Hague in 1677.

Benedict Spinoza, the first name being the conventionally latinized equivalent of the Hebrew *Baruch*, was first educated in the traditional Hebrew studies, and he spoke Spanish at school; he learnt Portuguese from his father, Latin from a German scholar, and Dutch from his neighbours. He was a Hebrew scholar and author of a Hebrew grammar; and his surviving library shows that he was a continuous reader of Spanish literature of all kinds. Little is known of his early scientific education, or of how he came to choose the highly skilled craft of lens-making as his profession; but it provided him with a livelihood in association with the new sciences, particularly optics, in which he was deeply interested. He could do his intricate work alone and as his own master.

Jewish orthodoxy, like Christian orthodoxy, had been profoundly shaken by the new ideas of the Renaissance and by the natural philosophy of Galileo, Kepler, Bacon and Descartes. Spinoza grew up among excommunications and recantations and heard first hand of many violent scenes of religious doubt and persecution. The Jews were not yet citizens in Holland and their leaders feared that the outbreak of free thought in their community would alarm the Dutch, who had already to contend with every variety of Christian schism sheltering within their borders. Amsterdam had become a centre of small sects and of violent religious discussions in many languages. To Spinoza, as to most strictly educated but critical Jews, the interpretation of the Bible presented an insurmountable obstacle; neither in its literal interpretation nor in the figurative or allegorical interpretations suggested by earlier Jewish philosophers could Biblical doctrine be made compatible with natural science and adult logic. Even as a very young man Spinoza was in the habit of acknowledging this incompatibility. Although he had no desire to agitate or to proselytize, he could not be persuaded by bribes or threats to renounce or to conceal his sceptical conclusions. He continued to attend the Synagogue at intervals and he always behaved as a natural member of the Jewish community. But his scepticism was too dangerous to be ignored and warnings were useless. He could not promise to pretend to believe what he did not believe. At the age of twenty-four and three years after his father's death, he was finally excommunicated with all the solemnity and violence of language which is appropriate to such occasions. He was an outcast from the only community to which he naturally belonged.

Stuart Hampshire, *Spinoza*, 1951

PUNISHMENT FOR THE DECEMBRISTS

Following the attempted revolution against Tsar Nicholas I by a number of noblemen in December 1825, the Supreme Criminal Court proposed a list of punishments for the 121 men found guilty.

On the basis of these considerations, the majority of the Court decided to submit to Your Imperial Majesty's consideration the following statement of sentences and punishments:

1. For all criminals who by the special nature and seriousness of their crimes cannot be included under any category, death through quartering.

2. For all criminals belonging to the first category, the penalty of death through beheading.

3. All criminals in the second category are to be given what in our laws is called political death, i.e., lay their heads on the scaffold and then be sent to forced labor in perpetuity.

4. Criminals in the third category, after deprivation of ranks and nobility, are to be sent to forced labor forever.

5. Criminals in the fourth, fifth, sixth, and seventh categories, upon deprivation of ranks and nobility, are to be exiled to forced labor for a specified period and, upon completion of this period, to perpetual settlement [in Siberia].

6. Criminals in the eighth category, after deprivation of ranks and nobility, perpetually banished to settlement [in Siberia].

7. Criminals in the ninth category, after deprivation of ranks and nobility, are to be enrolled as soldiers, without [right to] promotion.

8. Criminals in the tenth category, upon deprivation of ranks and nobility, are to be enrolled as soldiers with right to promotion.

9. Criminals in the eleventh category are to be deprived of ranks and enrolled as soldiers with right to promotion.

Quoted in Marc Raeff, *The Decembrist Movement*, 1966

ALEXANDER PUSHKIN SALUTES THE DECEMBRIST EXILES

Deep in the Siberian mine,
Keep your patience proud;
The bitter toil shall not be lost,
The rebel thought unbowed.

The sister of misfortune, Hope,
In the under-darkness dumb

Speaks joyfully courage to your heart:
The day desired will come.

And love and friendship pour to you
Across the darkened doors,
Even as round your galley-beds
My free music pours.

The heavy-clanging chains will fall,
The walls will crumble as a word;
And Freedom greet you in the light,
And brothers give you back the sword.

From *Poems of Five Decades*, tr. Max Eastman, 1955

A DECEMBRIST REPLIES

The sound of your prophetic harp,
Impassioned, came to us at last.
Swiftly our hands reached for the sword,
But found that shackles held them fast.

Yet, singer, fret not: we are proud
Of these our chains as of our fate.
Locked in our prison cells, we scoff
At the rulers of the State.

Our grievous toil will not be lost,
The spark will quicken into flame;
Our people, blindfolded no more,
A new allegiance will proclaim.

Beating our shackles into swords,
Liberty's torch we will relight,
And she will overwhelm the Tsars,
While nations waken in the night.

A. I. Odoevsky, 1827; from *Poems of Five Decades*, tr. Valentine Snow, 1955

FOUR JOYLESS YEARS

Fyodor Dostoevsky looks back on the effect of his banishment after being sentenced for revolutionary activity and undergoing mock execution in 1849.

I was guilty and I fully acknowledge it. I was convicted of intent to act against the regime (but no more than that). I was sentenced justly and in conformity with the law. My long, arduous, and painful experience has sobered me and, in many respects, changed my ideas. But then, then I was blind and I believed in various theories and utopias. When I left for Siberia, I at least had the consolation of having conducted myself honorably during the trial; I did not try to blame others for my crime and was even ready to sacrifice my own interests if I saw that a confession from me could shield others from misfortune. But I took it upon myself not to confess everything, and for that reason my punishment was of greater severity. For two years running prior to that I had been suffering from strange mental ills. I lapsed into hypochondria. There were even moments when I would lose my sanity. I was terribly irritable, hypersensitive, and prone to distort the most ordinary facts, investing them with a different appearance and dimension. But I felt that, although this disease did have a strong and pernicious effect upon my life, it would have been a poor and even shameful justification. Moreover, I didn't understand that too clearly then. Forgive me for giving you all these details. But be magnanimous and hear me out to the end.

Then came the period of penal servitude—4 years of a bleak, horrible existence. I lived with brigands, men devoid of human feeling, men with perverted values; and during all those four joyless years I did not see, nor could I possibly have seen, anything except the darkest and the ugliest aspects of life. I did not have by my side a single living creature with whom I could have exchanged a heartfelt word; I endured hunger, cold, sickness, work that was beyond my strength, and the hatred of my fellow convicts, who revenged themselves on me for my being a nobleman and an officer. But I swear to you, what caused me the greatest suffering was the fact that I came to understand my delusions, and the realization that I had been cut off from society by exile and that I could no longer be useful to it and serve it to the best of my abilities, aspirations, and talents. I know that I was condemned for my dreams, for my ideas.

> Fyodor Dostoevsky (1821–81), *Selected Letters*, ed. Joseph Frank and David I. Goldstein, tr. Andrew MacAndrew, 1987

THE DESTRUCTION OF THE CHEROKEE NATION

In [1828], Andrew Jackson replaced John Quincy Adams at the White House. As in more recent times, the cowboys had hijacked the republic. Jackson's United States would be no liberal utopia but a white settler conquest-state bent on expanding at the cost of Indians and blacks. The ideals the Cherokees had adopted with such fervor were no longer held by those in charge.

Emboldened by this, Georgia declared the Cherokee Nation's existence null and void. It became a crime for the Cherokee parliament to meet within state limits, which according to Georgia included New Echota, Etowah, and most other towns. Discovery of gold lent urgency to this aggression. Georgia made it illegal for Cherokees to dig their own minerals, while white prospectors, assisted by the brutal Georgia Guard, invaded their land. The Indians who ended up in white courts over the trouble that ensued were forbidden to testify—even in their own defense—on the grounds that they were not Christian. The Cherokees' federal agent pointed out that Muslims were allowed to testify in British courts, saying, 'The religion of the Cherokees is as good as that of Mahomet.' But his logic did no good. The real reason was that Indians were not white.

In 1830 Congress narrowly passed Jackson's Indian Removal Bill, which affected all of the Five Civilized Tribes: Cherokee, Cree, Choctaw, Chickasaw, and Seminole. One by one the others gave in and left; the Cherokees did not. John Ross, who had been elected Principal Chief in 1828, saw, as Dragging Canoe had seen sixty years earlier, that 'the advancing banners of the same greedy host' would follow the Indian everywhere. Determined to fight removal all the way, he went to Washington and took the Cherokee case to the Supreme Court.

While there, he met delegates from the Iroquois League and gave them a timely warning:

Brothers: The tradition of our Fathers . . . tells us that this great and extensive Continent was once the sole and exclusive abode of our race. . . . Ever since [the whites came] we have been made to drink of the bitter cup of humiliation; treated like dogs . . . our country and the graves of our Fathers torn from us . . . through a period of upwards of 200 years, rolled back, nation upon nation [until] we find ourselves fugitives, vagrants and strangers in our own country. . . .

It is one of history's darkest ironies that a Cherokee had saved Jackson's life in 1814. This man, Junaluska, went to Washington to make a personal appeal. Jackson listened impatiently, then said, 'Sir, your audience is ended, there is nothing I can do for you.' In the best Cherokee tradition, Junaluska kept his temper, but later, when he saw a woman die after being torn from her home, he raged: 'Oh my God if I had known . . . I would have killed him that day at the Horseshoe.'

In the summer of 1838 the United States army rounded up all 16,000 Cherokees and confined them for months in disease-infested camps. The trek west, begun that autumn, has been known ever since as the Trail of Tears. For the whole winter, the hungry, frostbitten people shuffled at bayonet point across a thousand miles of frozen woods and prairie. By the time it was over, 4,000—one quarter of the Cherokee Nation—had died.

Ronald Wright, *Stolen Continents: The Indian Story*, 1992

CHEATING THE NAVAHOS

A custom grew up of having horse races between the Navahos and the soldiers. All the Navahos looked forward to these contests, and on racing days hundreds of men, women, and children would dress in their brightest costumes and ride their finest ponies to Fort Wingate. On a crisp sunny morning in September several races were run, but the special race of the day was scheduled at noon. It was to be between Pistol Bullet (a name given Manuelito by the soldiers) on a Navaho pony, and a lieutenant on a quarter horse. Many bets were made on this race—money, blankets, livestock, beads, whatever a man had to use for a bet. The horses jumped off together, but in a few seconds everyone could see that Pistol Bullet (Manuelito) was in trouble. He lost control of his pony, and it ran off the track. Soon everyone knew that Pistol Bullet's bridle rein had been slashed with a knife. The Navahos went to the judges—who were all soldiers—and demanded that the race be run again. The judges refused; they declared the lieutenant's quarter horse was the winner. Immediately the soldiers formed a victory parade for a march into the fort to collect their bets.

Infuriated by this trickery, the Navahos stormed after them, but the fort's gates were slammed shut in their faces. When a Navaho attempted to force an entrance, a sentinel shot him dead.

What happened next was written down by a white soldier chief, Captain Nicholas Hodt:

The Navahos, squaws, and children ran in all directions and were shot and bayo-neted. I succeeded in forming about twenty men . . . I then marched out to the east side of the post: there I saw a soldier murdering two little children and a woman. I hallooed immediately to the soldier to stop. He looked up, but did not obey my order. I ran up as quick as I could, but could not get there soon enough to prevent him from killing the two innocent children and wounding severely the squaw. I ordered his belts to be taken off and taken prisoner to the post . . . Meanwhile the colonel had given orders to the officer of the day to have the artillery [mountain howitzers] brought out to open upon the Indians. The sergeant in charge of the mountain howitzers pretended not to understand the order given, for he considered it as an unlawful order; but being cursed by the officer of the day, and threatened, he had to execute the order or else get himself in trouble.

Dee Brown, *Bury My Heart at Wounded Knee*, 1971

DREYFUS AND HIS WIFE EXCHANGE LETTERS

Salvation Islands,
January 6th, 1897.

My dear Lucie,

Once more I feel the need to talk to you and let my pen run on. The uncertain equilibrium which I manage to maintain with difficulty through-out a long month of incredible suffering is upset as soon as I receive your dear letters, always so impatiently awaited. They awake in me a whole world of sensations and impressions that I have suppressed for thirty long days, and I ask myself in vain what can be the meaning of life when so many human beings are called upon to suffer in this way. Besides, I have endured so much these last few months that I come to you to warm my frozen heart. I know, too, darling, that I keep on saying the same things, and have done so since the first day of this strange drama, for my thought is single, like yours, and like the determination that must support and inspire us.

And when I come and chat with you like this for a few moments—oh, such fugitive moments, despite the fact that my thoughts never leave you for an instant, day or night—it seems as though I *live* this short space of time with you, feel your heart sighing against mine. And then I want to clasp you in my arms, take your hands, and say to you once more: 'Yes, all this is dreadful, but you must not let one moment of discouragement creep into your soul, any more than it does into mine. As I am a Frenchman and a father, you must be a Frenchwoman and a mother. The name our dear children bear must be washed clean of this horrible stain. There must not be left one single Frenchman who doubts our honour.'

That is our goal, every the same.

But, alas, if one can be stoical in the face of death, it is difficult to be so in the face of every day's suffering, and the lacerating pain of wondering when this dreadful nightmare will end. We have lived with it so long, if you can call it living when you are suffering without respite.

All this time I have lived in the hope, always doomed to disappointment, of a better to-morrow. I have struggled, not against the weaknesses of the flesh, for they leave me indifferent (perhaps because I am haunted by other preoccupations), but against weaknesses of the mind and heart. And then in those moments of unspeakable distress, of almost unbearable pain, all the greater for being kept under restraint, I feel that I want to cry out to you across the space that separates us: 'Ah, dear Lucie, run to those who direct our country's affairs and whose mission it is to defend us. Make them give you their warm and active support. Make them use every means in their power to shed light upon the dreadful mystery, and discover the truth. That is all we want.'...

*

February 1st, 1899.

My dear Alfred,

Your letter of December 24th, which I have just received, moved me very deeply. You can imagine how I devoured that dear letter. I read it and re-read it, and am not ashamed to tell you that I bathed it many times in my tears. Who would not have moments of weakness in a situation so sad and terrible as ours? For a long time I gave way to my emotion. I could not help it. I had waited so long for news. Until you have passed through such things, you do not realise what terrible suffering can be caused by anxiety. You feel so helpless to do anything for a creature who means all the world to you, and is dearer than life itself. You know that he is tortured by the most undeserved misfortune, and that he is in a situation where he needs so much to have a loving face near him. And you are left there, eating your heart out with anxiety, unable to do the least little thing to mitigate his sufferings. It is thoughts like these, added to our great grief, that sometimes make me utter cries of pain and rebellion.

You see, darling, my character is far less admirable than yours. You are a thousand times more to be pitied than I, and yet you endure your sufferings with a power of will and energy only to be found in a strong nature like yours. You never utter a complaint, never a word of bitterness against anybody. You show a nobility of soul that I admire beyond words. I wish I were capable of it, too, but alas, it seems beyond me. In this dreadful struggle it is *I* who ought to offer *you* words of calm and comfort, but actually *you* show *me* the path I should follow. And I ought to blush for shame, with your example before me, if I ever utter bitter words and let the cup of my heart run over.

I am all the more sorry to have given way to my feelings because there is no necessity to be discouraged. I am full of hope, and am absolutely convinced that the truth will be discovered and justice done, and that you will at long last receive the reparation due to you through the universal recognition of your innocence. Set your mind at rest, my beloved husband; the truth will come out, and France will have reason to be proud of the nobility of one of her sons. It all takes a long time, it is true, and your impatience is only too well justified, but what is time compared with the goal to be attained? . . .

Dreyfus: His Life and Letters, tr. Dr Betty Morgan, 1937

WEEP I COULD NO MORE

As the Boer War dragged on, the British introduced an aggressive policy to weaken the will of the Boers, who were mostly farmers, to continue. By 1900 the farms of men still fighting were burned, and their wives and children taken to centres which were christened 'concentration camps'.

Concentration camps in the Boer War must not be confused with the German camps of the Second World War. The British camps were set up for an entirely different reason and were meant to house the refugees in comfort and safety. However, their administration soon ran into such difficulties that conditions became very bad. The health of the occupants was a major problem. The biggest worry was that an epidemic of typhoid would break out . . .

Early in 1901 critical accounts of conditions in the camps began to reach Britain. Opposition papers were full of worrying reports about the way they were being run. Inspectors were ordered to visit the camps and report to the government. However, after the publication of Emily Hobhouse's heart-rending book and articles, it was felt that something more was needed to counteract the allegations of mismanagement. A commission of women was sent out to visit all the camps, and the government produced a Blue Paper with detailed reports of the situation in each. By this time there were 45 concentration camps. They varied in size, but the largest contained more than 5,000 people . . .

The exact number of Boers who died in the camps is still the subject of argument. After the war the official archivist of the Transvaal government, P. L. A. Goldman, fixed the figure at 27,927, of which more than 26,000 were women and children. . . . Since the entire Afrikander population of the two Republics was a good deal less than 100,000, the loss was catastrophic. . . .

An entry in [Alie Badenhorst's] diary during December 1901 reads:

I never thought to see with my own eyes so much misery . . . tents emptied by death. I went one day to the hospital and there lay a child of nine years to wrestle alone with death. I asked . . . where I could find the child's mother. The answer was that the mother had died a week before, the father is in [a prisoner-of-war camp in] Ceylon, that very morning her sister of 11 died. I pitied the poor little sufferer as I looked upon her . . . There was not even a tear in my own eyes, for weep I could no more. I stood beside her and watched until a stupefying grief overwhelmed my soul . . . I lamented like the prophet, 'I am the man that has seen affliction by the rod of His wrath.'

The chaplain of the Bethulie concentration camp kept a diary between August 1901 when he joined the staff of the camp and the end of October when he collapsed physically and mentally. It makes harrowing reading— the days filled with suffering and death, the nights broken by shrill whistles calling for another corpse to be taken to the mortuary tent:

O for a change of work! The continual cry is 'Minheer, kom tog heer' [Sir, please come here], 'Minheer, gaat tog daar' [Sir, please go there], and one grows weary of scenes of suffering and sorrow. . . . always face to face with helpless, hopeless, impotent despairing; always face to face with Decay, Change, Death; always the same close, stifling, little tent.

Emanoel Lee, *To the Bitter End*, 1986

LEOPOLD BLOOM AND THE IRISH NATIONALISTS

Bloom was talking and talking with John Wyse and he quite excited with his dunducketymudcoloured mug on him and his old plumeyes rolling about.
—Persecution, says he, all the history of the world is full of it. Perpetuating national hatred among nations.
—But do you know what a nation means? says John Wyse.
—Yes, says Bloom.
—What is it? says John Wyse.
—A nation? says Bloom. A nation is the same people living in the same place.
—By God, then, says Ned, laughing, if that's so I'm a nation for I'm living in the same place for the past five years.
So of course everyone had the laugh at Bloom and says he, trying to muck out of it:
—Or also living in different places.
—That covers my case, says Joe.
—What is your nation if I may ask? says the citizen.
—Ireland, says Bloom. I was born here. Ireland.
The citizen said nothing only cleared the spit out of his gullet and, gob, he spat a Red bank oyster out of him right in the corner.
—After you with the push, Joe, says he, taking out his handkerchief to swab himself dry.

—Here you are, citizen, says Joe. Take that in your right hand and repeat after me the following words.

The muchtreasured and intricately embroidered ancient Irish facecloth attributed so Solomon of Droma and Manus Tomaltach og MacDonogh, authors of the Book of Ballymote, was then carefully produced and called forth prolonged admiration. No need to dwell on the legendary beauty of the cornerpieces, the acme of art, wherein one can distinctly discern each of the four evangelists in turn presenting to each of the four masters his evangelical symbol, a bogoak sceptre, a North American puma (a far nobler king of beasts than the British article, be it said in passing), a Kerry calf and a golden eagle from Carrantuohill. The scenes depicted on the emunctory field, showing our ancient duns and raths and cromlechs and grianauns and seats of learning and maledictive stones, are as wonderfully beautiful and the pigments as delicate as when the Sligo illuminators gave free rein to their artistic fantasy long long ago in the time of the Barmecides. Glendalough, the lovely lakes of Killarney, the ruins of Clonmacnois, Cong Abbey, Glen Inagh and the Twelve Pins, Ireland's Eye, the Green Hills of Tallaght, Croagh Patrick, the brewery of Messrs Arthur Guinness, Son and Company (Limited), Lough Neagh's banks, the vale of Ovoca, Isolde's tower, the Mapas obelisk, Sir Patrick Dun's hospital, Cape Clear, the glen of Aherlow, Lynch's castle, the Scotch house, Rathdown Union Workhouse at Loughlinstown, Tullamore jail, Castleconnel rapids, Kilballymachshonakill, the cross at Monasterboice, Jury's Hotel, S. Patrick's Purgatory, the Salmon Leap, Maynooth college refectory, Curley's hole, the three birthplaces of the first duke of Wellington, the rock of Cashel, the bog of Allen, the Henry Street Warehouse, Fingal's Cave—all these moving scenes are still there for us today rendered more beautiful still by the waters of sorrow which have passed over them and by the rich incrustations of time.

—Show us over the drink, says I. Which is which?

—That's mine, says Joe, as the devil said to the dead policeman.

—And I belong to a race too, says Bloom, that is hated and persecuted. Also now. This very moment. This very instant.

Gob, he near burnt his fingers with the butt of his old cigar.

—Robbed, says he. Plundered. Insulted. Persecuted. Taking what belongs to us by right. At this very moment, says he, putting up his fist, sold by auction in Morocco like slaves or cattle.

—Are you talking about the new Jerusalem? says the citizen.

—I'm talking about injustice, says Bloom.

—Right, says John Wyse. Stand up to it then with force like men.

That's an almanac picture for you. Mark for a softnosed bullet. Old lardyface standing up to the business end of a gun. Gob, he'd adorn a sweepingbrush, so he would, if he only had a nurse's apron on him. And then he collapses all of a sudden, twisting around all the opposite, as limp as a wet rag.

—But it's no use, says he. Force, hatred, history, all that. That's not life for men and women, insult and hatred. And everybody knows that it's the very opposite of that that is really life.

—What? says Alf.

—Love, says Bloom. I mean the opposite of hatred. I must go now, says he to John Wyse. Just round to the court a moment to see if Martin is there. If he comes just say I'll be back in a second. Just a moment.

James Joyce, Ulysses, 1922

MUSTAFA KEMAL TURNS THE KURDS INTO SECOND-CLASS CITIZENS

As a first step towards the modern Turkey which was his vision, he promulgated a new constitution, just one year after the Treaty of Lausanne had laid down careful safeguards for minority groups. The largest of these, the Kurds, occupied about a third of the land mass of the new state of Turkey and made up about one fifth of the population. The Treaty of Lausanne, signed so soon after the bloody massacres of Armenians and the bitter war between Turks and Greeks, had stipulated that

no restriction shall be placed on the free use of any language by a Turkish national, neither in private relations nor in commerce, nor in matters of religion, press or publications, nor in public meetings. Notwithstanding the existence of an official language, Turkish nationals whose language is not Turkish will be given the right to oral use of their language before the tribunals.

Even when Mustafa Kemal had taken over in all but name, Turkey had agreed that this clause, and others like it protecting the rights of minorities, should become part of the fundamental law of the country, so that subsequent laws, regulations or decrees could not supersede them. With hands metaphorically on their hearts, the Turkish negotiators asked how they might be suspected of wanting to tamper with such laws; after all, there were seventy-five Kurdish MPs in the Grand National Assembly in Ankara, a clear indication that they spoke for the whole country. Certainly the provisions guaranteeing the right of free speech to minorities would be upheld.

That was in 1923. On 3 March 1924, having dissolved the Grand National Assembly, Mustafa Kemal issued a decree prohibiting the use of the Kurdish language, banning education in that language, and making illegal all publications in Kurdish. His aim was clearly to unify his country, to set all the peoples of Turkey on an even footing as they set off on their new modern adventure—secularization of the state, with the mystical dervish orders banned, the Latin alphabet replacing Arabic script, the fez and the veil, those symbols of submission to Islam, eliminated, the privileges of European states abolished, and pragmatic economic policies adopted. It was a recipe which proved hugely successful in transforming Turkey from the ailing heartland of a bankrupt empire into a modern state able to compete with its European neighbours; at the same time, by ignoring its largest minority group it laid the seeds of the trouble which today erupts in violence and bloodshed in the villages of the eastern provinces.

The Kurds became, overnight, second-class citizens in their own country. Living in the poorest regions of Turkey, they were still forced into additional expense each time they had to deal with authority: banned from using their own tongue, they had to have intermediaries to speak for them in all dealings with the state. They became ready recruits for the Turkish army, not always because they were poor and needed a living; sometimes too because young men were persuaded that it would be useful to learn the skills of their enemies, how to handle weapons, where to plant bombs. In the army those Kurds who joined at the instigation of separatists and nationalists had their prejudices reinforced: they had to put up with plenty of abuse, just as they did when they left their homeland for the cities of the west. Recruiting sergeants would ask them for the numbers of their caves when they took their addresses, and they had a hard time on the parade ground or ranges until they learnt enough Turkish to respond quickly to orders. The Turkish army was always the guardian and inheritor of Mustafa Kemal's ideas, the protector of his values; but in that army the Kurds were inferior beings, rarely rising to senior level unless they had become assimilated into the Turkish mainstream.

John Bulloch and Harvey Morris, *No Friends but the Mountains*, 1992

A LAST LETTER

The poet Osip Mandelstam had angered Stalin by writing a witty epigram about him. After being exiled to Voronezh he returned to Moscow but was rearrested in May 1938. This time he was sentenced to five years' forced labour near Vladivostok. Soon after this letter to his family was written, a group of criminal prisoners stole his rations and beat him up. He was driven nearly mad, and was forced outside his prison hut, where he begged for food 'like an animal'. He died on 27 December 1938.

Dear Shura! My address: Vladivostok, USVITL, barracks No. 11.

I got five years for counterrevolutionary activity by decree of the Special Tribunal. The transport left Butyrki Prison in Moscow on the 9th of September and we arrived on the 12th of October. I'm in very poor health, utterly exhausted, emaciated, and almost beyond recognition. I don't know if there's any sense in sending clothes, food, and money, but try just the same. I'm freezing without proper clothes.

Darling Nadenka, are you alive, my precious? Shura, write me at once about Nadya. This is a transit point. I wasn't picked for Kolyma. I may have to spend the winter here.

My dear ones, I kiss you. Osia.

Shurochka, one thing more. We've gone out to work these last few days. That has lifted my spirits. People are sent from our camp, as from a transit point, to regular camps. I was apparently 'sifted out' so I must get ready to spend the winter here. So please send me a telegram and wire me some money.

> Osip Mandelstam, *The Complete Critical Prose and Letters*, ed. Jane Gary Harris, tr. J. G. H. and Constance Link, 1979

A JEWISH BOY SURVIVES IN WARTIME BERLIN

Hidden dangers lurked everywhere. Every civilian was a potential Gestapo agent, every policeman a potential accomplice of the Gestapo. The sight of police barracks or prisons, whenever I chanced to ride past them, filled me with foreboding. I no longer dared to go visiting factories, not even those to which I had enjoyed free access for some time.

As the weeks went by, however, my agitation subsided. I had alerted my brothers and poor Kohn/Konn for nothing; the dreaded house-search failed to materialise. Nor did my visit to the electroplating works produce any unpleasant consequences for my parents or for my headmaster.

Soon the temptation was too strong for me: I went back to my old habit of frequenting various danger-spots in Berlin.

My brother Leon used to tell me I was being reckless. Yet basically we were both up to the same thing. Like myself, Leon defied all the laws of National Socialist ethnology by possessing an 'Aryan' skull and a nose that was not at all 'Jewish'. Consequently, we were attracted by the idea of being eye-witnesses in places where 'Jewish'-looking Jews could not venture without risk. The only difference was that Leon took it further than I did. He made himself a bogus uniform in which he even dared to enter the sports stadium and mingle with the SA and SS men when Goebbels was giving a speech.

The black boots and breeches looked as if he had been poured into them. No one would ever have thought that Leon had tailored his own 'SS trousers' from a couple of father's old overcoats. Roaring through the Tiergarten on his motorbike, he certainly looked more like an SS man than a student from the Jewish *Gymnasium*. Ah, but what if someone were to look more closely? Leon's get-up lacked the cap and badges of a real uniform. . . .

Leon ignored my warnings. He kept up this 'military' style of dress for years. During the war his bogus uniform was to play an important role, and not once was he stopped by police or SS patrols. However, we had no way of knowing that in 1938.

It was not simply the incompleteness of his disguise that aroused my misgivings. If he felt he needed that kind of camouflage for his safety, at least he ought also to have felt a certain revulsion against wearing it. Yet revulsion was the last thing he showed. On the contrary, he took the most elaborate care of his 'uniform'. A whole ritual surrounded the daily polishing of his boots to a mirror-like shine, and he never wearied of making little improvements to the outfit here and there. It seemed almost every day that I saw him standing in front of the mirror, examining the fit of his clothes with a critical eye. Tirelessly, he would unpick yet another seam, re-sew it, iron it flat, and try the garment on again. . . .

Towards evening, Leon came home from work. 'But you're not wearing your star!' I said to him in amazement.

'What, me walk around with a yellow star on my chest? I'm not daft! I'm not going to sabotage all my options for the future!'

This struck me as extremely dubious. Granted, in terms of the general perception of such matters, no one in our family looked 'Jewish'. That fact might possibly be of vital importance at some time in the future. Might it even justify the risk of infringing police regulations?

'But what do you do about it at work?' I wanted to know.

Leon proceeded to demonstrate. The yellow star on his coat was sewn on only halfway round. The top half thus formed a flap, which with the aid of an arrangement of press studs could be fixed in either the up or down position. In the down position, the star was completely invisible.

'But, Leon, isn't that dangerous?'

'Nowhere near as dangerous as walking round with it showing the whole time!' he retorted.

Ezra BenGershôm, *David*, 1988

COPING WITH THE SOUTH AFRICAN POLICE

I took my hat and went out; it was after midnight, I did not have a special Pass, Native public transport had stopped three hours ago. My pride had been hurt and I was too snobbish to lock myself in the servant's outdoor lavatory and spend the night there; I determined to brave the police and the tsotsis, to walk the nine miles to Sophiatown. Two hours later, on the Jan Smuts Avenue, I was surprised by a police block.

'Nag Pass, kaffir,' the white constable said, shining a torch in my face, 'Night Special.'

I pulled my hat off and came to military attention; I squeezed a sob into my voice, shook my body with fear, trembling before the authority confronting me.

'My baas, my crown,' I said, in my textbook Afrikaans. 'I have a School Pass, my baas.'

'Skool kinders is almal aan die slaap,' he said.

'Yes, my baasie,' I said. 'I was very stupid tonight, I was nearly led into the ways of the devil. This kaffir meid, my baas, was trying to trick me into sleeping in her room, but I know it is against the law, my baasie; so I said to her: the law says I must not sleep on the property of the white master. I know I didn't have a Special Pass, but I said to myself, this is wrong, you must go. This is the truth, my baasie.'

'Jy's'n goei kaffir,' he said, becoming sickeningly paternal, 'a very good kaffir. Let me see your Pass—you must be careful, these kaffir women are bad, very bad. You must learn good at school and be a good Native; don't run after these bad women and don't mix with the trouble-makers.'

'Hier is dit, my baas,' I said, 'the Pass.'

'Ek sien,' he said, looking at the Pass under the torch light. 'Now, tell the baas where you're going?'

'Sophiatown, my baas,' I said. 'I'm very sorry to be out so late, my baas; it's this kaffir meid, my baas, very bad; she delay me until it's too late for the buses, then she says I must sleep, but I say no, it's wrong; also I see, my baas, the clothes of a man, and I say to myself, trouble; but she try to stop me, say it belong to her brother, but I say she lie and I go home.'

'You must watch these meide,' the constable said, with fatherly concern. 'You watch out for them, they're the devil's work; now, listen here, weg is jy, gone with you.'

'Baie dankie, baasie,' I said, bowing my head several times, 'thank you very much, my baasie.'

'Don't let me catch you again,' he said, playfully kicking my bottom, but there was enough power behind it to make it playfully brutal.

'Thank you, my baasie.'

I was rubbing my hands over the spot where I was kicked, hopping forward and pretending a playful pain, all to the amusement of the white police constable and his African aides. Bloody swine, I mumbled through the laughing and the clowning. Two police blocks later, played with the same obsequiousness, I arrived home.

Bloke Modisane, *Blame Me on History*, 1963

SILENCING A TEACHER

The South African government's powers to 'ban' people whose political views it disliked were immense. The details of what the 'banned' person could or could not do varied according to the individual case. This is the banning order on Clive Nettleton, a leading anti-apartheid activist who later went to live in Britain.

TO: CLIVE JAMES LEE NETTLETON
(I. N. 360914995)
55, 10TH STREET
PARKHURST
JOHANNESBURG

NOTICE IN TERMS OF SECTION 9(1) OF THE INTERNAL SECURITY ACT, 1950 (ACT 44 OF 1950)

WHEREAS I, JAMES THOMAS KRUGER, Minister of Justice, am satisfied that you engage in activities which endanger or are calculated to endanger the maintenance of public order, I hereby, in terms of section 9(1) of the Internal Security Act, 1950, prohibit you for a period commencing on the date on which this notice is delivered or tendered to you and expiring on 28 February 1983, from attending within the Republic of South Africa or the territory of South-West Africa—

(1)   any gathering contemplated in paragraph (a) of the said section 9(1); or
(2)   any gathering contemplated in paragraph (b) of the said section 9(1), of the nature, class or kind set out below:

(a) any social gathering, that is to say, any gathering at which the persons present also have social intercourse with one another;

(b) any political gathering, that is to say, any gathering at which any form of State or any principle or policy of the Government of a State is propagated, defended, attacked, criticised or discussed;

(c) any gathering of pupils or students assembled for the purpose of being instructed, trained or addressed by you, or from giving any educational instruction in any manner or form to any person other than a person of whom you are a parent.

Given under my hand at CAPE TOWN this 27th day of April, 1978.

[J. KRUGER]

MINISTER OF JUSTICE

Note: The Magistrate, Johannesburg, has in terms of section 9(1) of the abovementioned Act been empowered to authorize exceptions to the prohibitions contained in this notice.

ASIMBONANGA

Robben Island, where Nelson Mandela was held for many years, was a maximum security prison for political offenders. It lies in Table Bay, and can clearly be seen from parts of Cape Town. This song was written by the South African musician, Johnny Clegg. The three names in the last verse are those of political activists who died at the hands of the South African police.

Asimbonanga [We have not seen him]
Asimbonang'uMandela thina [We have not seen Mandela]
Laph'ekhona [In the place where he is]
Laph'ehlehli khona [In the place where he is kept].

Oh the sea is cold and the sky is grey
Look across the island into the bay
We are all islands till comes the day
We cross the burning water.

A seagull wings across the sea
Broken silence is what I dream
Who has the words to close the distance
Between you and me?

Asimbonanga [We have not seen him]
Asimbonang'umfowethu thina [We have not seen our brother]

Laph'ekhona [In the place where he is]
La wafela khona [In the place where he died]
[Voice:] Steven Biko
[Voice:] Victoria Mxgenge
[Voice:] Neil Aggett
Hey wena [Hey, you]
Hey wena nawe [Hey, you, and you as well]
Sizofik a nini la' siyakhona [When will we arrive at our true
    destination?]

Johnny Clegg

A BRUTAL WARDER

During Nelson Mandela's quarter-century in prison, one of the more unpleasant characters was Warrant Officer Van Rensburg.

He would lean against our food table and think nothing of urinating right there if the urge took him. He could stand alongside his puddle and be totally unaffected by its stench and pollution. Each day he would choose his victim for persecution. One day Fikile Bam and I became the targets. 'I want to see you,' he announced at the end of the day and took us to the lieutenant and charged us for lazing on the job. *Te lui om te werk* was the official classification in Afrikaans. We defended ourselves and invited the lieutenant to come and examine the pile of stone that testified our work. 'They are small piles,' Van Rensburg countered. The lieutenant said he would see for himself, and we had an inspection *in loco*. Van Rensburg was shocked to see our large piles of broken rock. 'That's a whole week's work,' he protested, but his lie was obvious, and the disgusted lieutenant did what a superior prison officer rarely does, chastised his subordinate in the presence of prisoners. 'You are telling lies,' he said. It was a vindication that heartened all of us. . . .

In 1972 we were plagued by Colonel Badenhorst who had been brought out of retirement. He was rude beyond words, and lazy. It was his duty as commanding officer to carry out a daily inspection. He came once a month. If you complained, his stock reaction was to abuse you with the most scurrilous Afrikaans swear words. 'Jou ma se moer!' was a favourite. When three judges, Steyn, Corbett and Theron, visited us, I complained on behalf of the prisoners. Badenhorst threatened me in their presence. 'You are going to get into trouble,' he said. I pointed out to the judges that that was a typical example of what was going on, on Robben Island. Badenhorst was transferred.

Our strategy of not arguing with the prison warders when accused of misdemeanours, but waiting for them to initiate charges against us worked. We defended ourselves before the higher ups and won practically every time and this toned down the warders' aggression against us.

The warders also learnt that surliness on their part resulted in a 'go slow' on ours, that if they wanted our cooperation they had to approach us in a civil manner. Sergeant Opperman wanted more lime from the quarry. 'Gentlemen,' he addressed us, 'the heavy rain yesterday washed away the markings on the roads. There is an urgent need for lime. Can you help?' We did.

Quoted in Fatima Meer, *Higher Than Hope*, 1990

HOW AN ASTRONOMER SAVED HIS SANITY IN THE GULAG

If the first thing you see each and every morning is the eyes of your cellmate who has gone insane, how then shall you save yourself during the coming day? Nikolai Aleksandrovich Kozyrev, whose brilliant career in astronomy was interrupted by his arrest, saved himself only by thinking of the eternal and infinite: of the order of the Universe—and of its Supreme Spirit; of the stars; of their internal state; and what Time and the passing of Time really are.

And in this way he began to discover a new field in physics. And only in this way did he succeed in surviving in the Dmitrovsk Prison. But his line of mental exploration was blocked by forgotten figures. He could not build any further—he had to have a lot of figures. Now just where could he get them in his solitary-confinement cell with its overnight kerosene lamp, a cell into which not even a little bird could enter? And the scientist prayed: 'Please, God! I have done everything I could. Please help me! Please help me continue!'

At this time he was entitled to receive one book every ten days (by then he was alone in the cell). In the meager prison library were several different editions of Demyan Bedny's *Red Concert*, which kept coming around to each cell again and again. Half an hour passed after his prayer; they came to exchange his book; and as usual, without asking anything at all, they pushed a book at him. It was entitled *A Course in Astrophysics*! Where had it come from? He simply could not imagine such a book in the prison library. Aware of the brief duration of this coincidence, Kozyrev threw himself on it and began to memorize everything he needed immediately, and everything he might need later on. In all, just two days had passed, and he had eight days left in which to keep his book, when there was an unscheduled inspection by the chief of the prison. His eagle eye noticed immediately. 'But you are an astronomer?' 'Yes.' 'Take this book away from him!' But its mystical arrival had opened the way for his further work, which he then continued in the camp in Norilsk.

Alexander Solzhenitsyn, The Gulag Archipelago, 1973–5

A CHALLENGE FROM THE LABOUR CAMP TO THE SOVIET AUTHORITIES

And for the cry from the well of 'Mama!'
and for the cross knocked from the cathedral,
and for your lie of 'Telegram!'
when it's an order for arrest—
You will dream of me, Russia!
In the curse of your triumphs,
the toil of your impotence,
in your bragging, carousing.
The nausea of your hangover—
Why is it that fright breaks out?
All is lamented, all laid to rest—
Who is it, makes you suddenly flinch?
Fling blame at the murdered—
Deny it, weasel out with lies.
All the same, I'll come before you,
look straight in your eyes!

Irina Ratushinskaya, *Beyond the Limit*, tr. Frances Padorr Brent and Carol J. Avins, 1987

AN END TO CONTACT WITH FOREIGNERS

Dr Andrei Sakharov was the old Soviet Union's greatest nuclear scientist, but from the 1970s he also became its most prominent dissident. He and his wife, Yelena Bonner ['Lusia'], protested so strongly against President Brezhnev's invasion of Afghanistan in December 1979 that it was decided to silence them.

January 22 [1980] was a Tuesday, the day the theoretical physics seminar met at FIAN. I followed my customary routine, ordering a car from the Academy's motor pool and leaving home at one-thirty. I intended to stop first at the Academy commissary to pick up some groceries and send the driver back with them, but we never got past the Krasnokholmsky Bridge, where a traffic patrol car overtook us. The policeman signaled us to pull over and stopped in front of us. My driver, surprised, mumbled that he hadn't broken any law. He got out to meet the policeman, who saluted and began examining his papers. From the front seat, I had a good view of what was happening. Hearing the car's rear door open, I glanced around and saw two men get in, flashing red IDs marked 'MVD' (of course, they were actually KGB).

They ordered the driver to follow the traffic patrol car to the Procurator's Office on Pushkin Street. He obeyed without a word. We were traveling slowly, and I could see that there were no other cars on the bridge, which apparently had been closed to traffic. We turned into a side street, and as we passed a phone booth, I asked the driver to stop for a moment so that I could call Lusia. The KGB agents reacted instantaneously: one blocked the door handle; the other ordered the driver: 'Don't stop, keep moving.' Then he turned to me and added: 'You can phone from the Procurator's Office.'

The car pulled into the Procurator's courtyard. I asked the driver to return the shopping bag to my house, adding that we would be too late to stop at the commissary. I got out of the car and, ringed by KGB agents, was escorted to the fourth floor, where my 'chats' with Malyarov in 1973 and Gusev in 1977 had taken place. This time I was told to enter a door marked: 'Alexander Rekunkov, Deputy Procurator General.'

Rekunkov was seated behind a desk, facing the door. I don't remember what he looked like. Several other persons were seated at a table to my left, but they remained silent. Rekunkov invited me to be seated.

'Why didn't you send a summons instead of shanghaiing me?' I asked. 'I've always obeyed the Procurator's summonses.'

Rekunkov replied: 'I gave orders to have you brought here owing to the extraordinary circumstances and the great urgency involved. I have been instructed to read you a decree passed by the Presidium:

In view of A. D. Sakharov's systematic actions which discredit him as a recipient of State awards and in response to many suggestions made by the Soviet public, the Presidium of the USSR Supreme Soviet, acting on the basis of Article 40 of the General Regulations on Orders, Medals and Honorary Titles, has decided to deprive Andrei Dmitrievich Sakharov of the title Hero of Socialist Labor and all his State awards.

'It has been decided to banish A. D. Sakharov from Moscow to a place that will put an end to his contacts with foreigners,' Rekunkov continued. He looked up and added: 'The place that has been selected is Gorky, which is off limits to foreigners. Please sign here to acknowledge that you have been informed of the decree's contents.'

He handed me a typewritten sheet of paper on which I saw the last part of the decree and the typed signatures of Brezhnev and Mikhail Georgadze, the Presidium's secretary. It was undated and made no mention of banishment . . .

'Let's get to the practical details. You're to leave for Gorky at once. Your wife may accompany you.'

'Can I go home first?'

'No, but you may call your wife.'

'Where will we meet?'

'I can't tell you that. She'll be picked up. How much time will she need to pack?'

'I don't know; probably a couple of hours.'

'All right. She'll be picked up two hours after you call her.'

Andrei Sakharov, Memoirs, 1991

A NEW CELL FOR A PALESTINIAN IN AN ISRAELI GAOL

'You can take the bag off,' commanded the warden.

The handcuffs fastened tightly around my wrists made it painful to pull off the bag, which fitted closely around my head. It was like surfacing from deep under water. My eagerness to breathe freely and my curiosity to examine my surroundings were stronger than the pain in my wrists, however. For several moments I inhaled air in huge gulps, gasping for more. My vision had blurred so it took my eyes a while to accustom themselves to the light.

There wasn't much to see. The room reminded me of a walk-in closet where brooms and buckets and cleaning supplies are kept in a home. It was tiny, no more than four feet by three feet, and painted red with a high ceiling. A huge black bucket occupied one corner, almost one-fourth of the whole room. Next to it sat a dirty plastic jug, half full of drinking water. The floor was rough and wet.

Even after the heavy door had been closed, I remained standing in the center of the cubicle, waiting for it to open again. I thought I was only there temporarily and would soon be moved to the interrogation room. It was hard to realize this might be my new cell. More anxious than tired, I tried to recline in the driest corner of the cell, leaning my head back against the wall, and facing the door.

I closed my eyes trying to absorb it all. How strangely and rapidly everything shifted in life, instantly altering old conceptions and ideas. The previous cell, where I had spent the last fifteen days, seemed large and luxurious compared to this one. An hour ago it had seemed like the most hideous place in the world. I could barely tolerate it.

The moment the door of the cell had closed, I felt deserted. The rest of the world was on the other side, a united front against me. Then the old giant within me rose to protest: 'You are not alone! So many others are with you or struggling for you. Don't give in to abandoned feelings! Don't give in to the present moment! In this instant you make your own history, so do it the best way you can. Think of twenty years from now when you will sit around a table with family and friends telling the story of this moment. Think how proud you will be to have survived when the mention of this moment comes up. Don't complain! The more severe it is, the more glorious it will be. It is paradoxical that, for freedom fighters, the moments of prison are the most heroic of our memories. You may be confined inside four walls right now but don't confine yourself within wrong conceptions. That would only help your enemy to pull you down. Your family is not alone in missing you, and you are not alone in confinement! Thousands are in even worse situations. This is not a cell, this is a womb from which you shall be delivered, stronger, purer! Think of it as a womb!'

Salma Khadra Jayyusi, ed., *Anthology of Modern Palestinian Literature*, 1992

AN ENGLISH-LANGUAGE NEWSPAPER AND THE DISAPPEARED

When the Argentine military took power in the coup of 1976 they decided to deal with the threat from Marxist insurgency by arresting large numbers of possible left-wing sympathizers and murdering them in secret. More than ten thousand people died altogether. Many were unconnected with any Marxist group, and were arrested in mistake for someone else, or simply because they were young.

A mother came to the *Buenos Aires Herald* in the evening. She had tried to get help to find her daughter everywhere else. She had been to police stations, courts, hospitals; called influential friends and finally had gone to the newspapers. Each news editor in town had told her, quite unabashed, that he could do nothing and that she ought to try the English-language paper, the smallest in the city. It was known that the *ingleses* stuck their neck out. We were suspected of having the protection of the British and United States embassies, as if such missions were capable of protecting anything. Any argument appeared unaccountably solid when it was necessary to deflect responsibility in times of crisis. But she was told that the *Herald* was the only paper that would report the news of her daughter's disappearance. The publicity might help if she went back to the police stations, army depots, courts and rabbis that she had resorted to earlier in her hopeless pilgrimage.

She had been advised of her daughter's arrest by an anonymous caller using a public telephone not far from where the girl had been picked up. The caller had made sure he was speaking to the right person, apologised for not introducing himself, and described how and where the girl had been arrested.

The mother was short, plump, with hair slightly greying and with an almost unlined face. Her features were tender, as of fantasy mothers men and women conjure when their minds fly for refuge to a home long left.

Her hand was limp and dry as I took it with a politely muttered invitation that she come into the newsroom. She dropped into a chair with a tired sigh.

'I am the mother of a person who has disappeared; so please listen.' She apologised for coming. She was asking for only a little guidance, no help. 'I was told that this paper would publish something about what happened to her.' She paused and stared at me; I looked away. 'I don't want anything published now . . . I want you to help me find her.'

I told her I had been advised that she was coming, which was untrue; but it gave her the impression, even if a small one, that somebody else had cared about her as she had walked from another newspaper office, across the Plaza de Mayo and along the avenue south of Government House by the large mausoleum-like building of the army command and the turn-of-the-century anachronism that was the Custom House.

An office boy brought her a cup of tea and she hardly let it touch the desk top before she had raised it to her lips.

'I decided when I sat down that I had come for a chat with nice people and some comfort. Just the fact that you've invited me in makes you people better.' I glanced at my watch and wondered how long she would stay. Humanitarian consideration and newsroom deadlines were in conflict.

Her husband was under sedation since they had received the news. They had not seen their daughter for months and did not know what had happened to her husband, an engineer; she had been led into the 'political thing' by him. She sniffed at the hint of tears and opened her handbag; but instead of a handkerchief she produced a small crumpled paper with a list of all the names and addresses of places she had called at to try to find her daughter.

She sighed deeply at regular intervals, wondering aloud why there were people so cruel that they had decided that she should not know the where-abouts of the girl.

'When I was young, people were tortured, people were killed by police. But it was just one or two and people did not worry, because it was known that something strange was going on . . . they were involved in something . . . they were criminals, or anarchists . . . But now they are taking away people by the dozen, by the hundreds I think . . . I was told today, I suppose you know: there were over two hundred writs of habeas corpus filed in the central courts building last week . . . over two hundred in one week, just at the central courts, which cover only a small part of the federal capital . . . And the military authorities and police always answer the same: The person mentioned is not being held, there is no warrant for the arrest of the citizen in this jurisdiction . . . etc.

'I don't have a photograph, but you should have seen her . . . You would love her. Of course, you will say it is just her mother speaking, but she is beautiful, so tender, such a loving girl. And she was always such a friend to me.'

> Andrew Graham-Yooll, *A State of Fear: Memories of Argentina's Night-mare*, 1986

CONDEMNED TO SILENCE

The Argentine singer Mercedes Sosa was too famous for the military authorities to murder, but she was eventually forced to leave the country.

That night, halfway into my presentation, I noticed 'strange' incidents. My agent motioned to me to come closer; at the end of the song, I moved toward her. She offered me a glass of water. Right away, she said, 'The police came . . .' So what, I thought; the more the merrier. But the look on her face told me that they didn't buy a ticket, nor did they come to hear me. So I moved closer to the police and asked them straight out: 'Can you tell me what's happening?'

'What's happening is that you are singing subversive songs.'

'What do you mean, "subversive songs"? What's that all about?'

'Songs of protest, Marxist . . .'

'But these songs were taped in 1973 and I've been singing them every-where,' I said.

'I don't know what it's like in other places. But *here*, these songs are communist.'

'So then, why did you let me get on stage to perform? It would have been easier to prohibit me—and that's it.'

'We are the ones who decide what must be done here!'

I thought they would only write a report and cancel the rest of the performance. But the police officers' commands sounded ominous. I thought of one of those Nazi war movies, in which you see the police interrupt a meeting, holding the crowd at gunpoint, and the truth is, *I felt scared*.

All of a sudden, a policeman climbed on stage and started harassing, and I mean grossly harassing, me. I felt so humiliated, enraged. If words could kill, the police would have been dead when I shouted with such hatred: 'What are you doing, you shameless cowards!' It was obviously a setup. He was trying to provoke us so that when we fought back they could charge us with 'disorder and resisting authority.'

They dragged me off stage, separated the men and the women, and boarded everybody onto a bus after ordering all the passengers to get off. Since I was the 'most dangerous delinquent' they took me in a police truck. During the trip, the officer who had harassed me moved closer and, ashamed and confused, told me quickly, 'I'm sorry, Señora, but it was an order; I had to do it, or else.'

We arrived at the Second Precinct Jail in La Plata; Chief Ronconi mistreated us as expected. When I asked for an explanation, he told me that I shouldn't sing any more, that I should stop singing altogether, and he called me 'shitty nigger' and other such compliments.

They treated us like criminals; they photographed us, took our fingerprints, and started a file. People were scared; we couldn't go to the bathroom, or speak, or smoke. When one young man talked, the cop punished him so severely that he fell. The kid broke his neck. . . . That scared the cops, who were trying to minimize the incident. I asked them to let a woman with a feverish child go home; they paid no attention.

At six in the morning, the nightmare ended. Slowly, people regained liberty. Stricken, the men started leaving. More animated, the women saluted me, comforted me . . .

Weeks later, I had to perform in Cinema Premier, also in Buenos Aires: This time the tickets were sold beforehand, and I arrived at the theater happy, despite the fact that the newspapers refused to advertise the concert and the radio stations wouldn't play my music. I felt happy that day. I arrived at the theater and the people were getting ready to go in when I saw a police patrol: 'Again,' I thought. But no; again, yes, but in a different way.

'Someone telephoned, warning that there is a bomb inside. We are going to check.' They looked for hours. The people were getting impatient; we had to cancel the show, return their money.

What else could I do but leave? They've already bombed Guarany's house.
Daniel Chanal, another popular folk singer, was 'disappeared.'
And me? I was condemned to internal exile, silence . . .

> Mercedes Sosa, in *You Can't Drown the Fire: Latin American Women
> Writing in Exile*, ed. Alicia Partnoy, 1989

A CIRCULAR FROM THE IRANIAN EDUCATION MINISTRY

*The Bahá'í faith is regarded as deeply heretical in the Islamic Republic of Iran,
and after the revolution in 1979 the new government reversed the Shah's policy
of toleration towards the Bahá'ís.*

Referring to Decree No. 14973/2 dated 1st Tir 1358 and in view of your not
being a follower of one of the official and recognized religions of the
country, you were thus dismissed from the Ministry of Education; we state
the following:

The Ministry of Education, which has come into being only through the
justice of the Islamic Republic of Iran and the blood and martyrdom of
thousands of Muslims, men and women, cannot tolerate, like the previous
regime, the existence of followers of the Bahá'í sect in its Educational unit,
and in this way defile and deviate the minds and thoughts of innocent
students.

In view of the fact that, to the extent to which the environment of education is pure and undefiled, the schools can be mirrors of the effulgent
splendours of God, no doubt it cannot be tolerated that, as under the
previous regime, the Bahá'ís should be active in the educational activities of
the country. If you remember how many thousands of men and women
according to the guidance of the Muslim Ulamas suffered in exile, and
eventually quaffed the chalice of martyrdom, you will justly conclude that
the holy threshold of education should not be left to people like yourself,
who are against the best interests of Islam and are spreading false ideas.

In conclusion, I would like to remind you that the employment of Iranians
who are not followers of recognized religions, such as Muslims, Jews, Christians and Zoroastrians, in Government Offices is against the law.

Therefore, your dismissal according to the existing law is a minimum punishment. No doubt the maximum punishment will befall those who employed

you—who very shortly will be tried in the Islamic Revolutionary Court. Your previous salary payments made to you against the law are being considered, and in future the result of this will be announced to you.

(Signed)

Muhammad 'Ali Rajá'í, Guardian of the Ministry of Education of the Islamic Republic of Iran

THE EXPERIENCE OF EXILE

For some, to be out of a country where they have been mistreated is nothing short of a release. For others, it is a tragedy which they will never entirely overcome. Others again look for every opportunity to let the people back home know how successful they have been as a result of leaving. A proportion of exiles always seem to succeed wherever they go: refugees from Nazism in Hollywood, Syrian traders in West Africa or Latin America, Iranian royalists in Texas. Writers often find the change of atmosphere deeply stimulating, politicians obtain a new intensity of response from their exiled fellow countrymen. It says something for the drive and acumen of the kind of people who are likely to be exiled from their own country that they rarely seem to fail altogether in the countries of their adoption. And even if they decide to settle there permanently, they never forget their homeland.

SORROW ON THE JADE STEPS

The dew is white on the jade steps
At this late hour it soaks her silk stockings
Her curtain of glittering crystals drops
As she watches the autumn moon, clear as glass

Li Po (701–62), *Collected Poems*, 1986, tr. John Simpson

UNWILLINGLY, LADY WEN-CHI GETS USED TO THE NOMADIC LIFE

Part II

I sleep beside the stream, and sit on the ground;
The wind that blows from China tatters my clothes.
I use mutton-fat on my hair, but I rarely comb it.
I button the collar of my lambskin coat on the left, like the barbarians do;
With its lapels of fox-fur and its sleeves of badger, it smells unpleasant.
I wear these clothes all day, then sleep in them at night.
The felt screens in the *yurt* are constantly being taken down and put up,
    since we do not stay anywhere for long.
The days and nights are interminable: they seem never to pass.

It upsets me that spring is so short here.
In the lands of the nomads there are few flowers or willow-trees.
For all I know, heaven and earth might have been turned upside down.
Still, I can see the constellation of the Plough in the southern sky.
The names of everything, the sounds, and even the signs we make are
    completely different,
So I simply keep my mouth shut the whole time.
I make gestures with my hands for 'yes' and 'no', and for 'please' and
    'thank you';
As for expressing feelings, it's easier to use sign-language than to say
    something.

Both men and women carry bows and arrows,
And their ponies and sheep are all round, even in the frost and sleet,
So there's no chance of taking a step in any direction whatever.
It's no use doing anything secretly, or begging for an early death.
I listen sadly to the sound of the horn from Ch'iu-tzu,
And the lute from Sui-yeh makes a mournful sound in the night.
The moon climbs the cloudless sky:
I have to see my home again!

I remember when I was a pretty, spoiled child at home:
Someone brought me a valuable bird from far away, which I tamed.
Now that I am lost and abandoned, I think about my former home,
And I am sorry I didn't let my pet bird fly off to the forest.
The north wind blows loudly, the pale sun goes down,
And the stars stream past overhead until the new dawn in the nomads' sky.
Night and day I think about returning, but it's impossible;
My sad heart is like that bird in its cage.

In the former days, when Su Wu was kept prisoner by the Khan,
It is said that he sent a message back with the migrating geese.
Following Su Wu's example, I bite my finger to get blood for writing with,
And I pour out my ten thousand grievances into a letter.
But these bearded nomad youths are good horsemen:
They bend their bows and shoot the birds out of the sky, far and near,
So the geese of the frontier are scared of people.
How can I make my feelings heard from the ends of the earth?

I am angry at the indignities I have suffered, and revolted by the dreadful
    smells;
How I despise the nomads' steppe, and hate the nomads' sky!
When I became pregnant with the child of a barbarian I wanted to kill
    myself:
And yet once I had given birth, I felt the love of a mother for her baby.
He looks peculiar, and he makes strange sounds, but my hatred has turned
    to love.
From deep inside me, my heart goes out to him.
He is with me morning and evening;
I cannot help pitying the child my womb has borne and my hand has tended.

The days and months pass, time never stops;
Judging from the year-star, it must be almost twelve years now.
Winter or summer, the frost and sleet continue.

Each time the water freezes and the grass withers, I mark down another year.
In China there is a proper calendar for the phases of the moon,
But out here the sun, moon and stars just hang meaninglessly in the sky.
The migrating geese have passed over many times,
And I am broken-hearted as the moon wanes, then grows full again.

> From 'Eighteen Songs of a Nomad Flute' by Liu Shang (*c.* AD 770), tr. John Simpson

A WANDERING ANGLO-SAXON

A wanderer on earth, remembering hardships, the violent assaults of enemies, the extinction of loving family, spoke thus:

'Often I have had to bemoan my anxieties alone at each dawning. There is now not one living being to whom I dare plainly express my heart. I know, to be sure, that it is an excellent virtue in a man that he should bind fast his bosom and lock up the treasury of his thoughts, let him think as he wishes. A weary mind cannot resist fate, nor can rueful thought afford help. For this reason those caring for reputation often bind fast in their breast some sorrowful thing. So I, often wretchedly anxious, separated from my home, far from noble kinsfolk, have had to fasten my heart with fetters ever since, years ago, the darkness of the earth enfolded my generous and loving lord, and I, despondent, travelled away, oppressed by wintry anxiety, over the ambit of the waves; full of sorrow I was seeking the hall of a treasure-giving lord where, whether far or near, I might find the one who would acknowledge my love in the mead-hall or would comfort me in my friendlessness and win me over with good things . . .

'Then the heart's lacerations, sore in the wake of the loved ones, are the harder to bear. Sorrow is renewed. When the memory of kinsfolk passes through his imagination, the man greets his comrades with cheerful words, eagerly he watches them: they drift away again. The company of fleeting figures does not bring many familiar exclamations there. Anxiety is renewed in him who oft and again must drive his weary spirit on over the ambit of the waves.'

> From *The Exeter Book*, tr. S. A. J. Bradley, 1982

A NEW GAOLER FOR MARY QUEEN OF SCOTS

In January 1585, as fears grew of a Catholic plot to put Mary on the English throne, she was transferred to Tutbury, which she disliked intensely, and was

*placed in the charge of a much tougher and less sympathetic figure. It was to
be the final stage of her captivity.*

The harsh character of Sir Amyas Paulet, Mary's new jailer, was apparent
from his very first action. This was to take down from above her head and
chair that royal cloth of state by which she set such store, since it constituted a proof of her queenship. Paulet's reasoning was that as the cloth of
state had never been officially allowed, it must be removed, however long
it had been there. Mary first wept and protested vigorously, then retired to
her chamber in a mood of great offence; finally she secured the return of
the dais. The incident was typical of the man, who believed profoundly in
the letter of the law: 'There is no other way to do good to this people than
to begin roundly with them . . . whatsoever liberty or anything else is once
granted unto them cannot be drawn back again without great exclamation',
he wrote to London. Paulet came of a west country family, and his father
had been the governor of Jersey. He himself had been English ambassador
to the French court for three years, but had otherwise not enjoyed a particularly distinguished career; he was certainly not of the high rank of a
Shrewsbury, or a diplomat of great age and experience such as Sir Ralph
Sadler, whom he replaced. But he had been specially selected by Walsingham
for the task in hand, because, as all his contemporaries agreed, he was not
only a prominent Puritan but also a mortal enemy of the queen of Scots and
all she stood for. Walsingham understood his man; Paulet was quite immune to the charms of the queen of Scots and, unlike Knollys and even
Cecil, found her irritating and even tiresome as a character. Since honour
and loyalty were his gods, and these Mary Stuart seemed to offend with
every action, Paulet's Puritan conscience allowed him to hate her in advance. When they actually met, Paulet was able to transform charms into
wiles in his own mind; like Knox so many years before, he disliked his
captive all the more for her possible attractions.

   Paulet's instructions from London were clear: Mary's imprisonment was
to be transformed into the strictest possible confinement. She was not even
to be allowed to take the air, that terrible deprivation which she dreaded
so much, 'for that heretofore under colour of giving alms and other extraordinary courses used by her, she hath won the hearts of the people that habit
about those places where she hath heretofore lain . . .' In particular her
sources of untapped private letters and messages were to be stopped once
and for all; the only letters she was to be allowed to receive were those from
the French ambassador in London—and these Paulet read in any case and
stopped at will, as he thought proper. At no point in her captivity so far had
Mary been cut off so completely. Her correspondence with Beaton, her

ambassador in Paris, Morgan, Paget and her other foreign agents, had depended on a secret pipeline of letters, without which no foreign plotting could have taken place. During the whole of 1585, under the orders of the Elizabethan government, this pipeline was shut off, and Mary was totally deprived of the news she wanted so much.

Antonia Fraser, Mary Queen of Scots, 1969

TAKEN OFF IN THE PRIME OF YOUTH, 1712

Mr Spectator,

I write this to communicate to you a misfortune which frequently happens, and therefore deserves a consolatory discourse on the subject. I was within this half year in the possession of as much beauty and as many lovers as any young lady in England. But my admirers have left me, and I cannot complain of their behaviour. I have within that time had the small-pox: and this face, which (according to many amorous epistles which I have by me) was the seat of all that is beautiful in woman, is now disfigured with scars. It goes to the very soul of me to speak what I really think of my face; and though I think I did not over-rate my beauty while I had it, it has extremely advanced in its value with me, now it is lost. There is one circumstance which makes my case very particular; the ugliest fellow that ever pretended to me, was and is most in my favour, and he treats me at present the most unreasonably. If you could make him return an obligation which he owes me, in liking a person that is not amiable—But there is, I fear, no possibility of making passion move by the rules of reason and gratitude. But say what you can to one who has survived herself, and knows not how to act in a new being. My lovers are at the feet of my rivals, my rivals are every day bewailing me, and I cannot enjoy what I am, by reason of the distracting reflection upon what I was. Consider the woman I was did not die of old age, but I was taken off in the prime of youth, and according to the course of nature may have forty years after-life to come. I have nothing of myself left, which I like, but that I am, SIR,

Your most humble servant,
PARTHENISSA.
The Spectator, no. 306, 12 February 1712

AMONG THE FEMALE CONVICTS

John Nicol, having travelled most of the way round the world, was thinking of settling down after one last voyage. He wanted to see Australia, however, and

decided to join a transport ship which was bound there; though he did not, he said, like the idea of her cargo: women convicts.

I was appointed steward of the Lady Julian, commanded by Captain Aitken, who was an excellent humane man, and did all in his power to make the convicts as comfortable as their circumstances would allow. The government agent, an old lieutenant, had been discharged a little before I arrived, for cruelty to the convicts. He had even begun to flog them in the river. Government, the moment they learned the fact, appointed another in his place.

We lay six months in the river before we sailed; during which time, all the jails in England were emptied to complete the cargo of the Lady Julian. When we sailed, there were on board 245 female convicts. There were not a great many very bad characters; the greater number were for petty crimes, and a great proportion for only being disorderly, that is, street-walkers; the colony at the time being in great want of women.

One, a Scottish girl, broke her heart, and died in the river; she was buried at Dartford. Four were pardoned on account of his Majesty's recovery. The poor young Scottish girl I have never yet got out of my mind; she was young and beautiful, even in the convict dress, but pale as death, and her eyes red with weeping. She never spoke to any of the other women, or came on deck. She was constantly seen sitting in the same corner from morning to night; even the time of meals roused her not. My heart bled for her,— she was a countrywoman in misfortune. I offered her consolation, but her hopes and heart had sunk. When I spoke she heeded me not, or only answered with sighs and tears; if I spoke of Scotland she would wring her hands and sob, until I thought her heart would burst. I endeavoured to get her sad story from her lips, but she was silent as the grave to which she hastened. I lent her my Bible to comfort her, but she read it not; she laid it on her lap after kissing it, and only bedewed it with her tears. At length she sunk into the grave of no disease but a broken heart. After her death we had only two Scottish women on board, one of them a Shetlander. . . .

One day I had the painful task to inform the father and mother of one of the convicts, that their daughter, Sarah Dorset, was on board; they were decent-looking people, and had come to London to inquire after her. When I met them they were at Newgate; the jailor referred them to me. With tears in her eyes, the mother implored me to tell her, if such a one was on board. I told them there was one of that name; the father's heart seemed too full to allow him to speak, but the mother, with streaming eye, blessed God that they had found their poor lost child, undone as she was. I called a coach, drove to the river, and had them put on board. The father, with a trembling step, mounted the ship's side; but we were forced to lift the mother on board. I took them down to my berth, and went for Sarah Dorset; when I brought her, the father said, in a choking voice, 'My lost child!' and turned his back, covering his face with his hands; the mother sobbing, threw her hands around her. Poor Sarah fainted and fell at their feet. I knew not what to do; at length she recovered, and in the most heart-rending accents implored their pardon. She was young and pretty, and had not been two years from her father's house at this present time; so short had been her course of folly and sin. She had not been protected by the villain that ruined her above six weeks; then she was forced by want upon the streets, and taken up as a disorderly girl; then sent on board to be transported. This was her short but eventful history. One of our men, William Power, went out to the colony, when her time was expired, brought her home, and married her.

The Life and Adventures of John Nicol, Mariner, 1822

THE NORTH COUNTRY MAID

A north country maid up to London had strayed
Although with her nature it did not agree.
She sobbed and she sighed and she bitterly cried,
How I wish once again in the north I could be,
Where the oak and the ash and the bonny rowan tree
Are all growing green in my north country.

As sadly I roam, I remember my home
Where lads and young lasses are making the hay,
Where the birds sweetly sing and the merry bells ring
And the maidens and meadows are pleasant and gay,
Where the oak and the ash and the bonny rowan tree
Are all growing green in my north country.

No doubt should I please I could marry with ease,
Where maidens are fair many lovers will come,
But he whom I wed must be north country bred
And carry me back to my north country home,
Where the oak and the ash and the bonny rowan tree
Are all growing green in my north country.

Clayre, *100 Folk Songs and New Songs*

SHELLEY TELLS MARY WOLLSTONECRAFT HE WANTS TO GET AWAY FROM EVERYTHING

My greatest content would be utterly to desert all human society. I would retire with you and our child to a solitary island in the sea, would build a boat, and shut upon my retreat the flood-gates of the world. I would read no reviews, and talk with no authors. If I dared trust my imagination, it would tell me that there are one or two chosen companions beside yourself whom I should desire. But to this I would not listen—where two or three are gathered together, the devil is among them. And good, far more than evil impulses, love, far more than hatred, has been to me, except as you have been its object, the source of all sorts of mischief. So on this plan, I would be *alone*, and would devote either to oblivion or to future generations, the overflowings of a mind which, timely withdrawn from the contagion, should be kept fit for no baser object. But this it does not appear that we shall do.

The other side of the alternative (for a medium ought not to be adopted) is to form for ourselves a society of our own class, as much as possible in intellect, or in feelings; and to connect ourselves with the interests of that society. Our roots never struck so deeply as at Pisa, and the transplanted tree flourishes not. People who lead the lives which we led until last winter, are like a family of Wahabee Arabs, pitching their tent in the midst of London. We must do one thing or the other—for yourself, for our child, for our existence. The calumnies, the sources of which are probably deeper than we perceive, have ultimately, for object, the depriving us of the means of security and subsistence. You will easily perceive the gradations by which calumny proceeds to pretext, pretext to persecution, and persecution to the ban of fire and water. It is for this, and not because this or that fool, or the whole court of fools, curse and rail, that calumny is worth refuting or chastising.

> Percy Bysshe Shelley, *Essays, Letters from Abroad, Translations and Fragments*, ed. Mary Shelley, 1840

DAVID COPPERFIELD BECOMES A LITTLE LABOURING HIND

I know enough of the world now, to have almost lost the capacity of being much surprised by anything; but it is matter of some surprise to me, even now, that I can have been so easily thrown away at such an age. A child of excellent abilities, and with strong powers of observation, quick, eager, delicate, and soon hurt bodily or mentally, it seems wonderful to me that nobody should have made any sign in my behalf. But none was made: and

I became, at ten years old, a little labouring hind in the service of Murdstone and Grinby.

Murdstone and Grinby's warehouse was at the water-side. It was down in Blackfriars. Modern improvements have altered the place; but it was the last house at the bottom of a narrow street, curving down hill to the river, with some stairs at the end, where people took boat. It was a crazy old house with a wharf of its own, abutting on the water when the tide was in, and on the mud when the tide was out, and literally overrun with rats. Its panelled rooms, discoloured with the dirt and smoke of a hundred years, I dare say; its decaying floors and staircase; the squeaking and scuffling of the old grey rats down in the cellars; and the dirt and rottenness of the place; are things, not of many years ago, in my mind, but of the present instant. They are all before me, just as they were in the evil hour when I went among them for the first time, with my trembling hand in Mr. Quinion's.

Murdstone and Grinby's trade was among a good many kinds of people, but an important branch of it was the supply of wines and spirits to certain packet-ships. I forget now where they chiefly went, but I think there were some among them that made voyages both to the East and West Indies. I know that a great many empty bottles were one of the consequences of this traffic, and that certain men and boys were employed to examine them against the light, and reject those that were flawed, and to rinse and wash them. When the empty bottles ran short, there were labels to be pasted on full ones, or corks to be fitted to them, or seals to be put upon the corks, or finished bottles to be packed in casks. All this work was my work, and of the boys employed upon it I was one.

There were three or four of us, counting me. My working place was established in a corner of the warehouse, where Mr. Quinion could see me, when he chose to stand up on the bottom rail of his stool in the counting house, and look at me through a window above the desk. Hither, on the first morning of my so auspiciously beginning life on my own account, the oldest of the regular boys was summoned to show me my business. His name was Mick Walker, and he wore a ragged apron and a paper cap. He informed me that his father was a bargeman, and walked, in a black velvet head-dress, in the Lord Mayor's Show. He also informed me that our principal associate would be another boy whom he introduced by the—to me—extraordinary name of Mealy Potatoes. I discovered, however, that this youth had not been christened by that name, but that it had been bestowed upon him in the warehouse, on account of his complexion, which was pale or mealy. Mealy's father was a waterman, who had the additional distinction of being a fireman, and was engaged as such at one of the large theatres;

where some young relation of Mealy's—I think his little sister—did Imps in the Pantomimes.

No words can express the secret agony of my soul as I sank into this companionship; compared these henceforth every-day associates with those of my happier childhood—not to say with Steerforth, Traddles, and the rest of those boys; and felt my hopes of growing up to be a learned and distinguished man crushed in my bosom. The deep remembrance of the sense I had, of being utterly without hope now; of the shame I felt in my position; of the misery it was to my young heart to believe that day by day what I had learned, and thought, and delighted in, and raised my fancy and my emulation up by, would pass away from me, little by little, never to be brought back any more; cannot be written. As often as Mick Walker went away in the course of that forenoon, I mingled my tears with the water in which I was washing the bottles; and sobbed as if there were a flaw in my own breast, and it were in danger of bursting.

Charles Dickens, *David Copperfield*, 1849–50

THE LONELY HABITUÉ OF THE CAFE DE FLORE

There were not many people on whom Wilde could depend for companionship. Gide, a likely candidate in view of their long acquaintance, saw him only twice. The first time was by accident, when he heard a voice call, and saw it came from Wilde, sitting outside a café. Gide went over, intending to sit facing Wilde, with his back to the passersby; but Wilde insisted he sit beside him: 'I'm so alone these days.' After a pleasant conversation, Wilde suddenly said, 'You must know—I'm absolutely without resources.' Gide gave him some money and they arranged another meeting. That time Gide reproached him for having left Berneval without, as he had promised, writing a play. Wilde replied, 'One should not reproach someone who has been *struck*.' They did not meet again.

Other incidents fill in a sorry sequence. Henry Davray, Wilde's translator, passed in front of the Café de Flore one day in May 1898 when Wilde beckoned to him and insisted on his sitting down for a moment. Davray thought his appearance so broken down and harassed that he yielded, though he was in a great hurry to keep an appointment. Wilde said he had fled the boredom of his hotel room. He became less troubled when Davray sat down, and talked about all sorts of things, at the same time insisting that Davray should not go away and leave him. In the end Davray had to telephone to cancel his appointment. Wilde was so afraid of being alone that when Davray got up to go he went with him to the Luxembourg, walked through the gardens with him and made him sit down at another café on the Boulevard Saint-Michel. At last he confessed his embarrassment: 'I haven't a sou,' he said, then laughed. 'I'll give you security for some money,' and he took from his pocket a copy of Webster's *The Duchess of Malfi*, which he inscribed to his friend. Another writer, Frédéric Boutet, tells how in July 1899 he and a friend were walking along the boulevard Saint-Germain, and came upon Wilde seated at a café in torrential rain, which poured down on him, turning his straw hat into a candle-snuffer and his coat into a sponge, for the waiter, anxious to be rid of his last customer, had not only piled up the chairs but wound up the awning. Wilde could not leave because he could not pay for the three or four drinks he had taken to avoid going back to his squalid lodgings. As he wrote to Frances Forbes-Robertson, 'Like dear St Francis of Assisi I am wedded to poverty, but in my case the marriage is not a success. I hate the bride that has been given to me.' And to Frank Harris, 'A hole in the trousers may make one as melancholy as Hamlet, and out of bad boots a Timon may be made.'

Richard Ellmann, *Oscar Wilde*, 1987

MEAULNES LEAVES THE GOLDEN WORLD OF THE LOST DOMAIN

Already a line of carriages was advancing slowly through the darkness towards the gate in the wood. At their head walked a man in a goat-skin jacket holding a dark-lantern and leading the first horse by the bridle.

Meaulnes was in haste to find someone to give him a lift, in haste to be off. He had now a deep-seated dread of being left alone in the domain and shown up for a fraud.

When he reached the main entrance he found the drivers of the rearmost wagons adjusting the balance of their loads: passengers were being asked to stand while seats were drawn back or forward. Girls swathed in fichus got up with difficulty; rugs slipped from their laps; and as they stooped to retrieve them their faces looked strained in the disk of light cast by the carriage-lamps.

In one of these drivers Meaulnes recognized the young peasant who had offered him a lift.

'May I get in?' he called out.

But he himself had not been recognized. 'Which way are you going, mate?'

'Sainte-Agathe.'

'Then you'd better try Maritain.'

He searched among the belated travellers for a man he didn't know. In the end Maritain was identified as one of the group still drinking and singing in the kitchen.

'He's a rare one for a good time,' someone remarked. 'He'll be there till three in the morning.'

Meaulnes's thoughts flew, to the unhappy girl sick with anxiety, spending a feverish night while these louts filled her house with their singing. Where, he wondered, was her room? In what part of these mysterious precincts was her window to be seen? But no purpose could be served by delaying his departure. He must get away. Once back at Sainte-Agathe his impressions would sort themselves out; he would no longer be a schoolboy playing truant; he would be free to dream of they young lady of the château.

One by one the carriages moved away, their wheels grinding the sand of the long avenue. He saw them turn and disappear into the night laden with women in shawls and children swaddled in mufflers and already asleep. A large carriole set off; a wagonette in which women sat shoulder to shoulder—and Meaulnes was left standing in dismay on the threshold of the house. The only chance now was an old Berlin in charge of a peasant wearing a smock.

'Get in, then,' he said when Meaulnes had explained his plight. 'We're going your way.'

With difficulty Meaulnes opened the door of the ramshackle coach, making the window-pane rattle and the hinges creak. At one end of the seat two small children, a boy and a girl, were sleeping. The noise and the cold air woke them; they stretched, stared vaguely, shivered, and then huddled back into their corner and went to sleep again . . .

As the old carriage got into motion Meaulnes closed the door more gently and settled cautiously into the other corner of the seat. Then, avidly, he kept his eyes at the window trying to fix in memory the topography of the scene he was leaving behind and the route by which he had first come to it. In the dark he half saw, half guessed his surroundings as the carriage felt its way through garden and courtyard, past the stairway to his room, into the avenue, through the gateway, out to the road through the wood where the trunks of old fir trees went past the window in procession.

'We may overtake Frantz de Galais,' he thought, and his heart beat faster.

Abruptly the carriage swerved to avoid an obstacle in the narrow road. Out of the night something huge loomed up that looked like a house on wheels; it could only be a caravan which had been left standing there, within easy reach, during the festivities.

Once past this obstruction, the horses began to trot. Meaulnes was growing tired of peering through the window into a fog of darkness when suddenly, in the wood, there was a flash and a detonation. The horses broke into a gallop and at first Meaulnes was not sure whether the man on the box was trying to hold them in or urging them on. He tried to open the door, but it was stuck, and he shook it in vain . . . The children, awake now and frightened, pressed close to one another but made no sound. And while he was struggling with the door, his face close to the window-pane, the carriage-lamp flashing for an instant on a bend in the road revealed a white figure running, haggard and distraught. It was the pierrot of the fête, the strolling player still in costume, holding a body in his arms. Then everything was blotted out.

Inside the carriage, now hurtling through the night, the two children had again settled down to sleep. There was no one to whom Meaulnes could speak of the mysterious happenings of these last two days. For a long while he revolved in his mind all he had seen and heard until, weary and heavy-hearted, the young man too gave himself up to sleep, like a disconsolate child . . .

Alain-Fournier, Le Grand Meaulnes, 1913

DREAMERS

Soldiers are citizens of death's grey land,
  Drawing no dividend from time's tomorrows.
In the great hour of destiny they stand,
  Each with his feuds, and jealousies, and sorrows.
Soldiers are sworn to action; they must win
  Some flaming, fatal climax with their lives.
Soldiers are dreamers; when the guns begin
  They think of firelit homes, clean beds and wives.

I see them in foul dug-outs, gnawed by rats,
  And in the ruined trenches, lashed with rain,
Dreaming of things they did with balls and bats,
  And mocked by hopeless longing to regain
Bank-holidays, and picture-shows, and spats,
  And going to the office in the train.

Siegfried Sassoon, Collected Poems, 1976

SEPARATED BY SO LITTLE

What makes experience in the Great War unique and gives it a special freight of irony is the ridiculous proximity of the trenches to home. Just seventy miles from 'this stinking world of sticky trickling earth' was the rich plush of London theater seats and the perfume, alcohol, and cigar smoke of the Café Royal. The avenue to these things was familiar and easy: on their two-week leaves from the front, the officers rode the same Channel boats they had known in peacetime, and the presence of the same porters and stewards ('Nice to serve you again, Sir') provided a ghastly pretence of normality. One officer on leave, observed by Arnold Bennett late in 1917, 'had breakfasted in the trenches and dined in his club in London.'

The absurdity of it all became an obsession. One soldier spoke for everyone when he wrote home, 'England is so absurdly near.' Another, bogged down in the Salient in September, 1917, devoted many passages of his diary to considering the anomaly: 'I often think how strange it is that quiet home life is going on at Weybridge, and everywhere else in England, all the time that these terrific things are happening here.' Remembering the war fifty years afterwards and shaping his recollections into a novel, one participant discovers that the thing he finds especially 'hard to believe' about the war is this farcical proximity. On the way back up the line on a train, one officer returning from leave remarks to others in his compartment: 'Christ! . . . I was at *Chu Chin Chow* last night with my wife. Hard to believe, isn't it?' And the narrator observes:

> Hard to believe. Impossible to believe. That other life, so near in time and distance, was something led by different men. Two lives that bore no relation to each other. That was what they all felt, the bloody lot of them. . . .

At even the worst moments, when apparently nothing could live through the shelling, troops found the *Daily Mail* being peddled by French newsboys at the entrances to communication trenches, and buying it was a way, if not of finding out what was going on, at least of 'feeling at home' and achieving a laugh as well. There were other anomalous apparitions of 'London.' During the winter of 1914–15 a familiar sight just behind the line was a plethora of London heavy transport vehicles—brewer's trucks, moving vans, London buses—often with their original signs intact. 'You meet them,' says one observer, 'toiling along the greasy road with heavy loads of shells or food, their gay advertisements of Bass's Beer or Crosse and Blackwell scarred and dirtied by the war.' Some traditional civilian comforts might find themselves in odd circumstances. Major Frank Isherwood relied on Mothersill's seasickness preventative to mitigate the Channel crossings, and General J. L. Jack sniffed often at 'a smelling salts bottle given years ago by an old aunt without any thought of this purpose' to disguise 'the stench from the older corpses in our parapets.' Sassoon, perceiving that uncut wire was going to be one of the problems on July 1, 1916, devoted his last leave just before the Somme jump-off to shopping. At the Army and Navy Stores he bought two pair of wire-cutters with rubber-covered handles, which he issued to his company on his return. These were, he says, 'my private contribution to the Great Offensive.'

Paul Fussell, *The Great War and Modern Memory*, 1978

A LAST NIGHT TOGETHER

The poet Edward Thomas, a difficult and sometimes depressive man, had spent more than a year in the Army when he came back for what was to be his last leave in 1917. Later, when she wrote about it, Helen Thomas used the name 'David' for her husband and 'Jenny' for herself.

So we lay, all night, sometimes talking of our love and all that had been, and of the children, and what had been amiss and what right. We knew the best was that there had never been untruth between us. We knew all of each other, and it was right. So talking and crying and loving in each other's arms we fell asleep as the cold reflected light of the snow crept through the frost-covered windows.

David got up and made the fire and brought me some tea, and then got back into bed, and the children clambered in, too, and we sat in a row sipping our tea. I was not afraid of crying any more. My tears had been shed, my heart was empty, stricken with something that tears would not express or comfort. The gulf had been bridged. Each bore the other's suffering. We concealed nothing, for all was known between us. After break-fast, while he showed me where his account books were and what each was for, I listened calmly, and unbelievingly he kissed me when I said I, too, would keep accounts. 'And here are my poems. I've copied them all out in this book for you, and the last of all is for you. I wrote it last night, but don't read it now. . . . It's still freezing. The ground is like iron, and more snow has fallen. The children will come to the station with me; and now I must be off.'

We were alone in my room. He took me in his arms, holding me tightly to him, his face white, his eyes full of a fear I had never seen before. My arms were round his neck. 'Beloved, I love you,' was all I could say. 'Jenny, Jenny, Jenny,' he said, 'remember that whatever happens, all is well be-tween us for ever and ever.' And hand in hand we went downstairs and out to the children, who were playing in the snow.

A thick mist hung everywhere, and there was no sound except, far away in the valley, a train shunting. I stood at the gate watching him go; he turned back to wave until the mist and the hill hid him. I heard his old call coming up to me: 'Coo-ee!' he called. 'Coo-ee!' I answered, keeping my voice strong to call again. Again through the muffled air came his 'Coo-ee.' And again went my answer like an echo. 'Coo-ee' came fainter next time with the hill between us, but my 'Coo-ee' went out of my lungs strong to pierce to him as he strode away from me. 'Coo-ee!' So faint now, it might be only my own call flung back from the thick air and muffling snow. I put my hands up to my mouth to make a trumpet, but no sound came. Panic seized me, and I ran through the mist and the snow to the top of the hill, and stood there a moment dumbly, with straining eyes and ears. There was nothing but the mist and the snow and the silence of death.

Then, with leaden feet which stumbled in a sudden darkness that overwhelmed me I groped my way back to the empty house.

Helen Thomas, *World Without End*, 1931

NO ONE SO MUCH AS YOU

No one so much as you
Loves this my clay,
Or would lament as you
Its dying day.

You know me through and through
Though I have not told,
And though with what you know
You are not bold.

None ever was so fair
As I thought you:
Not a word can I bear
Spoken against you.

All that I ever did
For you seemed coarse
Compared with what I hid
Nor put in force.

My eyes scarce dare meet you
Lest they should prove
I but respond to you
And do not love.

We look and understand
We cannot speak
Except in trifles and
Words the most weak.

For I at most accept
Your love, regretting
That is all: I have kept
Only a fretting

That I could not return
All that you gave
And could not ever burn
With the love you have,

Till sometimes it did seem
Better it were
Never to see you more
Than linger here

With only gratitude
Instead of love—
A pine in solitude
Cradling a dove.

Edward Thomas (1878–1917), Collected Poems, 1936

WHAT NOW?

Isaac Bashevis Singer, having come to the United States from his native Poland, finds himself in an entirely alien society.

After a long hesitation I decided to take a walk. Outside, I made a mental note—there were two white columns at the front of the porch. No other house on the street had them. I walked slowly and each time glanced back at the house with the two columns. I had read accounts of spies, revolutionaries, of such explorers as Sven Hedin, Amundsen, and Captain Scott who wandered over deserts, ice fields, and jungles. They were able to determine their locations under the most bewildering conditions, and here I trembled about getting lost in such a tiny community as Seagate. I had walked, not knowing where, and had come to the beach. This wasn't the open sea, since I could see lights flashing on some faraway shore. A lighthouse cast its beams. The foamy waves mounted and crashed against a stony breakwater. The beach wasn't sandy but overgrown with weeds. Chunks of driftwood and vegetation spewed forth by the sea lay scattered about. It smelled here of dead fish and something else marinelike and unfamiliar. I trod on seashells. I picked one up and studied it—the armor of a creature that had been born in the sea and apparently had died there as well, or had been eaten despite its protection.

I looked for a star in the sky but the glow of New York City, or maybe Coney Island, made the sky opaque and reddish. Not far from the shore, a small boat tugged three dark barges. I had just come from eight days at sea, yet the ocean seemed as alien as if I were seeing it for the first time. I inhaled the cool air. Maybe simply walk into the sea and put an end to the whole mess? After long brooding, I headed back. It was my impression that I had been following a straight path, but I had already walked quite a distance back and the house with the white columns was nowhere in sight. I reached the fence that separated Seagate from Coney Island and spotted the policeman guarding the gate.

I turned around to go back. Someone had once advised me to always carry a compass. I'm the worst fumbler and clod under the sun, I scolded myself. A compass wouldn't have helped me. It would only have confused me further. Possible Freud might have unraveled my mystery. I suffered from a kind of disorientation complex. Could this have anything to do with my repressed sexual urges? The fact is that it was inherited. My mother and father lived for years in Warsaw and they never knew the way to Nalewki Street. When Father journeyed to visit the Radzymin Rabbi on the holidays, Joshua had to escort him to the streetcar and later buy his ticket and seat him in the narrow-gauge railroad running to Radzymin. In our house there hovered the fear of the outside, of Gentile languages, of trains, cars, of the hustle and bustle of business, even of Jews who had dealings with lawyers, the police, could speak Russian or even Polish. I had gone away from God, but not from my heritage.

What now? I asked myself. I felt like laughing at my own helplessness. I turned back and saw the house with the two white columns. It had materialized as if from the ground. I came up to the house and spotted my brother outlined within the illuminated window. He sat at a narrow table with a pen in one hand, a manuscript in the other. I had never thought about my brother's appearance, but that evening I considered him for the first time with curiosity, as if I weren't his brother but some stranger. Everyone I had encountered in Seagate this day had been sunburned, but his long face was pale. He read not only with his eyes but mouthed the words as he went along. From time to time, he arched his brows with an expression that seemed to ask, How could I have written this? and promptly commenced to make long strokes with the pen and cross out. The beginning of a smile formed upon his thin lips. He raised the lids of his big blue eyes and cast a questioning glance outside, as if suspecting that someone in the street was observing him. I felt as if I could read his mind: It's all vanity, this whole business of writing, but since one does it, one must do it right.

A renewed surge of love for my brother coursed through me. He was not only my brother but my father and master as well. I could never address him first. I always had to wait for him to make the first overture. I went back to my room and lay down on the sofa. I did not put on the light. I lay there in the darkness. I was still young, not yet thirty, but I was overcome by a fatigue that most probably comes with old age. I had cut off whatever roots I had in Poland yet I knew that I would remain a stranger here to my last day. I tried to imagine myself in Hitler's Dachau, or in a labor camp in Siberia. Nothing was left for me in the future.

Isaac Bashevis Singer, *Love and Exile: The Early Years—A Memoir*, 1985

THOMAS MANN WRITES FROM CHICAGO TO HERMANN HESSE IN GERMANY, 1941

I shall never forget our first visit to you after the upheaval, after the uprooting, after it became impossible for us to go home, and how your existence then filled me with envy but at the same time comforted me and gave me strength. That was long ago; we have learned to recognize an interlude as an era. In spite of everything we have lived, worked, and made our way, but of course when I think of Switzerland I always wonder whether I shall ever see it and Europe again. God only knows whether I shall last long enough and have the strength. I fear—if fear is the right word—that this process is going to roll on and on, and that when the waters recede Europe will have changed byeond recognition, so that one will hardly be able to speak of going home, even if it is physically possible. Actually it is as good as certain that this continent, many of whose inhabitants still dream of preserving their 'way of life' in isolation, will soon be drawn into the present changes and upheavals. How is one to think otherwise? The whole world hangs together; we are not as far apart as it seems—and that again is comforting and encouraging.

I am distressed to hear of your wife's grief and worry over her relatives and friends. The human misery these wretched history-makers are creating all around us cries to high heaven and has long been inexpiable; one no longer dares hope for any true and clear redress. But of this I am convinced: that all this misery will fall back on Germany at the end of its criminal adventures.

No one is immune. Monika, our second daughter, has lost her husband in the sinking of the *City of Benares*. She herself was saved, having spent twenty hours in the water, clinging—one wonders how it was possible—to the rim of a leaky lifeboat. Now she is with us in Princeton, quite broken. My brother Heinrich and our Golo have also arrived here safely. But we have not been able to get my wife's brother, who was a professor in Brussels, out of France.

> Hermann Hesse and Thomas Mann, *Correspondence, 1910–1955*, ed. Anni Carlsson and Volker Michels, tr. Ralph Manheim, 1976

SARTRE'S ENTHUSIASM FOR RESISTANCE EVAPORATES

Sartre needs only one brief dip into occupied Paris to be convinced of the need for direct action. 'That's what seemed to me the first thing to do on coming back to Paris—to create a resistance group; to try, step by step, to win over the majority to resistance and thus bring into being a violent movement that would expel the Germans.' This metamorphosis baffles his friends, especially Simone de Beauvoir, who, 'quite taken aback by the rigor of his moralism,' describes their first conversation and his new behavior in great detail: 'Did I buy things on the black market? A little tea occasionally, I told him. Even this was too much. I had been wrong to sign the paper stating that I was neither a Freemason nor a Jew. Sartre had always asserted his ideas, not to mention his likes and dislikes, in a most dogmatic fashion, whether verbally or through his personal actions. Yet he never formulated them as universal maxims. . . . The first evening he gave me yet another surprise. He had not come back to Paris to enjoy the sweets of freedom, he told me, but to *act*. How? I inquired, taken aback. We were so isolated, so powerless! It was precisely this isolation that had to be broken down, he said. We had to unite, to organize a resistance movement.'. . .

The first meeting . . . took place in a messy room of the Hôtel d'Egypte, Rue Gay Lussac. Dominique Desanti remembers: 'It was on the first floor, and we entered through the window, which gave us the illusion that we could escape more easily in case the police decided to arrest us. We were still innocent then.' Between the two groups, there is a clear understanding: to fight the Vichy regime and all collaborators, and to dissociate themselves, on the right, from the Gaullists, and, on the left, from the communists and their ridiculous pact. They decided to call the group 'Socialisme et Liberté' (Socialism and Freedom), because, Sartre explains, they must look ahead and elaborate a global plan for liberated France. They must open the way for the future, and organize socialism in view of the freedom that will come to power once fascism is defeated. Sartre views the end of the war as imminent. 'Oddly,' Dominique Desanti notes, 'he, a mature man, seemed much more optimistic than we who were ten years younger.'. . .

Sartre soon finds himself, neither an organizer nor a figurehead but simply an extra. Before leaving clandestine action, Sartre made a serious mistake: he agreed to write an article for *Comoedia*, the collaborationist weekly; in fact, according to Simone de Beauvoir, he may even have agreed to write an editorial for them on a regular basis, and hence to work for a paper that, every week, exhorted its readers to familiarize themselves with Germany, to love Kleist and Hölderlin, in short a paper that was trying to give credit to the thesis that all was well in France, France was having fun, its cultural life was thriving. No trace of the war, no trace of Nazi occupation. 'Max Jacob is dead,' a paragraph announces on the first page, no further data, no mention of the Jewish writer's deportation. Nevertheless, at the request of the editor-in-chief of the magazine, René Delange, Sartre agrees to write a piece about *Moby Dick*.

Annie Cohen-Solal, Sartre: A Life, 1987

YOU ARE AN OUTSIDER

The poet and writer Breyten Breytenbach was imprisoned in his native South Africa for planning terrorist acts. When he was released he went to live in Europe. He wrote this 'letter from exile' to Don Espejuelo in 1985.

What is it really like to be exercising the 'dur métier de l'exil', to be 'climbing up and down other people's staircases', to be 'changing countries more often than changing your shoes, despairing whether the revolt can ever bring injustice to an end'?

It is, when you are a writer, to be living *elsewhere* (*ailleurs*), to be writing *differently* (*autrement*). You live in an acquired linguistic zone like going dressed in the clothes of the husband of your mistress. It may be said that you are caught in a cleft mouth. You live and you write in terms of absence, of absent time (or in terms of a questioned present time). Not an imagined or remembered existence: more an absent presence. A state of instant reminiscence. With your tongue you keep searching for the aftertaste of remembered delicacies, and you may well imbue the tasteless fibres with an unexpected refinement. But the tongue keeps clacking against areas of dead palate. Your relationship with the world around you is that of the foreign observer. Or you turn in upon yourself, turn yourself over, observe the albino insects scurrying away from the light. And you taste a distaste, bloated as the tongue in its orifice of saying.

You risk the rupture of silence: either because the break with your milieu is finally too traumatic (you can't stand being painted into a corner), and the awareness of your declining faculties wears the few existing links down to nothingness; or (which is the same problem seen full face) you lose the sense of inevitability, you stop believing in the magic-making, you break with yourself. Writing, after all, is like breathing. Only more painful.

True, you never really relax. You never completely 'belong'. And yet—your situation is probably a blessing in disguise. Freedom, because that is where you're at, is a nasty taskmaster. You have so much more to learn. You are conscious of the *étrangeté* of life, and your senses are sharpened to needles with which you skewer the grey flesh of dull daily acceptances. Your head too is crammed with clichés and stereotypes, but at least you recognize them for what they are—in several languages! For better or for worse you are an outsider. You may be a mutant, for all you know—like a Jew in Poland or a Palestinian in Egypt or a Black in America! If so you are privileged. And, in a century of Displaced Persons and exiles and those fleeing famine or torture, you are in the position to share in and contribute to a historically important, and vital, human experience. (Not to say experiment.)

Take heart then. Lady Luck has smiled upon you!

Breyten Breytenbach, *End Papers*, 1986

A PUPIL FROM A POOR COUNTRY

I woke with a start. I was clutching my bed. My sheets were damp with sweat. Why had I been dreaming about tiffin at Dadar School for the Blind in Bombay, where I had been sent when I was not yet five, and which I had last attended more than six years ago? I was now grown up and in America. The wretched school in Bombay couldn't touch me now. But was this school going to be much different?

I consulted my Braille watch. It was only twelve-thirty. I couldn't have been asleep more than half an hour. I must not go back to sleep, I thought, or I'll have terrible dreams. I shall stay awake. It was my first night in Little Rock, where I had arrived after spending a couple of days in Washington with Mr. and Mrs. Dickens, filing papers to try to get my visitor's visa changed to a student visa. I was alone upstairs in the older boys' sleeping hall at the Arkansas School for the Blind—a long room with thirty identical iron beds, all but mine empty. The students weren't expected for two and a half weeks. In fact, it seemed that Mr. Woolly and his family and the night watchman were the only other people in the building. I could have been in Maine, with the di Francescos, I thought. Why had Mr. Woolly made me

come so early? He said he wanted me to familiarize myself with my surroundings. But how long did he think it would take someone to learn his
way around the school—essentially, one simple building? Any blind person
could master it in a matter of minutes. (Years later, Mr. Woolly explained,
'We were all eager to meet you. We didn't know you from Adam. I'm still
wondering at my brashness at having told you to come on over from India.
I thought if you arrived two or three weeks before school opened, you
could get used to us and we could get used to you.')

A few hours before I went to bed that first night, a longtime student at
the school, a boy I'll call Wayne Tidman, had taken me around. As we
walked up the circular school drive in the rain—the school was set on a
hillside just to the north of a busy street called West Markham—Wayne had
told me, 'I live in Little Rock. I'm the only boy from the school in town
now. That's why Mr. Woolly recruited me to show you around. I didn't use
to live in Little Rock, but then my mother got a divorce.' Wayne spoke fast,
in a nasal voice, and I had to strain to follow him.

'What's divorce?'

'You don't know what a divorce is? How old are you?'

'Fifteen.'

Wayne explained a divorce to me with obvious condescension, as if he
thought I had come from a really strange, backward place.

'I don't think we have it in India,' I said. Then I asked, 'But where is
your father?'

'I don't know—I never see him.'

It was my turn to feel superior.

'We're the same size, but you're much skinnier than I am, because you
come from a poor country,' Wayne said.

I didn't like his calling my country poor, but, of course, he was right. So
I contented myself with saying, 'I think you're older than I am.'

'Only a year.'

We climbed some steps onto the school's front porch.

'By the way, how did you go blind?' Wayne asked.

'From meningitis, when I was very small. And you?'

'I'm not blind, the way you are. I have nystagmus.' I didn't know what
that was, but I didn't dare ask. . . .

At home, we had worried whether the school I was going to might be
for Negroes. But it seemed that there was no way to find out from that
distance without risking bad feelings and jeopardizing my admission. We
had reasoned that if the school turned out to be for Negroes—and so
perhaps unsuitably poor for me—I could always change schools once I was

in America. I now asked Wayne, 'Is this school for Negroes or for whites? What color are you?'

Wayne didn't answer, and I was afraid that I had offended him. Suddenly, he said, his voice coming out almost in an angry spit, 'White, you fool! What do you think?'

I was relieved, even though I worried that I might have made an enemy of my very first American school friend.

'You ain't white, you know,' Wayne said after a while.

'My people are not dark-skinned, like the Dravidians, in South India,' I said. 'We're fair-skinned Aryans—we come from the North.'

'I don't know about all that. Here you're just white or not white, and I can see that you ain't white. You can't fool me.'

Ved Mehta, *Sound Shadows of the New World*, 1986

THE ADOPTED HOME IS NEVER HOME

There is an expression in English 'to make one's home' somewhere. I may be said to have made my home in England, but the English actually deny the right of the individual to make her home where she pleases. 'Do I detect an accent?' asks the optician/taxi-driver/door-to-door salesman. 'South Africa? New Zealand? Whereabouts in Australia? How long've you been over here?' I too detect an accent, an accent of smug ignorance and confident superiority. By ferreting out my accent my interlocutor reminds himself that greatly to his credit he is an Englishman, 'echt Englisch'.

I could answer that my ancestors came over with William the Conqueror. Instead, sullenly, I reply, '1964' nearly 30 years ago, and I have been paying taxes ever since. Do I regard Australia as home? Yeah, I guess I do but then, like many a child sleeping in a shop doorway, I regard the happiest day of my life as the day I ran away from home. It was a long day, because I didn't stop running till I fetched up in Europe. My ancestors were born in Lincolnshire, Ulster, Eire, the Ticino and Schleswig-Holstein. I have more right to live in any of those places than I do in Australia.

Australia is, was, and ever shall be someone else's country. The British delusion that they discovered it and claimed it for the British Empire has always depended upon a nonsensical description of the continent as *Terra nullius*, empty land, theirs for the planting of a piece of coloured cloth on a stick. The empire builders knew there were people in Australia; the definition of the country as *Terra nullius* relied upon the denial of human status to those people. The British people who were sent to make their homes there were also denied human status, being criminals.

They were greatly outnumbered by the people who were forced by poverty and oppression to make the unrepeatable journey half-way round the world, many of whom died or faced greater hardship in Australia than they would have had to endure in the old country. Whether convicts, indentured servants, soldiers, agricultural labourers or mineworkers, once they were dumped in someone else's country they had no option but to make a go of it, which meant not only that they had to defend a spurious claim to the land at the expense of its real owners but that they had to carry the guilt. For the vast majority there was never the option of going home. The Australian classic novel, *The Fortunes of Richard Mahony*, has for its hero the man who tried to go home. It traces the erosion of his personality by the gradual realisation that he is permanently exiled.

Colonialism is a continuing disaster founded on a mistake. The explosion of the European people that eclipsed and displaced the African nations and imposed a long agony on the indigenous peoples of the Americas cannot be undone. Europeans may die out in Europe because of their extreme reluctance to breed in any numbers, and their genetic presence in other countries will gradually be diluted, but the disrupted populations will never be able to reclaim a homeland so fundamentally changed as to be no longer home.

Just so, the migrant's adopted home is never home but the migrant is too changed to be welcome in her old country. Only in dreams will she see the skies of home. The ache of exile cannot be assuaged by travelling anywhere, least of all by retracing old steps looking for houses that have been bulldozed and landscapes that have disappeared under urban sprawl and motorway.

Home is the one place that you can keep strangers out of: home, like the Englishman's castle, cannot be penetrated by outsiders. Because the ideology of home justifies chauvinism and racism, it is as well that there is in creation no such place. The only unchanging place where we really will belong and all will be satisfied is heaven, and heaven cannot be brought about on earth. Failure to recognise the fact that earthly home is a fiction has given us the anguish of Palestine and the internecine raging of the Balkans. The ideology of home primes the bombs of the PPK and the IRA. The rest of us can face the fact that our earthly journey is a journey away from home. Exile being the human condition, no government subsidy can provide the chariot that will carry us home.

Germaine Greer, column in the *Guardian*, September 1993

LOOKING BACK AT THE BIRTHPLACE OF THE FORTUNATE

By the time this book is published I will be forty years old. When I left Sydney I boasted that I would be gone for five years. I was to be gone three times that and more. During that time most of those who came away have gone back. Before Gough Whitlam came to power, having to return felt like defeat. Afterwards it felt like the natural thing to do. Suddenly Australia began offering its artists all the recognition they had previously been denied. It took a kind of perversity to refuse the lure. Perhaps I did the wrong thing. Eventually fear plays a part: when you are too long gone, to return even for a month feels like time-travel. So you try to forget. But the memories keep on coming. I have tried to keep them under control. I hope I have not overdone it, and killed the flavour. Because Sydney is so real in my recollection that I can taste it.

It tastes like happiness. I have never ceased to feel orphaned, but nor have I ever felt less than lucky—a lucky member of a lucky generation. In this century of all centuries we have been allowed to grow up and grow old in peace. There is a Buster Keaton film in which he is standing around innocently when the façade of a house falls on him. An open window in the façade passes over his body, so that he is left untouched.

I can see the Fun Doctor juggling for us at Kogarah Infants' School. One of the balls hits the floor with a thud. Then what looks like the same ball lands on his head. I can hear the squeak that the mica window panels of the Kosi stove made when I scorched them with the red-hot poker. When Jeanette Elphick came back on a visit from Hollywood they drove her around town in a blue Customline with her new name painted in huge yellow letters along the side: VICTORIA SHAW. On Empire Night when we threw pieces of fibro into the bonfire they cracked like rifle shots. Every evening for weeks before Empire Night I used to lay my fireworks out on the lounge-room carpet, which became impregnated with the smell of gunpowder. Peter Moulton kept his fireworks in a Weetabix carton. On the night, a spark from the fire drifted into the carton and the whole lot went up. A rocket chased Gail Thorpe, who was only just back from therapy. She must have thought it was all part of the treatment.

At the Legacy Party in Clifton Gardens I got a No. 4 Meccano set. On hot nights before the nor'easter came you changed into your cossie and ran under the sprinkler. At Sans Souci baths I dive-bombed a jelly blubber for a dare. If you rubbed sand into the sting it hurt less. Bindies in the front lawn made you limp to the steps of the porch and bend over to pick them out. Sandfly bites needed Calomine lotion that dried to a milky crust. From Rose Bay at night you could hear the lions making love in Taronga Park.

If the shark bell rang and you missed the wave, you were left out there alone beyond the third line of breakers. Every shadow had teeth. Treading water in frantic silence, you felt afraid enough to run Christ-like for the shore.

At the Harvest Festivals in church the area behind the pulpit was piled high with tins of IXL fruit for the old age pensioners. We had collected the tinned fruit from door to door. Most of it came from old age pensioners. Some of them must have got their own stuff back. Others were less lucky. Hunting for cicadas in the peppercorns and the willows, you were always in search of the legendary Black Prince, but invariably he turned out to be a Redeye. The ordinary cicada was called a Pisser because he squirted mud at you. The most beautiful cicada was the Yellow Monday. He was as yellow as a canary and transparent as crystal. When he lifted his wings in the sunlight the membranes were like the deltas of little rivers. The sun shone straight through him. It shone straight through all of us.

It shone straight through everything, and I suppose it still does. As I begin this last paragraph, outside my window a misty afternoon drizzle gently but inexorably soaks the City of London. Down there in the street I can see umbrellas commiserating with each other. In Sydney Harbour, twelve thousands miles away and ten hours from now, the yachts will be racing on the crushed diamond water under a sky the texture of powdered sapphires. It would be churlish not to concede that the same abundance of natural blessings which gave us the energy to leave has every right to call us back. All in, the whippy's taken. Pulsing like a beacon through the days and nights, the birthplace of the fortunate sends out its invisible waves of recollection. It always has and it always will, until even the last of us come home.

Clive James, *Unreliable Memoirs*, 1980

THE DISTASTEFUL PRACTICALITIES OF HOSTAGE LIFE

Brian Keenan, a lecturer at the American University of Beirut, was taken hostage by Islamic fundamentalists in Lebanon in 1986.

Always in the morning I see the marks of the night's battle. Red lumps like chicken pox, all raging to be itched and scratched. I sit trying to prevent myself from scratching. The more I try to resist, the more difficult it becomes and the more demanding is my body for the exquisite pain of my nails tearing my own flesh. For some reason I do not understand, the feet and the backs of my fingers suffer the most from these insistent fleas. The pain of the bites on these tender areas can be excruciating. At times I exchange one pain for another. Deciding feverishly to tear and scratch the skin from my feet, and with it the pain of the bite, knowing that in the morning my feet will be a bloody mess and I will be unable to walk on this filthy floor. It's all so purposeless. I am naked in the dark and I try to wipe the perspiration from my skin. The night noise of these insects is insidious. I cannot bear much more. I thrust my body back upon the mattress and pull the filthy curtain over it to keep these things from feeding on my flesh. I cannot bear the heat and smell of this rag over my body like a shroud. I must content myself, let the mosquitoes feed and hope that having had a fill of me they will leave me alone to find some sleep . . .

I take up one of the magazines, *Time* or *Newsweek*, and tear one page from it. I set it on the floor beside my bed and squat down over it. I defecate on it. I defecate on the reason why I am being held in this asylum of a place and then I carefully wrap my excrement in a parcel and push it into the corner, knowing that if it is found I will suffer. Tomorrow I will lift this piece of myself and carry it with me in my pocket and cast it into that cockroach-filled hole in the ground. I cannot relieve myself at a fixed and set time. I am reduced to sleeping in the smell of my own filth. Excrement, sweat, the perspiration of a body and a mind passing through waves of desperation. All of everything is in this room. I am breaking out of myself, urges, ideas, emotions in turmoil are wrenched up and out from me; as with a sickness when nothing can be held down. I tell myself again and over again that this will pass. I convince myself at each day's down-plunging into an abyss of crushing despair that there will be an up day. I have forced myself to believe these doldrums will be followed by a few hours of euphoria in which the mind, tired of its own torment, drifts off to walk in some sun-lit field. I feel the soft pleasure of it, as a child must feel when its mother or father gently cradles it and rubs its tummy. Ups and downs, the tidal wave and undertow of days and hours of unending manic shifts. . . .

I have been and seen the nightmare exploding in the darkness. I am in the charnel house of history, I am ash upon the wind, a screaming moment of agony and rapture. I have ceased being. I have ceased becoming. Even banging my body against the wall does not retrieve me to myself.

I am alone, naked in a desert. Its vast expanse of nothingness surrounds me. I am where no other thing is or can be. Only the desert wind howling and echoing. There is no warming light. I am the moment between extremes. I feel scorching heat upon my skin and feel the freeze of night cut me to the bone, yet I also feel empty and insensible.

Many times I think of death, pray for it, look for it, chase after its rapturous kiss. But I have come to a point of such nothingness that even death cannot be. I have no more weeping. All the host of emotions that make a man are no longer part of me. They have gone from me. But something moves in this empty place. A profound sense of longing, not loneliness, simply longing.

In my corner I sit enclosed in the womb of light from my candle-flame. I lift my eyes and see a dead insect held in a cocoon made by a spider and I know that I too am cocooned here. Nothing can touch me nor harm me. I am in a cocoon which enfolds me like a mother cradling a child.

Brian Keenan, An Evil Cradling, 1992

PLUTARCH, AN ALIEN IN ROME, FINDS A SILVER LINING

Assume that exile is a calamity, as the multitude declare in speech and song. So too, many foods are bitter and pungent and irritate the taste; but by combining with them certain sweet and pleasant ingredients we get rid of the disagreeable savour. There are colours too, painful to the sight, and when confronted with them our vision is blurred and dazzled by their harshness and unrelieved intensity. Now if we have found that we could remedy this inconvenience by mingling shadow with them or turning our eyes aside and resting them upon something of a greenish and pleasant shade, the same can be done with misfortunes as well: they can be blended with whatever is useful and comforting in your present circumstances: wealth, friends, freedom from politics, and lack of none of the necessities of life.

Plutarch (c. AD 46–c.120), Moralia, tr. Philip H. de Lacy and Benedict Einarson, 1959

LISTENING TO A FLUTE IN YELLOW CRANE PAVILION

I was a wanderer when I came here
Thinking of my home in far-off Ch'ang-an.
From inside the Yellow Crane pavilion
I heard a beautiful flute playing 'Falling Plum Blossoms'
In the late spring, in a city beside the river.

Li Po (701–62), in Tang Dynasty Poetry, 1987, tr. Sam Hamill

VERSES, SUPPOSED TO BE WRITTEN BY ALEXANDER SELKIRK,
DURING HIS SOLITARY ABODE IN THE ISLAND OF JUAN
FERNANDEZ

I am monarch of all I survey,
　My right there is none to dispute;
From the centre all round to the sea,
　I am lord of the fowl and the brute.
Oh, solitude! where are the charms
　That sages have seen in thy face?
Better dwell in the midst of alarms,
　Than reign in this horrible place.

I am out of humanity's reach,
　I must finish my journey alone,
Never hear the sweet music of speech;
　I start at the sound of my own.
The beasts, that roam over the plain,
　My form with indifference see;
They are so unacquainted with man,
　Their tameness is shocking to me.

Society, friendship, and love,
　Divinely bestowed upon man.
Oh, had I the wings of a dove,
　How soon would I taste you again!
My sorrows I then might assuage
　In the ways of religion and truth,
Might learn from the wisdom of age,
　And be cheered by the sallies of youth.

Religion! what treasure untold
　Resides in that heavenly word!
More precious than silver and gold,
　Or all that this earth can afford.
But the sound of the church-going bell
　These valleys and rocks never heard,
Ne'er sighed at the sound of a knell,
　Or smiled when a sabbath appeared.

Ye winds, that have made me your sport,
　Convey to this desolate shore
Some cordial endearing report
　Of a land I shall visit no more.

My friends, do they now and then send
  A wish or a thought after me?
O tell me I yet have a friend,
  Though a friend I am never to see.

How fleet is a glance of the mind!
  Compared with the speed of its flight,
The tempest itself lags behind,
  And the swift-winged arrows of light.
When I think of my own native land,
  In a moment I seem to be there;
But alas! recollection at hand
  Soon hurries me back to despair.

But the sea-fowl is gone to her nest,
  The beast is laid down in his lair,
Ev'n here is a season of rest,
  And I to my cabin repair.
There is mercy in every place;
  And mercy, encouraging thought!
Gives even affliction a grace,
  And reconciles man to his lot.

William Cowper (1731–1800)

ALEXANDER SELKIRK ACCUSTOMS HIMSELF TO LIFE ON JUAN
FERNANDEZ

For eight long months Selkirk had lived in melancholy and horror, 'scarce
able to refrain from doing himself violence'. Day after day he had sat in
watch, his face towards the sea, until his eyes and the light failed him and
he could watch no more. By night he had lain shivering with terror at the
howlings of sea-monsters on the shore, and the first show of dawn lighting
up his great prison-house had roused him only to a sharper consciousness of
his forlorn and miserable state. He spent his time for weeks together roaming aimlessly about his island, staring, listening, weeping, talking to himself.

  As time went on, however, Selkirk's spirits began to revive, as human
spirits, please Heaven, are apt to revive even in the most adverse of circumstances. He vanquished his blues, he set to work, kept tally of his days, and,
like Orlando, cut his name in the trees. He fed plentifully on turtle until
he could no more stomach it except in jellies. He built himself two huts,
thatched them with grass and lined them with goatskins; the one for a
kitchen, the other wherein to sleep, to read, to sing Scots psalms and to

pray. Thus he became, he confessed, a better Christian than he had ever been before, or was likely to be again.

For warmth, cheer, and candle he burned the fragrant allspice wood, but had squandered nearly all his gunpowder before he got fire by rubbing two sticks together. He had no grain, physic, salt, ink, paper, or even rum. He fed on crawfish, goats' flesh, broiled or boiled, turnips—sown by Dampier— and a small black plum, difficult of access on the island's rocky heights. Of living things, apart from goats, he had the company only of seals, which in November came ashore to 'whelp and engender', their bleating and howling so loud that the noise of them could be heard inland a mile from the shore. Another creature strange to Selkirk was the sea lion, the hair of whose whiskers is 'stiff enough to make tooth-pickers'. Of birds there was only a sort of blackbird with a red breast, and the many-coloured humming-bird, 'no bigger than a large humble bee'.

So life went on. When his ammunition failed him, he came to run, barefoot, with such celerity that he had chased down and killed, he said, no less than 500 goats. After ear-marking and laming their young kids, he had set free as many more—beasts which Lord Anson was thus able to identify over thirty years afterwards. When his clothes fell off his back, Selkirk took to himself hairy breeches, and, unravelling the worsted of his worn-out stockings, hemmed himself shirts out of his scanty stock of linen, by means of a shred of goat sinew threaded through a nail. When his knife was worn to the back, he made substitutes out of hoop-iron, beaten thin and ground on the rocks.

Twice he narrowly escaped death, the first time from a fall of a hundred feet—he lay unconscious for three days and nights, a period which he afterwards computed by the appearance of the moon; and the second time from voyaging Spaniards, who, sighting his fire at sea, landed and pursued him. He hid himself in a tree-top and listened to them talking beneath. But rats were his worst enemy; they gnawed his calloused feet and his clothes, until he had bred up cats to teach them manners. These would 'lie about him in hundreds'. Thus best we picture him, praying aloud, singing and dancing with his kids and cats in the flames and smoke of his allspice wood, and the whole world's moon taunting and enchanting him in her seasons.

Walter de la Mare, *Desert Islands*, 1930

CRUSOE MAKES HIMSELF NEW CLOTHES, A HAT AND AN UMBRELLA

Within doors, that is, when it rained, and I could not go out, I found employment on the following occasions; always observing, that all the while I was at work, I diverted myself with talking to my parrot, and teaching him to speak, and I quickly learned him to know his own name, and at last to speak it out pretty loud, 'Poll,' which was the first word I ever heard spoken in the island by any mouth but my own. This, therefore, was not my work, but an assistant to my work; for now, as I said, I had a great employment upon my hands, as follows, viz., I had long studied, by some means or other, to make myself some earthen vessels, which indeed I wanted sorely, but knew not where to come at them. However, considering the heat of the climate, I did not doubt but if I could find out any such clay, I might botch up some such pot as might, being dried in the sun, be hard enough and strong enough to bear handling, and to hold anything that was dry, and required to be kept so; and as this was necessary in the preparing corn, meal, etc., which was the thing I was upon, I resolved to make some as large as I could, and fit only to stand like jars, to hold what should be put into them.

It would make the reader pity me, or rather laugh at me, to tell how many awkward ways I took to raise this paste; what odd, misshapen, ugly things I made; how many of them fell in, and how many fell out, the clay not being stiff enough to bear its own weight; how many cracked by the over-violent heat of the sun, being set out too hastily; and how many fell in pieces with only removing, as well before as after they were dried; and, in a word, how, after having laboured hard to find clay, to dig it, to temper it, to bring it home, and work it, I could not make above two large earthen ugly things (I cannot call them jars) in about two months' labour.

My clothes began to decay, too, mightily. As to linen, I had none a good while, except some chequered shirts which I found in the chests of the other seamen, and which I carefully preserved, because many times I could bear no other clothes on but a shirt; and it was a very great help to me that I had, among all the men's clothes of the ship, almost three dozen of shirts. There were also several thick watch-coats of the seamen's which were left indeed, but they were too hot to wear; and though it is true that the weather was so violent hot that there was no need of clothes, yet I could not go quite naked, no, though I had been inclined to it, which I was not, nor could abide the thoughts of it, though I was all alone.

The reason why I could not go quite naked was, I could not bear the heat of the sun so well when quite naked as with some clothes on; nay, the very heat frequently blistered my skin; whereas, with a shirt on, the air itself made some motion, and whistling under that shirt, was twofold cooler than without it. No more could I ever bring myself to go out in the heat of the sun without a cap or a hat. The heat of the sun beating with such violence, as it does in that place, would give me the headache presently, by darting so directly on my head, without a cap or a hat on, so that I could not bear it; whereas, if I put on my hat, it would presently go away.

Upon these views, I began to consider about putting the few rags I had, which I called clothes, into some order. I had worn out all the waistcoats I had, and my business was now to try if I could not make jackets out of the great watch-coats which I had by me, and with such other materials as I had; so I set to work a-tailoring, or rather, indeed, a-botching, for I made most piteous work of it. However, I made shift to make me two or three new waistcoats, which I hoped would serve me a great while. As for breeches or drawers, I made but a very sorry shift indeed till afterward.

I have mentioned that I saved the skins of all the creatures that I killed, I mean four-footed ones, and I had hung them up stretched out with sticks in the sun, by which means some of them were so dry and hard that they were fit for little, but others it seems were very useful. The first thing I made of these was a great cap for my head, with the hair on the outside, to shoot off the rain; and this I performed so well, that after this I made me a suit of clothes wholly of these skins, that is to say, a waistcoat, and breeches open at knees, and both loose, for they were rather wanting to keep me cool than to keep me warm. I must not omit to acknowledge that they were wretchedly made; for if I was a bad carpenter, I was a worse tailor. However, they were such as I made very good shift with; and when I was abroad, if it happened to rain, the hair of my waistcoat and cap being outermost, I was kept very dry.

After this I spent a great deal of time and pains to make me an umbrella. I was indeed in great want of one, and had a great mind to make one. I had seen them made in the Brazils, where they are very useful in the great heats which are there; and I felt the heats every jot as great here, and greater too, being nearer the equinox. Besides, as I was obliged to be much abroad, it was a most useful thing to me, as well for the rains as the heats. I took a world of pains at it, and was a great while before I could make anything likely to hold; nay, after I thought I had hit the way, I spoiled two or three before I made one to my mind; but at last I made one that answered indifferently well. The main difficulty I found was to make it to let down. I could make it to spread; but if it did not let down too, and draw in, it was not portable for me any way but just over my head, which would not do. However, at last, as I said, I made one to answer, and covered it with skins, the hair upwards, so that it cast off the rains like a penthouse, and kept off the sun so effectually, that I could walk out in the hottest of the weather with greater advantage than I could before in the coolest; and when I had no need of it, could close it, and carry it under my arm.

Daniel Defoe, *Robinson Crusoe*, 1719

CASANOVA FINDS ENTERTAINMENT IN LONDON

My table and my house were not enough for my happiness. I was alone, and the reader will understand by this that Nature had not meant me for a hermit. I had neither a mistress nor a friend, and at London one may invite a man to dinner at a tavern where he pays for himself, but not to one's own table. One day I was invited by a younger son of the Duke of Bedford to eat oysters and drink a bottle of champagne. I accepted the invitation, and he ordered the oysters and the champagne, but we drank two bottles, and he made me pay half the price of the second bottle. Such are manners on the other side of the Channel. People laughed in my face when I said that I did not care to dine at a tavern as I could not get any soup.

'Are you ill?' they said, 'soup is only fit for invalids.'

The Englishman is entirely carnivorous. He eats very little bread, and calls himself economical because he spares himself the expense of soup and dessert, which circumstance made me remark that an English dinner is like eternity: it has no beginning and no end. Soup is considered very extravagant, as the very servants refuse to eat the meat from which it has been made. They say it is only fit to give to dogs. The salt beef which they use is certainly excellent. I cannot say the same for their beer, which was so bitter that I could not drink it. However, I could not be expected to like beer after the excellent French wines with which the wine merchant supplied me, certainly at a very heavy cost.

In the evening as I was walking in St. James's Park, I remembered it was a Ranelagh evening, and wishing to see the place I took a coach and drove there, intending to amuse myself till midnight, and to find a beauty to my taste.

I was pleased with the rotunda. I had some tea, I danced some minuets, but I made no acquaintances; and although I saw several pretty women, I did not dare to attack any of them. I got tired, and as it was near midnight I went out thinking to find my coach, for which I had not paid, still there, but it was gone, and I did not know what to do. An extremely pretty woman who was waiting for her carriage in the doorway, noticed my distress, and said that if I lived anywhere near Whitehall, she could take me home. I thanked her gratefully, and told her where I lived. Her carriage came up, her man opened the door, and she stepped in on my arm, telling me to sit beside her, and to stop the carriage when it got to my house.

As soon as we were in the carriage, I burst out into expressions of gratitude; and after telling her my name I expressed my regret at not having seen her at Soho Square.

'I was not in London,' she replied, 'I returned from Bath to-day.'

I apostrophised my happiness in having met her. I covered her hands with kisses, and dared to kiss her on the cheek; and finding that she smiled graciously, I fastened my lips on hers, and before long had given her an unequivocal mark of the ardour with which she had inspired me.

She took my attentions so easily that I flattered myself I had not displeased her, and I begged her to tell me where I could call on her and pay my court while I remained in London, but she replied,—

'We shall see each other again; we must be careful.'

I swore secrecy, and urged her no more. Directly after the carriage stopped, I kissed her hand and was set down at my door, well pleased with the ride home.

> Jacques Casanova de Seingalt (1725–98), *Memoirs: In London and Moscow*, tr. Arthur Machen, 1894

SOMETHING SPOILS GIBBON'S SWISS IDYLL

Lausanne, 5th September 1785

I solemnly protest, after two years' trial, that I have never in a single moment repented of my transmigration. The only disagreeable circumstance is the increase of a race of animals with which this country has been long infested, and who are said to come from an island in the Northern Ocean. I am told, but it seems incredible, that upwards of forty thousand English, masters and servants, are now absent on the continent; and I am sure we have our full proportion both in town and country, from the month of June to that of October.

> Edward Gibbon (1737–94), *Collected Letters*

THE ENGLISH PROPHETESS OF MOUNT LEBANON

A. W. Kinglake's book Eothen *is one of the best travel books ever written, describing as it does the wanderings of an Old Etonian in the Middle East in the 1830s. The high point of his tour was a visit to Lady Hester Stanhope, granddaughter of Pitt the Elder. A feminist, mystic, and figure of fascination and moral disapproval in Britain, she had settled in what is now Lebanon and lived more or less Arab-fashion.*

At last I was ushered into a small apartment, which was protected from the drafts of air passing through the door-way by a folding screen; passing this, I came alongside of a common European sofa, where sat the Lady Prophetess.

She rose from her seat very formally—spoke to me a few words of welcome, pointed to a chair which was placed exactly opposite to her sofa, at a couple of yards distance, and remained standing up to the full of her majestic height, perfectly still, and motionless, until I had taken my appointed place; she then resumed her seat, not packing herself up according to the mode of the Orientals, but allowing her feet to rest on the floor, or the footstool; at the moment of seating herself she covered her lap with a mass of loose, white drapery, which she held in her hand. It occurred to me at the time, that she did this in order to avoid the awkwardness of sitting in manifest trowsers under the eye of an European, but I can hardly fancy now, that with her wilful nature, she would have brooked such a compromise as this.

The woman before me had exactly the person of a Prophetess—not, indeed, of the divine Sibyl imagined by Domenichino, so sweetly distracted betwixt Love, and Mystery, but of a good businesslike, practical, Prophetess, long used to the exercise of her sacred calling. I have been told by those who knew Lady Hester Stanhope in her youth, that any notion of a resemblance betwixt her, and the great Chatham, must have been fanciful, but at the time of my seeing her, the large commanding features of the gaunt woman, then sixty years old or more, certainly reminded me of the Statesman that lay dying in the House of Lords, according to Copley's picture; her face was of the most astonishing whiteness; she wore a very large turban, which seemed to be of pale cashmere shawls, so disposed as to conceal the hair; her dress, from the chin down to the point at which it was concealed by the drapery which she held over her lap, was a mass of white linen loosely folding—an ecclesiastical sort of affair—more like a surplice than any of those blessed creations which our souls love under the names of 'dress,' and 'frock,' and 'boddice,' and 'collar,' and 'habit-shirt,' and sweet 'chemisette.'

A couple of black slave girls came at a signal, and supplied their mistress as well as myself, with lighted tchibouques, and coffee.

The custom of the East sanctions, and almost commands some moments of silence whilst you are inhaling the first few breaths of the fragrant pipe; the pause was broken, I think, by my Lady, who addressed to me some inquiries respecting my mother, and particularly as to her marriage; but before I had communicated any great amount of family facts, the spirit of the Prophetess kindled within her, and presently, (though with all the skill of a woman of the world,) she shuffled away the subject of poor, dear Somersetshire, and bounded onward into loftier spheres of thought . . .

With respect to her then present mode of life, Lady Hester informed me, that for her sin, she had subjected herself during many years to severe penance, and that her self-denial had not been without its reward. 'Vain and false,' said she, 'is all the pretended knowledge of the Europeans—their Doctors will tell you that the drinking of milk gives yellowness to the complexion; milk is my only food, and you see if my face be not white.' Her abstinence from food intellectual, was carried as far as her physical fasting; she never, she said, looked upon a book, nor a newspaper, but trusted alone to the stars for her sublime knowledge; she usually passed the nights in communing with these heavenly teachers, and lay at rest during the day-time. She spoke with great contempt of the frivolity, and benighted igno-rance of the modern Europeans, and mentioned in proof of this, that they were not only untaught in astrology, but were unacquainted with the com-mon, and every day phenomena produced by magic art; she spoke as if she would make me understand that all sorcerous speels were completely at her command, but that the exercise of such powers would be derogatory to her high rank in the heavenly kingdom. She said, that the spell by which the face of an absent person is thrown upon a mirror, was within the reach of the humblest, and most contemptible magicians, but that the practice of such like arts was unholy, as well as vulgar.

In truth, this half-ruined convent, guarded by the proud heart of an English gentlewoman, was the only spot throughout all Syria and Palestine in which the will of Mehemet Ali, and his fierce Lieutenant was not the law. More than once had the Pasha of Egypt commanded that Ibrahim should have the Albanians delivered up to him, but this white woman of the mountain (grown classical, not by books, but by very pride,) answered only with a disdainful invitation to 'come and take them.'

A. W. Kinglake, Eothen, 1844

PIERRE BEZUHOV LEAVES FOR MOSCOW

After Prince Andrei's engagement to Natasha, Pierre, without any apparent reason, suddenly felt it impossible to go on living as before. Firmly con-vinced as he was of the truths revealed to him by his benefactor, and happy as he had been in his first period of enthusiasm for the task of improving his spiritual self, to which he had devoted so much ardour—all the zest of such a life vanished with the engagement of Andrei and Natasha, and the death of Bazdeyev, the news of which reached him almost at the same time. Nothing but the empty skeleton of life remained to him: his house, a brilliant wife who now enjoyed the favours of a very important personage, acquaintance with all Petersburg, and his duties at court with all their tedious formalities. And this life suddenly began to fill Pierre with unexpected loathing. He ceased keeping a diary, avoided the company of the brethren, took to visiting the club again, drank a great deal and renewed his association with the gay bachelor sets, leading such a life that the Countess Hélène found it necessary to bring him severely to task. Pierre felt that she was right, and to avoid embarrassing her went away to Moscow.

In Moscow, as soon as he set foot in his enormous house with the faded and fading princesses and the swarm of servants; as soon as, driving through the town, he saw the Iversky chapel with innumerable tapers burning before the golden settings of the icons, the Kremlin square with its snow undisturbed by vehicles, the sledge-drivers and the hovels of the slum district; saw the old Muscovites quietly living out their days, with never a desire or a quickening of the blood; saw the old Moscow ladies, the Moscow balls and the English Club—he felt himself at home in a haven of rest. Moscow gave him the sensation of peace and warmth that one has in an old and dirty dressing-gown.

Moscow society, from the old ladies to the children, welcomed Pierre like a long-expected guest whose place was always ready waiting for him. In the eyes of Moscow society Pierre was the nicest, kindest, most intelligent, merriest and most liberal-minded of eccentrics, a heedless, genial Russian nobleman of the old school. His purse was always empty because it was open to everyone.

Benefit performances, wretched pictures, statues, charitable societies, gipsy choirs, schools, subscription dinners, drinking parties, the freemasons, the churches, and books—no one and nothing ever met with a refusal from him, and had it not been for two friends who had borrowed large sums from him and now took him under their protection he would have parted with everything. At the club no dinner or *soirée* was complete without him. The moment he sank into his place on the sofa after a couple of bottles of Margaux he would be surrounded by a circle of friends, and the discussions, the arguments and the joking began. Where there were quarrels his kindly smile and apt jests were enough to reconcile the antagonists. The masonic dinners were dull and dreary when he was absent.

When he rose after a bachelor supper and with his amiable, kindly smile yielded to the entreaties of the festive party to drive off somewhere with them the young men would make the rafters ring with their shouts of delight and triumph. At balls he danced if a partner was needed. Young women, married and unmarried, liked him because he paid court to no one but was equally agreeable to all, especially after supper. '*Il est charmant, il n'a pas de sexe*,' they said of him.

Pierre was one of those retired gentlemen-in-waiting, of whom there were hundreds, good-humouredly ending their days in Moscow.

How horrified he would have been seven years before, when he first arrived back from abroad, if anyone had told him there was no need for him to look about and make plans, that his track had long ago been shaped for him and marked out before all eternity, and that, wriggle as he might, he would be what everyone in his position was doomed to be. He would not have believed it. Had he not at one time longed with all his heart to establish a republic in Russia? Then that he might be a Napoleon? Then a philosopher, then a great strategist and the conqueror of Napoleon? Had he not seen the possibility of and passionately desired the regeneration of the sinful human race, and his own progress to the highest degree of perfection? Had he not established schools and infirmaries and liberated his serfs?

But instead of all that, here he was, the wealthy husband of a faithless wife, a retired gentleman-in-waiting, fond of eating and drinking, fond, too, as he unbuttoned his waistcoat after dinner, of abusing the government a bit, a member of the Moscow English Club, and a universal favourite in Moscow society. For a long while he could not reconcile himself to the ideas that he was one of those same retired Moscow gentlemen-in-waiting he had so profoundly despised seven years before.

Leo Tolstoy, *War and Peace*, 1863–9

A RUSSIAN PROGRESSIVE GOES WEST

Although I have been seeing hardly anybody, one does unavoidably stumble on people here. In Germany I came across a Russian who resides abroad permanently and who makes a trip to Russia every year for about three weeks to collect his income and then returns to Germany, where he has a wife and children, who have all become Germanized. I once asked him, by the way, what prompted him to become an expatriate. This is what he replied, literally (and with irritable insolence):

'Here there is civilization, there—barbarism. Besides, there are no differences of nationality here: Yesterday I was traveling in a train and I couldn't tell a Frenchman from an Englishman or from a German.'

'And that, *in your view*, is progress?'

'Of course it is; there's no question about it.'

'But let me tell you that that is not so at all. A Frenchman is above all else a Frenchman and an Englishman an Englishman, and their highest ambition is to be themselves. More than that—that is their great strength.'

'That's not true at all. Civilization must level everything and we shan't be happy until we forget that we are Russians and until everyone is just like everyone else. Don't listen to Katkov [a Russian nationalist]!'

'You don't like Katkov, then?'

'He's a scoundrel.'

'Why?'

'Because he dislikes the Poles.'

'Do you read his magazine?'

'No, I never read it.'

I report the conversation verbatim. The man in question is one of those young progressives, although it would appear that he keeps very much to himself. Abroad, these people turn into growling, squeamish Pomeranian dogs.

> Fyodor Dostoevsky (1821–81), *Selected Letters*, ed. Joseph Frank and David I. Goldstein, tr. Andrew R. MacAndrew, 1987

THE NATION-BUILDER

I was the convict
Sent to hell,
To make in the desert
The living well:

I split the rock;
I felled the tree—
The nation was
Because of me.

> Mary Gilmore, 1918; from Robert Hughes, *The Fatal Shore*, 1987

AT HOME IN AFRICA

A freed American slave writes to a sympathetic white clergyman after reaching the newly created state of Liberia, in West Africa, which has been established for former slaves. He regards it as home.

> Cald[well], *May 20, 1849*

Rev'd Mr. Mclane

Sir: I write to inform you that I have got home Safe after 28 days and nine hours after we left Hamelton roads [Hampton Roads]. I can say that I thank God that I am at home in Africa. I found my family well. I never expect to contend with the collard man in America no more. If they come, well; if not [it is] well with me. I expect to die in Africa where the free air blows, for here are liberty. The Presadent had got home before I did. He has just come from ware from New Sess. [He] have broak up the great slave factory and liberated a great manny slaves. There was none of our men lost [and] none crippled. They burnt up a great many towns. [A] great many told me when I was in America that we could not take the Spanyards. We have got them in our town wating for tryal. It proved as in all of the wars that God is on our side & if he be for us who can be against us. We have been oppressed long enough. We mean to stand our ground & contend for our rights until we die. O if my cullarred friends would only believe and feel the love of liberty they would not stay in the United Sates. We are so Ignorant that they won't even believe when they see. You know well how it is. It is not worth while for me to say anything more on this. You wished me to write you how things were in your department. There is mighty great grumbling with the emigrants that went out with me. They say they can't get nothing to eat. They are all sick But have got up. They gives them no coffee, no sugar, no tea. They can't get more. They all like the contry but not the far[e]. [Of] Mrs. [Jane C.] Washington's people, Charles Starks is a smart man. I believe he will work to mentain his family. I have let him have coffee an sugar occasionly. I beg him not to write to his Mistis yet. [I told him] that they would do better when Mr. Lewis comes home. He is gone to the leward. Mr. [Marshall] Hoopper from North Carlina went down Saterday to see the captain to return Back. He could not get anything to eat here, a pint of meal a day. They told him they thought when Mr. Lewis came they wold give him more. He says he paid for It and wants It; if not, he will return to the United Stats. There is But one died, hellems wife from Lynchburg, Virginia. I don't think any more will die with the feaver. It is a great pity that you hadent some one that feel for the emigrants & see that they were tended too. But men becomes carless. Mr. Lewis is engage in the menopolist [trade monopoly] & he is gone down the co[a]st. I am appose to It & It makes hard for the poor man. He can't get a pound of tobacco without getting a haxet [hatchet] and get a musket with his getting a box. It is only good for the merchant. I have been Elected by the people for Representative since I come home. If I live I will do all I can to brake It up. Give my love to Mrs. McLane & all the children. I have not had time to get any lemon juce yet. I will send some by the next opportunity. I got my dogs all home safe except one I lost in pasage. William Butler that left Washington, he is liveing with his cousin, the Vice President. He has had the feaver and has got up. He is well satisfied. Good by. I have no more business in America. But I will talk with you here. I will be glad to hear from you any time and thank you for a bundle of news papers. My wife [sends] respect to you, hoping you are well. She says you must send her Chrismas gift. Yours truly,

Sion Harris

Slaves No More: Letters from Liberia 1833–1869, ed. Bell I. Wiley, 1980

AN ASYLUM FROM THE MOST GRINDING OPPRESSION
Liberia's Declaration of Independence, 26 July 1847.

We, the people of the Republic of Liberia, were originally inhabitants of the United States of North America.

In some parts of that country we were debarred by law from all rights and privileges of man—in other parts, public sentiment, more powerful than law, frowned us down.

We were everywhere shut out from all civil office.

We were excluded from all participation in the Government.

We were taxed without our consent.

We were compelled to contribute to the resources of a country which gave us no protection.

We were made a separate and distinct class, and against us every avenue of improvement was effectually closed. Strangers from other lands, of a colour different from ours, were preferred before us.

We uttered our complaints, but they were unattended to, or only met by alleging the peculiar institutions of the country.

All hope of a favourable change in our country was thus wholly extinguished in our bosoms, and we looked with anxiety for some asylum from the deep degradation.

The western coast of Africa was the place selected by American benevolence and philanthropy for our future home. Removed beyond those influences which oppressed us in our native land, it was hoped we would be enabled to enjoy those rights and privileges and exercise and improve those faculties which the God of nature has given us in common with the rest of mankind.

Under the auspices of the American Colonisation Society, we established ourselves here, on land acquired by purchase from the lords of the soil.

Liberia is not the offspring of grasping ambition, nor the tool of avaricious speculation.

No desire for territorial aggrandisement brought us to these shores; nor do we believe so sordid a motive entered into the high consideration of those who aided us in providing this asylum. Liberia is an asylum from the most grinding oppression.

In coming to the shores of Africa, we indulged the pleasing hope that we would be permitted to exercise and improve those faculties which impart to man his dignity; to nourish in our hearts the flame of honourable ambition; to cherish and indulge those aspirations which a beneficent Creator had implanted in every human heart, and to evince to all who despise, ridicule, and oppress our race that we possess with them a common nature; are with them susceptible of equal refinement, and capable of equal advancement in all that adorns and dignifies man.

Sir Harry Johnston, *Liberia*, 1906

THE MÉNAGE BURTON

In 1878 the London magazine The World *carried an interview with Sir Richard and Lady Burton at their flat in Trieste.*

Captain and Mrs. Burton are well, if airily, lodged in a flat composed of ten rooms, separated by a corridor adorned with a picture of our Saviour, a statuette of St. Joseph with a lamp, and a Madonna with another lamp burning before it. Thus far the belongings are all of the Cross; but no sooner are we landed in the little drawing-rooms than signs of the Crescent appear. Small but artistically arranged, the rooms, opening into one another, are bright with Oriental hangings, with trays and dishes of gold and silver, brass trays and goblets, chibouques with great amber mouthpieces, and all kinds of Eastern treasures mingled with family souvenirs. There is no carpet, but a Bedouin rug occupies the middle of the floor, and vies in brilliancy of colour with Persian enamels and bits of good old china. There are no sofas, but plenty of divans covered with Damascus stuffs. Thus far the interior is as Mussulman as the exterior is Christian; but a curious effect is produced among the Oriental *mise en scène* by the presence of a pianoforte and a compact library of well-chosen books.

Burton conducted his visitor through the apartment:

Leading the way from the drawing-rooms or divans, he takes us through bedrooms and dressing-rooms, furnished in Spartan simplicity with little iron bedsteads covered with bearskins, and supplied with reading-tables and lamps, beside which repose the Bible, the Shakespeare, the Euclid and the Breviary, which go with Captain and Mrs. Burton on all their wanderings. . . . The little rooms are completely lined with rough deal shelves, containing, perhaps, eight thousand or more volumes in every Western language, as well as in Arabic, Persian, and Hindustani. Every odd corner is piled with weapons, guns, pistols, boar-spears, swords of every shape and make, foils and masks, chronometers, barometers, and all kinds of scientific instruments. One cupboard is full of medicines necessary for Oriental expeditions or for Mrs. Burton's Trieste poor, and on it is written, 'The Pharmacy'. Idols are not wanting, for elephant-nosed Gunpati [Ganapati or Ganesa] is there cheek by jowl with Vishnu.

The most remarkable objects the journalist found in the rooms were the eleven rough deal tables that were scattered about. Each was covered with writing materials. Burton liked to have a separate table for each book on which he was working so that when he tired of one project he could move to another table and a new subject.

Asked why he lived on the fourth floor, Burton said, 'Why we live so high up may be easily explained. To begin with, we are in good condition, and run up and down the stairs like squirrels. We live on the fourth storey because there is no fifth.'

The visitor from the *World* also described how the Burtons spent their time:

The *ménage Burton* is conducted on the early-rising principle. About four or five o'clock our hosts are astir, and already in their 'den', drinking tea made over a spirit lamp, and eating bread and fruit, reading and studying languages. By noon the morning's work is got over, including the consumption of a cup of soup, the ablution without which no true believer is happy, and the obligations of Frankish toilette. Then comes a stroll to the fencing-school, kept by an excellent broad-swordsman, and old German trooper. For an hour Captain and Mrs. Burton fence in the school, if the weather be cold; if it is warm, they make for the water, and often swim for a couple of hours.

Then comes a spell of work at the Consulate. 'I have my Consulate,' the Chief explains, 'in the heart of the town. I don't want my Jack-tar in my sanctum; and when he wants *me*, he has usually been on the spree and got into trouble.' While the husband is engaged in his official duties, the wife is abroad promoting a Society for the Prevention of Cruelty to Animals, a necessary institution in Southern countries, where—on the purely gratuitous hypothesis that the so-called lower animals have no soul—the uttermost brutality is shown in the treatment of them. 'You see,' remarks your host, 'that my wife and I are like an elder and younger brother living *en garçon*. We divide the work. I take all the hard and scientific part, and make her do all the rest. When we have worked all day, and said all we have to say to each other, we want relaxation. To that end we have formed a little "mess", with fifteen friends at the *table d'hôte* of the Hotel de la Ville, where we get a good dinner and a pint of country wine made on the hillside for a florin and a half. By this plan we escape the bore of housekeeping, and are relieved from the curse of domesticity, which we both hate. At dinner we hear the news, if any, take our coffee, cigarettes, and *kirsch* outside the hotel, then go homewards to read ourself to sleep; and tomorrow *da capo*.'

The interviewer commented on the tameness of this life compared to their former adventures, but Burton replied, 'The existence you deprecate is varied by excursions. We know every stick and stone for a hundred miles around, and all the pre-historic remains of the countryside. Our Austrian Governor-General, Baron Pino de Friedenthal, is a first-rate man, and often gives us a cruise in the Government yacht. It is, as you say, an odd place for me to be in; but recollect, it is not every place that would suit *me*.'

The World, London, 1878; quoted in Byron Farwell, *Burton*, 1963

WHY ROBERT LOUIS STEVENSON PREFERS SAMOA

I do not think I shall come to England more than once, and then it'll be to die. Health I enjoy in the tropics; even here, which they call sub- or semi-tropical, I come only to catch cold. I have not been out since my arrival; live here in a nice bedroom by the fireside, and read books and letters from Henry James, and send out to get his *Tragic Muse*, only to be told they can't be had as yet in Sydney, and have altogether a placid time. But I can't go out! The thermometer was nearly down to 50° the other day—no temperature for me, Mr. James: how should I do in England? I fear not at all. Am I very sorry? I am sorry about seven or eight people in England, and one or two in the States. And outside of that, I simply prefer Samoa. These are the words of honesty and soberness. (I am fasting from all but sin, coughing, *The Bondman*, a couple of eggs and a cup of tea.) I was never fond of towns, houses, society, or (it seems) civilisation. Nor yet it seems was I ever very fond of (what is technically called) God's green earth. The sea, islands, the islanders, the island life and climate, make and keep me truly happier. These last two years I have been much at sea, and I have *never wearied*; sometimes I have indeed grown impatient for some destination; more often I was sorry that the voyage drew so early to an end; and never once did I lose my fidelity to blue water and a ship. It is plain, then, that for me my exile to the place of schooners and islands can be in no sense regarded as a calamity.

Robert Louis Stevenson (1850–94), *Letters*, ed. Sidney Colvin, 1901

THE DESIRE FOR THE UNKNOWN

Every day gets better for me, in the end I understand the language quite well, my neighbours (three close by, the others at various distances) regard me almost as one of themselves; my naked feet, from daily contact with the rock, have got used to the ground; my body, almost always naked, no longer fears the sun; civilisation leaves me bit by bit and I begin to think simply, to have only a little hatred for my neighbour, and I function in an animal way, freely—with the certainty of the morrow [being] like today; every morning the sun rises serene for me as for everyone, I become care-free and calm and loving. I have a natural friend, who has come to see me every day naturally, without any interested motive. My paintings in colour [and] my wood-carvings astonished him and my answers to his questions taught him something. Not a day when I work but he comes to watch me. One day when, handing him my tools, I asked him to try a sculpture, he gazed at me in amazement and said to me simply, with sincerity, that I was not like other men; and he was perhaps the first of my fellows to tell me that I was useful to others. A child. . . . One has to be, to think that an artist ·is something useful.

The young man was faultlessly handsome and we were great friends. Sometimes in the evening, when I was resting from my day's work, he would ask me the questions of a young savage who wants to know a lot of things about love in Europe, questions which often embarrassed me.

One day I wished to have for sculpture a tree of rosewood, a piece of considerable size and not hollow. 'For that,' he told me, 'you must go up the mountain to a certain place where I know several fine trees that might satisfy you. If you like, I'll take you there and we'll carry it back, the two of us.'

We left in the early morning.

The Indian paths in Tahiti are quite difficult for a European: between two unscalable mountains there is a cleft where the water purifies itself by twist-ing between detached boulders, rolled down, left at rest, then caught up again on a torrent day to be rolled down further, and so on to the sea. On either side of the stream there cascades a semblance of a path: trees pell-mell, monster ferns, all sorts of vegetation growing wilder, more and more impenetrable as you climb towards the centre of the island.

We went naked, both of us, except for the loincloth, and axe in hand, crossing the river many a time to take advantage of a bit of track which my companion seemed to smell out, so little visible [it was], so deeply shaded.— Complete silence,—only the noise of water crying against rock, monoton-ous as the silence. And two we certainly were, two friends, he a quite young man and I almost an old man in body and soul, in civilised vices: in lost illusions. His lithe animal body had graceful contours, he walked in front of me sexless. . . .

From all this youth, from this perfect harmony with the nature which surrounded us, there emanated a beauty, a fragrance (*noa noa*) that en-chanted my artist soul. From this friendship so well cemented by the mutual attraction between simple and composite, love took power to blossom in me.

And we were only . . . the two of us—

I had a sort of presentiment of crime, the desire for the unknown, the awakening of evil—Then weariness of the male rôle, having always to be strong, protective; shoulders that are a heavy load. To be for a minute the weak being who loves and obeys.

I drew close, without fear of laws, my temples throbbing.

The path had come to an end . . . we had to cross the river; my companion turned at that moment, so that his chest was towards me. The hermaphrodite had vanished; it was a young man, after all; his innocent eyes resembled the limpidity of the water. Calm suddenly came back into my soul, and this time I enjoyed the coolness of the stream deliciously, plunging into it with delight—'*Toe toe*,' he said to me ('it's cold'). 'Oh no,' I answered, and this denial, answering my previous desire, drove in among the cliffs like an echo. Fiercely I thrust my way with energy into the thicket, [which had] become more and more wild; the boy went on his way, still limpid-eyed. He had not understood. I alone carried the burden of an evil thought, a whole civilisation had been before me in evil and had educated me.

We were reaching our destination.—At that point the crags of the mountain drew apart, and behind a curtain of tangled trees a semblance of a plateau [lay] hidden but not unknown. There several trees (rose-wood) extended their huge branches. Savages both of us, we attacked with the axe a magnificent tree which had to be destroyed to get a branch suitable to my desires. I struck furiously and, my hands covered with blood, hacked away with the pleasure of sating one's brutality and of destroying something. In time with the noise of the axe I sang:

> 'Cut down by the foot the whole forest (of desires)
> Cut down in yourself the love of yourself, as a man
>   would cut down with his hand in autumn the Lotus.'

Well and truly destroyed indeed, all the old remnant of civilised man in me. I returned at peace, feeling myself thenceforward a different man, a Maori.

Paul Gauguin (1848–1903), Noa Noa—Voyage to Tahiti, 1961

BICYCLES, TELEPHONES, AND COLONEL CODY

After the death in their Kentish exile of her husband, Napoleon III, the Empress Eugénie took on a new lease of life. She was particularly interested in new gadgets.

Everyone was amazed by Eugénie's physical vitality. In the 1880s most of her friends, like Queen Victoria, had thought of her as 'the poor Empress' who had suffered so much and looked old, ill and haggard, and so different from the beautiful, carefree young Empress of the Tuileries and Saint-Cloud; to her young companions of the 1900s, she was the wonderfully active and high-spirited old lady whose youth was for them a legend, not a memory. When she was over seventy she learned to ride a bicycle, and though she did not take part in the races on *la piste*, she wobbled along slowly, with a servant walking alongside ready to catch her if she fell off. . . .

Eugénie installed the telephone at Farnborough Hill, and had an internal telephone system with telephones all over the house. She was very interested in Marconi's successful experiments with transatlantic wireless communication, and had wireless installed on her yacht. She bought a motor car, and like other employers at the time transformed her coachman into her chauffeur. She was always a little nervous in a car, because she was afraid that they would have an accident or run over a hen. In travelling, she showed the cautious side of her dare-devil temperament, and when catching a train insisted on arriving at the station long before the departure time.

When she was in Venice in July 1906, she decided that she must go, for the first time in her life, to see a film in a cinema. She persuaded her secretary, Piétri, and her companion, Miss Vesey, to take her to a small hall in a working-class district, where they sat on a hard wooden bench and watched a film about a comic thief and two clever dogs which must have been one of the early silent Hollywood farces.

Within a few miles of Farnborough Hill, Colonel Cody was carrying out experiments in aviation at the Balloon House in Aldershot. The Empress and her household visited him on several occasions, and saw his aeroplane; and when Cody and Colonel Capper made their experimental flight in an airship over Farnborough in 1907, Eugénie, with the Scotts, the Veseys, and the Marquis of Santa Cruz's daughter, the young Princess Metternich, went up to the tower at Farnborough Hill to watch the flight. They saw, through the September mist, the airship rise from Cove Common and pass over the house with Cody and Capper saluting the Empress as they passed, while she and her party waved their handkerchiefs at the airmen.

Jasper Ridley, Napoleon III and Eugénie, 1979

STEPHEN DEDALUS RECOGNIZES HIS ISOLATION

How foolish his aim had been! He had tried to build a breakwater of order and elegance against the sordid tide of life without him and to dam up, by rules of conduct and active interests and new filial relations, the powerful recurrence of the tides within him. Useless. From without as from within the waters had flowed over his barriers: their tides began once more to jostle fiercely above the crumbled mole.

He saw clearly too his own futile isolation. He had not gone one step nearer the lives he had sought to approach nor bridged the restless shame and rancour that had divided him from mother and brother and sister. He felt that he was hardly of the one blood with them but stood to them rather in the mystical kinship of fosterage, fosterchild and fosterbrother. . . .

— The soul is born, he said vaguely, first in those moments I told you of. It has a slow and dark birth, more mysterious than the birth of the body. When the soul of a man is born in this country there are nets flung at it to hold it back from flight. You talk to me of nationality, language, religion. I shall try to fly by those nets. . . .

— . . . You have asked me what I would do and what I would not do. I will tell you what I will do and what I will not do. I will not serve that in which I no longer believe, whether it call itself my home, my fatherland, or my church: and I will try to express myself in some mode of life or art as freely as I can and as wholly as I can, using for my defence the only arms I allow myself to use—silence, exile, and cunning.

James Joyce, The Portrait of an Artist as a Young Man, 1916

CONTACT WITH WESTERN EUROPE FOR A ZLOTY

I had heard about Franz Kafka years before I read any of his books from his friend Jacques Kohn, a former actor in the Yiddish theater. I say 'former' because by the time I knew him he was no longer on the stage. It was the early thirties, and the Yiddish theater in Warsaw had already begun to lose its audience. Jacques Kohn himself was a sick and broken man. Although he still dressed in the style of a dandy, his clothes were shabby. He wore a monocle in his left eye, a high old-fashioned collar (known as 'father-murderer'), patent-leather shoes, and a derby. He had been nicknamed 'the lord' by the cynics in the Warsaw Yiddish writers' club that we both frequented. Although he stooped more and more, he worked stubbornly at keeping his shoulders back. What was left of his once yellow hair he combed to form a bridge over his bare skull. In the tradition of the old-time theater, every now and then he would lapse into Germanized Yiddish—particularly when he spoke of his relationship with Kafka. Of late, he had begun writing newspaper articles, but the editors were unanimous in rejecting his manuscripts. He lived in an attic room somewhere on Leszno Street and was constantly ailing. A joke about him made the rounds of the club members: 'All day long he lies in an oxygen tent, and at night he emerges a Don Juan.'

We always met at the club in the evening. The door would open slowly to admit Jacques Kohn. He had the air of an important European celebrity who was deigning to visit the ghetto. He would look around and grimace, as if to indicate that the smells of herring, garlic, and cheap tobacco were not to his taste. He would glance disdainfully over the tables covered with tattered newspapers, broken chess pieces, and ashtrays filled with cigarette stubs, around which the club members sat endlessly discussing literature in their shrill voices. He would shake his head as if to say, 'What can you expect from such schlemiels?' The moment I saw him entering, I would put my hand in my pocket and prepare the zloty that he would inevitably borrow from me.

This particular evening, Jacques seemed to be in a better mood than usual. He smiled, displaying his porcelain teeth, which did not fit and moved slightly when he spoke, and swaggered over to me as if he were on-stage. He offered me his bony, long-fingered hand and said, 'How's the rising star doing tonight?'

'At it already?'

'I'm serious. Serious. I know talent when I see it, even though I lack it myself. When we played Prague in 1911, no one had ever heard of Kafka. He came backstage, and the moment I saw him I knew that I was in the presence of genius. I could smell it the way a cat smells a mouse. That was how our great friendship began.'

I had heard this story many times and in as many variations, but I knew that I would have to listen to it again. He sat down at my table, and Manya, the waitress, brought us glasses of tea and cookies, Jacques Kohn raised his eyebrows over his yellowish eyes, the whites of which were threaded with bloody little veins. His expression seemed to say, 'This is what the barbarians call tea?' He put five lumps of sugar into his glass and stirred, rotating the tin spoon outward. With his thumb and index finger, the nail of which was unusually long, he broke off a small piece of cookie, put it into his mouth, and said, '*Nu ja,*' which meant, One cannot fill one's stomach on the past.

It was all play-acting. He himself came from a Hasidic family in one of the small Polish towns. His name was not Jacques but Jankel. However, he had lived for many years in Prague, Vienna, Berlin, Paris. He had not always been an actor in the Yiddish theater but had played on the stage in both France and Germany. He had been friends with many celebrities. He had helped Chagall find a studio in Belleville. He had been a frequent guest at

Israel Zangwill's. He had appeared in a Reinhardt production, and had eaten cold cuts with Piscator. He had shown me letters he had received not only from Kafka but from Jakob Wassermann, Stefan Zweig, Romain Rolland, Ilya Ehrenburg, and Martin Buber. They all addressed him by his first name. As we got to know each other better, he had even let me see photographs and letters from famous actresses with whom he had had affairs.

For me, 'lending' Jacques Kohn a zloty meant coming into contact with Western Europe.

Isaac Bashevis Singer, 'A Friend of Kafka', *Collected Stories*, 1981

BERTIE WOOSTER ESCAPES HIS AUNT

I first got to know Corky when I came to New York. He was a pal of my cousin Gussie, who was in with a lot of people down Washington Square way. I don't know if I ever told you about it, but the reason I left England was because I was sent over by my Aunt Agatha to try to stop young Gussie marrying a girl on the vaudeville stage, and I got the whole thing so mixed up that I decided that it would be a sound scheme for me to stop on in America for a bit instead of going back and having long cosy chats about the thing with aunt. So I sent Jeeves out to find a decent apartment, and settled down for a bit of exile. I'm bound to say that New York's a topping place to be exiled in. Everybody was awfully good to me, and there seemed to be plenty of things going on, and I'm a wealthy bird, so everything was fine. Chappies introduced me to other chappies, and so on and so forth, and it wasn't long before I knew squads of the right sort, some who rolled in dollars in houses up by the Park, and others who lived with the gas turned down mostly around Washington Square—artists and writers and so forth. Brainy coves.

P. G. Wodehouse, *My Man Jeeves*, 1930

PRACTICALLY LIVING ON PRAIRIE OYSTERS

'Oh, hullo, Chris darling!' cried Sally from the doorway. 'How sweet of you to come! I was feeling most terribly lonely. I've been crying on Frau Karpf's chest. Nicht wahr, Frau Karpf?' She appealed to the toad landlady, 'ich habe geweint auf Dein Brust.' Frau Karpf shook her bosom in a toad-like chuckle.

'Would you rather have coffee, Chris, or tea?' Sally continued. 'You can have either. Only I don't recommend the tea much. I don't know what

Frau Karpf does to it; I think she empties all the kitchen slops together into a jug and boils them up with tea-leaves.'

'I'll have coffee, then.'

'Frau Karpf, Leibling, willst Du sein ein Engel und bring zwei Tassen von Kaffee?' Sally's German was not merely incorrect; it was all her own. She pronounced every word in a mincing, specially 'foreign' manner. You could tell that she was speaking a foreign language from her expression alone. 'Chris darling, will you be an angel and draw the curtains?'

I did so, although it was still quite light outside. Sally, meanwhile, had switched on the table-lamp. As I turned from the window, she curled herself up delicately on the sofa like a cat, and, opening her bag, felt for a cigarette. But hardly was the pose complete before she'd jumped to her feet again:

'Would you like a Prairie Oyster?' She produced glasses, eggs and a bottle of Worcester sauce from the boot-cupboard under the dismantled wash-stand: 'I practically live on them.' Dexterously, she broke the eggs into the glasses, added the sauce and stirred up the mixture with the end of a fountain-pen: 'They're about all I can afford.' She was back on the sofa again, daintily curled up.

She was wearing the same black dress to-day, but without the cape. Instead, she had a little white collar and white cuffs. They produced a kind of theatrically chaste effect, like a nun in grand opera. 'What are you laugh-ing at, Chris?' she asked.

'I don't know,' I said. But still I couldn't stop grinning. There was, at that moment, something so extraordinarily comic in Sally's appearance. She was really beautiful, with her little dark head, big eyes and finely arched nose—and so absurdly conscious of all these features. There she lay, as complacently feminine as a turtle-dove, with her poised self-conscious head and daintily arranged hands.

'Chris, you swine, do tell me why you're laughing?'

'I really haven't the faintest idea.'

At this, she began to laugh, too: 'You are mad, you know!'

'Have you been here long?' I asked, looking round the large gloomy room.

'Ever since I arrived in Berlin. Let's see—that was about two months ago.'

I asked what had made her decide to come out to Germany at all. Had she come alone? No, she'd come with a girl friend. An actress. Older than Sally. The girl had been to Berlin before. She'd told Sally that they'd certainly be able to get work with the Ufa. So Sally borrowed ten pounds from a nice old gentleman and joined her.

She hadn't told her parents anything about it until the two of them had actually arrived in Germany: 'I wish you'd met Diana. She was the most marvellous gold-digger you can imagine. She'd get hold of men anywhere— it didn't matter whether she could speak their language or not. She made me nearly die of laughing. I absolutely adored her.'

But when they'd been together in Berlin three weeks and no job had appeared, Diana had got hold of a banker, who'd taken her off with him to Paris.

'And left you here alone? I must say I think that was pretty rotten of her.'

'Oh, I don't know . . . Everyone's got to look after themselves. I expect, in her place, I'd have done the same.'

Christopher Isherwood, *Goodbye to Berlin*, 1939

GRAHAM GREENE'S DAILY LIFE IN WARTIME SIERRA LEONE

My house in Freetown stood on the flats below Hill Station, the European quarter, opposite a transport camp of the Nigerian Regiment which attracted flies and vultures. The house had been built by a Syrian and was remarkable for having a staircase and a first floor in this land of bungalows. It had been condemned by the medical officer of health, but houses were not easily obtainable now that the Army, the Navy and the Air Force had moved into Freetown. When the rains came I realized why it had been condemned: the ground on which it stood became a swamp. Between it and the sea stretched a few acres of scrub used as a public lavatory by the African inhabitants of the slum houses close by.

At six in the morning I would get up and have breakfast. The kitchen equipment was limited and once I was roused by the cries of my cook (who later went off his head completely); he was chasing my steward with a hatchet because the boy had borrowed the empty sardine tin in which the cook was accustomed to fry my morning egg. Life was very different from the blitzed London of my story, but it is often easier to describe something from a long way off.

At seven I would take my little Morris car and drive into Freetown, do my shopping at the stores—PZ or Oliphant's—and collect my telegrams at the police station to which I was fictitiously attached by my cover employment of CID Special Branch. They arrived in a code unintelligible to the police and were handed me by the Commissioner, a man at the end of his middle years, to whom I became greatly attached. Then I would drive home and decode the telegrams and reply to them as best I could, write my reports or rearrange the reports of others into an acceptable form—work was over by lunchtime, unless an urgent telegram arrived or a convoy had brought a bag to be opened and dealt with.

By the end of lunch in the full humid heat of the day I would take a siesta, my sleep disturbed by the heavy movements of the vultures on the iron roof above my head (I have seen as many as six perched up there, like old broken umbrellas). When one of them took off or landed it was as though a thief were trying to break through the iron roof. At four thirty I would have tea, then take a solitary walk along an abandoned railway track once used by European officials, halfway up the slopes below Hill Station. There was a wide view of the huge Freetown bay where sometimes the *Queen Mary* would be lying at anchor as though she had been hijacked from the North Atlantic, and the old *Edinburgh Castle*—now a naval depot ship—lay rotting on a reef of empty bottles. As the sun began to set the laterite paths turned the colour of a rose. It was the hour and the place I liked best.

When dusk began to fall it was time to turn home; I write 'home' for as one year ebbed away the house on the swamp where I lived alone really became home. I had to take my bath before night dropped suddenly at six, for that was the rat-hour. I had constructed a covered way between the house and the kitchen and this provided a bridge for the invaders. Once, a little late at six thirty, I found a rat making its toilet on the rim of the bath (the rats were always punctual) and I never bathed as late again. At night I would be woken under my mosquito-net by the rats swinging on the bedroom curtains.

Graham Greene, Ways of Escape, 1980

WITTGENSTEIN GETS A NEW JOB

For the first two years of war, a recurrent theme of conversation with Wittgenstein was his frustration at not being able to find work outside academic life. He found it intolerable to be teaching philosophy while a war was being fought, and wanted more than anything else to be able to contribute to the war effort. His chance to do so came through his friendship with the Oxford philosopher Gilbert Ryle. Gilbert's brother, John Ryle, was Regius Professor of Physics at Cambridge, but in 1940 he had returned to Guy's Hospital to help them prepare for the Blitz. In September 1941 Wittgenstein wrote to John Ryle asking to meet him at Guy's. Ryle invited him to lunch, and was immediately impressed. 'He is one of the world's famousest philosophers', he wrote to his wife. 'He wears an open green shirt and has a rather attractive face':

I was so interested that after years as a Trinity don, so far from getting tarred with the same brush as the others, he is overcome by the deadness of the place. He said to me 'I feel I will die slowly if I stay there. I would rather take a chance of dying quickly.' And so he wants to work at some humble manual job in a hospital as his war-work and will resign his chair if necessary, but doesn't want it talked about at all. And he wants the job to be in a blitzed area. The works department are prepared to take him as an odd job man under the older workmen who do all the running repairs all over the hospital. I think he realises that his mind works so differently to most people's that it would be stupid to try for any kind of war-work based on intelligence. I have written to him tonight to tell him about this job but am not trying to persuade him unduly.

Someday I must bring him and also one or two of the Canadians down to see you.

Wittgenstein clearly needed no undue persuasion, for a week or so after this letter was written he started work at Guy's. Not, however, as an odd-job man but as a dispensary porter.

John Ryle respected Wittgenstein's wish that his change of job from Professor of Philosophy at Cambridge to dispensary porter at Guy's Hospital should not be talked about, and does not seem to have mentioned to any of the staff at Guy's that the new porter was 'one of the world's famousest philosophers'. One indication of his discretion is that Humphrey Osmond, a good friend of Ryle's and the editor during the war of the in-house journal *Guy's Gazette* (and therefore always on the look-out for an interesting story), did not find out that Wittgenstein had been at Guy's until after the publication of Norman Malcolm's memoir in 1958. It is fortunate that Ryle kept his silence, for if the *Gazette* had run a 'Famous philosopher at Guy's' piece, there is no doubt that Wittgenstein would have reacted with the utmost rage. . . .

Wittgenstein's job as a porter was to deliver medicines from the dispensary to the wards, where, according to John Ryle's wife, Miriam, he advised the patients not to take them. His boss at the pharmacy was Mr S. F. Izzard. When asked later if he remembered Wittgenstein as a porter, Izzard replied: 'Yes, very well. He came and worked here and after working here three weeks he came and explained how we should be running the place. You see, he was a man who was used to thinking.' After a short while, he was switched to the job of pharmacy technician in the manufacturing laboratory, where one of his duties was to prepare Lassar's ointment for the dermatological department. When Drury visited Wittgenstein at Guy's, he was told by a member of staff that no one before had produced Lassar's ointment of such high quality.

Ray Monk, *Ludwig Wittgenstein: The Duty of Genius*, 1990

GENERAL DE GAULLE MAKES HIS FIRST BROADCAST FROM LONDON

The leaders who, for many years past, have been at the head of the French armed forces, have set up a government.

Alleging the defeat of our armies, this government has entered into negotiations with the enemy with a view to bringing about a cessation of hostilities. It is quite true that we were, and still are, overwhelmed by enemy mechanized forces, both on the ground and in the air. It was the tanks, the planes, and the tactics of the Germans, far more than their numbers that forced our armies to retreat. It was the German tanks, planes and tactics that took our leaders by surprise and brought them to their present plight.

But has the last word been said? Must we abandon all hope? Is our defeat final?—No!

Speaking in full knowledge of the facts, I ask you to believe me when I say that the cause of France is not lost. The very factors that brought about our defeat may one day lead us to victory.

For France is not alone! She is not alone! She is not alone! Behind her is a vast empire, and she can make common cause with the British Empire, which commands the seas and is continuing the struggle. Like England, she can draw unreservedly on the immense industrial resources of the United States.

This war is not limited to our unfortunate country. The outcome of the struggle has not been decided by the Battle of France. This is a world war. Mistakes have been made, there have been delays and untold suffering, but the fact remains that there still exists in the world everything we need to crush our enemies some day. Today we are crushed by the sheer weight of mechanized force hurled against us, but we can still look to a future in which even greater mechanized force will bring us victory. Therein lies the destiny of the world.

I, General de Gaulle, now in London, call on all French officers and men who are at present on British soil, or may be in the future, with or without their arms; I call on all engineers and skilled workmen from the armament factories who are at present on British soil, or may be in the future, to get in touch with me. Whatever happens, the flame of French resistance must not and shall not die. Tomorrow, I shall broadcast again from London.

Lord Gladwyn, *The History-Makers*, 1973; the broadcast was made at 6 p.m. on 18 June 1940

THE PROBLEMS OF OVERSEEING DE GAULLE AT THE MICROPHONE

Seven o'clock and still no script. My chief, Sir Alexander Cadogan, went off leaving me with strict instructions. Shortly after, it arrived. I found it brilliant, but it did violate several of my rules. Making the minimum changes and even so taking a very considerable risk, I rushed round to the Rubens Hotel, only to be told that the General had not yet finished his dinner. Just before eight he emerged, clearly in a bad temper, and gazing down on me said: '*Qui êtes-vous?*' I explained that I was a mere subordinate, but that owing to the late arrival of the text it had fallen to me to propose certain '*légères modifications*'. '*Donnez-les moi!*' Awful pause. '*Je les trouve ridicules,*' said the General. '*Parfaitement ri-di-cules.*' I felt bound to point out that it was now five past eight, that the delay was not my fault and that, not to put too fine a point on it, if he could not accept the '*modifications*' he would not be able to broadcast. The ultimatum succeeded. . . . '*Eh bien,*' he said, '*j'accepte, c'est ridicule, mais j'accepte.*'

Lord Gladwyn, *The History-Makers*, 1973

A QUESTION OF COMMUNICATION

At five to three the bell from the Cabinet room rang and I went in. Mr Churchill informed me that when de Gaulle arrived he would rise and bow slightly but would not shake hands with him. He would indicate by a gesture that the General was to sit opposite him, on the other side of the Cabinet table. No doubt as a supreme mark of disapproval, he announced that he would not speak to him in French, but would converse through an interpreter. 'And you,' he said, 'will be the interpreter.'

Punctually at 3 p.m. the General arrived. Churchill rose from his chair in the middle of the long Cabinet table, inclined his head slightly and gestured to the selected seat opposite him. De Gaulle seemed quite unabashed. He walked to his chair, sat down, gazed at the Prime Minister and said nothing.

'General de Gaulle, I have asked you to come here this afternoon.' Churchill stopped and looked fiercely at me. 'Mon Général,' I said, 'je vous ai invité de venir cet après-midi.'

'I didn't say Mon Général,' interrupted the Prime Minister 'and I did not say I had invited him.' Somehow I stumbled, with frequent interruptions, through the next few sentences.

Then it was de Gaulle's turn. After the first sentence he turned to me and I interpreted. 'Non, non,' he interjected, 'ce n'est pas du tout le sens de ce que je disais.' But it was.

Churchill said it was clear to both of them that if I could not do better than that I had better find somebody who could. So I escaped from the room with shame and telephoned to Nicholas Lawford at the Foreign Office. His French was immaculate. He arrived at the double and I showed him into the Cabinet room where no word had been spoken in the intervening minutes. It seemed no time at all before he emerged, red in the face and protesting that they must be mad: they had said he could not speak French properly and they would have to manage without an interpreter.

Lord Gladwyn, *The History-Makers*, 1973

A LITTLE CORNER OF PARIS IN LONDON

The Frenchmen who work in this section of the BBC make up as lively and as vivid a group of people as you could meet in the wisest and wittiest circles of any civilized capital. London hostesses fight in vain to lure them to dinner parties for any one of them would make the dullest evening sparkle. Some of them are brilliant and acrid French journalists; others are distinguished painters, writers, lawyers, scientists and politicians. For obvious reasons they are known now in France and even over here by pseudonyms. Until the war is over, they are not interested in social life. They prefer to sit in a stuffy canteen or an obscure Soho restaurant—eating with one hand and dashing off new ideas and embryo scripts with the other—to lingering over a Mayfair dinner table. They pride themselves on being a first-class *équipe*, combining the comradeship and discipline of a ship's crew with the readiness to play any part from lead to 'noises off' of a provincial repertory company. They make a little corner of Paris in the heart of London, an oasis of French clarity, French warmth and French gaiety—above all of passionate French love of country. For the *équipe* lives, thinks, works, eats, sleeps and dreams for one end only . . . the liberation of France. . . .

Every day, between 6.15 a.m. and midnight, eight French news bulletins and two-and-a-quarter hours of programme material goes out from London. It reaches not only France but Syria and the Near East, the Far East, Africa, Canada, and central and western Europe. Pierre Bourdan and Jean Marin, the news commentators, are two of the most popular figures in

France to-day and receive large packets of fan-mail, even from occupied France where it is highly dangerous to smuggle out letters to England. Jacques Duchesne, one of the leading spirits of the section, is famous for his nightly *réflexions*. Another favourite series is the weekly discussion by 'Les Trois Amis.' The three friends meet, talk out their witty conversation just as if they were sitting at a café table, work it into a script and broadcast it an hour or two later.

The BBC At War, 1944

CHOOSING TO BE DIFFERENT

From the dawn of my history I was so disfigured by the characteristics of a certain kind of homosexual person that, when I grew up, I realized that I could not ignore my predicament. The way in which I chose to deal with it would now be called existentialist. Perhaps Jean-Paul Sartre would be kind enough to say that I exercised the last vestiges of my free will by swimming with the tide—but faster. In the time of which I am writing I was merely thought of as brazening it out.

I became not merely a self-confessed homosexual but a self-evident one. That is to say I put my case not only before the people who knew me but also before strangers. This was not difficult to do. I wore make-up at a time when even on women eye-shadow was sinful. Many a young girl in those days had to leave home and go on the streets simply in order to wear nail varnish.

As soon as I put my uniform on, the rest of my life solidified round me like a plaster cast. From that moment on, my friends were anyone who could put up with the disgrace; my occupation, any job from which I was not given the sack; my playground, any café or restaurant from which I was not barred or any street corner from which the police did not move me on. An additional restricting circumstance was that the year in which I first pointed my toes towards the outer world was 1931. The tidal wave, started by the fall of Wall Street, had by this time reached London. The sky was dark with millionaires throwing themselves out of windows.

So black was the way ahead that my progress consisted of long periods of inert despondency punctuated by spasmodic lurches forward towards any small chink of light that I thought I saw. In major issues I never had any choice and therefore the word 'regret' had in my life no application.

As the years went by, it did not get lighter but I became accustomed to the dark. Consequently I was able to move with a little more of that freedom which T. S. Eliot says is a different kind of pain from prison. These crippling disadvantages gave my life an interest that it would otherwise never have had. To survive at all was an adventure; to reach old age was a miracle. In one respect it was a blessing. In an expanding universe, time is on the side of the outcast. Those who once inhabited the suburbs of human contempt find that without changing their address they eventually live in the metropolis. In my case this took a very long time.

Quentin Crisp, The Naked Civil Servant, 1968

A REASON FOR LIVING

Ian Paynter ('Bwana Panda') has just bought Luke Hardy's farm in recently independent Kenya. 'Watu' are Africans.

Joseph and Kimoi had been driven off in the lorry with their iron cots, bedding, pots and pans and cardboard suitcases loaded behind. They looked like men on the way to prison. Luke was leaving two servants for Ian. Mwangi, Luke explained, was as good a cook as old Joseph but Joseph's jealousy held him down to assistant and substitute when Joseph was on leave. Kimoi trained Beda and Beda was a perfectly capable houseboy. In case Ian wanted more servants; Ian interrupted to say he would never need more. Now Luke was ready to depart. He took only four worn suitcases as salvage from his entire adult life. Ian felt like bursting into tears which would disgrace him, Luke, Marlborough and the British Empire. Mwangi and Beda stood at the kitchen door weeping without shame.

Luke had not foreseen the anguish of this moment. It was as if Sue died a second time. He wanted to hurry away from the sight of Fairview and the pain of homesickness. Ian closed the door of the old Austin.

'Thank you for everything, sir.'

'Take care of the place, Paynter. Take care of it and find someone responsible to leave it to.'

'Leave it to?'

'You aren't immortal, you know. A place like this,' Luke said, with difficulty, 'a place like this deserves looking after.'

The Austin backfired and creaked down the drive. Ian watched its dust trail rising into the tall double row of eucalyptus that Luke and Sue had planted long ago. He watched until he could see no further sign of Luke. Depressed and aimless, he wandered on to the verandah, thinking he would take a look at his property before facing the tedious chore of sorting out the office. Some kind of miracle happened there in the morning sun. He saw no visions, heard no divine voice. The miracle was how he suddenly felt so happy, happier than he'd ever hoped to be again. He had a reason for living: fifty African families and land and stock and a house and garden to look after. And there was this wonderful feeling in him, like coming home.

The watu were bewildered by their new master, Bwana Panda. They had never seen a European, naked to the waist, sweating as they did, wield a pick and shovel alongside them. Bwanas kept clean and gave orders. They had never seen anyone, black or white, enjoying work like this Bwana. If he wasn't racing over the farm, pitching in on all the jobs, he was racing to Nakuru. Each time he went, more lorries full of cement timber roofing piping bricks fence wire machinery arrived at the farm, as well as more outside workmen to be hounded by that Sikh boss. There was no peace; everyone was running around as if in the middle of a forest fire.

When it rained for a week in March, the watu counted on a rest. Nobody wanted to get soaked and chilled, you couldn't be expected to work in the rain. Bwana Panda worked in the rain, soaked and chilled, driving them and himself. What's a little water, he said; dig drainage ditches along the roads while the ground is loose, pry out the rocks, get trenches ready for new piping, put up fence posts. Hurry, hurry, hurry. This wasn't the life they had known.

But Bwana Panda was not a bad man, by which they meant bad-tempered, their only standard for judging Europeans. He never shouted at them. Ian knew from the Oflag how it eats into a man's soul to be shouted at and unable to shout back. The watu gave him a nickname, as they did to all Europeans. They called him Soft Voice. It was a compliment.

Though Soft Voice was constantly crazily on the move, the watu had seen him stop his small truck and stand beside it for a moment in silence. They discussed this act and agreed that Soft Voice was praying. His God commanded him to stop anywhere, any time, and stare at Africa, praying. Ian looked at the land, mile after empty beautiful mile, stretched out to the smooth receding mountains and said to himself: I'm free, *I'm free.*

Martha Gellhorn, *The Weather in Africa*, 1978

PSYCHO, TOOTH, MAILMAN, AND LITTLE HITLER

In 1979 the American embassy in Tehran was overrun by Islamic students who held the diplomats hostage for 444 days. Moorhead Kennedy, one of the prisoners, describes their captors.

In January [1980] there had been a kind of sea change in the mood of our guards, the recognition that we were in for the long haul. 'Good morning, Mr. Kennedy,' said Little Hitler, as we called the most objectionable of the guards, 'how are you this morning?' And by mid-February we had been moved out of our cramped quarters in the basement to a comfortable room on the first floor. From its windows we could see high-rise buildings across Taleghani Avenue. From time to time, we had dinner by candlelight. And soon we received permission to speak to one another, and the full-time room guard was withdrawn. By then, too, we had come to know the students. Some told us their real names: Ahmad, the economist, who after the aborted rescue attempt in April 1980 was to become senior warden; Abbas, not one of the original guards, who used to listen to Louisa on the Voice of America ('Your wife,' he would tell me, 'is doing so much to effect your release'); Ali, known as Little Dwarf because he was so short, who tried to start a consolidated laundry service for the hostages. After two weeks of mismatched socks, we told him we would prefer to do our own. But he continued conscientiously supplying us with vitamin pills.

Others were known to us by their nicknames only. There was Tooth, for example, so named because of a conspicuous gap; his name we learned after our release, was Hossein Sheikholeslam. Psycho, our cook in the latter days of our captivity, was, we thought, well named; he made excellent lasagna. There were Croquet Mallet, Brillo Pad, and the Barber. But the most complex of all was Mailman. He was tall for an Iranian, and his real name was Hamid; on January 3, when he entered our room for the first time, he brought us letters from home.

The students were governed by committees, of which the security committee was clearly the most important. Other students, presumably from different committees, had specialized functions. Tooth dealt with our indoctrination. Whenever we moved, Mohammad the Mover seemed to be in charge. Mailman, who seemed to be the coordinator, told us that he was keeping files on each prisoner. He took a parental interest in his charges. When, for example, we asked about a colleague one of us had seen quite by accident in the washroom and who seemed depressed, Mailman responded, 'Yes, he has been depressed, but now he finally understands that he will not be shot. Besides, his wife has just sent him a lovely picture puzzle!'

Occasionally, Mailman's quest for our gratitude overstepped his authority. For example, he told us one day that we could receive food packages. We decided whose family was good for peanut butter, whose for pâté de foie gras, and wrote accordingly. Two weeks later Mailman came back, somewhat shamefaced. 'President Carter went on national TV to tell the American people not to send you food packages. We do not understand why he did that.' At another point, having forgotten his first explanation, Mailman told us that the students were refusing all food packages addressed to the hostages, on the theory that the CIA would poison the food and blame the students for murdering us.

Mail, being uncertain, was a constant strain. One day I lost my temper, and Mailman was furious. 'You will not curse me,' he said and stomped from the room. Later I apologized. The next day, Mailman appeared with some color photographs of my parents' home on the Maine coast, taken from a letter I was obviously not going to receive. 'I thought,' he said, 'that these would look nice on your wall.'

Moorhead Kennedy, *The Ayatollah in the Cathedral*, 1986

PLAYING GAMES WITH THE INTERROGATOR

Roger Cooper, a British businessman who had lived in Tehran for many years, was arrested on a trumped-up charge of spying in 1985. He was forced to 'confess' on Iranian television, but added so many absurd and inaccurate details that what he said was patently untrue.

To titillate Hosein and his masters I needed to spice my otherwise bald and unconvincing narrative with rumour and speculation. To help with this, and to justify my writing as a confession, however feeble, I introduced them to Colonel Dick Hooker, the man I claimed was my first and most influential contact in the British Intelligent [*sic*] Service. His name is based on Brigadier Ritchie-Hooke, a character in Evelyn Waugh's *Men at Arms* trilogy. His successor, Charles Knight, a man of about my age with some years of military experience in Germany and Oman, is named after Charles Ryder, the protagonist of *Brideshead Revisited*, while Knight's number two, Paul Penny, an academic with no military experience, is a thinly-veiled reference to Paul Pennyfeather in Waugh's *Decline and Fall*. I chose these names with care, knowing that if my confession was ever published my literary friends would spot the references, but confident that there would be few readers of Waugh's novels among Iranian intelligence officers . . .

Hooker became something of a father-figure in my mind. He was a composite of several real friends and acquaintances, thus making it easy for me to believe in him myself. He had lost an eye at Alamein as a subaltern in the Royal Welch Fusiliers, a regiment known to me because my uncle Robert Graves had served in it in the First World War; his eldest son, my cousin David, followed in his footsteps in the Second World War, losing his life in heroic circumstances in Burma. I knew that the regiment had not taken part in the North African campaign. I came almost to believe in the colonel's existence myself, and when Hosein once asked me what I would do when I was released I instinctively replied that I would go and see Hooker. In an idle moment I wrote a clerihew about him:

> Brigadier Ritchie-Hooke
> Is a character in a book.
> My Colonel Dick Hooker
> Should have won me the Booker.

A useful technique in countering some of Hosein's questions was the 'need-to-know' principle. Again and again I told him: 'That's a very interesting question, one I asked Colonel Hooker myself, in fact, but his answer was always the same. "There's no need for you to know, Cooper. Somebody one day might put you under pressure to reveal the answer and that would not be good, for you or for us. It's far better if you don't know."' I explained that this principle was now established in Western intelligence circles as the 'need-to-know principle', or even the 'Hooker principle'. Hooker was proud to have originated it when Montgomery took him on his staff after his eye operation. Hosein sniffed at this and said that in Islam combatants always trusted each other and would anyway never give away secrets to the enemy, even under torture. He immediately realized this was not the most tactful thing to have said, so he added, 'I don't mean that you are giving away secrets. It is our right to know about these things and you are doing your duty as a human being in telling us.'

One of the most successful products of my imagination was the mysterious 'Iran Committee' set up in Whitehall after the Revolution to co-ordinate government policy on Iran. Even in the Shah's day, Iranians believed that foreign politicians spent most of the waking hours plotting against their country, and my Iran Committee played nicely on this paranoia. Unfortunately the Hooker principle prevented me from knowing much about its deliberations, but I listed the main organizations I believed to be represented on it. The Iran Committee reported directly to Mrs Thatcher, of course.

Roger Cooper, *Death Plus Ten Years*, 1993

'WHO DO YOU WRITE FOR?'

The exiled Iraqi author Samir al-Khalil, whose real name is Kanan Makiya, was heavily criticized by the Palestinian writer Edward Said and others for criticizing Saddam Hussein in his book The Republic of Fear *at a time when*

Iraq was facing attack by the United Nations forces, headed by the United States, in the Gulf War of 1991.

Were you [Samir al-Khalil] thinking of visiting your original country, Iraq, carrying your American passport after your American army had installed itself there? You have no right to speak of Iraq and of those who live in it. Iraq and its people are as innocent of you as the wolf is innocent of the blood of Yousuf. You sit in the lap of luxury and in your hand is paper and pencil. This is all that you own. As for feeling and compassion [for Iraq], of that you have none. You should have denounced the attack which sent Iraq back into the twelfth century. Instead, you asked the barbarians to finish what they had started.

Now I don't want to get personal about any of this, but I urge you to look back into yourself and to direct yourself to God, the all-knowing and the all-powerful, especially in these holy days [Ramadhan], asking him for forgiveness for your sins. He is all-forgiving and merciful.

Editorial in *Al-Arab* newspaper

'I WRITE FOR MYSELF'

What is the connection between the passport one holds, the views one expresses, the books one writes, and one's innermost emotional and belief system, which is of course what constitutes one's identity? It so happens I don't have an American passport. Nor have I ever had one. However, after years of working hard at it, I succeeded in freeing myself from the restrictions imposed by that great bane of fourteen years of my adult life, that ball and chain upon my freedom: my Iraqi passport. The day I received the letter granting me British nationality in 1982 was one of the happiest in my life. Although I was fortunate enough to know what freedom was in many ways, on that particular day I tasted it. Now I could travel without restrictions, whether those imposed by the Iraqi state even while I resided abroad, or those imposed by harsh immigration policies and the occasional racist officer at a Western port of entry. Never again would I have to go to an Iraqi embassy, posting friends at the corner of the street to check up on whether or not I came out again. Many Iraqis, Palestinians, Syrians, and Lebanese in forced or voluntary conditions of diaspora and exile will identify with these feelings and with this personal experience. . . .

Iraqis, even those who wish me well, sometimes ask: 'Who do you write for?' They want to know whether I write to please a Western audience or whether I write as an Iraqi, 'on behalf of the people of Iraq.'. . .

A less sophisticated acquaintance of mine, an Iraqi businessman, was actually convinced that I played up the story of what was done to Iraqi Jews in 1969 in *Republic of Fear* only in order to sell more copies of the book. He approved of this marketing tactic on my part because of how much he hated Saddam Husain. Anything I did that would benefit 'our cause' was fine with him. His is a more sympathetic way of expressing basically the same way of thinking as those non-Iraqi Arab-Americans who thought of Samir al-Khalil during 1991 as a 'self-hating Arab' who wrote critically about the Arab world in order to curry favor with publishers and book reviewers in the West.

In a similar vein, Edward Said has criticized my writing for being 'unsympathetic' to Arabs and advancing the thesis that the violence in the Middle East is inscribed in Arab genes. In the same interview on intellectuals and the Gulf war, Said spoke approvingly of a popular source of conspiratorialism in the Arab world, namely, asking of every piece of writing: 'who is this person really speaking *for*? As they say in Arabic, *min warrah?*, "who's behind him?" ' The fundamental difference between myself and Said can be boiled down to the fact that whereas I reject the very asking of such questions of any human being, he approves of them.

Kanan Makiya, Cruelty and Silence, 1993

NO POLITICS AT AGA REZA'S

In Kensington High Street, heading west beyond the cinema, there's a row of shops, all brightly lit up like you might see in the Middle East somewhere. They're open at all hours. One sells fruit, another one sells meat, another bread, cakes, and pastry. Some of them are owned by a man everyone knows as Aga Reza; used like this, 'Aga' means something like uncle. And as a result the whole parade of shops is called Aga Reza's, even the shops he doesn't own. The coloured light-bulbs, red, white, and green, festooned all over the front of these shops tell you what nationality Aga Reza's caters for: Iranians, of course. There are around a quarter of a million Iranians in London, most of them exiles from the time the Shah fell. Many of them are seriously rich, which explains why these shops are in Kensington.

But there are all sorts of other Iranians in London too. For a start, there is the official community, quite large, which centres on the embassy and the official Iranian school and the mosques and so on. They're the ones who support the Islamic government back in Tehran. Then there are the Mujaheddin, the supporters of a fierce opposition group which has carried out hundreds of bomb attacks back in Iran, is backed by Saddam Hussein's

Iraq, and even invaded Iran in tanks and armoured personnel carriers at the end of the Iran–Iraq war in 1988. Then there are the intellectuals, who don't support any of these groups and are often in some danger from the government in Tehran: there have been several murders of Iranian dissidents in London.

The curious thing is that they all do their shopping at Aga Reza's. It's the only place in London where they can get real Iranian bread, and all the goodies that you need if you are to celebrate Now Ruz (the Persian New Year) properly, and the right kind of meat and the right kind of water melons. They sell specially pre-cooked and frozen Persian dishes, like *fezanjun*, that are hard to get the right ingredients for.

But what's important is that Aga Reza won't allow any political arguments in his shops. If anyone gets into a fight with anyone else, they're asked to leave the premises: and that means no bread, no *fezanjun*, and nothing for Now Ruz. So you see them all lining up there peaceably: the rich ladies in their fur coats, the government people with buttoned-up shirts and no tie who haven't shaved in a long time, and the easy-dressed writers in jeans and sports jackets. And whatever they might think about each other, or want to do to each other, they don't say it or do it in Aga Reza's. They just wait politely and say 'after you' and walk away quietly afterwards, carrying their shopping-bags.

Conversation with Tira Shubart

THE END OF EXILE

Once, it seemed, exile was a lengthy death sentence. The autocracy against which you had rebelled was likely to outlive you; that, at any rate, was the experience of the men and women of 1848–9, and for most of their predecessors. For their successors, however, things were rather different. The exiles of 1905 returned in triumph to the Russia of 1917, though for many of them in the long run, this proved to be a death sentence too. The exiles of 1940 in France entered Paris four years later and the others who had been driven out of Hitler's European empire soon followed. The collapse of Soviet Communism brought about a mass return of exiles to Eastern Europe, and with the ending of apartheid thousands of South Africans went home too. Nowadays we have come to expect that autocracies will fall and that exile is likely to be temporary rather than a permanent condition. For those who returned, the joy of seeing their homes again sometimes faded fast: so much had changed, so few friends remained, and things rarely went as well with the triumphant new regimes as everyone had hoped. Yet even when society has grown sour with the changes, inflation is high and there is a temptation to call the old autocrats back to help with clearing up the mess they themselves originally created, the moment of return is something to be remembered with a quiet pleasure which lasts when the pains of exile have finally faded.

A SECOND INCA IS MURDERED

*Manco Inca, nephew of Atahuallpa, the Inca monarch whom the Spaniards
put to death in 1533 during their conquest of Peru, succeeded to the throne soon
afterwards with Spanish support. But the Spaniards began mistreating him,
beating him and raping his wives, and at last he escaped from his capital,
Cuzco, and set up a rebel kingdom at Vilcabamba, in the rain forest. There,
at his court in Vitcos, a group of Spanish renegades killed him.*

When the seven fugitives first reached Vitcos, Manco's officers wanted to
kill them immediately. It was the Inca who allowed them to remain alive
and to stay as his guests, provided they were stripped of their arms. He used
to play games with them, and a favourite pastime was throwing horseshoe
quoits. They were enjoying such a game when Diego Méndez suddenly
produced a hidden dagger. He fell upon the Inca from behind as he was
about to throw a horseshoe. Méndez and his companions then repeatedly
stabbed the man whose hospitality had saved their lives. The nine-year-old
Titu Cusi was with his father at the time, and later reported: 'My father,
feeling himself wounded, tried to make some defence, but he was alone and
unarmed and there were seven of them with arms. He fell to the ground

covered with wounds and they left him for dead. I was only a small boy, but seeing my father treated in this way I wanted to go to him to help him. But they turned furiously upon me and hurled a lance which only just failed to kill me also. I was terrified and fled among some bushes. They searched for me but failed to find me.' Native attendants ran to the bleeding Inca, but he died three days later. His heartbroken subjects embalmed Manco's body and took it from Vitcos to Vilcabamba.

The Spanish assassins ran for their horses and galloped off on the road to Cuzco. They rode all night, but missed the path through the forested hills and camped in a large thatched building. The Indians of Vitcos had meanwhile sent runners to alert the forces marching against Cotamarca. The runners met these returning with their prisoners. Rimachi Yupanqui turned back with a contingent of forest archers and caught the Spaniards on a forest path. Some assassins were dragged from their horses; others retreated into the building, but the Indians piled firewood at the entrances and set fire to it. Any assassins who were not burned to death were speared or shot as they ran out of the flaming building.

So ended Manco Inca. The heroic warrior who had so frequently confronted Spanish forces and eluded Spanish pursuers fell to Spanish treachery. He was stabbed in the back by men whose lives he had spared and who had enjoyed his hospitality for two years—the same men who had stabbed his enemy Francisco Pizarro. His death was a tragic loss for the natives of Peru. Manco was the only native prince whose royal lineage and stubborn courage enjoyed the respect of Spaniards and Indians alike. With the disgrace of the Pizarros, Manco could certainly have negotiated a return to Spanish-occupied Peru on favourable conditions. But, as an indomitable patriot, he might have preferred to rule his tiny but independent Inca state in Vilcabamba.

John Hemming, *The Conquest of the Incas*, 1970

THE EXECUTION OF MARY QUEEN OF SCOTS

Against the black velvet of the chair and dais her figure, clad in black velvet, was almost lost. The grey winter daylight dulled the gleam of white hands, the glint of yellow gold in her kerchief and of red gold in the piled masses of auburn hair beneath. But the audience could see clearly enough the delicate frill of white lace at her throat, and above it, a white heart-shaped petal against the blackness, the face with its great dark eyes and tiny wistful mouth. This was she for whom Rizzio had died; and Darnley, the young fool; and Huntly, and Norfolk, and Babington and a thousand nameless men on the moors and gallows of the north. This was she whose legend had hung over England like a sword ever since she had galloped across its borders with her subjects in pursuit. This was the last captive princess of romance, the Dowager Queen of France, the exiled Queen of Scotland, the heir to the English throne and (there must have been some among the silent witnesses who thought so) at this very moment, if she had her rights, England's lawful queen. This was Mary Stuart, Queen of Scots. For a moment she held all their eyes, then she sank back into the darkness of her chair and turned her grave inattention to her judges. She was satisfied that her audience would look at no one else . . .

The Dean of Peterborough was even more nervous than Mr Beale. She let him repeat his stumbling exordium three times before she cut him contemptuously short. 'Mr Dean,' she told him, 'I shall die as I have lived, in the true and holy Catholic faith. All you can say to me on that score is but vain, and all your prayers, I think, can avail me but little.'

This, she was sure, was the one weapon which would not turn in her hand. She had been closely watched at Fotheringhay, but not so closely that she could have no word from the daring subtle men who slipped in and out of the Channel ports in disguise. The north was Catholic, they said, and the west; and even here in the heretic's own strongholds, even in the Midlands, even in London, more and more turned daily to the ancient faith. While the heir to the throne was a Catholic, likely to succeed without a struggle on her heretic cousin's death, those thousands had been quiet; but now should the heretic slay her orthodox successor surely they would rise in their wrath to sweep away all this iniquity. And there were Catholic kings beyond the seas who would be more eager to avenge the Queen of Scots dead than ever they had been to keep her alive . . .

So she held the crucifix high, visible all down the long hall, as she flung defiance at her judges, and her voice rose with a kind of triumph above the voice of the Dean of Peterborough, always higher and clearer than his rising tones, arching over the vehement English prayers the mysterious dominating invocations of the ancient faith. The Queen's voice held on for a minute after the clergyman had finished. Her words were in English now; she was praying for the people of England and for the soul of her royal cousin Elizabeth; she was forgiving all her enemies. Then for a moment her ladies were busy about her. The black velvet gown fell below her knees revealing underbodice and petticoat of crimson silk, and she stepped forward suddenly, shockingly, in the colour of martyrdom, blood red from top to toe, against the sombre background. Quietly she knelt and bowed herself low over the little chopping-block. 'In manus tuas, domine . . .' and they heard twice the dull chunk of the axe.

There was one more ceremony to accomplish. The executioner must exhibit the head and speak the customary words. The masked black figure stooped and rose, crying in a loud voice: 'Long live the Queen!' But all he held in his hand that had belonged to the rival queen of hearts was a kerchief, and pinned to it an elaborate auburn wig. Rolled nearer the edge of the platform, shrunken and withered and grey, with a sparse silver stubble on the small shiny skull was the head of the martyr. Mary Stuart had always known how to embarrass her enemies.

Garret Mattingley, *The Defeat of the Spanish Armada*, 1958

AN IRISH GENERAL IN THE FRENCH ARMY ON TRIAL FOR HIS LIFE

James O'Moran left Elphin, Co. Roscommon, in 1752, imbued with a powerful hatred of the English and the Penal Laws they had imposed on Ireland. He joined the French army and rose to the rank of General. When the Revolution came he was at first promoted, but during the Terror he was accused of failing to attack Ostend and was arrested. He wrote this letter the night before being tried and guillotined.

Citizen Minister,

Without wealth or relatives or friends, the only consolation now remaining to me lies in a serene conscience and in that justice which I request that you will claim for my cause to enable me to refute the charges brought against me. I wish to outline and verify those facts which alone should determine the opinion and verdict of all true Republicans on my civil and military conduct. I am not an intriguer nor an adventurer nor a plotter. I swear that my heart is entirely devoted to the sacred observance of the laws and decrees of the National Convention. I make bold to assert, too, that the Republic does not possess within its gates a more zealous defender. . . . Between my wife and myself I do not possess 14,000 francs in the world. Greed and love of glory do not go together.

Forty-one years of unbroken and stainless service ought to be enough to establish the character of such as I am, scarred with many wounds. In all those battles where I have personally commanded, in those expeditions which I have carried out, I can congratulate myself that I have on every occasion overcome the satellites of despots and tyrants. Not once have I met with check or defeat.

I fought with the success that befitted the arms of the Republic to assert the independence and liberty of America; my thoughts and hopes have gone even further than this on many occasions to achieve the complete triumph of Liberty and Equality. I call to witness the glorious annals of the Republic and those brave battalions which, under my command, have gained so much fame.

There still remains with me the cherished dream that I shall some day be able to give my life to free my own native land from the tyrannical oppression of the savage English government, under which a poverty-stricken number of my class have grievously suffered for many centuries.

The proud and triumphant position in which the Republic stands at this moment strengthens in every way that hope of mine; outlawed from my native land on account of my activities in France, I leave it to you to imagine how dear the Republic is to me and how I pray from day to day that I may see my own country adopt with enthusiasm its principles of government.

Divested of all prejudices, a Republican from principle and character, my conduct has been incorruptible. Who can with truth glory in having manifested as much love and patriotism? My morality is known and my soul tells me that you yourself, my comrade-in-arms, and all the citizens of the Republic who have known me for forty-one years, are ready to acknowledge the purity of my principles.

I have just been informed, Citizen Minister, that I shall be brought before the Revolutionary Tribunal for trial to-morrow. My defence is almost entirely contained in my correspondence and papers. I require witnesses, too, for that defence. I beg of you, therefore, to help me to procure all these essentials. Surely after forty years of service, I have some right to demand such an act of justice—and there is not a moment to be lost.

Salut et fraternité,

Coniergerie, 5th March   O'MORAN.
(*Second year of the Republic*) [*1794*]

Richard Hayes, *Irish Swordsmen of France*, 1934

A GRUDGING FUNERAL

Napoleon died on 5 May 1821 of cancer of the stomach in his prison on St Helena. He was only 51. Many of his admirers, like William Hazlitt, believed that even in death he was treated with petty vindictiveness by the governor.

Napoleon lay in state in his little bedroom which had been converted into a funeral chamber. It was hung with black cloth brought from the town. It was this circumstance which first apprised the inhabitants of his death; for till then every one had believed in the report of the Governor that 'General Buonaparte was doing well.' The corpse, which had not been embalmed for want of means and which was of an extraordinary whiteness, was placed on one of the camp-beds, surrounded with little white curtains which served for a sarcophagus. The blue cloak which Napoleon had worn at the battle of Marengo covered it. The feet and the hands were free; the sword on the left side, and a crucifix on the breast. At some distance was the silver vase containing the heart and stomach which were not allowed to be removed. At the back of the head was an altar, where the priest in his stole and surplice recited the customary prayers. All the individuals of Napoleon's suite, officers and domestics, dressed in mourning, remained standing on the left. Dr Arnott had been charged to see that no attempt was made to convey away the body.

For some hours the crowd had besieged the doors; they were admitted, and beheld the inanimate remains of Napoleon without disorder, and in respectful silence. The officers of the 20th and 66th Regiments were admitted first: then the others. The following day (the 7th) the throng was greater; the troops, the inhabitants, even women came, in spite of a ridiculous order to the contrary. Antommarchi was not allowed to take the heart of Napoleon to Europe with him; he deposited that and the stomach in two vases, filled with alcohol and hermetically sealed, in the corners of the coffin in which the corpse was laid. This was a case of tin, lined with a mattress, furnished with a pillow, and covered with white satin. There not being room for the hat to remain on his head, it was placed at his feet, with some eagles, the pieces of French money coined during his reign, a plate engraved with his arms, etc. The coffin was closed, carefully soldered up, and then fixed in another case of mahogany, which was enclosed in a third, made of lead, which last was fastened in a fourth of mahogany, which was sealed up, and fastened with iron-screws. The coffin was exposed in the same place as the body had been, and was covered with the cloak that Napoleon had worn at the battle of Marengo. The funeral was ordered for the morrow; and the troops were to attend in the morning by break of day. . . .

This took place accordingly: the Governor arrived first, the Rear-Admiral soon after; and shortly all the authorities, civil and military, were assembled at Longwood. The day was fine, the people crowded the roads, music resounded from the heights; never spectacle so sad and solemn had been witnessed in these remote regions. At half-past twelve, the grenadiers took hold of the coffin, lifted it with difficulty, and succeeded in removing it into the great walk in the garden, where the hearse awaited them. It was placed in the carriage, covered with a pall of purple velvet and with the cloak which the hero wore at Marengo. The Emperor's household were in mourning. . . . While this was doing, the crowd fell upon the willows, which the former presence of Napoleon had already rendered objects of veneration. Every one was ambitious to possess a branch or some leaves of these trees, which were henceforth to shadow the tomb of this great man; and to preserve them as a precious relic of so memorable a scene. The Governor and Admiral endeavoured to prevent this mark of enthusiasm, but in vain. The Governor, however, took his revenge by interdicting all access to the tomb, and surrounding it with a barricade, where he placed a guard to keep off all intruders. . . .

The French were not allowed to mark the spot with a tomb-stone or with any inscription. The Governor opposed this, as if a tomb-stone or an inscription could tell the world more than they knew already.

William Hazlitt, *Life of Napoleon*, 1830

THE CREMATION OF SHELLEY

Percy Bysshe Shelley and two companions were drowned off Viareggio in Italy in July 1822. The local authorities buried the two bodies they found in the sand of the seashore, but Lord Byron, Leigh Hunt, and the unpleasant, toadying Edward Trelawny decided to give Shelley a more fitting send-off.

The following morning Trelawny, who had spent the night at the inn in Viareggio, proceeded to the spot about a mile down the beach toward Massa where Shelley was buried in the sand. The markings were not accurate, and it was more than an hour before a spade struck the skull. In the meantime, Byron and Hunt had arrived. . . .

In his later *Recollections,* when a growing hostility to Byron caused him to 'remember' things which were not in his early narratives, Trelawny said: 'Byron asked me to preserve the skull for him; but remembering that he had formerly used one as a drinking-cup, I was determined Shelley's should not be so profaned.' But that pious thought is not recorded in any of his contemporary manuscript narratives. In one he says: 'Lord B. wished much to have the skull if possible—which I endeavoured to preserve—but before any part of the flesh was consumed on it . . . on attempting to move it—it broke to pieces—it was unusually thin and strikingly small.'

After Trelawny started the fire under the corpse, the ceremony of casting oil and spices on the flame proceeded as before. Trelawny later told W. M. Rossetti: 'When I threw the incense, wine and oil on the pile, I uttered an incantation, saying: "I restore to nature through fire the elements of which this man was composed, earth, air, and water; everything is changed, but not annihilated; he is now a portion of that which he worshiped."—Byron, who was standing by my side, said: "I knew you were a Pagan, not that you were a Pagan Priest; you do it very well."'

Hunt could not bear to witness the gruesome scene and remained in the carriage. Byron soon wandered away and swam out to the *Bolivar*, which was anchored about a mile and a half from shore. Trelawny kept watch over the tremendous fire, which burned fiercely for three hours. . . .

Trelawny placed the ashes in the box and sealed it. Then they all went in the carriage to Viareggio, where, apparently overcome by the two days of fascinating horror, they dined and drank heavily before returning to Pisa. Hunt recalled the reaction that took place: 'On returning from one of our visits to the sea-shore, we dined and drank; I mean, Lord Byron and myself; dined little, and drank too much. Lord Byron had not shone that day, even in his cups, which usually brought out his best qualities. As to myself, I had bordered upon emotions which I have never suffered myself to indulge, and which, foolishly as well as impatiently, render calamity, as somebody termed it, "an affront, and not a misfortune." The barouche drove rapidly through the forest of Pisa. We sang, we laughed, we shouted. I even felt a gaiety the more shocking, because it was real and a relief.'

The whole experience of the cremation was etched on Byron's memory. He wrote to Moore ten days later: 'We have been burning the bodies of Shelley and Williams on the sea-shore. . . . You can have no idea what an extraordinary effect such a funeral pile has, on a desolate shore, with mountains in the back-ground and the sea before, and the singular appearance the salt and frankincense gave to the flame. All of Shelley was consumed, except his *heart*, which would not take the flame, and is now preserved in spirits of wine.'

Leslie A. Marchand, *Byron: A Biography*, vol. 3, 1959

THE EXECUTION OF STODDART AND CONOLLY

When the British army suffered its worst disaster in Afghanistan in 1842, British power was humiliated throughout Asia. In Bokhara the Emir took the opportunity to execute the two British officers who had been kept under terrible conditions in his prison. Some months later the news reached the British embassy in Tehran.

It was brought by a young Persian, once employed by Arthur Conolly, who had just returned from Bokhara. Conolly and Stoddart, whose plight had been all but forgotten in the wake of the Kabul catastrophe, were, he reported, both dead. It had happened, he said, back in June, when Britain's reputation as a power to be feared in Central Asia was at rock bottom. Furious at receiving no reply to his personal letter to Queen Victoria, and no longer worried by any fear of retribution, the Emir of Bokhara had ordered the two Englishmen, then enjoying a brief spell of freedom, to be seized and thrown back into prison. A few days later they had been taken from there, with their hands bound, and led into the great square before the Ark, or citadel, where stood the Emir's palace. What followed next, the Persian swore, he had learned from the executioner's own lips.

First, while a silent crowd looked on, the two British officers were made to dig their own graves. Then they were ordered to kneel down and prepare for death. Colonel Stoddart, after loudly denouncing the tyranny of the Emir, was the first to be beheaded. Next the executioner turned to Conolly and informed him that the Emir had offered to spare his life if he would renounce Christianity and embrace Islam. Aware that Stoddart's forcible conversion had not saved him from imprisonment and death, Conolly, a devout Christian, replied: 'Colonel Stoddart has been a Mussulman for three years and you have killed him. I will not become one, and I am ready to die.' He then stretched out his neck for the executioner, and a moment later his head rolled in the dust beside that of his friend.

News of their brutal murder sent a wave of horror through the nation, but short of sending another expedition across Afghanistan to deal with this petty tyrant, there was precious little that could be done about it. Even at the risk of losing further face in Central Asia, the Cabinet decided that it would be better if the whole unfortunate affair were quietly forgotten.

Twenty years later a poignant footnote was added to the story of Conolly and Stoddart. Through the post one day a small parcel arrived at the home of Conolly's sister in London. It contained a battered prayer book which had been in her brother's possession throughout his captivity, and had evidently brought comfort to him and Stoddart during their long and painful ordeal. On the end-papers and in the margins were penned in a tiny hand details of their misfortunes. The last of these entries ended abruptly in mid-sentence. The prayer book had eventually found its way into the hands of a Russian living in St Petersburg who had managed to track down Conolly's sister.

Peter Hopkirk, *The Great Game*, 1993

DEATH OF AN EMPIRE-BUILDER

George Hayward, an explorer and player in 'The Great Game' between Britain and Russia for control of Central Asia, fell foul of a local chieftain in the

Pamir mountains in 1869 and was murdered. One account, which was retailed by one of his murderers, was turned into a poem—'He Fell Among Thieves'— by the laureate of romantic imperial endeavour, Sir Henry Newbolt.

'Ye have robb'd,' said he, 'ye have slaughter'd and made
    an end,
  Take your ill-got plunder, and bury the dead:
What will ye more of your guest and sometime friend?'
    'Blood for our blood,' they said.

He laugh'd: 'If one may settle the score for five,
  I am ready; but let the reckoning stand till day:
I have loved the sunlight as dearly as any alive.'
    'You shall die at dawn,' said they.

He flung his empty revolver down the slope,
  He climb'd alone to the Eastward edge of the trees;
All night long in a dream untroubled of hope
    He brooded, clasping his knees.

He did not hear the monotonous roar that fills
  The ravine where the Yassîn river sullenly flows;
He did not see the starlight on the Laspur hills,
    Or the far Afghan snows.

He saw the April noon on his books aglow,
  The wistaria trailing in at the window wide;
He heard his father's voice from the terrace below
    Calling him down to ride.

He saw the gray little church across the park,
  The mounds that hid the loved and honour'd dead;
The Norman arch, the chancel softly dark,
    The brasses black and red.

He saw the School Close, sunny and green,
  The runner beside him, the stand by the parapet wall,
The distant tape, and the crowd roaring between,
    His own name over all.

He saw the dark wainscot and timber'd roof,
  The long tables, and the faces merry and keen;
The College Eight and their trainer dining aloof,
    The Dons on the daïs serene.

He watch'd the liner's stem ploughing the foam,
　He felt her trembling speed and the thrash of her screw;
He heard the passengers' voices talking of home,
　He saw the flag she flew.

And now it was dawn. He rose strong on his feet,
　And strode to his ruin'd camp below the wood;
He drank the breath of the morning cool and sweet;
　His murderers round him stood.

Light on the Laspur hills was broadening fast,
　The blood-red snow-peaks chill'd to a dazzling white;
He turn'd, and saw the golden circle at last,
　Cut by the Eastern height.

'O glorious Life, Who dwellest in earth and sun,
I have lived, I praise and adore Thee.'
　　A sword swept.
Over the pass the voices one by one
　Faded, and the hill slept.

Sir Henry Newbolt (1862–1938)

A LAST LETTER FROM EDWARD LEAR

Villa Tennyson | San Remo | 29 November 1887

My dear Lord Aberdare,

　I have been wanting to know how your hand is now—if quite recovered, or still giving trouble? But I am little able now a days to write albeit I have a great deal of writing to get through.

　For, whoever has known me for 30 years has known that for all that time my Cat Foss has been part of my solitary life.

　Foss is dead: & I am glad to say did not suffer at all—having become quite paralyzed on all one side of him. So he was placed in a box yesterday, & buried deep below the Figtree at the end of the Orange walk & tomorrow there will be a stone placed giving the date of his death & his age (31 years,)—(of which 30 were passed in my house.)

> Qui sotto è sepolto il mio buon
> Gatto Foss. Era 30 anni in casa
> mia, e morì il 26 Novembre
> 1887, di età 31 anni.

[Here lies buried my good cat Foss. He was 30 years in my house, and died on 26 November 1887, at the age of 31 years.]

All those friends who have known my life will understand that I grieve over this loss. As for myself I am much as usual, only suffering from a very bad fall I had on Novr. 5th—having risen, the Lamp having gone out, & the matches misplaced, so that I could not find them.

The effects of this fall have lasted several days—but now—THANK GOD THURSDAY 29TH are beginning to cause less worry. Salvatore has the stone for Foss, & the Inscription, & I suppose in a day or two all will be as before, except the memory of my poor friend Foss. . . .

Let me know before long how your hand is now. I have lost many friends latterly, among these, Harvie Farquhar, brother of Mrs George Clive.

My love to all of you. | Your's affectionately
Edward Lear.

Edward Lear (1812–88), *Selected Letters*, ed. Vivien Noakes, 1988

A SIXTH-CLASS FUNERAL FOR OSCAR WILDE

[Lord Alfred] Douglas, to whom Ross had telegraphed, arrived on 2 December. He was chief mourner at the funeral, '*un enterrement de 6e classe.*' The coffin was cheap, and the hearse was shabby . . . The Reverend Cuthbert Dunne said the requiem mass at St Germain-des-Prés, only a side door being opened for the mourners. Four carriages followed the hearse. (It bore the number 13.) . . . At the graveside there was an unpleasant scene, which none of the principals ever described—perhaps some jockeying for the role of principal mourner. When the coffin was lowered, Douglas almost fell into the grave. John Gray, who was not there, wrote a poem in 1931, 'The Lord Looks at Peter,' which is a kind of elegy for Wilde:

> A night alarm; a weaponed crowd;
> One blow, and with the rest I ran,
> I warmed my hands, and said aloud:
> I never knew the man.

He was buried in the eleventh grave in the seventh row of the seventeenth section at Bagneux on 3 December. A simple stone, with an iron railing around it, bore the inscription from the Book of Job:

Oscar Wilde
RIP Oct 16th 1854–Nov 30th 1900
Job xxix Verbis meis addere nihil audebant et super illos
stillebat eloquium meum.

That is, 'To my words they durst add nothing, and my speech dropped upon them' (Douai Version). Ross wrote to one of Wilde's friends, 'He was very unhappy, and would have become more unhappy as time went on.' Wilde's humiliations were at an end.

Richard Ellmann, *Oscar Wilde*, 1987

FR. ROLFE'S PAPERS: MATERIAL FOR A HUNDRED SCANDALS

Rolfe died penniless on 26 October 1913. His last benefactor, Revd Stephen Justin, had spent more than £1000 on him but received nothing in exchange.

The British Consul, Mr Gerald Campbell, was called to take charge of the dead man's belongings, and wrote to his brother:

Your brother had been in good health and spirits of late, and dined at his usual restaurant, Hotel Cavaletto, on Saturday night, leaving there about 9 p.m. with a friend, Mr Wade-Browne, who occupied rooms in his apartment. On Sunday the latter called out to him, but receiving no answer thought that he was still asleep. Towards three o'clock in the afternoon he went into his bedroom and found your brother lying dead upon the bed. He was fully dressed and it would seem that he had died in the act of undoing his boots and had fallen on the bed, knocking down the candle, which, fortunately, went out. The English doctor was called in but could do nothing beyond helping Mr Wade-Browne to notify the authorities and summon your brother's usual medical attendant. The police came in the evening and removed the body to the Hospital Mortuary and locked up the apartment. The following morning the hospital doctor certified that the cause of death was in all probability heart failure. This diagnosis was subsequently confirmed.

Searching through the dead man's papers for the address of his relatives, the horrified Consul found letters, drawings and notebooks sufficient to cause a hundred scandals, which showed plainly enough what Fr. Rolfe's life had been. Even his business affairs were utterly disordered. Herbert Rolfe, who had journeyed from England to bury his brother, could make nothing of them; despite Mr Justin's help, Fr. Rolfe died, as he lived, insolvent.

A. J. A. Symons, *The Quest for Corvo*, 1934

LYING IN THE DARK

At the centre of Joseph Conrad's portrait of perverted imperialism, The Heart of Darkness, *is the figure of Mr Kurtz: an idealist overwhelmed by his own greed.*

'The brown current ran swiftly out of the heart of darkness, bearing us down towards the sea with twice the speed of our upward progress; and Kurtz's life was running swiftly, too, ebbing, ebbing out of his heart into the sea of inexorable time. The manager was very placid, he had no vital anxieties now, he took us both in with a comprehensive and satisfied glance: the "affair" had come off as well as could be wished. I saw the time approaching when I would be left alone of the party of "unsound method." The pilgrims looked upon me with disfavour. I was, so to speak, numbered with the dead. It is strange how I accepted this unforeseen partnership, this choice of nightmares forced upon me in the tenebrous land invaded by these mean and greedy phantoms. . . .

'His was an impenetrable darkness. I looked at him as you peer down at a man who is lying at the bottom of a precipice where the sun never shines. But I had not much time to give him, because I was helping the engine-driver to take to pieces the leaky cylinders, to straighten a bent connecting-rod, and in other such matters. I lived in an infernal mess of rust, filings, nuts, bolts, spanners, hammers, ratchet-drills—things I abominate, because I don't get on with them. I tended the little forge we fortunately had aboard; I toiled wearily in a wretched scrap-heap—unless I had the shakes too bad to stand.

'One evening coming in with a candle I was startled to hear him say a little tremulously, "I am lying here in the dark waiting for death." The light was within a foot of his eyes. I forced myself to murmur, "Oh, nonsense!" and stood over him as if transfixed.

'Anything approaching the change that came over his features I have never seen before, and hope never to see again. Oh, I wasn't touched. I was fascinated. It was as though a veil had been rent. I saw on that ivory face the expression of sombre pride, of ruthless power, of craven terror—of an intense and hopeless despair. Did he live his life again in every detail of desire, temptation, and surrender during that supreme moment of complete knowledge? He cried in a whisper at some image, at some vision—he cried out twice, a cry that was no more than a breath—

' "The horror! The horror!"

'I blew the candle out and left the cabin. The pilgrims were dining in the mess-room, and I took my place opposite the manager, who lifted his eyes to give me a questioning glance, which I successfully ignored. He leaned back, serene, with that peculiar smile of his sealing the unexpressed depths of his meanness. A continuous shower of small flies streamed upon the lamp, upon the cloth, upon our hands and faces. Suddenly the manager's boy put his insolent black head in the doorway, and said in a tone of scathing contempt—

' "Mistah Kurtz—he dead." '

Joseph Conrad, The Heart of Darkness, 1902

NEVILE 'TITTY' TITMARSH—HOPELESS DIPLOMAT

During the whole later part of the war he remained in South America, passing from place to place. At one awful moment, owing to the death of the Minister, he was left in charge. It took at least three weeks before someone could be hurried there to take his place. In the interval he sent a long and expensive telegram to the Foreign Office which, had it been taken seriously, would have involved us in war with the Republic of Colombia. It was not taken seriously, least of all by Titty himself. On the next day he sent an even longer and more expensive telegram, saying that 'on mature consideration' he had made a mistake. He was told to shut up and to send no more telegrams. For the rest of the war Titty remained a silent little name upon a list. In the spring of 1920 he came home on leave. He was then down for promotion to the rank of Counsellor, but the Foreign Office, most long-suffering of institutions, had had enough. Titty was to be offered the alternative between resignation and a very subordinate post at Addis Ababa. He came to see me in my room at the Foreign Office; he was on his way upstairs to interview the Private Secretary: I knew what they were going to say to him, but I retained a discreet and ominous silence. Titty was a little alarmed: he kept glancing at the watch which was strapped to his hairy little wrist: at two minutes to 12.0 he jumped up brightly. 'Good luck,' I said to him. He promised to look in afterwards and tell me the result.

At 12.15 a delighted Titty opened the door and sat down on the edge of my table. 'I must first light a cigarette,' he said, and the long black holder was produced. 'You know,' he began at last, 'such a tremendous bit of luck; they have offered me a job at Addis Ababa under Bognor. I am to start at once.' 'So you accepted?' 'Well, of course I accepted. I have always wanted to go to Abyssinia, and Bognor is such an awfully nice chap.' I looked at Titty curiously; I really think that he was being sincere . . .

It took several weeks for him to reach Abyssinia, and it was a month or two before Bognor's letters of protest began to arrive. They increased in volume and intensity. The Private Secretaries remained obdurate. And then one morning there came two telegrams from Bognor. Titty had caught influenza and was seriously ill. Titty a few hours later was dead. The will that he left behind him was so inaccurate and confused that it entailed protracted litigation.

A year later I lunched next to Bognor at the Marlborough Club. I asked him about Titty. He adopted the 'poor little fellow' attitude, and assumed a restrained and Anglican manner when telling the circumstances of his death. 'I think,' he concluded, 'it was a mercy in disguise. The little blighter, you know . . .' I was angry at this. I had since the Constantinople days increased in self-confidence. There was now no reason why I should be polite to Bognor. I was not polite. 'Why,' I asked, my colour rising, 'do you call him a little blighter?' 'Oh, well,' he hesitated in surprise, 'really, you know, between you and me and the doorpost he wasn't quite . . .' I looked round that ugly dining-room; at the Landseer prints presented by King Edward; at those courtly servants; at those courtly old gentlemen with their clean linen and their pearl tie-pins: I turned to Bognor. 'It is people like you,' I said in a loud and angry voice, hoping to reach the ears of the eminent courtier opposite, of the distinguished Civil Servant beyond, 'who make diplomacy ridiculous: you simply aren't real at all: you have got no reality: you're merely bland: that's what you are, and you're smug, you're bloody smug: absolutely bloody.'

Bognor looked at me in astonishment. 'You see,' I added, 'compared to you, Titty was a real person. You must *feel* that?' I asked him earnestly, 'surely you *feel* somewhere that Titty was more of a personality than your-self?'

He changed the subject. 'I see,' he remarked blandly, 'that George Clerk is going to Prague.'

Harold Nicolson, *Some People*, 1927

THE MURDER OF LEON TROTSKY

On 20 August 1940 a man known as 'Jacson' came to Trotsky's house in Mexico. Everyone in the household was aware of the danger from Stalin's assassins, but 'Jacson' had managed to persuade everyone that he was a genuine disciple. He had brought an article he had written, and he asked Trotsky, who was looking after his pet rabbits, to read it.

Shortly after 5 p.m. he was back at the hutches, feeding the rabbits. Natalya, stepping out on a balcony, noticed an 'unfamiliar figure' standing next to him. The figure came closer, took off the hat, and she recognized 'Jacson'. ' "Here he is again," it flashed through my mind. "Why has he begun to come so often?" I asked myself.' His appearance deepened her foreboding. His face was grey-green, his gestures nervous and jerky, and he pressed his overcoat to his body convulsively.

'Lev Davidovich was reluctant to leave the rabbits and was not at all interested in the article', Natalya relates. 'But controlling himself, he said: "Well, what do you say, shall we go over your article?" Unhurriedly, he fastened the hutches and took off his working gloves. . . . He brushed his blue jacket and slowly, silently, walked with myself and "Jacson" towards the house. I accompanied them to the door of L.D.'s study; the door closed and I went into the adjoining room.' As they entered the study, the thought 'this man could kill me' flashed across Trotsky's mind—so at least he told Natalya a few minutes later when he lay bleeding on the floor. However, thoughts like this must have occurred to him sometimes—only to be dismissed—when strangers visited him singly or in groups. He had resolved not to let his existence become cramped by fear and misanthropy; and so now he suppressed this last faint reflex of his self-protective instinct. He went to his desk, sat down, and bent his head over the typescript.

He had just managed to run through the first page, when a terrific blow came down upon his head. 'I had put my raincoat . . . on a piece of furniture', 'Jacson' testifies, 'took out the ice-axe, and, closing my eyes, brought it down on his head with all my strength.' He expected that after this mighty blow his victim would be dead without uttering a sound; and that he himself would walk out and vanish before the deed was discovered. Instead, the victim uttered 'a terrible, piercing cry'—'I shall hear that cry all my life', the assassin says. His skull smashed, his face gored, Trotsky jumped up, hurled at the murderer whatever object was at hand, books, inkpots, even the dictaphone, and then threw himself at him. It had all taken only three or four minutes. The piercing, harrowing cry raised Natalya and the guards to their feet, but it took a few moments for them to realize whence it had come and to rush in its direction. During those moments a furious struggle went on in the study, Trotsky's last struggle. He fought it like a tiger. He grappled with the murderer, bit his hand, and wrenched the ice-axe from him. The murderer was so confounded that he did not strike another blow and did not use pistol or dagger. Then Trotsky, no longer able to stand up, straining all his will not to collapse at his enemy's feet, slowly staggered back. When Natalya rushed in, she found him standing in the doorway, between the dining-room and the balcony, and leaning against the door frame. His face was covered with blood, and through the blood his blue eyes, without the glasses on, shone on her sharper than ever; his arms were hanging limply. ' "What has happened?" I asked. "What's happened?" I put my arms around him...'

' "Natasha, I love you." He uttered these words so unexpectedly, so gravely, almost severely that, weak from inner shock, I swayed towards him.' 'No one, no one,' she whispered to him, 'no one, must be allowed to see you without being searched.' Then she carefully placed a cushion under his broken head and a piece of ice on his wound; and she wiped the blood off his forehead and cheeks. . . .

The nurses began to undress him for the operation, cutting with scissors his jacket, shirt, and vest, and unstrapping the watch from his wrist. When they began to remove his last garments, he said to Natalya 'distinctly but very sadly and gravely': 'I do not want them to undress me . . . I want you to undress me.' These were the last words she heard from him. When she finished undressing him, she bent over him and pressed her lips against his. 'He returned the kiss. Again. And again he responded. And once again. This was our final farewell.'

Isaac Deutscher, The Prophet Outcast: Trotsky 1927–1940, 1963

IN THE CONDEMNED CELL

Albert Camus' 'Outsider', having committed murder, has been sentenced to death. When the prison chaplain comes to see him in the condemned cell, he refuses to repent. What follows is a powerful statement of existentialist alienation.

Then, for some reason, something exploded inside me. I started shouting at the top of my voice and I insulted him and told him not to pray for me. I'd grabbed him by the collar of his cassock. I was pouring everything out at him from the bottom of my heart in a paroxysm of joy and anger. He seemed so certain of everything, didn't he? And yet none of his certainties was worth one hair of a woman's head. He couldn't even be sure he was alive because he was living like a dead man. I might seem to be empty-handed. But I was sure of myself, sure of everything, surer than he was, sure of my life and sure of the death that was coming to me. Yes, that was all I had. But at least it was a truth which I had hold of just as it had hold of me. I'd been right, I was still right, I was always right. I'd lived in a certain way and I could just as well have lived in a different way. I'd done this and I hadn't done that. I hadn't done one thing whereas I had done another. So what? It was as if I'd been waiting all along for this very moment and for the early dawn when I'd be justified. Nothing, nothing mattered and I knew very well why. He too knew why. From the depths of my future, throughout the whole of this absurd life I'd been leading, I'd felt a vague breath drifting towards me across all the years that were still to come, and on its way this breath had evened out everything that was then being proposed to me in the equally unreal years I was living through. What did other people's deaths or a mother's love matter to me, what did his God or the lives people chose or the destinies they selected matter to me, when one and the same destiny was to select me and thousands of millions of other privileged people who, like him, called themselves my brothers. Didn't he understand? Everyone was privileged. There were only privileged people. The others too would be condemned one day. He too would be condemned. . . . Didn't he understand that he was condemned and that from the depths of my future . . . I was choking with all this shouting. But already the chaplain was being wrested from me and the warders were threatening me. He calmed them though and looked at me for a moment in silence. His eyes were full of tears. Then he turned away and disappeared.

Once he was gone, I felt calm again. I was exhausted and I threw myself onto my bunk. I think I must have fallen asleep because I woke up with stars shining on my face. Sounds of the countryside were wafting in. The night air was cooling my temples with the smell of earth and salt. The wondrous peace of this sleeping summer flooded into me. At that point, on the verge of daybreak, there was a scream of sirens. They were announcing a departure to a world towards which I would now be forever indifferent. For the first time in a very long time I thought of mother. I felt that I understood why at the end of her life she'd taken a 'fiancé' and why she'd pretended to start again. There at the home, where lives faded away, there too the evenings were a kind of melancholy truce. So close to death, mother must have felt liberated and ready to live her life again. No one, no one at all had any right to cry over her. And I too felt ready to live my life again. As if this great outburst of anger had purged all my ills, killed all my hopes, I looked up at the mass of signs and stars in the night sky and laid myself open for the first time to the benign indifference of the world. And finding it so much like myself, in fact so fraternal, I realized that I'd been happy, and that I was still happy. For the final consummation and for me to feel less lonely, my last wish was that there should be a crowd of spectators at my execution and that they should greet me with cries of hatred.

Albert Camus, The Outsider, 1942, tr. Joseph Laredo, 1982

FAR FROM EVERYTHING HE LOVES

On 26 July 1980, eighteen months after he had been driven from the throne of Iran, the Shah lay dying in Cairo. His twin sister Ashraf, who was closer to him than anyone, was with him.

Princess Ashraf later gave her own account of her brother's death to *Paris Match*. She said she watched her brother's electrocardiogram as if her own life depended on it. 'Following the movement of the needles, I felt my own heart beat, my own pulse run.' By midnight it was clear that his heart was beating more and more slowly. Ashraf said, 'My spirit was completely confused, but one thought dominated all others: I must leave with him. I must not stay.' She asked Dr. Pirnia how long she gave him. Five or six hours was the reply.

I told myself that I ought to take something at once if I wanted to leave at the same time as him. . . . All that I wanted was to end our life as we had begun it— together. Like a robot I went to my room and swallowed a mixture of sleeping pills and Valium. I lay down as if to go to sleep. But sleep did not come. I stayed wide-awake and I asked myself the question which had been haunting me for months, 'What kind of justice is it that forces my brother to live his last moments in exile, in a little hospital bed, far from everything he loves?' I know today that it is a question to which I will never find an answer.

The Queen and the children came to the bedside at various times during the night. Dr. Pirnia was also there, and so was the Shah's valet, Amir Pourshoja, who had served him for twenty-five years, had a weak heart, and was in a state of total grief about his master. Ardeshir Zahedi remained in the room all night. Before the Shah lost consciousness, Zahedi said to him, 'You are in shock. You will get better.'

The Shah replied, 'No, you don't understand. I'm dying.' He held Zahedi's hand and watched the drip going into his arm. Before dawn he went into a coma. He died just before 10 o'clock in the morning of July 27, 1980.

At the moment of death, Zahedi and Mark Morse were standing at the end of the bed. Amir Pourshoja leaned his head against the wall and began to weep so fiercely that the others were afraid for him.

The doctors removed the drips from the Shah's body. The Queen asked Dr. Pirnia to take off the Shah's ring and give it to her. She also took a small copy of the Koran from under the pillow. An Egyptian nurse closed his eyes. Farah and his son Reza kissed him on the cheek. His body was taken to the morgue; someone snatched a photograph and sold it to *Paris Match*.

William Shawcross, *The Shah's Last Ride*, 1989

THE COLLAR

I struck the board, and cry'd, No more.
                    I will abroad.
          What? shall I ever sigh and pine?
My lines and life are free; free as the rode,
          Loose as the winde, as large as store.
               Shall I be still in suit?
          Have I no harvest but a thorn
          To let me bloud, and not restore
          What I have lost with cordiall fruit?
                    Sure there was wine
Before my sighs did drie it: there was corn
          Before my tears did drown it.
          Is the yeare onely lost to me?
               Have I no bayes to crown it?
No flowers, no garlands gay? all blasted?
                    All wasted?
          Not so, my heart: but there is fruit,
                    And thou hast hands.
          Recover all thy sigh-blown age
On double pleasures: leave thy cold dispute
Of what is fit, and not. Forsake thy cage,
                    Thy rope of sands,
Which pettie thoughts have made, and made to thee
          Good cable, to enforce and draw,
                    And be thy law,
     While thou didst wink and wouldst not see.
                    Away; take heed:
                    I will abroad.
Call in thy deaths head there: tie up thy fears.
                    He that forbears
               To suit and serve his need,
                    Deserves his load.
But as I rav'd and grew more fierce and wilde
                    At every word,
Me thoughts I heard one calling, *Child!*
               And I reply'd, *My Lord.*

                    George Herbert (1593–1633), 'The Collar'

THE PRODIGAL SON COMES TO HIMSELF

And when he had spent all, there arose a mighty famine in that land; and he began to be in want.

And he went and joined himself to a citizen of that country; and he sent him into his fields to feed swine.

And he would fain have filled his belly with the husks that the swine did eat: and no man gave unto him.

And when he came to himself, he said, How many hired servants of my father's have bread enough and to spare, and I perish with hunger!

I will arise and go to my father, and will say unto him, Father, I have sinned against heaven, and before thee,

And am no more worthy to be called thy son: make me as one of thy hired servants.

And he arose, and came to his father. But when he was yet a great way off, his father saw him, and had compassion, and ran, and fell on his neck, and kissed him.

And the son said unto him, Father, I have sinned against heaven, and in thy sight, and am no more worthy to be called thy son.

But the father said to his servants, Bring forth the best robe, and put it on him; and put a ring on his hand, and shoes on his feet:

And bring hither the fatted calf, and kill it; and let us eat, and be merry:

For this my son was dead, and is alive again; he was lost, and is found. And they began to be merry.

Luke, 15

PENELOPE IS FINALLY CONVINCED THAT ODYSSEUS HAS COME BACK

Odysseus, having killed his wife's suitors, appears before her. But the need for caution over so many years has left its mark, and she sets him one last test.

Circumspect Penelope said to him in answer:
'You are so strange. I am not being proud, nor indifferent,
nor puzzled beyond need, but I know very well what you looked like
when you went in the ship with the sweeping oars, from Ithaka.
Come then, Eurykleia, and make up a firm bed for him
outside the well-fashioned chamber: that very bed that he himself
built. Put the firm bed here outside for him, and cover it
over with fleeces and blankets, and with shining coverlets.'
So she spoke to her husband, trying him out, but Odysseus
spoke in anger to his virtuous-minded lady:
'What you have said, dear lady, has hurt my heart deeply. What man
has put my bed in another place? But it would be difficult

for even a very expert one, unless a god, coming
to help in person, were easily to change its position.
But there is no mortal man alive, no strong man, who lightly
could move the weight elsewhere. There is one particular feature
in the bed's construction. I myself, no other man, made it.
There was the bole of an olive tree with long leaves growing
strongly in the courtyard, and it was thick, like a column.
I laid down my chamber around this, and built it, until I
finished it, with close-set stones, and roofed it well over,
and added the compacted doors, fitting closely together.
Then I cut away the foliage of the long-leaved olive,
and trimmed the trunk from the roots up, planing it with a brazen
adze, well and expertly, and trued it straight to a chalkline,
making a bed post of it, and bored all holes with an auger.
I began with this and built my bed, until it was finished,
and decorated it with gold and silver and ivory.
Then I lashed it with thongs of oxhide, dyed bright with purple.
There is its character, as I tell you; but I do not know now,
dear lady, whether my bed is still in place, or if some man
has cut underneath the stump of the olive, and moved it elsewhere.'
    So he spoke, and her knees and the heart within her went slack
as she recognized the clear proofs that Odysseus had given;
but then she burst into tears and ran straight to him, throwing
her arms around the neck of Odysseus, and kissed his head, saying:
'Do not be angry with me, Odysseus, since, beyond other men,
you have the most understanding. The gods granted us misery,
in jealousy over the thought that we two, always together,
should enjoy our youth, and then come to the threshold of old age.
Then do not now be angry with me nor blame me, because
I did not greet you, as I do now, at first when I saw you.
For always the spirit deep in my very heart was fearful
that some one of mortal men would come my way and deceive me
with words. For there are many who scheme for wicked advantage ...
    She spoke, and still more roused in him the passion for weeping.
He wept as he held his lovely wife, whose thoughts were virtuous.
And as when the land appears welcome to men who are swimming,
after Poseidon has smashed their strong-built ship on the open
water, pounding it with the weight of wind and the heavy
seas, and only a few escape the gray water landward
by swimming, with a thick scurf of salt coated upon them,
and gladly they set foot on the shore, escaping the evil;

so welcome was her husband to her as she looked upon him,
and she could not let him go from the embrace of her white arms.
Homer, The Odyssey, Book XXIII, tr. Richmond Lattimore, 1991

ODYSSEY, BOOK TWENTY-THREE

Now has the rapier of iron wrought
The work of justice, and revenge is done.
Now spear and arrows, pitiless every one,
Have made the blood of insolence run out.
For all a god and all his seas could do
Ulysses has returned to realm and queen.
For all a god could do, and the grey-green
Gales and Ares' murderous hullabaloo.
Now in the love of their own bridal bed
The shining queen has fallen asleep, her head
Upon her king's breast. Where is that man now
Who in his exile wandered night and day
Over the world like a wild dog, and would say
His name was No One, No One, anyhow?
Jorge Luis Borges, Collected Poems, tr. Robert Fitzgerald, 1979

LADY WEN-CHI RETURNS HOME AT LAST

Part III

If you drop a broken bottle down a well, it is gone for good.
With no hope in sight, I had given up any thought of returning.
It never occurred to me that a messenger might come from far away,
    asking for names:
The Chinese he speaks, so pleasing to the ear, brings happy news.
So often in the past my spirit had wandered homewards in my dreams,
But each time when I awoke I was more unhappy than ever.
Now that I am faced with the things I dreamt about
Sorrow takes the place of joy, and my emotions become too strong
    for me.

On either side of me my children pull at my clothes:
I cannot take them with me, yet I shall miss them terribly if I leave
    them behind.
My emotions are so mixed: to go home, yet to leave in sorrow.
I must abandon my children if I leave.

There are ten thousand miles of mountains and rivers between here
    and the border,
And once I have gone I will never hear from my children again.
My face is bathed in tears as I face the setting sun;
I have stood there all day, looking first one way then the other.

It isn't that I'm ashamed of my nomad children:
Everyone thinks of their children with love.
The ten fingers on your hand are of different lengths,
But it hurts just as much to cut one off as another.
When I return, I shall be reunited with my family,
And this part of my life will be as distant as the dead are from the living.
The south wind blows across ten thousand miles to touch my heart;
My heart will follow the wind across the River Liao.

My feelings are hard to define:
Then I was sorry to be leaving my home—now I hate going back.
I can't understand these emotions of anxiety and sorrow,
And all I feel is a sharp knife in my heart.
Sorrow mixed with joy is not a good emotion.
My reactions are mixed, and I keep asking myself
'If it wasn't fate that preordained our marriage,
Then how is it that I love and trust my enemy so much?'

On my way here, all I noticed was the vast blue sky.
Now I'm returning, I realize how distant the nomad's land is.
Since the sky is overcast it is hard to know where the sun sets,
But the geese must be flying south.
If you look out across the sands, it is easy to become confused;
So we watch the geese, both near and farther away.
Long before our journey ends there are no more horse tracks,
No other people in sight, just the yellow grass of the steppe.

We have crossed thousands of miles under the nomads' sky,
Seeing only the yellow sand and the white clouds above.
Our horses are hungry, and race across the snow to crop the grass.
The men are thirsty: they break the ice to get drinking water.
At Yen-shan we start seeing bonfires and a fort,
And the sound of military drums tells us it is a Chinese garrison.
We gather ourselves together and ride on, knowing the Emperor's
    domain lies ahead of us.
That is where my life is, now that I have managed not to die among
    the nomads.

I return to my house and see my family.
The fields and gardens are overgrown, but the spring grass is green.
You can light a bright candle from ashes,
And in the cool waters of a spring you can wash the mud from a
    piece of jade.
I take up my towel and comb, and rediscover the rituals and correct
    behaviour;
And when I touch the household gods again I can live or die without
    regret.
It has been twelve years from the time I went through the pass to my
    return;
And now I have told all my sorrows in this Song of a Nomad Flute.

Liu Shang (c. AD 770), tr. John Simpson

DISILLUSION

Slowly and sadly
The river flows
On its long journey
To the sea.
A solitary wild goose
Calls under the moon,
And the night
Is agleam with frost.

If for ten long years
You have wandered
In the distant lands
Of the earth,
Be not in too much haste
To seek
News of your faraway home.

Wang Tso (fl. c.1360)

AN UNENTHUSIASTIC WELCOME FOR MARCO POLO

And so 'they returned unharmed to Venice, with great riches and with an
honorable retinue. Which was the year of the Lord 1295, giving thanks unto
God, who had conducted them to their home safe, and rescued from many
dangers.'

At last they reached their home, which was, as Ramusio quaintly states,

In the district of San Giovanni Chrisostomo, as today it can still be seen, which at that time was a most beautiful and very high place . . . and when they arrived there the same fate befell them as befell Ulysses, who, when after twenty years he returned from Troy to Ithaca, his native land, was recognized by none.

They knocked at the door, for they had learned that some of their relatives had moved in and were dwelling there comfortably as in their own homes. Those who responded to their summons did not know them. The travelers had been away nearly twenty-six years, and, though vague reports of their wanderings may have drifted back to Venice during the earlier part of their protracted absence, as the years had rolled by and they had never returned they had long been given up as dead.

The Polos found it almost impossible to convince their kinsfolk of their identity. The long duration of their absence, the many hardships and worries that they had suffered, had changed their faces and their appearance entirely. 'They had an indescribable something of the Tartar in their aspect and in their way of speech, having almost forgotten the Venetian tongue. Those garments of theirs were much the worse for wear, and were made of coarse cloth, and cut after the fashion of the Tartars.' The dwellers in their house refused to believe that these rough men, who in no way resembled the handsome, well-dressed gentlemen who had sailed from Venice to Acre in 1271, were Messer Nicolo Polo, his brother Messer Maffeo, and his son Marco. No, they were too shabby, too down-at-the-heels, and all in all too disreputable to be taken at their word. One of these who met them at the door was most likely Maffeo, the young half-brother of Marco. They had never seen each other, nor did Marco know that Maffeo existed. For Maffeo, like Marco himself, had been born after his father had left Venice. Finally, with much misgiving and doubt, the doors were grudgingly thrown open, and the three adventurers were hesitatingly permitted to set foot once again in their own house.

> Henry H. Hart, *Venetian Adventurer: Being an Account of the Life and Times and of the Book of Messer Marco Polo*, 1942

PROSPERO PREPARES TO LEAVE HIS BARE ISLAND

PROSPERO (*to Alonso*)
  Sir, I invite your highness and your train
  To my poor cell, where you shall take your rest
  For this one night; which part of it I'll waste

With such discourse as I not doubt shall make it
Go quick away: the story of my life,
And the particular accidents gone by
Since I came to this isle. And in the morn
I'll bring you to your ship, and so to Naples,
Where I have hope to see the nuptial
Of these our dear-belovèd solemnized;
And thence retire me to my Milan, where
Every third thought shall be my grave.

ALONSO   I long
To hear the story of your life, which must
Take the ear strangely.

PROSPERO   I'll deliver all,
And promise you calm seas, auspicious gales,
And sail so expeditious that shall catch
Your royal fleet far off. (*Aside to Ariel*) My Ariel, chick,
That is thy charge. Then to the elements
Be free, and fare thou well.   *Exit Ariel*

                              Please you, draw near.
                              Exeunt [*all but Prospero*]

Epilogue

PROSPERO

Now my charms are all o'erthrown,
And what strength I have's mine own,
Which is most faint. Now 'tis true
I must be here confined by you
Or sent to Naples. Let me not,
Since I have my dukedom got,
And pardoned the deceiver, dwell
In this bare island by your spell;
But release me from my bands
With the help of your good hands.
Gentle breath of yours my sails
Must fill, or else my project fails,
Which was to please. Now I want
Spirits to enforce, art to enchant;
And my ending is despair
Unless I be relieved by prayer,
Which pierces so, that it assaults
Mercy itself, and frees all faults.

As you from crimes would pardoned be,
Let your indulgence set me free.

He awaits applause, then exit
William Shakespeare, *The Tempest*, Act V, 1611

KING CHARLES COMES INTO HIS OWN

Tuesday.—At the House of Commons. Resolved, That the king's Majesty
be desired to make a speedy return to his Parliament, and to the exercise
of his kingly office.

May 9, 1660. Wednesday.—Ordered by the Lords and Commons that
general Montague do receive the commands of the king's Majesty for the
disposal of the fleet in order to his Majesty's return.

The Lords agreed to the vote for his Majesty's return to the Parliament
and kingly office. . . .

On Monday . . . his Majesty came into Rochester. . . . The mayor and
corporation of the city presented his Majesty with a bason and ewer of silver
gilt, of good value, which was well received. His Majesty took his journey
from Rochester betwixt four and five in the morning. . . . At Blackheath the
army was drawn up, where his Majesty received them, giving out many
expressions of his gracious favour to the army, which were received by loud
shoutings and rejoicings. Several bonfires were made as his Majesty came
along, and one more remarkable than the rest for bigness where the States'
arms were burned.

The solemnity of this day was concluded with an infinite number of
bonfires . . . there were almost as many bonfires in the streets as houses
throughout London and Westminster. And among the rest in Westminster
a very costly one was made, where the effigies of the old Oliver Cromwell
was set up upon a high post with the arms of the Commonwealth, which,
having been exposed there a while to the public view, with torches lighted
that every one might take better notice of them, were burnt together. . . .

1660, May 12, London.—The citizens never had such trading in their
lives, their shops are fuller of customers than commodities.

W. F. Taylor, *England under Charles II, from the Restoration to the Treaty
of Nijmegen, 1660–1678*, 1889

CHARLES MAKES A PROMISE

My Lords,

I am so disordered by my journey, and with the noise still sounding in
my ears (which I confess was pleasing to me, because it expressed the

affections of my people), as I am unfit at the present to make such a reply as I desire. Yet thus much I shall say unto you, that I take no greater satisfaction to myself in this my change, than that I find my heart really set to endeavour by all means for the restoring of this nation to their freedom and happiness; and I hope, by the advice of my Parliament, to effect it. Of this also you may be confident, that, next to the honour of God, from whom principally I shall ever owe this Restoration to my Crown, I shall study the welfare of my people, and shall not only be a true Defender of the Faith, but a just assertor of the laws and liberties of my subjects.

Arthur Bryant, *The Letters, Speeches and Declarations of King Charles II*, 1931

FROM ALEXANDER SELKIRK TO ROBINSON CRUSOE, AND FROM JUAN FERNANDEZ TO ENGLAND

His feet restored to shoes, and his tongue to its original English, Alexander Selkirk sailed away as mate of the *Duke*. She was crammed with booty in the shape of wine and brandy taken from a Spanish prize; and a mutiny broke out which her commander ingeniously suppressed by making one ringleader flog the other. Selkirk came home safe but weary to England in October 1711, and after the publication of Captain Woodes Rogers' book, *A Cruising Voyage Round the World*, in the following year, seems to have enjoyed, or at any rate to have endured, a passing notoriety. He was interviewed by Prue's wayward and enchanting husband Richard Steele, and was made the subject of a paper in the *Englishman*, from which most that we know about him is derived.

Better still, but less certainly, Selkirk is said to have actually met in Bristol at the house of a Mrs. Damaris Daniel (seductive name) yet another and a more notorious journalist, a man—as his enemies described him when about twenty years previously he had been 'wanted', and at £50 reward—'a man middle-sized and spare . . . of a brown complexion, and dark-brown-coloured hair, but wears a wig; a hooked nose, a sharp chin, grey eyes, and a large mole near his mouth'. This man, though in the well-known portrait his chin is almost femininely rounded and the mole appears to be missing, was Daniel Defoe. And rather more than two centuries ago—on April 25th, 1719—Defoe being then about sixty years of age—forty-eight years older, that is, than a boy of twelve!—Samuel Johnson ten, the first George five years on the throne, and the South Sea Bubble on the eve of bursting, appeared *The Life and Strange Surprizing Adventures of Robinson Crusoe, of York, Mariner . . . Written by Himself.*

Walter de la Mare, *Desert Islands*, 1930

ROBINSON CRUSOE TAKES HOME SOME MEMENTOES

When I took leave of this island, I carried on board, for relics, the great goat-skin cap I had made, my umbrella and my parrot; also I forgot not to take the money I formerly mentioned, which had lain by me so long useless that it was grown rusty or tarnished, and could hardly pass for silver till it had been a little rubbed and handled; as also the money I found in the wreck of the Spanish ship.

And thus I left the island, the 19th of December, as I found by the ship's account, in the year 1686, after I had been upon it eight and twenty years, two months, and nineteen days, being delivered from this second captivity the same day of the month that I first made my escape in the *barco-longo*, from among the Moors of Sallee.

In this vessel, after a long voyage, I arrived in England, the 11th of June, in the year 1687, having been thirty and five years absent.

Daniel Defoe, Robinson Crusoe, 1719

A NOT SO VERY HAPPY RETURN

John Nicol at last came back to Scotland, but had problems avoiding the press-gang and made a not particularly successful marriage. Above all, he missed the sea. In his old age, short of money, he turned to writing the story of his life.

I arrived in Edinburgh just twenty-five years after I had left it to wander over the globe. I had been only twice there, once at the end of the American war, when I found my father dead, and my brothers wanderers. After my return from the voyage with Captain Portlock, I remained only a few days, and just passed through the city. When in the Edgar, I never had been on shore. I scarce knew a face in Edinburgh. It had doubled itself in my absence. I now wandered in elegant streets where I had left corn growing;—everything was new to me. I confess, I felt more sincere pleasure and enjoyment in beholding the beauties of Edinburgh, than ever I felt in any foreign clime, for I now could identify myself with them. I was a Scotchman, and I felt as if they were my own property. In China, in Naples, in Rio Janeiro, or even in London, I felt as a stranger, and I beheld with only the eye of curiosity. Here I now looked on with the eye of a son, who is witnessing the improvements of his father's house. Little did I at this time think I should wander in these very streets to pick up a few coals to warm my aged limbs!—but everything is wisely ordered by that Power who has protected me in dangers when I thought not of Him.

I felt myself, for a few weeks after my arrival, not so very happy. As I had anticipated, there was scarcely a friend I had left that I knew again; the old were dead, the young had grown up to manhood, and many were in foreign climes. The Firth of Forth, which, in my youth, appeared a sea to my inexperienced mind,—Arthur Seat, and the neighbouring hills,—now seemed dwindled to insignificance, in comparison to what I had witnessed in foreign parts. Because they were my native scenery, I felt hurt that any other country should possess more imposing objects of their kind. But they were Scotch, and I loved them still. I could not settle to work, but wandered up and down. At length I fell in with a cousin of my own. We had been playfellows, and a friendly intimacy had continued until I went to sea. I fixed my affections on her, and we were married. I gave her my solemn promise never again to go to sea during her life. I then thought sincerely of settling, and following my trade. I bought a house in the Castle-Hill, and furnished it well; then laid in a stock of wood and tools. I had as much work as I could do for a soap-work at the Queensferry. For one year my prospects were as good as I could have wished, and I was as happy as ever I had been in my life. But in a few months after, the war broke out again, and the press-gang came in quest of me. I could no longer remain in Edinburgh and avoid them. My wife was like a distracted woman, and gave me no rest until I sold off my stock in trade and the greater part of my furniture, and retired to the country. Even until I got this accomplished I dared not to sleep in my own house, as I had more than one call from the gang. . . .

I hoped that every month would put a period to the war, and I would be allowed to return to Edinburgh. But peace still seemed to recede from Britain. Year after year I looked for it in vain. When the weather was good, night after night have I sat, after my day's labour, by the old windmill in Bartholomew's field, first gazing upon Edinburgh, that I dared not reside in, then upon the vessels that glided along the Forth. A sigh would escape me at my present lot. My promise to Margaret kept me from them, (my word has ever been my bond,) or I should assuredly have gone to sea again. I was like a bird in a cage, with objects that I desired on every side, but could not obtain. . . .

For eleven years I lived at Cousland. Year followed year, but still no views of peace. I grew old apace, and the work became too heavy for me. I was now fifty-eight years of age, and they would not have taken me, had I wished to enter the service. I therefore removed to Edinburgh, and again began to work for myself. . . . I never had any children by my cousin during the seventeen years we lived together. Margaret, during all that time, never gave me a bad word, or made any strife by her temper; but all have their faults. I will not complain; but more money going out than I by my industry could bring in, has now reduced me to want in my old age. . . .

In the month of August, last year, a cousin of my own made me a present of as much money as carried me to London. I sailed in the Hawk, London smack. I was only a steerage passenger; but fared as well as the cabin passengers. I was held constantly in tow by the passengers. My spirits were up. I was at sea again. I had not trod a deck for twenty years before. I had always a crowd around me, listening to my accounts of the former voyages that I had made. Every one was more kind to me than another. I was very happy.

The Life and Adventures of John Nicol, Mariner, 1822

A GREAT, BUT NOT A HARDENED, SINNER

When Allworthy returned to his lodgings, he heard Mr Jones was just arrived before him. He hurried therefore instantly into an empty chamber, whither he ordered Mr Jones to be brought to him alone.

It is impossible to conceive a more tender or moving scene, than the meeting between the uncle and nephew, (for Mrs Waters, as the reader may well suppose, had at her last visit discovered to him the secret of his birth.) The first agonies of joy which were felt on both sides, are indeed beyond my power to describe: I shall not therefore attempt it. After Allworthy had raised Jones from his feet, where he had prostrated himself, and received him into his arms, 'O my child,' he cried, 'how have I been to blame! How have I injured you! What amends can I ever make you for those unkind, those unjust suspicions which I have entertained; and for all the sufferings they have occasioned to you?' 'Am I not now made amends?' cries Jones, 'Would not my sufferings, if they had been ten times greater, have been now richly repaid? O my dear uncle! this goodness, this tenderness over-powers, unmans, destroys me. I cannot bear the transports which flow so fast upon me. To be again restored to your presence, to your favour; to be once more thus kindly received by my great, my noble, my generous ben-efactor'—'Indeed, child.' cries Allworthy, 'I have used you cruelly.'—He then explained to him all the treachery of Blifil, and again repeated expres-sions of the utmost concern, for having been induced by that treachery to use him so ill. 'O talk not so', answered Jones; 'indeed, sir, you have used me nobly. The wisest man might be deceived as you were, and, under such a deception, the best must have acted just as you did. Your goodness displayed itself in the midst of your anger, just as it then seemed. I owe everything to that goodness of which I have been most unworthy. Do not put me on self-accusation, by carrying your generous sentiments too far. Alas, sir, I have not been punished more than I have deserved; and it shall be the whole business of my future life to deserve that happiness you now bestow on me; for believe me, my dear uncle, my punishment hath not been thrown away upon me: though I have been a great, I am not a hardened sinner; I thank Heaven I have had time to reflect on my past life, where, though I cannot charge myself with any gross villainy, yet I can discern follies and vices too sufficient to repent and to be ashamed of; follies which have been attended with dreadful consequences to myself, and have brought me to the brink of destruction.' 'I am rejoiced, my dear child,' answered Allworthy, 'to hear you talk thus sensibly; for as I am convinced hypocrisy (good Heaven how have I been imposed on by it in others!) was never among your faults, so I can readily believe all you say. You now see, Tom, to what dangers imprudence alone may subject virtue (for virtue, I am convinced, you love in a great degree). Prudence is indeed the duty which we owe to ourselves; and if we will be so much our own enemies as to neglect it, we are not to wonder if the world is deficient in discharging their duty to us; for when a man lays the foundation of his own ruin, others will, I am afraid, be too apt to build upon it.'

Henry Fielding, *The History of Tom Jones, a Foundling,* 1749

AFTER EIGHTEEN YEARS, CASANOVA GOES HOME

Casanova re-entered Venice the 14th September 1774 and, presenting himself, on the 18th, to Marc-Antoine Businello, Secretary of the Tribunal of the Inquisitors of State, was advised that mercy had been accorded him by reason of his refutation of the *History of the Venetian Government* by Amelot de la Houssaie which he had written during his forty-two day imprisonment at Barcelona in 1768. The three Inquisitors, Francisco Grimani, Francesco Sagredo and Paolo Bembo, invited him to dinner to hear his story of his escape from The Leads.

In 1772, Bandiera, the Republic's resident at Ancona, drew this portrait of Casanova:

'One sees everywhere this unhappy rebel against the justice of the August Council, presenting himself boldly, his head carried high, and well equipped. He is received in many houses and announces his intention of going to Trieste and, from there, of returning to Germany. He is a man of forty years or more,' [in reality, forty-seven] 'of high stature and excellent appearance, vigorous, of a very brown color, the eye bright, the wig short and chestnut-brown. He is said to be haughty and disdainful; he speaks at length, with spirit and erudition.' [Letter of information to the Very Illustrious Giovanni Zon, Secretary of the August Council of Ten at Venice. 2 October 1772.]

Returning to Venice after an absence of eighteen years, Casanova renewed his acquaintance with many old friends, among whom were:

Angela Toselli, his first passion. In 1758 this girl married the advocate Francesco Barnaba Rizzotti, and in the following year she gave birth to a daughter, Maria Rizzotti (later married to a M. Kaiser) who lived at Vienna and whose letters to Casanova were preserved at Dux.

C ... C ..., the young girl whose love affair with Casanova became involved with that of the nun M ... M ... Casanova found her in Venice 'a widow and poorly off.'

The dancing girl Binetti, who assisted Casanova in his flight from Stuttgart in 1760, whom he met again in London in 1763, and who was the cause of his duel with Count Branicki at Warsaw in 1766. She danced frequently at Venice between 1769 and 1780.

Mlle. X ... C ... V ..., really Giustina de Wynne, widow of the Count Rosenberg, Austrian Ambassador at Venice. 'Fifteen years afterwards, I saw her again and she was a widow, happy enough, apparently, and enjoying a great reputation on account of her rank, wit and social qualities, but our connection was never renewed.'

Callimena, who was kind to him 'for love's sake alone' at Sorrento in 1770.

Marcoline, the girl he took away from his younger brother, the Abbé Casanova, at Geneva in 1763.

Father Balbi, the companion of his flight from The Leads.

> Jacques Casanova de Seingalt (1725–98), *Memoirs*, vol. ii, tr. Arthur Machen, 1894

KING LOUIS XVIII IS WELCOMED TO FRANCE BY NAPOLEON'S ARMY

Half way across, the vessel that bore the King passed from the naval escort of the English into the midst of the cortège of French boats and vessels. He found his country advancing towards him on the waves, and he entered in triumph into the harbour of Calais. The guns of the French coast had been answering from daylight the guns of Dover. The downs, the capes, the jetties, the tongues of earth running into the sea, the walls and the towers of Calais, were all covered with a people who awaited the King as a salvation and a hope. No division existed at that moment, either in the mind or the hearts of the French people: and those who had neither souvenir nor affection for the old monarchy had, at least, no repugnance. Manifestations of joy arose from the crowd which flocked forth from their houses. The earth itself, and the walls, by the sound of bells and cannons, seemed to participate in this emotion of the human kind. Louis XVIII, melted to tears, and shrewd in calculating even his sincere impressions, scattered about him, to all the deputations and to all the spectators, which surrounded his vessel, those happy expressions in which the sentiment springs from the circumstance, to fly from mouth to mouth. He possessed himself of his new country by the felicity of his answers, and fixed the enthusiasm of others in expressing his own. Nature seemed to have created him for such moments as this. He was the natural genius of such solemnities. . . . He found, on the whole route to Paris, at Boulogne, at Montreuil, at Abbeville, and at Amiens, the same people, the same sympathising expression of countenance, the same enthusiasm of the populace, and the same unanimity of hope. He felt, in the spontaneous and universal trembling of joy of his country, that he was the master of his people.

The marshals of Napoleon, and those most intimate with him, had hastened to meet the King before his arrival at Compiègne to secure to themselves his earliest regards, and be the first to gain the confidence of the future reign. There was Marshal Berthier, who for twelve years had not quitted the tent or the cabinet of the Emperor; and Marshal Ney, his most intrepid lieutenant on the field of battle, of whom the Emperor had said,— 'I have three hundred millions in gold in the vaults of my palace, and I would give them all to ransom the life of such a man.' These showed themselves the most eager in the presence of his successor. Marshal Ney, on horseback with his colleagues round the royal coach, flourished his sword over his head, and cried aloud, as he showed the King to the people, 'Vive le Roi! There he is, my friends,—the legitimate King! the real King of France!'

> Alphonse de Lamartine, *History of the Restoration of the Monarchy in France*, 1851

A RESERVED REUNION

Alfred Dreyfus left his prison on Devil's Island, where he had spent four years in suffering and near-silence, and was brought back to France. The process of exoneration was starting: but it would not be completed until 1906, when he was awarded the Legion of Honour; and at first when the ship brought him back his ill-treatment continued.

On the night of June 30, in the midst of a torrential rainstorm, he was ordered to jump from the cruiser's side ladder into a small dinghy; he injured both legs, and, as the boat headed toward the coast, he was seized by fever and chills. Finally, at 2:15 on the morning of July 1, he set foot on French soil. But instead of the festive homecoming he had imagined, he arrived on a dark, deserted beach and found only the 'anxious faces' of policemen and mounted troops. Hurried into an open carriage and taken to a special train, he traveled in the company of thirteen policemen and four detectives—all silent. Nearly three hours later the train stopped between stations, and the prisoner was transferred to yet another carriage. Only at dawn, as the procession galloped through the streets of a large provincial city and toward a military prison, did Dreyfus learn that he had disembarked near Quiberon, on the southern coast of Brittany, and that he had been taken to Rennes, the place, he thought, where his innocence would be proclaimed and his 'nightmare' would end.

If his return had been 'sinister,' a letter awaiting him in prison promised hope. 'I want you to receive a word from me when you arrive,' Lucie had written, 'and I want you to know that I am close by, in the same city, with my heart beating with joy and emotion.' Through a local Protestant pastor, the Dreyfuses had rented the house of a widow, Madame Godard, for the duration of the captain's retrial; shaded by trees and surrounded by a high wall with an iron gate, the house was situated on the same narrow street as the military prison. Lucie's note, written while her husband was en route to France, described him traveling closer to Rennes, 'each hour, each minute,' until the couple 'found themselves in each other's arms.' Lucie had acknowledged in letters to Devil's Island that they would be 'much older,' in many ways, when they finally met again, and that their 'characters would be markedly different.' But she had also admitted that they now shared 'something more than the immense fondness' they had always known; they shared 'an indefinable feeling created by the community of our sufferings.'

Less than three hours after arriving in Rennes, Dreyfus learned that his wife would meet him in a few minutes in an adjoining room. Suddenly, uncontrollably, he cried ('tears I had not known for such a long time'). In pain from the injuries sustained a few hours before, and physically and mentally exhausted, he was unprepared for the one reunion he had dreamed about through every day and night in exile. 'Taking hold' of himself as he had done prior to meetings with Lucie at Cherche-Midi, Santé, and Saint-Martin de Ré, he fought back his tears and joined his wife for the first time since the early spring of 1895.

'There are no words with enough intensity,' he later wrote, 'to describe the emotions we felt upon seeing each other again. There was everything, joy and grief.' But mostly there was silence as the couple, in the presence of a guard, tried to 'read on each other's face the traces of pain.' For Lucie, who wanted to speak 'of a thousand things, of the children, of the family, of those who love us both,' there was the fear that her husband could not support the weight of it all so soon; and for the prisoner, whose monologues on Devil's Island had been 'whispered' to Lucie's photograph, to his 'talisman,' there was the awkwardness of dialogue and the paralysis of embarrassment over his physical condition. On the morning of his arrest nearly five years before, he must have been at the peak of physical health; more wiry than muscular, he had profited from holidays on the Normandy coast and morning gallops through the Bois de Boulogne. He had strength and stamina. But now the ill-fitting suit from Cayenne seemed to hang on his body, as if from a mannequin, and though he was only thirty-nine, his thinning hair had gone almost completely white. Since his early bouts with malaria, he suffered sudden flushes of fever that turned his sallow face bright red and exaggerated his prominent cheekbones. His voice was strangled and almost inaudible; not only had years of silence damaged his larynx and vocal chords, but malnutrition and disease had inflamed his gums and rotted his teeth. He could utter only raspy, hissing sounds. To maintain a facade of dignity during his reunion with Lucie—to appear the 'Stoic' she had always admired—he forced himself to remain as quiet and motionless as possible.

'The meeting between the prisoner and his wife was . . . less sensational than one would have supposed,' went a police report from Rennes, 'and the couple seems to have been particularly reserved.' But Lucie knew the meaning of that 'reserve,' and though she rushed to telegraph allies in Paris with the good news of the captain's arrival ('Saw my husband this morning,' she informed Maître Demange, 'found him well morally and physically'), she confessed her concerns in private to family and close friends. After arranging for daily one-hour visits to the military prison, she began another letter-writing campaign designed to raise her husband's spirits and prepare him for the trial scheduled to begin on August 7. 'My poor friend,' she wrote on the day of their first meeting, 'you have not spoken for nearly five years, and you have suffered every martyrdom.' But 'you are still valiant and courageous,' she added, and 'worthy of all the admiration, all the numerous testimonials I have received for you from France and the entire world.'

Michael Burns, *Dreyfus: A Family Affair 1789–1945*, 1992

GENERAL DE GAULLE'S POLITICAL CORONATION IS INTERRUPTED

The first shots were heard as the General's triumphant cortège, slowly patting the rejoicing crowd, entered the Place de la Concorde on its way from the Arc de Triomphe to Notre-Dame. It was nearly 4 p.m. on that 'coronation' day, 26 August 1944.

The city was still swarming with enemies and well within reach of German artillery and aircraft. Was not 'the man of 18 June' taking an almost insane risk in seeking, by such a demonstration of popular legitimation, to consolidate his heroic 'legitimacy' of 1940 and thus forge 'the unity of the nation'? Was the whole exercise to end in panic? Were the 'political reefs' that he had felt under his feet as he walked the full length of the Champs-Elysées even sharper than he had suspected?

It took twenty minutes or so for the ill-assorted cortège of jeeps, 'half-tracks', tanks and old Citroën *tractions avant*—led by the open car that de Gaulle had insisted on using—to reach Notre-Dame, after a brief stop-off in front of the Hôtel de Ville. In the meantime, those who were already being called the *tireurs de toit*, or roof marksmen, seemed to have given up any idea of upsetting the great celebration.

But the head of the provisional government had no sooner set foot on the cathedral square than the gunfire resumed louder than ever. He entered the nave through a mass of bodies that had thrown themselves to the ground in fear:

It was immediately apparent to me that this was one of those contagious shooting matches which high feeling sometimes sets off in over-excited troops on the occasion of some fortuitous or provoked incident. Nothing could be more important than for me not to yield to the panic of the crowd. I therefore went into the cathedral. Without electricity, the organ was silent, and the shots echoed inside the structure.

As he took up position in front of the chair reserved for him, General Leclerc, waving his baton, stopped one of his soldiers firing in the direction of the vaults, while Claude Hettier de Boislambert snatched the pistol from a man who was pointing it at one of the stained-glass windows, convinced, he said, that someone was hiding behind it. Nevertheless, bullets whistled through the air and pieces of stone flew off, wounding some people.

What the ceremony may have lacked in calm, it gained in eloquence: what a leader, people would say, to emerge intact from that new 'murder in the cathedral'! Those who tried to disturb the 'crowning' of the man who embodied Free France had nothing to show for their pains. If provocation was intended, it was certainly a miscalculation: everyone knew that Charles de Gaulle was always at his best when confronting danger.

In any case, however fervent his *Magnificat* may have been, the General still had his eyes peeled and his suspicions alerted. Who was responsible? Ten years later, when writing his *Mémoires de guerre*, he felt able to point the finger. Rejecting the hypothesis of 'snipers on the roofs, German soldiers or members of the Vichy militia', Charles de Gaulle laid the blame squarely on 'people who wanted to justify the maintenance of revolutionary power and the deployment of physical force'. It seemed that 'an attempt had been made to create the impression that threats still lurked in the shadows, that the resistance organizations must remain armed and vigilant, that COMAC, the Parisian Liberation Committee (CPL) and the neighbourhood committees were still to take the responsibility for police action, justice and the purging of collaborators in order to protect the people against dangerous conspiracies.'

Jean Lacouture, *De Gaulle: The Ruler 1945–70*, 1991

A WARM WELCOME FOR A RADICAL

William Cobbett, who began life as a plough-boy and became a passionate critic of the Establishment and a gifted pamphleteer, had gone to America in 1817 to avoid prosecution for demanding reform of the British political system. By 1819 he judged that it was safe to return. The welcome he received persuaded him that he should stand for Parliament, but he had to wait until the Reform Bill in 1832.

After twenty-one days' sailing over a sea almost as smooth as the beautiful Long Island Lake, I arrived at Liverpool, on a Sunday evening, [in November 1819]. We were not permitted to land until Monday about two o'clock. There had been a great multitude assembled on the wharf the whole of the day; and, when I landed, I was received with cheers and with shakings of the hand, which made me feel that I was once again in England. I soon learned that the whole country of Lancashire was in a stir to give me a hearty welcome. The news of my arrival, upon reaching Bolton, was announced by a man, who went round the town with a bell. He stopped at different parts of the town, and, after ringing his bell, said: 'Our countryman, William Cobbett, is arrived at Liverpool in good health.' This man, for this act, was taken before a Magistrate.

On Sunday, the 28th of November, I, accompanied by [my sons] William and John, left Liverpool, on my road to Manchester, which I had been invited to visit, and where I had been invited to partake of a dinner on the Monday. We proceeded on our way to an Inn at a little hamlet called Irlam, which was within ten miles of Manchester. There we slept, and, the next morning prepared to get into our coach and to go to receive the welcome intended for us. A deputation had arrived to accompany us on the way, when, not to my surprise at all, arrived a messenger on horseback with a notification from the Borough-reeves and Constables of Manchester and Salford, interdicting any further advance toward the Town! It would have been really criminal in me to proceed, for the purpose of receiving marks of approbation, and without any other purpose, when there manifestly would have been danger to the lives of some persons or other if the military had been brought out to obstruct my entrance into Manchester.

We went back to Warrington and took the road to London; not, however, before I took an opportunity to make a short address to about two hundred persons who had assembled round the Inn, some of whom had come on foot all the way from Manchester. I shall never forget the looks of these men, and, indeed, of these women, for there were some of both sexes. My hand yet reminds me of the hard squeezes I had from them; and, [it is well known,] how great a favourite of mine a hard squeeze of the hand is.

We arrived at Coventry late on the evening of the 30th. When I came down into a front room of the house to breakfast, [the next day,] I found a great number of persons assembled in the street opposite the house; and finding that they were there for the purpose of seeing me, I informed them that I should set off in precisely an hour. When we started a great number followed us to a distance of about a mile out of the city, where there was an open space on the side of the road, surrounded by some high banks. Having drawn the chaise up in a suitable position, and having placed myself upon the outside of the chaise on the foot-board, I found myself surrounded by several thousands of persons of both sexes, the females forming a very beautiful battalion, many of them with children in their arms, in one part of the circle, not mixed among the men, while other persons were running towards us not only along the track of the chaise from the city, but in all directions over the fields and meadows. This was not a meeting. There had been nothing done to call it together. It was spontaneous, it was collected of itself, by the mere sound of my name. Never did I behold any spectacle in my whole life that gave me so much pleasure as this.

William Cobbett, *Autobiography*, ed. William Reitzel, 1947

THE RECALL

I am the land of their fathers.
In me the virtue stays.

I will bring back my children,
After certain days.

Under their feet in the grasses,
My clinging magic runs.
They shall return as strangers.
They shall remain as sons.

Over their heads in the branches
Of their new-bought, ancient trees,
I weave an incantation
And draw them to my knees.

Scent of smoke in the evening.
Smell of rain in the night—
The hours, the days and the seasons,
Order their souls aright,

Till I make plain the meaning
Of all my thousand years—
Till I fill their hearts with knowledge,
While I fill their eyes with tears.

Rudyard Kipling (1865–1936)

HOME-COMING

I have returned, I have passed under the arch and am looking around. It's
my father's old yard. The puddle in the middle. Old, useless tools, jumbled
together, block the way to the attic stairs. The cat lurks on the banister. A
torn piece of cloth, once wound around a stick in a game, flutters in the
breeze. I have arrived. Who is going to receive me? Who is waiting behind
the kitchen door? Smoke is rising from the chimney, coffee is being made
for supper. Do you feel you belong, do you feel at home? I don't know,
I feel most uncertain. My father's house it is, but each object stands cold
beside the next, as though preoccupied with its own affairs, which I have
partly forgotten, partly never known. What use can I be to them, what do
I mean to them, even though I am the son of my father, the old farmer?
And I don't dare knock at the kitchen door, I only listen from a distance,
I only listen from a distance, standing up, in such a way that I cannot be
taken by surprise as an eavesdropper. And since I am listening from a
distance, I hear nothing but a faint striking of the clock passing over from
childhood days, but perhaps I only think I hear it. Whatever else is going

on in the kitchen is the secret of those sitting there, a secret they are keeping from me. The longer one hesitates before the door, the more estranged one becomes. What would happen if someone were to open the door now and ask me a question? Would not I myself then behave like one who wants to keep his secret?

> Frank Kafka (1883–1924), *The Complete Short Stories*, tr. Tania and James Stern, 1991

LEOPOLD BLOOM COMPLETES HIS ODYSSEY

What act did Bloom make on their arrival at their destination?

At the housesteps of the 4th of the equidifferent uneven numbers, number 7 Eccles street, he inserted his hand mechanically into the back pocket of his trousers to obtain his latchkey.

Was it there?

It was in the corresponding pocket of the trousers which he had worn on the day but one preceding.

Why was he doubly irritated?

Because he had forgotten and because he remembered that he had reminded himself twice not to forget.

What were then the alternatives before the, premeditatedly (respectively) and inadvertently, keyless couple?

To enter or not to enter. To knock or not to knock.

Bloom's decision?

A stratagem. Resting his feet on the dwarf wall, he climbed over the area railings, compressed his hat on his head, grasped two points at the lower union of rails and stiles, lowered his body gradually by its length of five feet nine inches and a half to within two feet ten inches of the area pavement and allowed his body to move freely in space by separating himself from the railings and crouching in preparation for the impact of the fall.

Did he fall?

By his body's known weight of eleven stone and four pounds in avoirdupois measure, as certified by the graduated machine for periodical selfweighing in the premises of Francis Froedman, pharmaceutical chemist of 19 Frederick street, north, on the last feast of the Ascension, to wit, the twelfth day of

May of the bissextile year one thousand nine hundred and four of the christian era (jewish era five thousand six hundred and sixtyfour, mohammadan era one thousand three hundred and twentytwo), golden number 5, epact 13, solar cycle 9, dominical letters C B, Roman indiction 2, Julian period 6617, MCMIV.

Did he rise uninjured by concussion?

Regaining new stable equilibrium he rose uninjured though concussed by the impact, raised the latch of the area door by the exertion of force at its freely moving flange and by leverage of the first kind applied at its fulcrum, gained retarded access to the kitchen through the subadjacent scullery, ignited a lucifer match by friction, set free inflammable coal gas by turning on the ventcock, lit a high flame which, by regulating, he reduced to quiescent candescence and lit finally a portable candle.

What discrete succession of images did Stephen meanwhile perceive?

Reclined against the area railings he perceived through the transparent kitchen panes a man regulating a gasflame of 14 CP, a man lighting a candle of 1 CP, a man removing in turn each of his two boots, a man leaving the kitchen holding a candle.

Did the man reappear elsewhere?

After a lapse of four minutes the glimmer of his candle was discernible throngh the semitransparent semicircular glass fanlight over the halldoor. The halldoor turned gradually on its hinges. In the open space of the doorway the man reappeared without his hat, with his candle.

Did Stephen obey his sign?

Yes, entering softly, he helped to close and chain the door and followed softly along the hallway the man's back and listed feet and lighted candle past a lighted crevice of doorway on the left and carefully down a turning staircase of more than five steps into the kitchen of Bloom's house.

James Joyce, *Ulysses*, 1922

ALFRED DOBLIN RETURNS TO GERMANY, 1945

When I came back—I didn't come back. You are no longer who you were when you went away, and you will no longer find the home you once had. You don't know that when you leave. You are given a hint of it only on the way back, and you see it when you enter your home. Then you know everything, and behold: yet not everything. . . .

And there, now, is the Rhine. What occurs to me? In the past, 'Rhine' had been a word pregnant with meaning. Now all I think of is 'war' and 'strategic border,' bitter thoughts. All that remains of the iron railway bridge is lying in the water like a felled elephant. I think of Niagara Falls, that unparalleled flood of water back in the huge, vast country of America I left behind.

Calm, alone in the car, I cross the current. . . .

. . . and am in Germany. I pick up the newspaper lying next to me: When am I entering this country that I left on that fateful day of March 3, 1933? What is the date? I lower the paper in shock, and then look again: it is the 9th of November. It is the date of the 1918 Revolution, the date of its failure, of a failed revolution—at that time I was also on my way from France to Germany, the date wouldn't let me be: I wrote four novels on that November, 1918, in my last years of exile. What does this date mean to me? Will everything be as bad this time as it was then, shouldn't, mustn't there be a new start this time, a true one?

The bell of 'November 9' has tolled. I am venturing into the land that I spent my life in and that I left, left its suffocating air and fled with the feeling: it is for the best. And this is the country I left, and it seems to me as though I am gazing into my past. Germany has suffered what I was able to escape. Now it is clear: a moloch sprung up here, he made his presence known, he straddled this land arrogantly, raging, destructively—and see what he has left behind. They had to beat him to death with clubs.

There are neatly planted fields here, Germany is an orderly country. The people are industrious, they always were. They have cleared the fields and smoothed the paths. The German forest, so often honored in song! The trees are bare, though some still have their autumnal foliage (take a look at this, you Californians, these are the beech and chestnut trees you dreamed of under your wonderful palms by the ocean. How are you doing? There they stand.)

Now I see piles of rubble, holes in the ground, craters created by shells and bombs, the skeletons of houses behind them. Then again (in bright rows) bare fruit trees, staked up. An undamaged sawmill, the houses near it destroyed.

Children stand in the field and wave to the train. The sky is overcast. We pass clusters of crushed and burned cars, their bodies twisted and demolished. In the distance a dark line appears, it is mountains, the Black Forest, we are traveling at a distance along the base of them.

There are neat piles of bluish bulbs, turnips that have been dug up. We are in Achern. There are factories with many chimneys, they are undamaged, but none is smoking. It all makes a sad, lifeless impression. Something happened here once, but now it is over.

There are pretty little houses with red-shingled roofs. The steam of the locomotive gathers in white clumps outside my window and dissolves in tufts. We pass through Ottersweier, a tin sign says KAISER'S COUGH CARA-MELS, a sign from peaceful times when one did something for one's cough. Then come bigger houses, the first group of people, a troop of soldiers waving the French tricolor. I read the town signs: STEINBACH, BADEN, SINZHEIM, BADEN-OOS. That station is terribly crowded; many people are changing trains there. Baden-Baden. I have arrived.

I have arrived; but where? I wander with my suitcase through German streets. (Nightmares during exile: I have been spirited away to this place, I see Nazis, they are coming toward me to interrogate me.)

I shiver: someone beside me is speaking German. Someone is speaking German on the street! I don't look at the streets and the people as I did before. There is a cloud over everything that happened, and also over what I carry within me: twelve dismal years of pain. One escape after another. Sometimes I shudder, sometimes I have to look away in my bitterness.

And then I see their pain and see that they have not yet experienced what it is they have experienced. It is intolerable. I want to help.

Alfred Doblin, *Destiny's Journey*, tr. Edna McCown, 1992

AFTER THE HOLOCAUST

Ben Helfgott, aged 15, and his 12-year-old cousin Gershon survived the con-centration camp at Theresienstadt and were liberated. As they passed through Czechoslovakia the two boys, emaciated and alone in the world, were treated with sympathy and generosity. Now they were back in Poland, and were wait-ing at Czestochowa station for the train to their home town, Piotrkow.

Hundreds of people were milling around talking and gesticulating excitedly when suddenly two Polish officers accosted us. 'Who are you? What are you doing here?' Somewhat taken aback and surprised, we replied, 'Can't you see? We are survivors from the concentration camps and we are returning to our home town.' To our amazement, they asked for some proof which we immediately produced in the form of an Identity Card which had been issued to us in Theresienstadt, the place of our liberation.

They were still not satisfied and ordered us to come with them to the police station for a routine check. It seemed rather strange to us, but we had nothing to fear. Fortified by our experience in Czechoslovakia and believing in a better world now that the monster that tried to destroy the people of Europe was vanquished, we walked along with the two officers

chatting animatedly about the great future that was in store for the people
of Poland.

The streets were deserted and darkness prevailed as there was still a curfew
after midnight and street lighting was not yet restored. My cousin and I
were tiring as we carried our cases which contained clothing we had received from the Red Cross.

Casually, I asked, 'Where is the police station? It seems so far.' The reply
was devastating and shattering: 'Shut your f... mouth you f... jew'!!!!!

I was stunned, hardly believing what I had just heard. How could I have
been so naive; so gullible? The Nazi cancer was removed but its tentacles
were widespread and deeply rooted. How had I lulled myself into a false
sense of security?

I believed what I wanted to believe. I had experienced and witnessed so
much cruelty and bestiality yet I refused to accept that man is wicked. I was
grown up in so many ways, yet I was still a child dreaming of a beautiful
world. I was suddenly brought back to reality and began to fear the worst.
Here I was in the middle of nowhere, no one to turn to for help.

At last we stopped at a house where one of the officers knocked at the
gate which was opened by a young Polish woman. We entered a room
which was dimly lit by a paraffin lamp, and we were ordered to open our
suitcases. They took most of the clothing and announced that they would
now take us to the police station. It seemed inconceivable to me that this
was their real intention, but we had no choice and we had to follow events
as they unfolded.

As we walked in the dark and deserted streets, I tried desperately to
renew conversation so as to restore the personal and human touch, but it
was to no avail. I endeavoured to conceal and ignore my true feelings and
innermost thoughts, pretending to believe that they were acting in the
name of the law, but they became strangely uncommunicative.

After what seemed an eternity, we arrived at a place that looked fearfully
foreboding. The buildings were derelict and abandoned; there was no sign
of human habitation; all one could hear was the howling of the wind, the
barking of the dogs and the mating calls of the cats.

The two officers menacingly extracted the pistols from their holsters, and
ordered us to walk to the nearest wall.

Both my cousin and I felt rooted to the ground unable to move.

When, at last, I recovered my composure, I emitted a torrent of desperate
appeals and entreaties. I pleaded with them, 'Haven't we suffered enough?
Haven't the Nazis caused enough destruction and devastation to all of us?
Our common enemy is destroyed and the future is ours. We have survived

against all odds and why are you intent on promoting the heinous crimes that the Nazis have unleashed. Don't we speak the same language as you? Didn't we imbibe the same culture as you?'

I went on in the same vein speaking agitatedly for some time. Eventually, one of the officers succumbed to my pleas and said, 'Let's leave them. They are after all still boys.' As they put away their pistols, they made a remark which still rings loud in my ears. 'You can consider yourselves very lucky. We have killed many of your kind. You are the first ones we have left alive.' With this comment they disappeared into the dark of the night.

Martin Gilbert, *The Holocaust*, 1987

A SHORT ANSWER

As the revolution in Iran reached its height, Ayatollah Khomeini flew back to Tehran from his exile in Paris on the night of 31 January 1979. The television journalists on board his plane were allowed forward to film him.

The Ayatollah was sitting at the front of the first class compartment, on the left-hand side, looking out of the window: there were no impurities at this height. The whirring of the camera—we were still using film then, rather than video—caught his attention, and he turned to face us. He was utterly calm and passionless. I asked him a question, a routine enough one about his emotions on returning; his son Ahmad, sitting next to him, translated it into Farsi. The Ayatollah lowered his head without answering, and looked out of the window again.

A few minutes later, a better-phrased question from a French correspondent elicited the most famous remark of the trip.

'We are now over Iranian territory. What are your emotions after so many years of exile?'

'*Hichi*,' was the answer: 'Nothing.'

John Simpson, *Behind Iranian Lines*, 1988

SAKHAROV GETS THE CALL TO RETURN TO MOSCOW

In 1986, after seven years of exile in the 'closed' city of Gorky, the leading Soviet dissident Andrei Sakharov and his wife Yelena Bonner ('Lusia') received the benefits of Mikhail Gorbachev's new policy of glasnost, *or openness.*

December 15 was the twenty-fifth anniversary of my father's death. That evening, Lusia was sewing as we watched television. Shortly after ten, the doorbell rang. It was too late for the postman, and no one else ever came to see us. A search? Two electricians escorted by a KGB agent entered the apartment. They had orders to install a phone. (We thought it might be a provocation and that we should refuse, but we said nothing.) The KGB man warned us, 'You'll get a call around ten tomorrow morning.'

Lusia and I made all sorts of wild guesses. Would someone try to interview me? There had already been two requests: a letter from *Novoye Vremya* (New Times) in September, and a proposal from *Literaturnaya gazeta* in November, passed along by Ginzburg. I'd refused both offers—I had no wish to give an interview 'with a noose around my neck.'

On December 16, we stayed at home until three in the afternoon, waiting for a call. I was just getting ready to go out for bread when the phone rang, and I answered. (My report of the ensuing conversation is based on my diary, with some comments added.)

A woman's voice: 'Mikhail Sergeyevich will speak with you.'

'I'm listening.'

I told Lusia, 'It's Gorbachev.' She opened the door to the hallway, where the usual chatter was going on around the policeman on duty, and shouted, 'Quiet, Gorbachev's on the phone.' There was an immediate silence.

'Hello, this is Gorbachev speaking.'

'Hello, I'm listening.'

'I received your letter. We've reviewed it and discussed it. [I don't remember his exact words about the other participants in the decision process, but he didn't mention names or positions.] You can return to Moscow. The Decree of the Presidium of the Supreme Soviet will be rescinded. A decision has also been made about Elena Bonnaire.'

I broke in sharply: 'That's my wife!' It was an emotional reaction, not so much to his mispronunciation of her name as to his tone. I'm glad I interrupted his speech.

Gorbachev continued: 'You can return to Moscow together. You have an apartment there. Marchuk is coming to see you. Go back to your patriotic work!'

I said, 'Thank you. But I must tell you that a few days ago, my friend Marchenko was killed in prison. He was the first person I mentioned in my letter to you, requesting the release of prisoners of conscience—people prosecuted for their beliefs.'

Gorbachev: 'Yes, I received your letter early this year. We've released many, and improved the situation of others. But there are all sorts of people on your list.'

I said, 'Everyone sentenced under those articles has been sentenced illegally, unjustly. They ought to be freed!'

Gorbachev: 'I don't agree with you.'

I said, 'I urge you to look one more time at the question of releasing persons convicted for their beliefs. It's a matter of justice. It's vitally important for our country, for international trust, for peace, and for you and the success of your program.'

Gorbachev made a noncommittal reply.

I said, 'Thank you again. Goodbye.' (Contrary to the demands of protocol, I brought the conversation to a close, not Gorbachev. I must have felt under stress and perhaps subconsciously feared that I might say too much.) Gorbachev had little choice, so he said, 'Goodbye.'

Andrei Sakharov, *Memoirs*, 1991

TWENTY YEARS AFTER

Le Ly Hayslip fought for the Viet Cong in central Vietnam, and was tortured, raped, and imprisoned. Eventually she and her sons went to America and settled there. After twenty years she decided to go back and meet the father of one of her children.

> *Morning, March 30, 1986:*
> *The Korean Air Departure Gate,*
> *Los Angeles International Airport*

I promise my boys I will come back, but who can be certain? My oldest son, Jimmy, a strong young man with a Vietnamese father he's never seen, blinks back tears. My youngest son, Alan, cries openly—the way he did when I left him on his first day at school in San Diego: a scared little boy whose mother was going away, perhaps forever. My middle son, Tommy, born in Vietnam but now a good American teenager, has pretended his classwork is too important to see his mother off at the airport; although that mother knows he's probably too proud to have his brothers see him cry. Like all the men in my life, they feel more than they can show.

Still, I know just what they are going through. I, too, want to see my mother again. A Vietnamese daughter's duty is to care for her parents; to be close when she is needed. I have not seen or spoken to my mother for almost a generation. An ocean and a war have come between us. I ask my boys, 'Wouldn't you do the same thing for me?' They are good sons and answer yes, even though their teary eyes make it clear they wished that I, as my mother's child, was less dutiful than they.

'What if the Communists won't let you out of the country?' Jimmy asks. He knows all about my life before coming to America. He knows that the Vietnamese father who sired him twenty years before is expecting me in

Saigon, a place now called Ho Chi Minh City. He knows I left Vietnam with a Viet Cong death warrant on my head. 'What if they throw you into prison?'

'Then I will get by in prison, eh?' I rub his clean black hair the way all boys hate their mothers to do. I said I would get by—survive and do the best I could—because it's true. That was how I've lived all my life. Because of that, I am surprised my American boys think I would say such a thing just to cheer them up. I cannot say what I really fear: that I will be imprisoned as soon as I step off the plane and see neither my mother nor my sons again. I will save those tears for the window of the big jet airplane. Instead, I say what I said to little Alan a few years ago in that frosty American school yard: '*Me di nghe con.*' (Your mother loves and leaves you.)

Past Midnight, April 4, 1986:
Lobby of the Continental Hotel HCMC

Anh has seen his son grow up in my photos and now he sits back in his chair in the lobby of the 'new' Continental and we look each other straight in the eye. I am dead tired, but I don't want to say good night and end our reunion. I study his face as he studies mine, the way tenants eye an old house in which they used to live. We have both withstood twenty seasons—twenty winter moonsoons—since we last laid eyes on each other. We must rediscover each other the way one climbs an old staircase—carefully, groping for footholds along the way. I see the light of compassion in his face, though his manner since coming to this state-run hotel has been guarded. Perhaps the Communist clerks make him nervous. Then again, maybe it's me.

'Well,' I say, trying to seem relaxed about everything, 'you've done okay for yourself, brother Anh.' He protests but I continue. 'No, no, I mean it. You fit well with the old regime, it's true, but you found your way with the new one, too. Not everybody can say that. You have nothing to be ashamed of. Just to be happy, like me, that fate or luck or god has brought you in one piece to enjoy this moment, eh?'

He regards me intently and we both feel a spark pass between us—shall we go up to my room or not?—but it quickly dies, snuffed from both sides. He *has* become my brother—the brother of my soul—and I his soul sister. Knowing it or not, he gave me a son and helped put me on a life course that brought me to America. For that I can't be anything but grateful.

We embrace, patting each other on the back affectionately (one cannot kiss goodbye, even innocently, in front of the prudish party minions) and I watch Anh mount his scooter and disappear into the night.

Le Ly Hayslip, *When Heaven and Earth Changed Places*, 1990

IN FREIER LUFT

At the Nico Malan opera house in Cape Town the performance of Beethoven's *Fidelio* is approaching the end of Act I. Leonora asks the keeper of the gaol to allow the political prisoners out of their cells to exercise in the garden of the fortress. Slowly, wonderingly, the prisoners come on stage and look about them in the sunlight. Quietly, they sing the words that few people can hear entirely unmoved:

> O welche Lust, in freier Luft
> Den Atem leicht zu heben!
> Nur hier, nur hier ist Leben!
> Der Kerker eine Gruft.
> (What pleasure to breathe free air! Here alone is life!
>   Prison is a tomb.)

Then the First Prisoner takes up the theme:

> Wir wollen mit Vertrauen
> Auf Gottes Hilfe bauen!
> Die Hoffnung flüstert sanft mir zu:
> Wir werden frei, wir finden Ruh.
> (With faith we will place our trust in God's help. Hope softly
>   whispers to me: we shall be free, we shall find peace.)

It was 30 miles from the opera house to Victor Verster prison, near the town of Paarl, where Nelson Mandela was still being held. The announcement had been made on the afternoon of Saturday 10 February 1990 that he was to be freed the following day, after twenty-seven years in gaol. The prisoner's chorus finished. For a moment or two there was silence in the opera house. Then the audience burst out in a storm of cheering and applause. Many were in tears. The audience was largely composed of English-speaking whites, and therefore almost by definition in the South African context political liberals. The relevance of the music to Mandela's release was overwhelming. The longest-serving political prisoner in South Africa would soon breathe the free air once again. . . .

On the day he was released from Victor Verster prison, near Paarl, his tall figure and impassive face rode serenely on the surface of all the excitement and noise and turbulence around him. Thin and fragile, his hair mostly white, he no longer looked anything like the photographs of a quarter of a century before. But his face seemed young and unlined. His years in prison had sheltered him from the world.

It was hard not to remember *Fidelio* as the whitish dust of the Cape swallowed up the line of cars taking him back to the world:

Nur hier, nur hier ist Leben!
Wir werden frei, wir finden Ruh.

On the way to Cape Town, for once out of sight of the television cameras, the crowd by the roadside thinned out for a while. It was almost empty country with a few scattered farms, all owned by whites. Mandela saw a white family standing by the roadside and asked the driver to stop. There were four of them: a couple and their two children. The man had a camera, and had been hoping to get a picture of Mandela's car as it swept past. Instead he found himself talking to the released hero for several minutes, while Mandela picked up the two children and played with them. In the end he asked someone to take his photograph with the couple and their children, using the man's camera. Then he got back into his car and drove on.

John Simpson, *Despatches from the Barricades*, 1990

ENTERING BY THE FRONT DOOR

Joe Slovo, the leader of South Africa's Communist Party and *bête noir* of the country's conservative whites, yesterday stepped on to the tarmac of Cape Town airport after 27 years in exile.

'As I was saying before I was rudely interrupted ... we are getting close,' he said.

Mr Slovo arrived in a chartered Zambian jet with six African National Congress colleagues, including Alfred Nzo, the secretary-general; Joe Modise, its guerrilla commander; Thabo Mbeki, its international spokesman; and Ruth Mompati, head of the women's section.

Nearly half the executive of the ANC, which was banned and hunted by South Africa's security forces until a few weeks ago, are back in the country. Only five are formally part of the team due to negotiate with the government when talks begin on Wednesday.

Mr Mbeki wept as he stood next to his 80-year-old father, Govan Mbeki, an ANC veteran who spent 23 years in prison before his release in 1987.

'We who left by the back door ... have now entered the very front door of South Africa,' said Mr Slovo, the highest-ranking white in the ANC.

Dozens of white policemen in uniform listened as the ANC leaders gave their first press conference in an airport lounge. Several plain-clothes officers with guns and earphones kept watch.

Mr Nzo said he brought a message of reconciliation for the white community. 'They have nothing to fear from a democratic South Africa.'

Mr Slovo said the ANC delegation had been struck during the flight from Lusaka by 'how big this land is, how beautiful it is and how much room there is for everyone'.

> Barry Streak, 'Pretoria's Bogeyman Returns from Exile', the *Guardian*, 28 April 1990

BACK IN THE FOLD

Rugby Union is the religion of white, Afrikaans-speaking South Africans, and throughout the 1970s and 1980s they had to practise it at home, since the policy of apartheid made South African teams unacceptable in the outside world. When apartheid was abandoned, the South African Rugby team could travel again. In November 1992 it came back to Twickenham to play England, after a gap of 22 years.

Gerrie Hoffman is 39 and from Pretoria. He came to Britain last week with his wife for the last two matches of the Springbok's tour of Britain—the test at Twickenham yesterday and the match against England North in Leeds on Tuesday. I met him in the Castle Tavern, a South African watering hole near Paddington station, wearing a padded bomber jacket in green and gold with the words South Africa written in bold lettering across the back.

Mr Hoffman's mother wasn't so sure things had changed. When she saw her son and daughter-in-law off from Jan Smuts airport last weekend she asked her son to be careful and discreet. And perhaps it would be a good idea to leave the jacket behind. He laughed her off. When Mr Hoffman arrived at Heathrow wearing the jacket, he said, an Englishman came to him, shook his hand and offered to carry his luggage. He also wanted to buy the jacket.

There were hundreds of South Africans wearing jackets like Gerrie Hoffman's in London yesterday and even more in silly gold hats and green scarves. They were like any mob of international rugby supporters, high-spirited and perhaps a bit tipsy. They were back in the fold.

If evidence were required of the respectable coming-out of South African rugby, you needed only to wander through the West Stand car park at Twickenham before England's 33–16 victory. Beside a van with an English rose on one side and a Springbok symbol on the other was a gaggle of white South Africans chewing *biltong* (dried spiced meat) and *boerewors* (farmer's sausage) who had been banned or jailed under South Africa's apartheid laws. Enemies of the state, forced to live in exile, they had now come to cheer their country, they said.

The men in the van made a curious team. The host was Donald Woods, the former South African newspaper editor best known for his friendship with Steve Biko, the Black Consciousness leader who died in police custody. Mr Woods was declared a banned person and fled the country in 1978. Another journalist, Benjamin Pogrund—now working for the *Independent*—was prosecuted in the 1960s for exposing the horrific jail conditions for blacks and political prisoners. There was Colin Legum, a veteran Africa correspondent, banned for 28 years from entering South Africa; Randolph Vigne, a member of the underground African Resistance Movement, who escaped a police round-up in 1962; Clive Nettleton [see pp. 194–5], another exile and former student leader who was branded a subversive; and Donald Card, a former member of the security police who was responsible for hunting down and jailing ANC activists before striking up a friendship with Donald Woods.

There is still a hint of white supremacy around the game. Blacks, you are told, play soccer; they are no good at rugby. In the Castle Tavern you are made sharply aware how important rugby is to South Africa's whites; rugby memorabilia is the only decoration, and it covers ceilings and walls: old jerseys, souvenirs from last year's rugby World Cup in Britain and France. Everywhere there is beer—cans of it in ice tubs with wheels such as you see in the rugby clubs of Australia and New Zealand.

There were no blacks in the Castle Tavern. The bouncers, however, were black which I suppose added a touch of home. In the middle of the scrum was a young man wearing a T-shirt with the legend: 'Fuck the Whales, Save the Whites.' I got the impression from this Springbok tour that the whites were doing very well, thank you. For the first time they feel loved.

Michael Fathers, *The Independent on Sunday*, 15 November 1992

THE PALESTINIAN'S JOURNEY HOME

Tired of being lost in life,
tired of endless journeying,
constant moving and shifting,
the winding of the exile's road,
tired of waiting for sunrise
with unfulfilled promises
anchoring our days.
Finally we've risen to create our own fate
spinning a new sun from
the light of the struggle.

Let the tents of humiliation burn!
Braving the battering storm,
we enter the realm
of the impossible!
Fashioning a new road, and
new songs of resistance
whose melodies millions will breathe
marching repeating:
To our land we return
  to sit beside our own hearths
  toasting bread and remembering

We'll renew old times when life was radiant
and listen to the old relating ancient tales,
of the brave ones who rejected humiliation.
Return to Galilee, to Hebron
to Gaza, to Jericho!
Ride the impossible, return to stay
Your country calls you, don't look away.

Taha Abd al-Ghani Mustafa, tr. Salwa Jabseh and Naomi Shihab Nye, from
An Anthology of Modern Palestinian Literature, 1992

WHAT WAS ONCE BLOODY SANTIAGO

Before the coup by General Pinochet in Chile in 1973, Miguel Littin was one
of the country's chief film-makers. Like so many other people, he went into exile.
A decade later, while the Pinochet regime was still in power, he decided to pay
his native country a clandestine visit.

Contrary to what we had heard in exile, Santiago was a radiant city, its
venerable monuments splendidly illuminated, its streets spotlessly clean and
orderly. If anything, armed policemen were more in evidence on the streets
of Paris or New York than here. Starting at the historic Central Station,
designed by the same Gustave Eiffel who built the tower in Paris, the
endless Bernardo O'Higgins Boulevard flowed before our eyes like a river
of light. Even the wan little streetwalkers did not seem as destitute and sad
to me as they used to. All at once, the Moneda Palace loomed into view
on my side of the taxi like an unwelcome apparition. The last time I saw
it, the building was still a burned-out shell covered with ashes in the after-
math of the coup. Restored and once more in use, it now looked like a
dream palace at the foot of a French garden.

The grand symbols of the city paraded by us. The Union Club, where the country's prominent *momios* met to pull the strings of traditional politics, the university with its darkened windows, the imposing palace of the National Library, the Paris department store. Beside me, Elena was trying to convince the driver to take us to the El Conquistador Hotel. He insisted on taking us to another hotel, which probably paid him a commission. She was tactful with him, careful not to offend or arouse suspicion, since many Santiago taxi drivers are known to be police informers. I was too dazed to help her persuade him.

As we approached the center of the city, I stopped admiring the material splendor with which the dictatorship sought to cover the blood of tens of thousands killed or disappeared, and ten times that number driven into exile, and instead concentrated on the people in view. They were walking unusually fast, perhaps because curfew was so close. No one spoke, no one looked in any specific direction, no one gesticulated or smiled, no one made the slightest gesture that gave a clue to his state of mind. Wrapped in dark overcoats, each of them seemed to be alone in a strange city. Faces were blank, revealing nothing, not even fear. My mood began to change and I couldn't resist the temptation to get out and lose myself in the crowd. Elena tried to dissuade me, but she couldn't argue with me as vehemently as she would have liked, for fear the driver would overhear. In the grip of uncontrollable emotion, I had the taxi stop and jumped out, slamming the door.

Heedless of the imminent curfew, I walked along Calle Estado, Calle Huérfanos, and through a new zone for pedestrians, closed to traffic, that resembles Calle Florida in Buenos Aires, Via Condotti in Rome, the Place de Beaubourg in Paris, and the Zona Rosa in Mexico City. It was another of the amenities of the dictatorship, yet despite the benches inviting rest and conversation, the gaiety of the lights, and the well-kept flowers in handsome planters, a grim reality showed through. Only on the street corners were there people talking, in low tones inaudible to the prying ears of the dictatorship. There were peddlers and a large number of children begging, but what most caught my attention were the evangelical preachers trying to sell the formula for eternal happiness. Then, all at once, turning into Calle Huérfanos, I saw my first policeman. A *carabinero* was pacing the sidewalk and several more were in a guard booth nearby. I felt an icy hollow in the pit of my stomach and my knees began to buckle. It infuriated me to think that the mere sight of a *carabinero* could so frighten me. However, I quickly realized from their anxious expressions as they watched the passersby that also the policemen were nervous, and this offered some consolation.

They had good reason to be. A guard booth on the same spot had been blown up by the underground only a few days before. . . .

Just then, somebody passed singing Pablo Milanés's song: *I will again walk the streets of what once was bloody Santiago.* I forgot my clandestine situation and returned for a moment to being myself. I had an irrational impulse to identify myself, to shout out my name, to tell the world that it was my right to be home.

> Gabriel Garcia Marquez, *Clandestine in Chile: The Adventures of Miguel Littin,* tr. Asa Zatz, 1987

A SLEEP-WALKER IN PRAGUE

Karel Kyncl was a leading figure in the opposition to the regime in Czechoslovakia, and came to London in 1982. After Communism collapsed in Czechoslovakia in November 1989, Kyncl went home on the official plane of the country's new president: the playwright and former dissident Václav Havel, some of whose work could be published only in the magazine Kyncl had worked for in London, Index on Censorship.

Till 1968, I used to be a foreign correspondent for Czechoslovak Radio and travelled quite a lot by air. I had developed a snobbish idea of relaxation: to sit at the aircraft's window and watch the earth below while slowly sipping scotch and soda.

After the Soviet tanks crushed the Prague Spring in August 1968, I was banned as a journalist and prevented from travelling anywhere. Instead, from time to time I was imprisoned. I spent 22 months in the notorious Ruzyně prison, in shouting distance from the main Prague airport which bears the same name. Each and every day of those 22 months I lived through an additional torment of my own making: on hearing the roar of aircraft engines, I began to crave a scotch and soda, which—as you might know— is in rather short supply in prisons.

Shortly before our plane from London Heathrow landed at Prague Ruzyně earlier this year, I remembered that Pavlovian 'conditioned reflex' vividly. I glimpsed the familiar prison buildings. The flight attendant was kind enough to bring me a drink. I was on board the presidential special, with Václav Havel who was returning from state visits to France and Britain. The drink was not a scotch and soda but a beer. (Austerity measures, you know.) But it worked.

After an absence of seven years, I strolled through Prague like a sleep-walker. I listened to my compatriots who had begun to realise how dreadful the devastation by the totalitarian system had been. Though still enchanted by their newly acquired freedom and eager to use it, the morning-after feeling was one of a crushing burden from the past and the pressure of new responsibilities. It was dawning on them that they are now on their own, that they have to decide the course of events, and that there are not many people in the country experienced enough to tell them where to start.

Václav Havel characterised the new existential feelings of Czechs and Slovaks. For half a century they had been crawling in a poorly-lit tunnel where movement was restricted by limits which they knew intimately. Now they are in a large sun-lit square which also has boundaries but—blinded by the sun—nobody can see them. People would love to be told about those limits; they do not understand that they have to find them on their own even at the cost of a bloody nose.

The metaphor fits; I would only add to it. When, after spending a couple of months in one prison cell, I was transferred to another cell, I felt a strong nostalgia. The old cell was known territory; I was in touch with my neighbours by Morse code, I knew the characters of the wardens. I knew my possibilities and limitations. My transfer was a journey into the unknown, and potentially dangerous; yes, one really can yearn for an old cell or a poorly-lit tunnel when one emerges from it into a large, sun-lit—but totally unknown—square.

*

I started this article on a personal note; allow me now to finish it with two remarks of the same kind. First, working at *Index on Censorship* for the last seven years and being in constant touch with the Communist Eastern Europe, I was sure that I understood pretty well the harmful consequences of information barriers in general and censorship in particular. After having a unique opportunity (which I never expected to get) to return to Czechoslovakia just as it emerges from a nightmare, I must confess that I hugely underestimated the terrible results of isolation. Talking to people there, you find yourself often having to explain the very basics of those democratic realities which are known even to the schoolchildren of the happier countries in Western Europe. And in this connection, I have in mind not only the 'men from the street'; it applies to intellectuals as well, despite samizdat, free radio broadcasts from the West and tons of smuggled literature. There is obviously no substitute for the individual experience, for the free contest between ideas. I stated earlier that 'Eastern European nationalism will keep the rest of Europe busy for a long time to come'. Nationalism is not the only problem. However, it will demand, on the part of democratic societies, a great effort in patience in the coming years. An effort which clearly will be useful to the whole continent.

And second, on my two returns from Prague, in April and August, I was able to enjoy again that snobbish relaxation of mine, to sit by the window of the plane sipping my scotch and soda. The second time it was as the brand old-new London correspondent for Czechoslovak Radio, a job I started on 1 September. Since that day, I have been trying to tell listeners in Czechoslovakia about the situation in Britain. It is an immense task, especially when one knows the serious and fateful limitations of journalism but—I assure you—it is child's play compared with my former difficulties when I was trying to inform the world about the Kafkaesque nature of Eastern Europe in the pages of *Index on Censorship*.

> Karel Kyncl, 'Pavlov, Prague Airport and the Sleepwalker's Memories of Going Home', *Index on Censorship 10*, 1990

FROM A NONPERSON TO A PERSON AGAIN

Dr Oliver Sacks found that some of his patients, turned into virtual zombies by the condition Post-Encephalitic Parkinsonism, could be brought back to intelligence and life by the use of the drug L-DOPA. One of the best results was shown in the case of Mrs Magda B.

Mrs B. was seated, motionless, in her wheel chair, when first seen by me: akinesia was so extreme at this time that she would sit without blinking, or change of facial expression, or any hint of bodily movement, for the greater part of the day. She showed a habitual dropped posture of the head, but was able to combat this for brief periods. There was little or no cervical rigidity. She appeared to have a bilateral nuclear and internuclear ophthalmoplegia, with alternating exotropia. Mrs B. was sweating very freely, showed a greasy seborrhoeic skin, and moderately increased lacrimation and salivation. There were rare attacks of spontaneous lid-clonus or closure, but no spontaneous blinking at all. Mrs B. was virtually aphonic—able to produce a faint 'Ah!' with great effort, but not to articulate a single word audibly: she had been speechless for more than ten years, and severely hypophonic for at least fifteen years before this.

She showed profound facial masking—at no time during the initial examinations did any hint of facial expression appear—was scarcely able to open the mouth, to protrude the tongue beyond the lip-margin, or to move it at all within the mouth from side to side. Chewing and swallowing were feeble and slowly performed—the consumption of even a small meal would take more than an hour—but there were no signs of bulbar or pseudo-bulbar palsy.

All voluntary movements were distinguished by extreme slowness and feebleness, with almost no involvement of 'background' musculature, and a tendency to premature arrest of movements in mid-posture. When raised from her chair—for Mrs B. was quite unable even to inaugurate the act of rising by herself—she stood as motionless as a statue, although she was unable to maintain her balance, due to an irresistible tendency to fall backwards. Stepping was not only impossible, but somehow seemed *unthinkable*. If she closed her eyes, while standing or sitting, she at once dropped forward like a wilted flower.

Mrs B. was thus profoundly incapacitated, unable to speak and almost unable to initiate any voluntary motion, and in need of total nursing care. Added to the motor problems were a striking apathy and apparent incapacity for emotional response, and considerable drowsiness and torpor for much of the day. Conventional anti-Parkinsonian drugs had been of very little use to her, and surgery had never been considered. She had been regarded for many years as a 'hopeless' back-ward post-encephalitic, with no capacity for rehabilitation. She was started on L-DOPA on 25 June.

2 July. After one week of treatment (and on a dose of 2 gm. L-DOPA daily), Mrs B. started *talking*—quite audibly—for the first time in many years, although her vocal force would decay after two or three short sentences, and her new-found voice was low-pitched, monotonous, and uninflected. . . .

Previously indifferent, inattentive, and unresponsive to her surroundings, Mrs B. became, with each week, more alert, more attentive, and more interested in what was taking place around her.

At least as dramatic as the motor improvement, and infinitely moving to observe, was the recovery of emotional responsiveness in this patient who had been so withdrawn and apathetic for so many years. With continued improvement of her voice, Mrs B. became quite talkative, and showed an intelligence, a charm, and a humour, which had been almost totally concealed by her disease. She particularly enjoyed talking of her childhood in Vienna, of her parents and family, of schooldays, of rambles and excursions in the country nearby, and as she did so would often laugh with pleasure at the recollection, or shed nostalgic tears—normal emotional responses which she had not shown in more than twenty years. Little by little Mrs B. emerged as a *person*, and as she did so was able to communicate to us, in vivid and frightening terms, what an *unperson* she had felt before receiving L-DOPA. She described her feelings of impotent anger and mounting depression in the early years of her illness, and the succeeding of these feelings by apathy and indifference: 'I ceased to have any moods,' she said. 'I ceased to care about anything. Nothing *moved* me—not even the death of my parents. I forgot what it felt like to be happy or unhappy. Was it good or bad? It was neither. It was nothing.'

Oliver Sacks, *Awakenings*, 1985

PERFECTLY AT HOME IN A THIRD-WORLD PRISON

Roger Cooper, after spending five years, three months, and twenty-five days in an Iranian prison for 'spying', was put on a plane for London in March 1991.

It must have been well after two when David suggested we should try to get some sleep, and he soon dropped off. I calculated that by now we must be safely out of Iran, but felt happier when I saw day breaking over the foothills of the Caucasus in eastern Turkey. Exhausted as I was, sleep was out of the question as we chased a cold dawn across the Balkans and the Alps to Frankfurt.

The London flight was packed with commuting businessmen, none too happy when a BBC television crew came forward from Club Class to interview me as I tucked into a substantial German breakfast of beefsteak and omelette. A pop star across the aisle looked cross when he realized they were not interested in him. Knowing how tight the BBC always are on expenses, I assumed the TV people were there by coincidence; only when I learned that they had taken the flight simply to get the first interview with me did it dawn on me that my release must be a big news story. The interviewer told me that there would be a press conference at Heathrow, so I spent the last quarter of an hour trying to prepare myself.

Gisu and Paul met me at the plane and we were taken to a VIP lounge for a family reunion. Much of what followed in the next few days is a blur, but my half-brother George's report to the FRCS recorded the highlights:

Roger's appearance was shocking. He looked thin, pale, stooped and tired. Close up, his face had a paper-like quality, without expression, but his voice was strong, full of vigour and pleasure. He telephoned his father, posed with a glass of champagne, but had a sip of tea. The Foreign Office told him of the enormous interest from the media and he chose to hold a press conference there and then. The room was so full that the family couldn't get in, and the noise of cameras, questions and laughter drowned out most of Roger's answers for us. From the news bulletins later it was clear his performance had been a great success. His most quoted remarks were 'sheer bloody-mindedness' (in reply to how he had survived) and 'Anyone who has been to an English public school and served in the ranks of the British army is perfectly at home in a Third World prison'.

The latter remark, although it had more than a grain of truth, was not as spontaneous as it appeared, having been thought up on the plane as we came in to land.

Roger Cooper, *Death Plus Ten Years*, 1993

CHAMPAGNE AT EVENSONG

John McCarthy was kidnapped in Beirut in 1986 and held hostage for five years. During that time his friends, led by Jill Morrell and Chris Pearson, campaigned tirelessly for his release. It came in August 1991.

We all crowded into a tiny room at the Russell Hotel to watch the BBC news for the first television pictures of John; the presenter, Philip Hayton, was grinning all over his face. I'd decided long before that this moment belonged to us; we wanted to share it among ourselves. No camera was going to film me watching John for the first time. John was making his statement to the press. 'Well, hallo,' he said, and those two words carried more of John than anything else he could have said. I couldn't believe how well he looked or how composed he seemed. He appeared exactly the same as when I last saw him. He was slightly tense, and looked nervous, but his statement was flawless. His voice sounded wonderful, slightly husky, but clear and strong, not the croaky whisper we'd heard from other hostages. He even seemed to have a tan. How on earth had he managed to turn up looking like that? It was absolutely, typically, unmistakably, John. Chris's voice was incredulous. 'For the last five years we've been trying to tell people he's been going through hell and he turns up looking like he's been on a health farm.' Someone else said, 'Frankly he looks a damn sight better than we do!' Everyone in the room cheered. We were all on the edge of hysteria, laughing, crying, hugging one another. It was wonderful, the only moment of the whole day that we had to ourselves. I glanced around at other people's faces to make sure that this was real, that it was John I was watching and that he was, finally, free.

John's release seemed to be one purely joyous moment that the whole country felt it could celebrate. Bells rang out in churches, announcements were made at the Oval cricket ground where everyone stood and cheered, and over the Tannoy at the London Underground. TV news bulletins were dominated by it, and extended their air time. Cars bearing yellow ribbons were tooting their horns at each other. The BBH [Bring Back The Hostages] building was wrapped in a huge yellow ribbon and the final poster, with the slogan: 'John McCarthy still counts', which had gone up only a few weeks before, was immediately amended. Now it read: 'John McCarthy is free. The other hostages still count.' At Broxted Church, the vicar, Jack Filby, served champagne at evensong. For months afterwards, people would tell me the story of where they were when they'd heard the news, as if it was a significant moment in their lives. After the last of the interviews was over, at about 7.30 p.m., Chris, Karen and I travelled down to RAF Lyneham in a chauffeur-driven hire car. . . .

Frustration was tempered only by my mounting nerves. More minutes ticked slowly by, and then an RAF officer came towards Chris and me and told us to follow him. I held Chris's hand tightly as we walked down the corridors for what seemed like miles. 'This is it, this is it,' I was thinking. Suddenly, we were at the entrance to the annexe containing John's suite. A group of men were standing outside and as we got nearer, I saw Pat, Roby and an RAF officer. They wanted Chris and I to go in together, but all at once I realized that Chris was deliberately blocking their way and at the same time shoving me through the door before they could stop him.

I was in the room. John was standing there, looking very small, but filling the whole room. He was smiling, shyly, and walking towards me. We hugged one another, and I was knocked sideways by the sensation of feeling him, of smelling his skin. I didn't know what year it was, where I was, or what I was supposed to say.

'You're back,' I said.

'Yes,' he said, 'I'm back.'

Minutes later, Chris came into the room, and he and John hugged. Chris was crying, saying something like, 'I missed you, it's good to see you', and then suddenly we were all sitting down, chatting, as normal as anything. I was aware that John was doing most of the talking and that his eyes looked dilated. I didn't say much; I felt no need to say anything at all. A wonderful peace had come over me. All tension was gone. Nothing mattered at all, only sitting here, listening to John talk, watching him move. It was like watching an old silent film and then seeing it come to life and fill the room. It was entrancing, magical, and, at the same time, it all felt very, very normal. At one point John reached over and took my hand, and the moment blotted out everything else. . . .

When it came to the time to leave, John pulled me into a separate room and we had another few minutes alone. All I remember is that John said, 'As far as I'm concerned, the plans we had still stand.' John wanted us to be together; finally I knew for sure. I was happier than I'd ever been. I didn't know what was going on around me, I didn't have a clue what the next few days or weeks were going to bring, but at that moment, I didn't care. All that mattered was that I still felt the same for John, John still felt the same for me; everything was all right. He was alive, he was safe and he was home.

Jill Morrell and John McCarthy, *Some Other Rainbow*, 1993

RETURN OF THE EXILE

You have come back on the currents and the tides
After spending long years in the barbarous east.
How great are the sorrows of exile?
More in number than the pearls in the sea.

Li Po (701–62), *Collected Poems*, 1986, tr. John Simpson

ACKNOWLEDGEMENTS

The editor and publishers are grateful for permission to reproduce the following copyright material:

Said Aburish, from *The St George Hotel Bar*. Reprinted by permission of the author.

Alain-Fournier, from *Le Grand Meaulnes* (Penguin, 1986).

Paul Albury, from *The Story of the Bahamas* (Macmillan Caribbean, 1975).

Claribel Alegria, from *You Can't Drown the Fire: Latin American Women Writing in Exile*, ed. Alicia Partnoy. Reprinted by permission of Cleis Press.

Anon., 'Jim Jones Is Sent to Botany Bay', reprinted in *How Strong the Roots: Poems of Exile*, ed. Howard Sergeant (Evans Brothers, 1981).

From *Anthology of Modern Palestinian Literature*, ed. Salma Khadra Jayyusi (Columbia University Press, 1992).

Herbert Aptheker, from *A Documentary History of the Negro People in the United States* (Citadel Press, 1969).

James Baldwin, from *Notes of a Native Son*. Reprinted by permission of the James Baldwin Estate and Beacon Press.

Alan Bennett, from *An Englishman Abroad*, © Alan Bennett 1982.

Hector Berlioz, from *Memoirs*, trans. David Cairns. Reprinted by permission of Victor Gollancz Ltd. and Alfred A. Knopf.

Peter Bland, 'A Sonnet For Exiles' from *How Strong The Roots: Poems of Exile*, ed. Howard Sergeant (Evans Brothers, 1981).

Jorge Luis Borges, 'In the drawing room's quiet . . .' from *Poems*, trans. Ben Belitt, and 'Now has the rapier of iron wrought . . .' from *Collected Poems*, trans. Robert Fitzgerald. Copyright Jorge Luis Borges.

Breyten Breytenbach, from *End Papers* (Faber & Faber, 1986).

Dee Brown, from *Bury My Heart At Wounded Knee*. Reprinted by permission of the Peters Fraser & Dunlop Group Ltd.

From *The BBC at War* (BBC Publications, 1944).

John Bulloch and Harvey Morris, from *No Friends but the Mountains* (Viking, 1992) © John Bulloch and Harvey Morris, 1992, 1993. Reprinted by permission of Penguin Books Ltd.

Michael Burns, from *Dreyfus: A Family Affair 1789–1945* (Chatto & Windus). Reprinted by permission of David Higham Associates Ltd.

Albert Camus, from *The Outsider*, trans. Joseph Laredo. (Hamish Hamilton 1982, first published as *L'Etranger*, 1942), translation © Joseph Laredo 1982. Reprinted by permission of Penguin Books Ltd.

Jung Chang, from *Wild Swans*. Reprinted by permission of HarperCollins Publishers Ltd. and Toby Eady Ltd., London.

Johnny Clegg, 'Asimbonanga' (EMI Records).

Annie Cohen-Salal, from *Sartre: A Life*. Reprinted by permission of Reed Consumer Books Ltd. and Pantheon Books, a division of Random House Inc.

Roger Cooper, from *Death Plus Ten Years*. Reprinted by permission of HarperCollins Publishers Ltd. and Rogers, Coleridge & White.

Quentin Crisp, from *The Naked Civil Servant*, reprinted by permission of Fontana, an imprint of HarperCollins Publishers Ltd. and Radala & Associates, London.

C. Day-Lewis, from *The Aeneid*, trans. © C. Day-Lewis 1967. Reprinted by permission by the Peters Fraser & Dunlop Group Ltd.

Walter de la Mare, from *Desert Islands* (1930). Reprinted by permission of the Literary Trustees of Walter de la Mare and the Society of Authors as their representative.

Isaac Deutscher, from *The Prophet Outcast: Trotsky 1927–1940* (Oxford University Press, 1963).

Alfred Doblin, from *Destiny's Journey*, trans. Edna McCown (Paragon House, New York, 1992).

John W. Dodds, from *The Year of Paradox*. Reprinted by permission of Henry Holt.

Fyodor Dostoevsky, from *Selected Letters of Fyodor Dostoevsky*, ed. Joseph Frank and David I. Goldstein, trans. Andrew MacAndrew, © 1987 Rutgers, the State University. Reprinted by permission of Rutgers University Press.

Richard Ellmann, from *Oscar Wilde* (Hamish Hamilton, 1987) © Richard Ellmann 1987.

Merle Fainsod, from *Smolensk under Soviet Rule* (Unwin Hyman, 1958).

Michael Fathers, in *The Independent on Sunday*, Nov. 1992. Reprinted by permission.

Leonid Vladimirovich Finkelstein, trans. in Michael Glenny and Norman Stone, *The Other Russia* (Faber & Faber, 1990).

Antonia Fraser, from *Mary Queen of Scots* (1969). Reprinted by permission of Weidenfeld & Nicolson Ltd.

Paul Fussell, from *The Great War and Modern Memory* (Oxford University Press, 1978).

Paul Gauguin, from *Noa Noa—Voyage To Tahiti* (Bruno Cassirer, 1961).

Martha Gelhorn, from *The Weather in Africa* (Eland, 1984).

William Gerhardie, from *Memories of St Petersburg, A BBC Talk* (1953).

Ezra Ben Gershon, from *David*, © Ezra Ben Gershon 1988.

Martin Gilbert, from *Churchill: A Life*. (William Heinemann, 1991). Reprinted by permission of Curtis Brown, London; from *The Holocaust*. Reprinted by permission of Fontana, an imprint of HarperCollins Publishers Ltd.

Lord Gladwyn, from *The History Makers* (Sidgwick & Jackson, 1973). Reprinted by permission of the author.

Andrew Graham-Yool, from *A State of Fear: Memories of Argentina's Nightmare* (Eland, 1986).

Graham Greene, from *The Honorary Consul* (The Bodley Head) and *Ways of Escape*. Reprinted by permission of David Higham Associates Ltd.

Germaine Greer, in *The Guardian*, Sept. 1993, © 1993 Germaine Greer. Reprinted by permission of Aitken & Stone.

Sion Harris, from *Slaves No More: Letters from Liberia 1833–1869*, ed. Bel I. Wiley (University of Kentucky, 1980).

Le Ly Hayslip, from *When Heaven and Earth Changed Places* (Penguin, 1990).

John Hemming, from *The Conquest of the Incas* (Macmillan, 1970).

Alexander Herzen, from *My Past and Thoughts*, trans. Constance Garnett. Reprinted by permission of Chatto & Windus Ltd.

Herman Hesse and Thomas Mann, from *Correspondence 1910–1955*, ed. Anni Carlsson and Volker Michels, trans. Ralph Manheim. Reprinted by permission of Peter Owen Ltd.

Christopher Hibbert, from *Edward VII: A Portrait* (Penguin, 1991).

Stuart Hampshire, from *Spinoza* (Faber & Faber, 1951).

Ernest Hemingway, from *A Moveable Feast*, © Ernest Hemingway 1964. Reprinted by permission of Jonathan Cape Ltd. and Macmillan Publishing Co. Inc.

Grainne Henry, from *The Irish Military Community in Spanish Flanders* (1992). Reprinted by permission of Irish Academic Press.

Ronald Hingley, from *The Russian Mind* (1978) and *Dostoevsky: His Life And Work*, © Ronald Hingley. Reprinted by permission of the Peters Fraser & Dunlop Group Ltd.

Homer, from *The Odyssey*, trans. Richard Lattimore, translation © Richard Lattimore 1991. Reprinted by permission by HarperCollins.

Peter Hopkirk, from *The Great Game*. Reprinted by permission of John Murray (Publishers) Ltd. and Kodansha America Inc.

A. E. Hotchner, from *Sophia: Living and Loving—Her Own Story*. Reprinted by permission of Transworld Publishers.

Robert Hughes, from *The Fatal Shore*. Reprinted by permission of Harvill, an imprint of HarperCollins Publishers Ltd. and Alfred A. Knopf Inc.

348   *Acknowledgements*

Michael Ignatieff, from *The Russian Album* (Chatto & Windus, 1987). Reprinted by permission of Random House UK Ltd., Sheil Land Associates Ltd. and Viking Penguin Inc.

Christopher Isherwood, from *Goodbye to Berlin* (Granada, 1977).

Clive James, from *Unreliable Memoirs* (Cape/Picador). Reprinted by permission of the Peters Fraser & Dunlop Group Ltd.

Josephus, from *The Jewish War*, trans. G. A. Williamson, rev. E. Mary Smallwood (Penguin, 1959, 2nd rev. edn. 1981), © G. A. Williamson, 1954, 1969, © E. M. Smallwood, 1981. Reprinted by permission of Penguin Books Ltd.

James Joyce, from *Ulysses*, copyright © 1934 and renewed 1962 by Lucia and George Joyce. Reprinted by permission of Random House, Inc. and the Society of Authors as the literary representative of the Estate of James Joyce.

Salem Jubran, 'Singer of Wind and Rain', trans. Lena Jayyusi and Naomi Shihab Nye, from *An Anthology of Palestinian Literature*, ed. Salma Khadra Jayyusi (Columbia University Press, 1992).

Franz Kafka, from 'Home Coming', from *Description of a Struggle*, trans. by Tania and James Stern, © 1958 by Schocken Books Inc. Reprinted by permission of Schocken Books, published by Pantheon Books, a division of Random House, Inc. Also by permission of Minerva Publishers.

Brian Keenan, from *An Evil Cradling*, © Brian Keenan 1992. Reprinted by permission of Random House UK and Curtis Brown Ltd.

Alexander Kerensky, from *The Kerensky Memoirs: Russia and History's Turning Point* (Cassell, 1966).

Moorhead Kennedy, from *The Ayatollah in the Cathedral* (Hill and Wang, 1986).

Jack Kerouac, from *On The Road* (Penguin Books 1972, first published by Andre Deutsch), © Jack Kerouac, 1955, 1957. Reprinted by permission of Penguin Books Ltd.

Susan Maclean Kybett, from *Bonnie Prince Charlie* (Unwin Hyman, 1988).

Karel Kyncl, 'A Sleep-walker In Prague' from 'Pavlov, Prague Airport and the Sleepwalker's Memories of Going Home', *Index on Censorship 10*, 1990.

Jean Lacouture, from *The Ruler: De Gaulle*. Reprinted by permission of Harvill, an imprint of HarperCollins Publishers Ltd. and Éditions du Seuil, Paris.

Dalai Lama, from *Freedom in Exile: The Autobiography of His Holiness the Dalai Lama of Tibet* (1990). Reprinted by permission of Hodder & Stoughton Ltd.

Philip Larkin, from *Collected Poems* (1988). Reprinted by permission of Faber & Faber Ltd.

Emanoel Lee, from *To the Bitter End: A Photographic History of the Boer War 1899–1902* (Viking, 1985), © Emanoel Lee 1985. Reprinted by permission of Penguin Books Ltd.

Dmitry Vladimirovich Lekhovich, trans. in Michael Glenny and Norman Stone, *The Other Russia* (Faber & Faber, 1990).

Amin Maalouf, from *The Crusades Through Arab Eyes*. Translation © Jon Rothschild 1984 (Al-Saqui Books).

Osip Mandelstam, from *The Complete Critical Prose and Letters*, trans. J. G. H. and Constance Link (Ardis, 1979).

Leslie A. Marchand, from *Byron: A Biography*, vol. 3, and *Byron: Selected Letters and Journals*. Reprinted by permission of John Murray (Publishers) Ltd.

Ian McIntyre, from *The Expense of Glory: A Life of John Reith*. Reprinted by permission of HarperCollins Publishers Ltd.

Kanan Makiya, from *Cruelty and Silence*. Reprinted by permission of Jonathan Cape Ltd. and Makiya Associates.

Gabriel Garcia Marquez, from *Clandestine in Chile: The Adventures of Miguel*, trans. Asa Zatz (Henry Holt & Co.).

Garrett Mattingly, from *The Defeat of the Spanish Armada*, © 1959 by Garrett Mattingly. Copyright renewed 1987 by Leonard H. Mattingly. Reprinted by permission of Houghton Mifflin Co. and Jonathan Cape Ltd. All rights reserved.

W. Somerset Maugham, from 'The Traitor' (William Heinemann, 1951). Reprinted by permission of Reed Consumer Books Ltd. and A. P. Watt Ltd. on behalf of the Royal Literary Fund.

Fatima Meer, from *Higher than Hope* (Hamish Hamilton, 1990). Reprinted by permission of Penguin Books Ltd. and Sheil Land Associates.

Ved Mehta, from *Sound Shadows of the New World* (William Collins).

Henry Miller, from *Tropic of Cancer*. Reprinted by permission of Grafton, an imprint of HarperCollins Publishers Ltd. and Curtis Brown Ltd., London.

Bloke Modisane, from *Blame Me On History* (Penguin Bookds 1990, first published by Thames and Hudson), © William B. Modisane 1963. Reprinted by permission of Penguin Books Ltd.

Ray Monk, from *Ludwig Wittgenstein: The Duty of Genius*. Reprinted by permission of Jonathan Cape Ltd. and Rogers, Coleridge & White.

Jill Morrell and John MacCarthy, from *Some Other Rainbow* (Bantam, 1993). Reprinted by permission of Transworld Publishers Ltd.

Taha Abd al-Ghani Mustafa, 'The Palestinian's Journey Home', trans. Salwa Jabseh and Naomi Shihab Nye, from An Anthology of Modern Palestinian Literature (Columbia University Press, 1992).

John Julius Norwich, from *Byzantium: The Apogee* © John Julius Norwich, 1991. Reprinted by permission of Penguin Books Ltd. and Alfred A. Knopf.

Thomas Pinney (ed.), from *Kipling's India: Uncollected Sketches 1884–1888* (Macmillan, 1986).

Plutarch, from *Moralia*, trans. Philip H. de Lacy and Benedict Einarson (Heinemann, 1959).

Po Chu-I, from *Chinese Poems*, trans. Arthur Waley, translation © Arthur Waley 1946. Reprinted by permission of George Allen & Unwin Ltd., a division of HarperCollins Publishers Ltd.

Li Po, 'Listening to a Flute on a Spring Night in Lo-Yang', copyright 1987. Translation copyright 1987 by Sam Hamill. Reprinted from *Banished Immortal — Visions of Li T'ai-Po*. With the permission of White Pine Press, Fredonia, New York, USA.

Ezra Pound, from *Ezra Pound: Letters 1907–41*, ed. D. D. Paige (Faber & Faber, 1951).

Irina Ratushinskaya, from *Beyond the Limit*, trans. Frances Padorr Brent and Carol J. Avins (Northwestern University Press, 1987).

Jasper Ridley, from *Napoleon III and Eugénie*. Reprinted by permission of Constable Publishers and Viking Penguin, New York.

Sir Steven Runciman, from *The Fall of Constantinople* (Penguin, 1965).

Oliver Sacks, from *Awakenings*. Reprinted by permission of Gerald Duckworth of Co. and Curtis Brown, London.

Andrei Sakharov, from *Memoirs*, © Andrei Sakharov 1989. Reprinted by permission of Random House UK Ltd. and Alfred A. Knopf Inc.

Siegfried Sassoon, 'Dreamers' from *Collected Poems* (Faber & Faber, 1976). Reprinted by permission of G. T. Sassoon and Viking Penguin Inc.

Paul Scott, from *Staying On* (Granada, 1982).

William Shawcross, from *The Shah's Last Ride*, © William Shawcross 1989. Reprinted by permission of Chatto & Windus Ltd. and Simon & Schuster Inc.

Pyotr Petrovich Shilovsky, trans. in Michael Glenny and Norman Stone, *The Other Russia* (Faber & Faber, 1990).

John Simpson, from *Behind Iranian Lines* (Robson, 1988) and *Despatches from the Barricades* (Robson, 1990). Reprinted by permisson.

Isaac Bashevis Singer, from *Collected Stories* (Penguin, 1968), and *Love and Exile: The Early Years, A Memoir*. Reprinted by permission of A. M. Heath on behalf of the author and Lescher and Lescher.

Alexander Solzhenitsyn, from *The Gulag Archipelago*, © Alexander Solzhenitsyn. Reprinted by permission of M. Claude Durand and HarperCollins.

Mercedes Sosa, from *You Can't Drown the Fire: Latin American Women Writing in Exile*, ed. Alicia Partnoy. Reprinted by permission of Cleis Press.

Allister Sparks, from *The Mind of South Africa* (William Heinemann, 1990). Reprinted by permission of Reed Consumer Books Ltd. and Carol Smith Literary Agency.

Gertrude Stein, from *What are Masterpieces* (Pitman Publishing, 1970), © The Estate of Gertrude Stein.

Barry Streak, 'Pretoria's Bogeyman Returns from Exile', *The Guardian*, 28 Apr. 1990, © *The Guardian*. Reprinted with permission.

Countess Natalya Sumarohov-Elston, trans. in Michael Glenny and Norman Stone, *The Other Russia* (Faber & Faber, 1990).

Virgil, from *The Aeneid*, trans. C. Day-Lewis, translation © C. Day-Lewis 1967. Reprinted by permission of the Peters Fraser & Dunlop Group Ltd.

Robert Penn Warren, from *All the King's Men* (Penguin, 1971).

Evelyn Waugh, from *Put Out More Flags* (Chapman & Hall, 1943), and from *Brideshead Revisited* (Chapman & Hall, 1945). Reprinted by permission of the Peters Fraser & Dunlop Group Ltd.

P. G. Wodehouse, from *My Man Jeeves* (1930). Reprinted by permission of A. P. Watt on behalf of the Trustees of the Wodehouse Trust No. 3 and Century Hutchinson.

Thomas Wolfe, from *You Can't Go Home Again* (Penguin, 1989).

Ronald Wright, from *Stolen Continents*, © 1992 Ronald Wright. Reprinted by permission of John Murray (Publishers) Ltd. and Houghton Mifflin Inc., New York.

Any errors or omissions in the above list are entirely unintentional. If notified the publisher will be pleased to make any necessary corrections at the earliest opportunity.

INDEX OF AUTHORS

INDEX OF EXILES

Note: References are to names of exiles; places and topics are only included for those passages where exiles are not identified by name.